Economic Diversity in Contemporary Timor-Leste

ECONOMIC DIVERSITY IN CONTEMPORARY TIMOR-LESTE

Edited by

Kelly Silva, Lisa Palmer and Teresa Cunha

Leiden University Press

The Open Access edition was made possible by a grant from the University of Melbourne.

Cover design: Andre Klijsen
Cover illustrations: Woman working at Beloi market, Atauro, 2022 (Photo: Kelly Silva); Ai Hulun ritual, Maubisi-Mauloko, Ainaro, 2012 (Photo: Lisa Palmer); Water buffalo on Wailili main road, Baucau, 2022 (Photo: Lisa Palmer)
Lay-out: Crius Group

ISBN 978 90 8728 395 7
e-ISBN 978 94 0060 440 7 (e-PDF)
https://doi.org/10.24415/9789087283957
NUR 692

Printed and bound by CPI Group (UK) Ltd, Croydon, CR0 4YY

To the memory of James Scambary and Lucas da Costa

Table of Contents

List of Illustrations and Tables 9

Introduction 11
Kelly Silva, Lisa Palmer and Teresa Cunha

GLIMPSES OF THE COLONIAL ECONOMY 43

Chapter 1. The colonial bazaar in 'Portuguese Timor': the taming of the 'savage marketers' 45
Lúcio Sousa

Chapter 2. Indexing social space: A marketplace in Timor-Leste 65
David Hicks

Chapter 3. Flirting with Ford, reverting to race? Housing, urban planning and the making of an economic and social order in Portuguese Timor in trans-colonial perspective, 1959-1963 85
Alex Grainger

LOCAL ECONOMIC DYNAMICS 105

Chapter 4. On the existence and persistence of the social category of *atan* in contemporary Timor-Leste 107
Susanna Barnes

Chapter 5. The *serimónia* network: economic mobilisation through rituals in the hamlet of Faulara, Liquiçá 123
Alberto Fidalgo-Castro and Enrique Alonso-Población

Chapter 6. Household decision-making processes and family resources: A case study from Viqueque 147
Josh Trindade and Ivete de Oliveira

Chapter 7. Gift economy and the acknowledgement of debt: (On) Living and eating with 'mystical' actors in Timorese houses 161
Renata Nogueira da Silva

Chapter 8. The work of women in Eluli and land economies in Timor-Leste 177
Teresa Cunha and Mina Bessa

ECONOMIC TRANSFORMATIONS 193

Chapter 9. Land and diet under pressure: The impacts of Suai Supply Base in Kamanasa kingdom 195
Brunna Crespi

Chapter 10. The socio-cultural benefits of emerging market-based instruments for carbon in Timor-Leste 215
Lisa Palmer and Sue Jackson

Chapter 11. China's engagement in Timor-Leste's economy 235
Laurentina 'Mica' Barreto Soares

Chapter 12. Migrant work and homecoming: Experiences of Timorese seasonal workers 255
Ann Wigglesworth and Abel Boavida dos Santos

Chapter 13. Refashioning Fataluku origin houses 275
Andrew McWilliam

Chapter 14. The *frente ekonomika* (economic front): Timorese perspectives on seasonal work in Australia 295
Michael Rose

About the Authors 313

Index 317

List of Illustrations and Tables

Illustrations

Fig. 1.1: A Timorese market (date unknown)	50
Fig. 2.1: Marketplace	76
Fig. 2.2: Market in 1966 showing selling rows	76
Fig. 5.1: Family tree of the household in 2009	127
Fig. 5.2: Percentage of ritual movements (names in Tetum)	128
Fig. 5.3: Percentage of ritual movements by type (according to Table 5.1)	129
Fig. 5.4: Family tree of the fertility-givers' group (*ego* is 6)	130
Fig. 6.1: Schematic representation of decision-making process at household level	153
Fig. 6.2: Factors influencing household (HH) decision making	154
Fig. 7.1: The preparation of the sacred food offered to *bosok*	161
Fig. 8.1: Map of Timor-Leste	178
Fig. 9.1: The different levels of appropriation of territory in Kamanasa	200
Fig. 10.1: Baguia forestscape	220
Fig. 12.1: Satisfaction with SWP experience	264
Fig. 13.1: Image of Twin Houses (*le amarua)*	280
Figs. 13.2 and 13.3: New style *Le ia valu* house	286

Tables

Table 0.1: Timor-Leste state budget/expenditure	27
Table 1.1: Regional markets in 1911	53
Table 2.1: Commodities bought and sold in Viqueque market	73
Table 5.1: Name and type of ritual recorded	125
Table 5.2: Redistribution of ritual gains	132
Table 5.3: Neighbours' contributions	133
Table 5.4: Fertility-takers' contributions	136
Table 5.5: Collection made during the negotiation of the bridewealth in Ermera	138
Table 11.1: Statistics on China's trade with Timor-Leste from 2013-2019 (US$'000)	241

Table 11.2: Statistic on Timor-Leste's export (including re-export) to and import from China between 2004 and 2019 (US$'000) 242
Table 11.3: Statistics on Timor-Leste's Trade Deficit 2004-2019 (US$'000) 243
Table 12.1: Numbers of Timorese SWP workers per year up to 2017 259

Introduction

Kelly Silva, Lisa Palmer and Teresa Cunha

Abstract

The introduction to this volume challenges hegemonic, market-driven analyses which characterise Timor-Leste's economy as weak, homogeneous and disformed and elucidates the agentive cultural institutions, logics and practices which underpin and mobilise diverse Timorese economic ecologies. It begins from the assumption that capitalism and its market economy is only one regime, among others, of production, exchange, distribution and consumption that people rely on to make their living. Developing the idea of the interdependencies of economic diversity, it outlines the processes through which an assemblage of institutions and their localised and historical relationships are mobilised for reproducing collective life. It introduces the ways in which subsequent chapters analyse this economic diversity and presents an overview of the ways in which they pattern out across diverse spatio-temporal contexts.

Keywords: Diverse economies; economic interdependencies; Timor-Leste; history; culture

I follow Hirokazu Miyazaki (2013) and others in suggesting that to take the economy seriously in part means to take seriously people's fantasies about it.

—Appel 2017, 312

For some time, narratives and projects aimed at improving and diversifying economic activities in Timor-Leste have been the leitmotivs of a number of development programs. Framing such endeavours are several assumptions about Timor-Leste's economy, namely, that it is unproductive, weak and unfair; that most of it is made up of subsistence agriculture benefitting male interests (Brogan and TOMAK 2016); and that it is excessively dependent on oil and state spending (World Bank Group 2018; Scheiner 2015). To overcome this state of affairs, endless diagnoses and prognoses are undertaken by national and international experts, simultaneously building the received truth that the local economy is underdeveloped and blaming it as a purveyor of poverty and for the country's low position in the Human Rights Development Index. Out of these narratives, a picture of Timor-Leste's economy as one in need of private/public investment and regulatory control emerges—processes, it is argued, that would make it more productive and diverse.

Various phenomena have been mobilised to make sense of this picture and to legitimise this constructed truth. On the one hand, a lack of proper physical, legal, financial and other institutional infrastructure is pointed out. On the other, the supposedly negative effects of local practices and values are cited as explanations for many of the constraints on economic growth in the country: Timor-Leste's people expend too much time on ritual practices (Alonso-Población et al. 2015; Silva 2017); the fertility rate is too high (Burke 2020); 'primitive' agriculture techniques prevail, perpetuating a lack of skills. Low productivity rates and idleness are also often cited (DFAT 2014, 4, 32; Akta 2012). To counter this, economic pedagogies of multiple origins are promulgated by governance institutions with the aim of turning Timor-Leste's citizens into active economic agents (Silva 2017) in neoliberal terms.[1]

As elsewhere in the world, measurement of the strength, weakness, growth or stagnation of Timor-Leste's economy is made possible by the crafting and management of indexes, numbers and percentages that supposedly record all activities of production, service and consumption (World Bank Group 2018). GDP (gross domestic product), GNI (gross national income), the poverty rate, and life expectancy at birth are exemplary of the serial global forms by which national economies are measured and crafted (Appel 2017; World Bank Group 2020, 34).

The *Timor-Leste Economic Report 2020* reveals some of the variables taken into consideration in depicting the current state of Timor-Leste's economy. These include 1) public expenditure, 2) private sector activity, 3) consumption related taxes, 4) fiscal sector activities, 5) commercial credit, and 6) domestic (national) revenue (World Bank Group 2020, 1-10). Importantly, households are represented as acting exclusively as units of consumption or recipients of state transfers. No productive activities are endowed to them (World Bank Group 2020, 20) despite the fact that households—and, within them, women carrying out all sorts of work and care—produce the most important economic asset in the world: persons.

In making the above observation, we do not only refer to the reproductive potential of women's bodies. As Federici (2019) and Cunha and Valle (2021) argue, the unpaid care provided mostly by women in the domestic realm is the very bedrock, the very infrastructure, of capitalism and the market society.[2] Yet, it continues to be silenced and made invisible by the hegemony of economics. A 2020 Oxfam report (one among many such reports) presents an important counterpoint to this hegemony: "The monetary value of women's unpaid care work globally for women aged 15 and over is at least $10.8 trillion annually—three times the size of the world's tech industry" (Oxfam International 2020, 8).

At development sector or academic events in Dili—such as the Timor-Leste Studies Association Conference—questions are sometimes asked about how local economic activities have been internalised, measured or even considered in indexes such as those aforementioned, but such questions cannot be answered. Some interlocutors recognise that the various phenomena that comprise local economies in rural areas cannot be measured because state-centred or market-driven institutions lack the tools to consider them (Guteriano Neves, pers. comm.). Activities such as growing food for self-consumption, exchanges performed in ritual contexts, barter among households or families, work exchanges, and women's domestic and communitarian work for productive and reproductive ends are not considered or measured by default. Such phenomena teach us a very important lesson: what has been glossed as the Timor-Leste economy does not correspond to the real economy in Timor-Leste at all.

This volume provides data, narratives and analyses that allow us to understand that the idea of a single economy in Timor-Leste is inaccurate. In other words, the economic relations within the country cannot be reduced to what has been depicted as Timor-Leste's economy in official narratives. We argue that it is critical to dissociate the idea of economy in Timor-Leste from its national inscription into a Timor-Leste market-based national economy, because the latter is unable to take account of economic facts that are outside and beyond the market-driven frame.

By doing so, we aim to complicate current imaginaries about the relevant economic dynamics in the country and bring to the fore fragments of the following occurrences: 1) local, community-based economic values and arrangements; 2) community-based entanglements with the market-driven economy;[3] 3) the colonial and postcolonial governance praxis by which a market-driven economy has been promoted in the country; and 4) the dramatic and creative ways by which local people have responded to transformations in the economic dynamics to which they are exposed. Hence, this collection contributes to replacing hegemonic, market-driven images of Timor-Leste's economy as pale, disformed and homogenised with a demonstration of the myriad ways in which economic relations in Timor-Leste are diverse, complex and socially embedded.

Our analysis is framed by a specific way of conceiving 'economy'. Economy is understood as a set of production, exchange, distribution and consumption procedures by which populations and institutions (including nation-states but not limited to them) guarantee their reproduction by replenishing people and things (Polanyi [1944] 2000). Such replacements are the product of articulations between diverse regimes and relations of production, exchange, distribution and consumption (Gibson and Graham 1996) among which the market regime is only one. These articulations create contextual equilibriums in order to respond to the aspirations and needs of the social whole. Therefore, on the basis of such a paradigm, we argue that economic relations in Timor-Leste are made up of particular interdependencies or, as we term them, economic ecologies.

This way of conceiving economy entails a critical widening of the phenomena we conceive as comprising an economy. Domestic work like cooking is an economic occurrence; care in the sphere of the family or of the community, producing the conditions of life, is also an economic reality; so too are barter experiences, *tara bandu* (ritual resource regulation) and other socio-ecological services carried out by ritual mediations, marriage exchanges (be they glossed as *barlake* or not), growing food for self-consumption, interpersonal relations of clientelism and dependency, and individual and collective ways of organising and deploying labour. For example, any time a funeral occurs in rural Timor-Leste, the event mobilises a whole neighbourhood and the households connected to it through labour and exchange obligations concerned with raising funds, killing animals and offering ritual services. This is an economic event (see Chapter 5, this volume). None of these phenomena are considered in any productive way when state-centred institutions discuss Timor-Leste's economy.

The recovery of the etymological origins of the word economy—the governance of home—is apposite here. While reminding us that economic experiences in the world far exceed the singularly capitalist one (Cunha 2015), it also highlights that what is presumed to be at stake in many governance strategies about the economy in Timor-Leste (and beyond) is merely building and maintaining a capitalist market society. Yet, at a grassroots or local economy level, capitalism might be much less decisive than what dominant and orthodox economic science makes us believe.[4]

Importantly, our proposed analytical frame does not deny that most of the East Timorese population face deprivation and poverty, even though the very idea of poverty might be questioned because it is measured, partially, on the basis of people's engagement with Western-origin systems and institutions (see, e.g., Lundahl and Sjöholm 2019, 1-33). While recognising that the material reproduction of Timorese life is very difficult for much of the population, we argue that it could be still worse if community-based economic institutions did not exist. Despite all the political and ecological catastrophes to which Timor-Leste's peoples have been subjected over time, their existence, resistance and resilience has been ensured, by and large, by relying on these local institutions (see Chapters 5, 6, 7, and 8).

Data provided in Part 3 of this collection, and in many political debates in Timor-Leste, show us that most people in the country aspire to engage in the market economy through wage labour and/or finding a way out of subsistence agriculture. These aspirations align with the notion of an agrarian transition (Bernstein 2010)—a model of social change that predicted that societal transformation and technological innovations would involve the exit of the masses from rural areas and agricultural activities towards urban settlements and waged work. Challenging this notion, we assume that a society of fully paid employment will not succeed in Timor-Leste, as it does not exist anymore anywhere in the world (Li 2014; Ferguson 2015; Ferguson and Li 2018). Not by chance, the question presented by Appel (2017, 309) is fundamental: "On what fictions and forgetting does the making of a thing called a national economy depend?".

Of course, the typical phenomenon of a capitalist market-driven economy are everywhere in Timor-Leste. We do not intend to deny or underestimate these. Even in the most remote villages, people take part in local and foreign produce markets, sell and purchase commodities by the mediation of money, take out microcredit loans and look for wage labour. But none of these facts are spontaneous developments derived from a supposed natural evolution of social dynamics—which as Polanyi ([1944] 2000) argued is based on the fallacious idea that the capitalist market is the natural and inevitable evolution of the economic life all around the world. On the contrary, they are products of multiple governance practices and interventions carried out since colonial times that entangle in both positive and negative ways Timor-Leste's resources and people in global economic markets and make them dependent on the latter. It is by these governance practices—the colonial and postcolonial—that state-building has occurred.

The analytical framework proposed here takes a critical stance in relation to both local, community-based economic forms, and global, capitalist market-driven ones. We distance ourselves from any romanticism towards these economic institutions, recognising that they are both structured by power relations which generate and reproduce hierarchies, inequalities and exclusions, even if in different intensities and ways (Meillassoux 1981). For instance, criticism of the exploitation of the domestic work of dependents in Timorese households, on one hand, and land expropriation resulting from capitalist mega-projects, on the other hand, are both carefully discussed in the book (see Chapters 4 and 9, this volume).

State-building, techno-science and national economies

The reduction of economic dynamics in Timor-Leste to a national representation of it has to do with elective affinities existing between modern state-building and the development of the global market capitalism elsewhere in the world. Broadly speaking, the global expansion of market exchanges and commercial linkages demand the pacification of various political conflicts and a certain monopoly and centralisation of power and global finances that is now performed by state and transnational actors (Elias 1993; Polanyi [1944] 2000).

Over time, the monopolisation of power by nation-states came to be nourished by political anxieties about the rationalisation of power. To manage these anxieties, a complex apparatus for producing knowledge for the betterment of governance practices came into existence. This included the emergence of statistics (the etymology of that word is revealing: stat-istic) and the systematic development of territorial and population maps (Mitchell 2002). In response to this epistemic anxiety, and in parallel with the very development of the modern nation-state, proposals for the development of a science aimed at measuring the production, exchange and consumption of wealth emerged. It was called economics and it was immersed in liberal and market fantasies of the ideal society:

> The national economy is, therefore, in the first instance an epistemological project of the state, born in a geopolitical moment in which Western powers were looking for tools to manage the Great Depression, pay for war, and respond to imperial decline. It was at this moment that states increasingly took explicit responsibility for economic activities nominally within their borders and sought statistical tools like per capita income, national income accounting, and GDP through which to know and manage their new charge (Stiglitz, Sen, and Fitoussi 2010; Vanoli 2005). As Chris Hann and Keith Hart (2011, 34) put it, 'states claimed the right to manage money, markets, and accumulation in the national interest; and this is why today 'the economy' primarily refers to the country we live in'. (Appel 2017, 297-298)

These umbilical relations between modern state-building and economics have conditioned the very idea of the economy. This reminds us, too, that economics respond to political anxieties related to the legitimation of state power. Consequently, we need to reflect on the emergence of national economies from the outside in; that is, we need to discuss certain extra-economic facts (called externalities in contemporary dominant economic thought) that were imposed in shaping state economic constitutions. In this perspective, laws, property rights, international conventions, and measurement tools such as the census and statistics all perform important roles in the making of national economies.

Importantly, we need to consider the performative role of the epistemic products that economics bring into existence. In Austin's (1999) terms, these have perlocutionary effects so as to build the reality that they, supposedly, only represent. So, when World Bank or International Monetary Fund (IMF) reports affirm the feeble character of Timor-Leste's economy, they are actually building that national economy and predicating it as poor, fragile and weak. This is possible because of fetishisation—the assignment of superhuman qualities to certain facts—which marks people's attitudes towards economics. Nourishing these attitudes are the claims of exclusive technical expertise by those called economists and also the faith placed in technical science on the part of the general population.

If the idea of economy in Timor-Leste cannot be reduced to the 'official' national economy, what phenomena constitute the former? In the following section we bring to the fore facts of a community-based economy that demand greater attention if we are interested in widening our perspectives about social reproduction at the grassroots or local economy level. All of these phenomena and associated institutions are, in varied ways, present in the chapters comprising this collection.

After presenting a range of institutions and phenomena that characterise a community-based economy, we briefly outline the ways in which East Timorese people have become enmeshed with capitalist processes and its market society over time. We then examine the ways in which these multiple local and global institutions and phenomena are now the bedrock of economic ecologies in Timor-Leste. We conclude by outlining the structure of the collection and the chapters comprising it.

Unmasking community-based economies

A number of scholars of Timor-Leste have directly or indirectly argued for the need to make visible the community-based economies that contribute to, and underpin, heterogenous community life across the country (Traube 2007; McWilliam 2011, 2020; Palmer 2010, 2015; Silva 2016, 2017; Carroll-Bell 2015; Fidalgo-Castro 2015; Batterbury et al. 2015; Barnes 2017; Trindade and Barnes 2018; Gibson et al. 2018). Drawing on the work of economic anthropologists, sociologists and geographers (such as Appadurai 1986; Gudeman 2001, 2008, 2016; Gregory 1982; Sousa Santos 2014; Cunha 2014; Gibson-Graham 2005, 2006), they have highlighted the diverse ways in which community-based economies have been, and continue to be, central to Timor's livelihood practices. They also show how these dynamic and always socially and historically contingent economies are masked or even denigrated by those who characterise them as ancillary or as a burden to society. Through long-term ethnographic work, these scholars discern diverse and often highly localised economic logics that allow life to function and pattern out across, between, and within Timor's diverse rural and urban contexts.

One area of concern has been the interrelationships between the logic of the gift (or customary exchange) and the logic of commodities (or market-based approaches). McWilliam (2011, 2020, this volume), drawing on Gudeman (2001, 2008, 2016), has argued that Fataluku communities in the far east of Timor-Leste, including their international diaspora, have chosen in the post-independence era to support their community economic relations for their own sake. These 'high relationship economies' (Gudeman 2016) are distinguished by their attention to mutuality and exchange rather than market-based self-interest. McWilliam's work is informed as well by Gregory (1982) who argues that careful ethnographic attention is needed to unpack the usually stark contrasts between logics of commodity and gift exchange. Reworking Mauss's ([1923] 1990) theory on the classic gift or debt economy as an exchange of inalienable things between persons who are in a state of reciprocal dependence, Gregory (1982) focuses on the importance of discerning the distances between relationships that are created through transactions. He argues that, by paying attention to these dynamic kin and non-kin relationships, distinctions between 'gift' and 'commodity' exchange emerge as extreme points on a continuum rather than binary opposites. A single object of exchange may be considered a gift within one setting, but a commodity within another, as Appadurai (1986) also highlighted.

Other scholars have drawn on Gibson-Graham (2005, 2006) to ask why we do not pay as much attention to examining already existing alternative forms of socio-economic organisation. Gibson-Graham's work encourages us to pay close attention to "non-capitalist economic spaces" and to ask what can be learnt from what is already there (Gibson-Graham 2006, x). Palmer (2010, 2015), for example, has argued that Timor-Leste's independence-era resurgence of customary exchange relations and *lulik* (Tetum: sacred, forbidden, taboo) comprises a re-normalisation of long suppressed potencies and practices across diverse community economies. At the same time, these powerful and dynamic (never quite settled) customary processes (McWilliam, Palmer, and Shepherd 2014) are being given new form by the uncertainties, opportunities and contingencies of the country's post-independence political and economic transition to a largely neoliberal economy and governance regime. Such customary assemblages continually rub up against, and produce interpretations and variations of, the market-based economy and attendant institutions across the country (Palmer 2015; Palmer and McWilliam 2019).

In order to explore in regionally specific ways the "persistent practices of interdependence built on a diversity of social, cultural, economic and ecological relations", Gibson et al. (2018, 4) elucidate a range of geographically located "keywords" or indigenous economic concepts. Using this keywords approach to reveal "economic practices animated by place-based ethics of care-full exchange, reciprocity and redistribution" (Gibson et al. 2018, 4), they draw on Sousa Santos (2014, 184) to argue that reproducing such normally absent keyword/conceptual categories to understand "an economy" is "a necessary prelude to generating a 'sociology of emergence'". The aim of this endeavour is to enlarge the formal idea of economy "by adding to the existing reality the realistic possibilities and future expectations it contains" (Sousa Santos 2014, 184).

Drawing from conceptual categories and keywords in the Timor region, Kehi and Palmer contribute to this task by evoking the concept of *hamutu moris hamutu mate* (together in life, together in death), a concept that they argue underpins customary social and economic relations in this setting:

> Life cycle events and commemorations are part of a vibrant complex of practices glossed in the Timorese language of Tetum Terik as the interplay between *hamutu moris hamutu mate* (together in life, together in death). In the process, people across East Timor (also West Timor) generate densely woven inter-relationships of spiritual ecology with ancestors, living relatives, their local environments and the Most Sacred One (*Nai Luli Waik*). Social and spiritual life and livelihoods are enacted and reproduced through careful attention to

> these relations for the sake of "intergenerational well-being", or a pervasive concern for sustaining and nourishing social and spiritual relations that stretch across the past, present and future. Families of particular lineages are organised around origin groups linked to particular ancestral houses and local spirit ecologies which embed these families in intimate, intergenerational social, spiritual, political and economic relationships with their extended kin from other ancestral houses. The alliances formed includes the obligation of members of each 'house' to perform particular ritual duties at each other's life and death based ceremonies and assist with house-based associated rituals and agricultural practices which are inseparable from spiritual life. (Gibson et al. 2018, 7)

Among other things, the institution *hamutu moris hamutu mate* presents us with new arrangements of categories for conceiving economic relations. First, it allows for a positive outlook on debts (notwithstanding the often onerous and frequently inter-generational burden these debts create (cf. Silva and Simião 2017)). Only those who are in a position to become a creditor of a debt participate in the *hamutuk*. In other words, it is a cooperative work that indicates that the people involved are mutually committed to recognising the debt that represents their interdependence. It is not a matter of symmetrical reciprocity in work, but, rather, the certitude that, when you are accepted into the group to work together, your place in the community and in the world is being recognised. In this sense, the worst that can happen to a person is not being accepted into the *hamutuk* because it means that she/he/they is not qualified with sufficient respect and dignity to make other people in debt of her/his/their work. Being excluded from a sense of *hamutuk* is, therefore, the social and symbolic confirmation that her/his/their collective personhood is hurt or obliterated.

Second, the *hamutuk* can only be understood if we consider another concept of time and economy. The *hamutuk* work (i.e., those human activities that are carried out together [human and non-human] on/with the land/water) cannot be bought or sold because it involves a relationship with the sacred character of the land/water.[5] This goes against the grain of the so-called modern and so-called Western anthropocentrism in which nature, especially land, is property (Polanyi [1944] 2000) prone to endless alienation and exploitation (Cunha and Bessa, this volume; Valle 2019).

Economic versions of this arguably pan-Timorese concept of *hamutuk* are explored by Fidalgo-Castro and Alonso-Población, Silva and Cunha and Bessa in this volume. In these chapters, diverse economic household relations are shown to form a fundamental institution among people whose social reproduction is not capitalist and where the family is the main unit of production, consumption and, to a large extent, distribution. Yet, the further a capitalist economy intrudes, the more families lose the role of being a production unit (Crespi, this volume) and the institution of the family loses part of its essential social function. Nonetheless, some of this change might be welcomed in some contexts. For example, Barnes (this volume) explores how historical ties of dependency, related to the potentially exploitative household category of servants or slaves (*atan*), also underpin the customary economy.

While these economic ecologies are often excluded from mainstream economic discourse in Timor-Leste, the autonomy and strength of community-based systems is, as many of the authors cited above argue, also an outcome of broader, more-than-human economies in which customary systems are embedded (Palmer and McWilliam 2019). In Timor-Leste (as in many other places), ancestral spirits and other more-than-human agents are taken into consideration in economic life. These economies can be understood as comprising more-than-human communities, with a diversity of beings and potencies deeply embedded in understandings of more-than-human mutuality and social relations. Understanding 'nature' as a part of these inclusive more-than-human social arrangements requires that people be constantly attuned to obligations and reciprocity across human and non-human realms. It requires careful attention to a more-than-human and relational ethics of care and responsibility (Jackson and Palmer 2015; Palmer and Jackson, this volume).

The relational ethics of *hamutu moris hamutu mate* infuse diverse understandings of labour and property that guide the more-than-human practices through which both materials and relations are continually transacted and exchanged. Yet, in their encounters with newer or more dominant economic arrangements (Gibson et al. 2018), a distinct dynamism continually shapes these diverse economic ecologies. As Gibson et al. (2018, 11) write:

> What collectively situates them together on a plane of potentiality is, among other things, their inherent sociality and flexibility, their commitment to more than human wellbeing and their unique temporalities. The enduring value of these various practices, relations and knowledges is reinforced by their persistence, creative adaptability and resistance to appropriation. These relations, practices and associated knowledges and cosmovisions are by no means isolated, traditional or static, although their historical roots run deep. Rather, these relations and practices reveal the creative negotiation communities in this interconnected part of the world have long pursued in response to external forces and agents of change (cf. Langton et al. 2006).

Inspired by the keywords approach of Gibson et al. (2018), we distil a non-exhaustive set of core economic institutions and phenomena that pervade customary life in Timor-Leste but which are not considered in neoclassical economic accounts of the country. The following economic institutions orient our approach to this collection and pervade many of its chapters:

- *Marriage-based exchange*: Timor-Leste is a house-based society and relationships between fertility-giving and fertility-taking houses underpin the Timorese customary economy. These more-than-human economies are embedded in a meshwork of multi-generational configurations in which the sum of the parts is always greater than the two houses concerned. Debts arising from the exchange processes are negotiated between houses in front of the ancestors and are usually settled and reconciled over the long term (often inter-generationally) through a series of highly strategic negotiations and exchanges.

- *Kinship and economy*: the multi-generational relationships between fertility-takers and fertility-givers create a rich array of interdependent economic relations involving both ritual and everyday obligations and acts of patronage, production, consumption and distribution. The types of kinship relation at stake (however close or distant they may be) help to determine the ways in which people comport themselves and the manner in which obligations and debts are activated and settled. This is not necessarily a fair or equitable economy but it is one with its own economic logics.
- *Wealth in knowledge*: this concept refers to two processes. First, the idea that people, specifically customary leaders, actively build compositions of dependents endowed with specific knowledge, such as magical and healing knowledge, genealogical and ritual knowledge, geographic knowledge and labouring (Guyer and Beliga 1995, 102). Second, that people's knowledge of their local environment, social relations and histories is learned through everyday practices of being together, doing, crafting and observing. This is a tacit knowledge transferred and grown inter-generationally (Ingold 2011).
- *Co-dependency*: the knowledge referred to above is co-dependent on recognising wider sets of more-than-human social relations, some of which stretch well outside a given locality. These co-dependencies acknowledge, rather than elide, the structure and agency of the social relations that animate them.
- *More-than-human care*: this concept refers to the obligations that co-dependent relations create for economies of care and community that value reciprocity and the continual attunement to signs of non-care or displeasure, especially in relation to the ancestral realm.
- *More-than-human economy*: the co-dependent relations between certain groups of people, their ancestors and their environment hinges on the recognition of a more-than-human economy in which people are constantly indebted to, and seek the assistance of, the ancestral and nature spirit realm for the wellbeing and vitality of their families and their livelihoods (T: *matak malirin*). These debts have uneven material affects.
- *Commons*: the more-than-human sociality that underpins house-based kinship and economic connections includes the notion of a more-than-human commons as well. This commons refers to the spaces and practices through which people and other beings come together to negotiate power arrangements and people's socially and historically contingent claims to material and immaterial resources.

- *Women and social reproduction*: women's role in these community-based economies is critical to their functioning. Their function and agency is central to social reproduction and economic production, consumption and distribution at the household and community level. While they play a less public role in the ritual economy, a woman's natal house is honoured and invoked in all life-affirming and death rituals. In patrilocal systems, male ritual leaders state that it is incumbent upon them to skilfully negotiate ritual outcomes that meet the approval of the female members of their house, including their wives. Women's roles in these rapidly changing processes of social production and reproduction are increasingly the subject of cross-scalar intervention, especially concerning the power, fertility and educational aspirations of younger women and girls.
- *Wealth in people* (Kopytoff 1986): across Timor-Leste, people are preoccupied with drawing together and holding close vast networks of people. Close and distant family members and neighbouring households are frequently called on to assist with the labour and/or resources required to run large agricultural and/or ritual events or to assist with burdensome or unexpected household expenses. The more people who are associated with a network, the larger the available pool of resources and support. While, in some cases, poorer live-in 'relations' carry out the bulk of domestic duties, the expectation is that the owner of the house will also then have certain obligations to resource and/or support the family networks of that person. Changing economic circumstances challenges these practices and assumptions; however, works by Mauss ([1923] 1990), Lévi-Strauss (2003) and Godelier (1982), among others, indicate that, among many people, wealth is the product of the possibility of distributing goods and people and not simply of their accumulation (as the hegemonic ideology of the Euro-American world would lead us to believe).

To sum up, by community-based economy we mean the complex of economic relations involving production, exchange, distribution and consumption of goods, services and people undertaken on the basis of kinship, neighbourhood or other community bounds for the sake of these very relations (Gudeman 2008). The material and immaterial reproduction of the community by various means and in a long-term perspective is the main source of aspiration and anxiety within this economic domain. This particular economic sphere (Bohanann 1955) is embedded in other social institutions and exists to allow them to reproduce (Polanyi [1944] 2000).

Institutions that make up community-based economy are not imagined as economic facts, necessarily. They act as *total social facts* (Mauss [1923] 1990) and often legitimise themselves in non-economic phenomena, such as kinship, religion, neighbourhood bonds, political relations and various symbolic governance systems.

For East Timorese people, at least four different institutions make up the community-based economy: the nuclear or extended-family, the household, neighbour-based groups and origin houses (*uma lisan*), the basic unit of exogamy. Transactions occurring in the community take into consideration a more-than-human economy wherein the potency of place, ancestors and other supernatural beings are considered.

Resources assessed by market operation, including money derived from wage labour and the sale of commodities, are often turned into resources to nourish the community-based economy. Importantly, in such an economic sphere, women have pivotal roles.

Capitalism and the market economy in Timor-Leste: a brief history

If it is true that the idea of economy in Timor-Leste very much exceeds what the concept of Timor-Leste's national economy suggests, it is also undeniable that there have been growing entanglements between Timorese livelihoods and the market economy during the twentieth and twenty-first centuries. As elsewhere in the world, it seems that colonial and postcolonial state-building in the country has much to do with the enforcement of governance policies aimed at reworking the webs of mutuality and the economic interdependencies in which people have been involved in order to make them more and more dependent on market-driven institutions (Polanyi [1944] 2000).

Among other things, policies aimed at reinforcing capitalism as a mode of production and the market as a sort of social organisation in the country have added new layers of density to the already complex set of local economic institutions and phenomena through which Timorese people make their living.

Others have comprehensively investigated the historical development of Timorese involvement in market and capitalist processes (Gunn 1999; Clarence-Smith 1992; Shepherd 2013, Figueiredo 2018; Lundahl and Sjöholm 2019) and our intention here is not to restate this in any substantive way. Rather, in our brief outline of key historical events and processes, our aim is to reframe the metanarrative through which these events and processes have often been presented. That is to say, we do not consider these events and processes to be the genitors of economy in Timor-Leste; instead, we argue that they should be understood as the means by which capitalism and the market economy—as particular modes of economic and societal organisation—have been introduced into a country already redolent in other modes of economic and societal organisation. Further, given that the geographical, ecological and political conditions of colonial and postcolonial Timor-Leste have been, and are, very diverse, we also argue that these market and capitalist processes have not manifest themselves in any homogenous spatial or temporal way.

Through the centuries and in uneven ways across Timor-Leste, facts as diverse as Christianity, tax paying, 'village making' (*aldeamentos*), land grabbing, schooling, forced displacement of people, lawmaking, monetary policies, moralising narratives and statistical studies have all been conduits for the transposition and immersion of a capitalist and market ethos into the minds and bodies of Timorese people.

Between the sixteenth and eighteenth centuries, most of the Portuguese and missionary actions on the island consisted of building alliances with local elites so as to access sandalwood, then a high value commodity exchanged in the incipient global market (Thomaz 2002). The then strong dominance of Chinese merchants in the region obliged those acting in the name of Portugal to subordinate and coordinate their interests with the former.

Later on, taxes were important devices for fostering the replacement of the webs of economic interdependence through which Timorese people made their living. As elsewhere, the monetisation of taxes—enforced as of 1906 by means of *impostos de capitação* (per capita taxes)—was an important vector for people's engagement with the market economy, forcing people to work for colonial agents in exchange for money or simply to not be arrested. The introduction of cash crops, especially coffee, and the related colonial policies to turn these into major export products, was another important contribution to capitalist expansion in the colony. Such efforts entailed the first systematic and large-scale processes of land grabbing (Shepherd and McWilliam 2013; Fitzpatrick, McWilliam, and Barnes 2012).[6] Regimes of forced labour were also important economic events in the history of colonial Timor and were strictly connected with the regimes of citizenship then existing. The 1899 Indigenous Labor Regulations (*Regulamento do Trabalho dos Indígenas*) and the 1936 *Rules for Indigenous Work in Timor* (*Regulamento do Trabalho Indígena na Colônia de Timor*) along with similar legislation functioned as technologies of resource management—in this case, of people—with economic impacts.[7]

This intertwined character of state-building and market making is made clear in Sousa's chapter in this collection. Sousa demonstrates the instrumental role assigned to local bazaars by colonial authorities in Portuguese Timor as devices for imposing a colonial order, and the market as the regime of exchange associated with it. Markets, as time-space of commodified trade, did not emerge spontaneously across the territory; such a phenomenon was enforced by colonial administration as a governance strategy that facilitated control over indigenous power structures to standardise people's mobility and set the use of space and time in an orderly administrative fashion. It also fostered new habits of dealing with resources and established certain expected economic behaviour for local people.

During World War II (WWII), much of the scant modern infrastructure in the territory was destroyed by the invasion of Timor by Australian and Japanese troops. After WWII, attempts to develop a colonial capitalism in Portuguese Timor were undertaken by means of various government practices. Pluriannual development plans were elaborated and carried out so as to foster the emergence of a local elite entrepreneurial class. Between the end of WWII and the civil war in 1975, a Chinese trader middle class also established itself in the country, as did numerous small-scale industries. Activities then undertaken by the state included the promotion of credit policies; the expansion of agriculture, veterinary assistance and schooling; housing policies; urban planning; price and inflation control; statistical registers; and attempts at mineral prospecting and exploration. Grainger's chapter in this collection investigates instances of colonial housing policy development after WWII, examining how these policies intersected with other economic, social and moral anxieties at the time. Grainger argues that competing colonial ideologies like racism and lusotropicalism as well as Fordism (a technique for organising large-scale production) all played a role in the development of plans for Timorese housing.

In the years after the Indonesian invasion in 1974, an increase in public spending and investment in infrastructure such as roads and schools became the hallmark of Indonesian governance of the territory. Beyond state propaganda and control, the aim was to increase Timorese people's involvement in the Indonesian economy and market society. Across the country, the number of schools, local health clinics and other state apparatuses increased greatly between 1975 and 1999, and the number of civil servants also grew exponentially. Meanwhile, the Indonesian army and police, as the state institutions with the strongest presence in Timor Timur, conditioned all governance practices carried out in the territory.

Transmigration policies and the appropriation of state apparatuses by people from other Indonesian provinces meant that the development policies undertaken during the occupation were redirected away from benefitting East Timorese people. These processes further exposed the reality that the enlargement of state and public policies was primarily undertaken in the interests of Indonesian and non-East Timorese people. Meanwhile, the ongoing violence of the military occupation seriously damaged state policies aimed at enlarging market institutions in the country. The continuous suspicion of the East Timorese towards all public policies, programs and institutions led by the Indonesian state—and the fact that these were marked by corruption and collusion—saw little engagement between these initiatives and the East Timorese people (Mubyarto et al. 1991, 50). In this period, the Chinese trader middle class and the small-scale industry existing during the Portuguese administration were destroyed in the first years of the occupation (Mubyarto et al. 1991, 50).

At the turn of the twenty-first century, Timor-Leste as an independent country came to life in a state of outstanding precariousness and vulnerability. Militia attacks in the aftermath of the 1999 popular referendum caused the destruction of most of the infrastructure developed by the Indonesian state. Between 1999 and 2006, humanitarian and development aid institutions played pivotal roles in the reconstruction of the country and in the development of new state-building processes (Silva 2012), supporting endless studies and proposals to forge the legal apparatuses to allow a market society to be transposed to the new country.

In 2007, the new country gained financial sovereignty through the royalties flowing from its vast offshore oil and gas revenues. Since then, the Timor-Leste state has made enormous investments in developing large-scale infrastructure like the South Coast Industrial Corridor and Complex and the Special Administrative Region of Oecussi (RAEOA)/Special Zone of Social Market Economy of Timor-Leste (ZEESM-TL). It is hoped that such mega-projects will trigger economic growth in the near future by providing wage labour to the enormous mass of supposedly unemployed East Timorese citizens (Bovensiepen 2018). Pension payments and direct cash transfers by means of government welfare programs, as well as microcredit initiatives, are increasingly providing post-conflict dividends to the poorer section of Timorese society. At the same time, they are also rapidly entangling people in further countrywide market production and consumption practices. Microcredit institutions have influenced the expansion of a monetised economy in the country and have also contributed to the replacement of webs of mutuality and the economic independencies in which people and their house societies participate. Not by chance, while legitimating their activities as ways to release Timorese women from kinship dependence, these very policies risk making them dependent on higher level financial institutions (Silva and Simião 2017).

The authoritative role that institutions like the IMF and World Bank perform in the arena of international development assistance in Timor-Leste has conditioned public policies and imposed models of neoliberal social organisation in the country. These models give heightened space and importance to the development of the private sector as well as to opening the economy to national and transnational capital in strategic areas like education, health, manufacturing, agricultural production, infrastructure and social security. Such institutional frames ensure that the country becomes further entangled in webs and vacillations of global capital.

Examining Timor-Leste's state budget/expenditure over a period of a decade and a half allows us to see how this global political economy has translated into domestic reality. Table 0.1 contains data documenting 2004/2005 and 2019 state spending in the selected areas of public social policies, defence and police forces, infrastructure and extractive activities.

Table 0.1. Timor-Leste state budget/expenditure

2004/2005 total spending: $65,471,167.05			2019 total spending: $1,233,357,598.67		
Ministries	**Subtotal**	%	**Ministries**	**Subtotal**	%
Agriculture, Forest Fisheries	$1,342,837.08	2.05	Agriculture and Fisheries	$12,635,239.23	1.02
Education, Culture Youth and Sports	$13,396,503.10	20.46	Education, Youth and Sports	$78,911,871.77	6.40
Health	$7,769,571.77	11.87	Health	$42,223,415.42	3.42
Sect. Labour Solidarity	$455,207.80	0.70	Social Solidarity and Inclusion	$54,792,385.36	4.44
Sect. of State Commerce Industries	$152,521.29	0.23	Tourism, Commerce and Industries	$5,314,584.17	0.43
Planning Finance	$4,346,768.96	6.64	Planning and strategic investment	$12,311,641.13	1.00
			Veterans	$96,999,167.34	7.86
Sect. of State for Defence	$4,494,273.43	6.86	Defence	$30,528,750.25	2.48
Interior	$7,777,688.24	11.88	Interior	$47,974,610.98	3.89
			Oil and natural resources	$24,894,571.36	2.02
			Commission for the Administration of the Infrastructure Fund	$276,902,289.79	22.45

Source: Timor-Leste Ministry of Finance. 'Budget Transparency Portal'. Accessed 5 January 2020. www.mof.gov.tl/budget-spending/budget-transparency-portal/?lang=en. Figures originally drawn from www.budgettransparency.gov.tl/publicTransparency (site discontinued).

Alarmingly for a highly ruralised post-conflict country, the percentage of the budget allocated to health, education and agriculture has significantly decreased over this period. The Interior and Defence ministries also had a remarkable reduction in their budget, but a new ministry in the area of post-conflict societal management and control (Roll 2018), the Ministry of Veterans, was created with an important share of the total budget.

The largest share of this budget in 2019 was allocated to infrastructure and mega-project spending. Given the difficulties of attracting international investment, most of Timor-Leste's economy (as a market economy) has been derived from, and depends on, state spending. Hence, during the last 20 years, Timor-Leste's economic policies have been based on the promise of prosperity through extractive activities and associated infrastructure (Bovensiepen 2018). Few investments have been made in smaller-scale productive activities such as small business and agriculture development (Scheiner 2015). Meanwhile, Timorese migrant and seasonal labour has burgeoned in overseas markets, becoming the second most important source of income in the country's market economy (McWilliam 2020; Wigglesworth and Santos, this volume). In other words, the overseas migrant and seasonal labourer experience seems to have become a pivotal part of the East Timorese involvement with the market society.

Not by chance, the final three chapters in this book deal with particular dimensions of the East Timorese overseas and seasonal labourer experience in Australia, the United Kingdom and Korea. By means of a comprehensive analysis, in different ways, these three chapters allow us to see how these phenomena are a means to promote the values and skills characteristic of a market society. Such experiences also reinforce urbanisation—most of the returnees stay in Dili because that is where market opportunities are concentrated—increasing people's dependency on money and wage labour and, ironically, given the nature of the seasonal agricultural labour overseas, contributing to the ongoing devaluing of livelihood activities such as agriculture in Timor-Leste.

Nonetheless, Timorese people have demonstrated a great willingness to embrace their growing enmeshment with the market economy. For example, Wigglesworth and Santos (this volume) show how young Timorese returnees engaging in market opportunities can contribute to extending the rural economy beyond subsistence agriculture. Meanwhile, McWilliam's chapter in this collection provides an important counterpoint by demonstrating that resources gained in migrant work carried out by Fataluku people in the UK have also been invested in the reproduction of mutual obligations among kin groups regarding life cycle rituals and the delayed revival of ceremonial origin houses.[8] McWilliam attributes this to a Fataluku cultural pragmatism (among other variables) and the successful accommodation between mutuality and market that characterises their contemporary economic dynamic. Michael Rose's chapter, in turn, points to the fact that some Timorese people make sense of their seasonal migrant worker experience by inscribing themselves in a narrative of national struggle for independence: they see their labour journey overseas as shaping an economic front (*frente ekonomika*) of resistance and resilience in the ongoing collective process of nation building.

Towards economic ecologies in Timor-Leste

Contemporary accounts of Timor-Leste's market economy are unanimous in pointing out its fragility and its excessive dependency on oil and gas revenues (La'o Hamutuk 2020). The unemployment index continues to be mobilised to prove the deficient character of the national economy and to legitimise multiple efforts to improve so-called productive activities and foster an entrepreneurial ethos among the population (Silva 2017).

Discussing the state of Timor-Leste's economy, Lundahl and Sjöholm (2019) argue that accounting for these variable unemployment/employment figures depends on whether or not analysts fully consider the labour force involved in agriculture and works carried out in the domestic sphere. If we consider unemployment only on the basis of those who are jobseekers, the statistical figures for unemployment are much lower than the figures arising when we take into consideration those who are not seeking jobs, but still are in vulnerable livelihood conditions. Agricultural activity involves between 63 and 68 per cent of all labour in the country depending on the data source considered (Lundahl and Sjöholm 2019, 146). According to the 2013 labour force survey, less than 30 per cent of job positions in the country involve paid work. As Lundahl and Sjöholm (2019, 143, 156) argue, "the unemployment concept is dubious in a country where few can afford to be formally unemployed".

While agreeing with Lundahl and Sjöholm's (2019) criticisms of the validity of these figures concerning employment/unemployment and their weaknesses in depicting the reality of economic dynamics in Timor-Leste, we also draw on their analysis to tell another story. For us, figures on employment and unemployment in Timor-Leste are poor indicators of economic dynamics because most people make their living through a much more complex array of local economic institutions than those considered in hegemonic economic analysis.

By taking into consideration the diverse institutions, phenomena and events mentioned above, we analyse economic relations in contemporary Timor-Leste by means of the concept of economic ecologies—that is, the historised, localised, heterogeneous and complex combinations of knowledge, production, distribution, exchange and consumption by which people and things are replenished and more-than-human well-being is ensured. As with Timor-Leste's diverse local complexes of governance and spiritual ecologies (Silva 2014; Palmer and McWilliam 2019), economic ecologies do not form a singular (economic) system per se: their constituent parts retain considerable autonomy and coexist in time and space, running in parallel. Following Gudeman (2008), three transaction domains constitute the economic ecologies: the community-based economic institutions, the market economy and the market finance or the trade of money[9]. So, economic dynamics are generated by people's opportunities, choices or non-choices to engage in each of these economic domains.

Across the globe, diverse ethnographies of economies have long demonstrated that the separation between the dynamics of production, exchange, distribution and consumption is not universal. For example, in many societies, domestic production is characterised by the fact that the production unit is also the consumer unit (Sahlins 1972), although this does not mean that the domestic unit is self-sufficient. The fact that households often do not produce all that is needed (in quantity and/or quality) for their whole reproduction compels them to exchange.[10] Thus, certain models of reproduction, including Timor-Leste's community-based economies, purposefully show the correlations between the dynamics of production, exchange, distribution and consumption. At the same time, these systems are exploited by capitalist practices that work to make the dependency between the spheres of production, circulation and consumption invisible.[11]

In this collection, we seek to expand upon these entanglements and bring these models into conversation. To do this we draw on the concept of *economic ecologies*—a concept that goes beyond the fact of diversity to demand careful attention to, and the elucidation of, embedded more-than-human social relations and interdependencies. We ask how these 'hidden' socio-economic and socio-ecological rationalities are already embedded with capitalist economies and how increased attention to their salience might help reshape lives and livelihoods in more sustainable and life affirming ways (cf. De Jong 2013; Tsing 2015).

Our choice for economic ecologies instead of economy aims at producing at least three main effects: 1. To mark our distance and difference from hegemonic neoclassic narratives which reduces all economic diversity to a market-driven economy glossed as economy; 2. To highlight the multiple and diverse phenomena which allow material and immaterial reproduction to occur in each particular context; and 3. To draw out the intersectionality of these economic instances that create the necessity for multiple relational layers within economic life.

We embrace this concept fully aware of the fact that many of the institutions making up local economic ecologies are a sort of living ruins (Santos 2018, 29-30)—institutions carved out in the past (be it close or distant) that capitalism has damaged but not completely destroyed or colonised. We think here of relationships of care and donation, of cooperative and mutualist practices, and even of the various systems of government-sanctioned communal use and enjoyment of the land that continue to exist across the region and the globe (Gibson et al. 2018). In Timor-Leste, this sense of mutuality and the commons is actively and explicitly informed by a more-than-human sociality, one that underpins house-based kinship assemblages and associated spiritual and economic ecologies (Palmer 2015, 2020). It is through these assemblages that people and other beings come together to negotiate arrangements and claims to material and immaterial resources.

From this perspective, capitalism and the market economy is only one regime, among others, of production, distribution and consumption that people rely on to make their living. Capitalism coexists with other institutions, such as those discussed above: marriage exchanges, more-than-human co-dependency and wealth in people and knowledge.

Thus, we deploy the concept of economic ecologies as a tool in a wider search for epistemological justice. We argue for an acknowledgment of the rationality and intrinsic value of non-market economic praxis and the ways in which these institutions and phenomena interpret, contribute to and sometimes even solve the problems and challenges that life, in all its interdependent spheres, presents. For us, inventorying, understanding and valuing these non-market praxes in Timor-Leste is also a political act: expanding the spectrum of possible solutions to the present challenges faced by the world.

Structure and chapter outlines

This book is structured in three parts. The first, 'Glimpses of the colonial economy', provides insight into colonial governance attempts to transpose market economic practices into the country and unveils localised subversions of such efforts. Sousa reveals how local markets, as we know them today, are colonial inventions through which colonial authorities attempted to effect their authority and occupation over the territory. These formalised colonial bazaars were devices for taming and incorporating a reluctant Timorese population and other mavericks into a colonial order. As a political undertaking, this process was activated to influence and control indigenous power structures, standardise people's mobility, and set the use of space and time in an orderly administrative fashion. Nevertheless, Sousa argues, the bazaars were places of dissent and resilient native practices. This is elucidated through a historical analysis of concrete bazaar dynamics, including the expectations, interactions and duplicity of Timorese and Portuguese actors.

In a similar vein, Hicks shows us a concrete experience of dissent around colonial projects of order through an analysis of the Viqueque market during the years 1966-1967. Hicks points out how the space occupied by the weekly emporium offered a forum in which ethnicity, social hierarchy, gender, cockfighting and religious affiliation played out visually, presenting a physical replication of the social distinctions that defined the contemporary character of the village and the subdistrict it served. His subsequent comparison between colonial and postcolonial market organisation in Viqueque suggests that ethnicities, gender and other social identity markers have become much less relevant in market dynamics. Hicks argues that this is a response to nation-building anxieties.

Colonial attempts to create a socio-economic order via urban planning and housing are analysed in Grainger's chapter. His study provides an epistemological window to better understand the control of domestic spaces and indigenous labour, as well as trans-colonial cooperation after WWII. Reporting on a regional housing study tour backed by the colonial state, Grainger reveals tensions in alignment of the diverse ideologies that underpinned popular housing plans and policies in colonial Timor-Leste: Fordism, lusotropicalism, tropical architecture and racism. This amalgam of ideologies and associated constraints in their application reveals the controversies bound up in the making of a rational administration in 'Portuguese Timor'. Colonial land titling and zoning are shown to be fundamental governance devices embedded with ideas and practices of urban planning, economy and mobility.

Part 2 brings to the fore the local institutions and practices that comprise the economic ecologies existing among East Timorese people. On the basis of different case studies and theoretical approaches, a rich array of values and relationships are made explicit to challenge statist and other 'common sense' representations of local economies as weak or sub-developed. In different ways, the chapters distil and make visible particular sets of power relations, patterns of inequality and a vibrant more-than-human economy.

It is no accident that we begin such a discussion with an analysis by Barnes of the Tetum category *atan* (slave/servant). The persistence and, at the same time, the discomfort this category triggers in research dialogues about Timor-Leste signals its historical and contemporary importance. Barnes calls attention to the different meanings such a category evokes and alerts us to its specificities before Euro-centric notions of 'slave' and 'slavery'. Based on a literature review, the category of *atan* emerges as a floating signifier evoking particular relationships of dependency, servitude (bondage) and even slavery or property. On the basis of her own and other ethnographic research, Barnes points out deep anxieties about *atan* ancestry in a range of settings and contexts, including those involving social differentiation and status recognition. Barnes also argues that *atan* is a category that highlights the importance and uneven effects of ideas of rights and wealth in people in Timor-Leste and elsewhere. Her analysis of this fundamental economic phenomenon blurs the boundaries between orphan/domestic, servant/slave, person/possession and kin/non-kin.

Fidalgo-Castro and Alonso-Población analyse how people from Faulara (Liquiçá Municipality) mobilise goods and money by mechanisms other than market transactions, namely rituals. In this chapter, rituals function as a pivotal economic fact, serving both as a source of economic security and of redistribution embedded in kinship and everyday social networks. By exploring how a particular household deals with and records their ritual commitments across time, the chapter demonstrates that wellbeing is enabled through debt relations with others and the ways these relations form a social and economic safety net. Taking this broader perspective of what constitutes economy as a category linked to ritual practice, Fidalgo-Castro and Alonso-Población avoid considering kinship related rituals as discrete units of analysis, and tease out some of the unseen functions of regimes of ritual exchange, including the ways in which they actively shape sociality and economy.

Following on from this, Trindade and Oliveira draw our attention to decision-making processes at the household level. Building on a study of household decision-making centred around farming, management of livestock and financial management in the Viqueque district, the authors argue that cultural differentiations at this scale have very often been neglected within the literature. The spatialised social differentiation bound up in Timorese sacred houses (*Uma Lulik*) and the complementarity this entails between male and female members of the house is drawn upon to document how decisions are made at the household level in relation to family resources. Who decides where to farm, what kind of crops are grown, how livestock is utilised and how a family's money is spent are linked to complex understandings of sociocultural norms and practices in the household and wider kinship space.

The operation of a more-than-human economy, based on gift and debt exchange, emerges sharply in Nogueira da Silva's chapter. She discusses household feeding routines in ordinary and extraordinary contexts in Same, Manufahi. Nogueira da Silva argues that the stages of making and consuming food are, among other things, moments of communion—with the creator (*Maromak*), with the ancestors (*bei'ala*) and with the sacred house (*Uma Lulik*). Within these moments, relationships between humans and non-humans are co-constituted by a constant giving and receiving of food—a process in which debt and the expectation of reciprocation are deliberate parts. Nogueira da Silva reminds us that food ingestion is a form of productive consumption through which life is generated materially and immaterially. She also explores the difference between cooking procedures for foods that will be consumed by humans and spirits. The foods offered to non-human agents are offered half-raw (or half-cooked) and, thus, like their recipients, 'appear to be in a liminal state between a natural state and a cultured one'.

Cunha and Bessa's chapter, the last in Part 2, draws on a twofold ecofeminist assumption: 1) in Timor-Leste, the vital relationship between people and the land is constitutive of both Timorese sociability and Timorese views of themselves and the world; and 2) as elsewhere, many of the land-associated works are the responsibility of women. This land work carried out by women generates, among other things, fundamental socio-economies for the subsistence of bodies, food for the spirit and a celebration of life that existed, exists and will exist. Cunha and Bessa explore how these land works performed by women produce goods, services, memories, identities, affections, bonds, food and objects; in other words, the plentiful resources that are essential for the endless flow of life. They also argue that such embedded socio-economies have a great capacity to resist a neoliberal capitalist hegemony by defining for themselves what abundance is and by practising another economy of desire. This economy of desire points to sobriety as the opposite of neoliberal austerity: sobriety at the centre is life in all its manifestations.

Finally, the third part of this book explores the economic transformations derived of the entanglement between local economies and broader market endeavours. In various ways, the new economic ecologies deriving from these assemblages are analysed as exemplary of the contemporary vitality and resilience of Timorese people and their capacity to generate new ways of organising life and economic relations.

Crespi discusses the impacts of building the Suai Supply Base on the economic dynamics of Kamanasa kingdom. Her focus is on issues related to land appropriation by the state and the ways in which this is linked to new phenomena concerning local diet and increased monetisation. Arguing that this project is a vehicle for the commodification of the economy, Crespi explores structural changes that are affecting existing social systems, especially as this concerns territoriality, trade and diet. With the transfer of the land to the project challenging local practices and notions of land ownership, Crespi explains how the state's plans for the base, and the ways in which the state deals with local expectations and knowledge relating to the land, have created tensions among local populations. She explores the community's fears and expectations about these matters and, finally, discusses the economic changes derived from compensation policies.

Palmer and Jackson explore the sociocultural benefits of emerging market-based instruments for carbon in Timor-Leste. Through an analysis of the market and community-economy interactions and values of a reforestation program in Baguia in the Matebian mountain range, the chapter highlights the opportunities and tensions faced by farmers and their extended kin networks in relation to their fields and forests. Palmer and Jackson argue that these new arrangements are an important facet of Baguia's emergent post-conflict local economy. Elucidating a diversity of understandings about labour and (private) property, they show how a range of practices of care are already subtly woven into the program's operations. They argue that these highly localised and particular relations between people and nature, and between people and people, might be better foregrounded to underpin the carbon trading scheme, triggering a range of other social and cultural benefits as well as biodiversity exchanges.

Barreto Soares examines China's economic activities in post-independence Timor-Leste since 2002. Her analysis focuses on both Chinese state and non-state actors and their varied levels of immersion in Timor-Leste's economy over the past two decades. Soares argues that non-state Chinese actors are represented, in particular, by the overseas Chinese community resident in Timor-Leste. Further, that the presence and economic activities of Chinese state and non-state actors has significantly changed Timor-Leste's economic landscape. The economic bolstering provided by the Chinese state within Timor-Leste is shown, in part, to reflect an emerging battleground for the competing economic and geopolitical interests of major powers. Meanwhile, overseas Chinese, particularly Chinese newcomers and, to some extent, the historical Timorese-Chinese community, are shown, to varying extents and with varying effects, to be involved in new forms of economic and settler colonialism. More recent arrivals of Chinese nationals have settled in strategic locations, becoming, as in the past, key players in different economic activities across the country.

Wigglesworth and Santos analyse how migrant work has provided an opportunity for Timorese youth to support their families. On their return to Timor-Leste, Timorese seasonal workers invest time and money in contributing to their family's home improvement and daily living expenses. Wigglesworth and Santos argue that this migration experience represents an opportunity for families enmeshed in a subsistence economy to be lifted out of poverty. They also analyse the impact of this migration on social change in Timor-Leste and argue that the migration experience creates new perspectives for many returned workers on gendered relations and how best to respond to the immediate economic needs of their families.

In the next chapter, McWilliam continues an examination of the theme of economic transformations as this relates to the customary economy and the remittance landscape. Focusing on the progressive refashioning of Fataluku origin houses, McWilliam argues that a widespread feature of the post independence landscape of Timor-Leste has been the sustained revival of traditional practices of economic mutuality and a return to custom' especially among many rural communities; further, that Fataluku-speaking customary communities in the far east of the country have been able to continue their engagement with the rebuilding and restoration of their ancestral house traditions in part because of the opportunities imparted by a remittance economy. The progressive re-appearance of these distinctive Fataluku origin houses across the landscape highlights the readiness of origin groups to commit their limited resources to their reconstruction. Reflecting too on the innovative changes that kin groups have made to these traditional forms of construction in recent years, McWilliam argues that this is also an outcome of a characteristic pragmatism that epitomises Fataluku cultural adaptation to changing circumstances and the embrace of modernity, highlighting what is arguably a successful accommodation between mutuality and the market

The final chapter in this collection focuses on the Timorese perspectives on seasonal work in Australia. Rose examines Timorese ideas about seasonal and other remittance work being a part of a new *frente ekonomika* (economic front) and continuing the East Timorese struggle for independence through greater economic autonomy. Drawing on close ethnographic work, Rose develops the theoretical premise that policy relating to labour migration should be attentive to the perspectives of those who participate in it or aspire to it. In order to better understand the varied and uneven impacts of such programs (including implied or real corruption emerging from Timorese patron-client relations), Rose argues that researchers need to find ways of engaging more deeply with those who do the work, listening carefully to their stories and grievances in all their cultural and linguistic distinctiveness.

Acknowledgements

We are deeply grateful to all our East Timor interlocutors for the insights and lessons they have shared with us over the years. We thank Ana Carolina Ramos de Oliveira, who provided critical editorial assistance for this collection. We also thank all the authors who contributed to this collection and reviewers for their valuable critiques. Recognition is also due to the institutions which funded the symposium "Economic Dynamics in Contemporary Timor-Leste", held by Universidade de Brasília in 2018, which triggered the editorial effort resulting in this book: Coordination for the Improvement of Higher Education Personnel (Coordenação de Aperfeiçoamento de Pessoal de Nível Superior – CAPES), the Brazilian National Council for Scientific and Technological Development (Conselho Nacional de Desenvolvimento Científico e Tecnológico – CNPq) and the Federal District Research Foundation (Fundação de Apoio a Pesquisa do Distrito Federal – FAP-DF). We also would like to acknowledge the financial assistance of the Australian Research Council via Grant (DP190100875), of CAPES (via Academic Excellence Program – PROEX) and the Faculty of Science at the University of Melbourne who supported open access publication.

Notes

1 Neoliberal capitalism emerged after the developmentalism of the 1970s (Sachs 2000), marked by the global rise of the financial sector and by the dynamics of a territorially expansionist system in which the growth of capital-bearing debt interest was an essential political dimension (Streeck 2013; Rodrigues, Santos, and Teles 2016; Fernández 2016). On neoliberal subjectivities, it is assumed that individual initiative driven by individualistic interests is the core condition of development and entails a belief that this is the only way to organise economic life. Reciprocity and mutuality are seen as obstacles to self-realisation and richness.

2 For the purpose of clarification, here we use the term market economy or market society to mean the capitalist market economy and the hegemonic capitalist market society.

3 We define community-based economies as the social relations that have an economic value, meaning: 1) producing, distributing and consuming whatever is considered as essential to live well and 2) the material reproduction of life taking place within a group of people that nourish bounds of co-dependency among themselves.

4 De Jong´s (2013) analysis of the relatively minimal impact of Indonesia's 1998's economic crisis on everyday life in two villages in Tana Toraja is exemplary of this.

5 Karl Polanyi's theorisation (1957, 72) about the invention of the work as a commodity is also instructive here. To Polanyi, work is just another name for human activity and is associated with life itself, which in turn is not produced in order to sell labour but for completely different reasons.

6 In fact, it seems that the very nature of coffee plant production provoked changes in the land tenure in Timor. On the basis of extensive fieldwork in Ermera, Oviedo (2019, 57) brings to the fore people's memory about how coffee changed their agriculture practices. The fact that coffee trees produce annually and that people sold their production to colonial brokers worked to reinforce people's attachment to the land plots where coffee trees were grown, whereas previously agriculture praxes were more nomadic and dispersed. A similar process is identified by Li (2014) in her analysis of transformations in land tenure in Sulawesi, Indonesia.

7 Local government ordinance no. 439, of June 2, 1936. For more details see Figueiredo 2018, 482-483.

8 De Jong (2013) points to a similar trend among Torajans immigrants who go abroad or to other Indonesian provinces.

9 It is worth noting that the trade of money by means of local money lenders—at very high rates—is a common practice in Timor-Leste. Microcredit finance institutions also play a similar role.

10 Sahlins (1972) attributes the following predicates to what he calls the domestic production mode: underproduction; priority for the production of use values; social division of labour based on sex and age; a more unitary productive process (in comparison with the capitalist mode of production); absence of private property; inclination towards maximum dispersion, which since it is self-contained, manifests in the absence of centralised political authority; etc.

11 Initiatives such as fair trade have explored the connection between production and consumption dynamics as a particular strategy for adding value to goods. For a discussion of fair trade initiatives in Timor-Leste, see Silva, Ferreira, and Gosaves (2020).

References

Alonso-Población, E., A. Fidalgo-Castro and M. J. Pena-Castro. 2018. "Bargaining kultura: Tensions between principles of power acquisition in contemporary Timor-Leste." *Sociologus* 68 (2): 107-24. https://doi.org/10.3790/soc.68.2.107.

Akta no regulamentu Tara bandu Distrito Ermera. Mimeo, 2012.

Appadurai, A. 1986. "Introduction: Commodities and the Politics of Value." In *The Social Life of Things: Commodities in Cultural Perspective*, edited by A. Appadurai, 3-63. Cambridge: Cambridge University Press. Doi.org/10.1017/CBO9780511819582.003.

Appel, H. 2017. "Toward an Ethnography of the National Economy." *Cultural Anthropology* 32 (2): 294-322. Doi.org/10.14506/ca32.2.09.

Austin, J. L. 1999. *How to Do Things with Words.* London: Harvard University Press.

Barnes, S. 2017. "Customary Renewal and the Pursuit of Power and Prosperity in Post-Occupation East Timor: A Case Study from Babulo, Uato-Lari." PhD diss., Monash University.

Batterbury, S., L. Palmer, T. Reuter, D. A. Carvalho, B. Kehi and C. Cullen. 2015. "Land access and livelihoods in post-conflict Timor-Leste: No magic bullets." *International Journal of the Commons* 9 (2 [September]): 619-647. Doi.org/10.18352/ijc.514.

Bernstein, H. 2010. *Class Dynamics of Agrarian Change.* Boulder: Kumarian Press.

Bohannan, P. 1955. "Some principles of exchange and investment among the Tiv." *American Anthropologist* 57 (1): 60-70.

Bovensiepen, J. 2018. "Introduction: Political and Spiritual Visions of the Future." In *The Promise of Prosperity. Visions of the Future in Timor-Leste*, edited by J. Bovensiepen, 1-28. Canberra: ANU Press. Doi.org/10.22459/PP.2018.

Brogan, K. and TOMAK (To´os ba Moris Di´ak). 2016. *Gender Equality and Social Inclusion Analysis.* Mimeo. Dili: TOMAK. Tomak.org/wp-content/uploads/2016/11/TOMAK-gender-and-social-inclusion-analysis.pdf. Accessed 10 December 2020.

Burke, L. 2020. "Planning Reproduction: Preparing for Life and the Future in Maubisse". In *Proceedings of the Understanding Timor-Leste 2019 Conference,* edited by S. Farram, D. M. da Silva, L. F. Soares, N. C. Mendes, C. Fernandes, M. B. Soares, U. Pinto, H. Loney, R. L. Williams, C. N. Nabais, M. Leach and contributors. Melbourne/Dili: Timor-Leste Studies Association.

Carroll-Bell, S. 2015. "Development alternatives in Timor-Leste: Recasting modes of local engagement." *Bijdragen tot de taal-, land- en volkenkunde/Journal of the Humanities and Social Sciences of Southeast Asia* 171 (2-3): 312-345. Doi.org/10.1163/22134379-17102006.

Clarence-Smith, W. G. 1992. "Planters and smallholders in Portuguese Timor in the nineteenth and twentieth centuries, Indonesia circle." *Indonesia Circle. School of Oriental & African Studies Newsletter* 20 (57): 15-30.

Cunha, T. 2014. *Never trust Sindarela. Feminismos, Pós-colonialismos, Moçambique e Timor-Leste.* Coimbra: Edições Almedina.

Cunha, T. 2015 *Women inPower Women. Outras economias criadas e lideradas por mulheres no Sul não-imperial.* Buenos Aires: CLACSO.

Cunha, T. and L. de P. Valle. 2021. "A pandemia na vida das mulheres: Uma reflexão feminista a partir de Moçambique e Brasil." *Revista de Educação Pública* 30: 1-20.

De Jong, E. 2013. *Making a Living between Crisis and Ceremonies in Tana Toraja. The Practice of Everyday Life of a South Sulawesi Highland Community in Indonesia.* Leiden, Boston: Brill.

DFAT. 2014. *TOMAK – To'os Ba Moris Diak. Farming for Prosperity. Investment concept.* Canberra: Department of Foreign Affairs and Trade. Available at: https://www.dfat.gov.au/about-us/business-opportunities/Pages/proposed-program-in-timor-leste-tomak-farming-for-prosperity-investment-concept. Accessed 17 March, 2022.

Elias, N. 1993. *O processo civilizador.* Rio de Janeiro: Jorge Zahar Ed.

Federici, S. 2019. *O ponto zero da revolução.* São Paulo: Editora Elefante.

Fernández, G. O. Z. 2016. *Alternativas al poder corporativo. 20 propuestas para una agenda de transición en disputa con las empresas transnacionales.* Barcelona: Icaria Editorial.

Ferguson, J. 2015. *Give a Man a Fish. Reflections on the New Politics of Distribution.* London: Duke University Press. doi.org/10.1515/9780822375524.

Ferguson, J., and T. M. Li. 2018. "Beyond the 'Proper Job': Political-Economic Analysis after the Century of Labouring Man." PLAAS Working Paper 51, Institute for Poverty, Land and Agrarian Studies, University of the Western Cape, Cape Town.

Fidalgo-Castro, A. 2015. "Dinámicas Políticas y Económicas En El Dominio Ritual y La Vida Cotidiana En Timor Oriental. Estudios de Caso Desde La Aldeia de Faulara" PhD diss., Universidade da Coruña.

Figueiredo, F. 2018. *Timor-Leste. A Presença Portuguesa desde a Reocupação à Invasão Indonésia (1945-1975)*. Lisboa: Ancora Editora.

Fitzpatrick, D., A. McWilliam, and S. Barnes. 2012. *Property and Social Resilience in Times of Conflict: Land, Custom and Law in East Timor*. Surrey & Burlington: Ashgate.

Gibson-Graham, J. K. 1996. *O fim do capitalismo (como nós o conhecemos). Uma crítica feminista de economia política*. Lisboa: Instituto Piaget.

Gibson-Graham, J. K. 2005. "Surplus possibilities: Postdevelopment and community economies." *Singapore Journal of Tropical Geography* 26 (1): 4-26. doi.org/10.1111/j.0129-7619.2005.00198.x.

Gibson-Graham, J. K. 2006. *A Postcapitalist Politics*. Minneapolis: University of Minnesota Press.

Gibson, K., R. Astuti, M. Carnegie, A. Chalernphon, K. Dombroski, A. R. Haryani, A. Hill, B. Kehi, L. Law, I. Lyne, A. McGregor, K. McKinnon, A. McWilliam, F. Miller, C. Ngin, D. Occeña-Gutierrez, L. Palmer, P. Placino, M. Rampengan, W. Lei Lei Than, N. I. Wianti and S. Wright. 2018. "Community Economies in Monsoon Asia: Keywords and Key Reflections." *Asia Pacific Viewpoint* 59 (1): 3-16. doi.org/10.1111/apv.12186.

Gluckman, M. (1958) 1987. "Análise de uma situação social na Zululândia moderna." In *Antropologia das Sociedades Contemporâneas*, by B. F. Bianco, 227-267. São Paulo: Global Universitária.

Godelier, M. 1982. *La production des grand homes*. Paris: Librarie Arthéme Fayard.

Gregory, C. 1982. *Gifts and Commodities*. London: Academic.

Gudeman, S. 2001. *The Anthropology of Economy: Community, Market and Culture*. Oxford: Blackwell.

Gudeman, S. 2008. *Economy's Tensions: The Dialectics of Community and Market*. New York: Berghahn Books.

Gudeman, S. 2016. *Anthropology and Economy*. Cambridge: Cambridge University Press. doi.org/10.1017/CBO9781316442739.

Gunn, G. 1999. *Timor Lorosa'e. 500 anos*. Macau: Livros do Oriente.

Guyer, J., and S. Beliga. 1995. "Wealth in people as wealth in knowledge: Accumulation and composition in Equatorial Africa." *The Journal of African History* 36 (1): 91-120. doi.org/10.1017/S0021853700026992.

Hayek, F. 1998. *Law, Legislation and Liberty: A New Statement of the Liberal Principles of Justice and Political Economy*. London: Routledge.

Ingold, T. 2011. *Being Alive: Essays on Movement, Knowledge and Description*. London: Routledge. doi.org/10.4324/9780203818336.

Jackson, S. and L. Palmer. 2015. "Reconceptualising ecosystem services: Possibilities for cultivating and valuing the ethics and practices of care." *Progress in Human Geography* 39 (2): 122-145. doi.org/10.1177/0309132514540016.

Kopytoff, I. 1986. "The Cultural Biography of Things: Commoditization as Process." In *The Social Life of Things: Commodities in a Cultural Perspective*, edited by A. Appadurai, 64-92. Cambridge: Cambridge University Press. doi.org/10.1017/CBO9780511819582.004.

Langton, M., O. Mazel and L. Palmer. 2006. "The 'spirit' of the thing: The boundaries of aboriginal economic relations at Australian Common Law." *The Australian Journal of Anthropology* 17 (3): 307-321. doi.org/10.1111/j.1835-9310.2006.tb00066.x.

La'o Hamutuk. 2020. *Rights and Sustainability*. Dili: La'o Hamutuk. www.laohamutuk.org/econ/briefing/RightSustainCurrentEn.pps. Accessed 4 December 2020.

Lévi-Strauss, C. (1959) 2003. *As estruturas elementares do parentesco*. São Paulo: Editora Vozes.

Li, T. M. 2014. *Land's End: Capitalist Relations on an Indigenous Frontier*. Duham: Duke University Press. doi.org/10.1215/9780822376460.

Lundahl, M and F. Sjöholm. 2019. *The Creation of the East Timorese Economy. Volume 2: Birth of a Nation*. Cham, Switzerland: Palgrave Macmillan. doi.org/10.1007/978-3-030-22052-5.

Mauss, M. (1923) 1990. *The Gift: The Form and Reasons for Exchange in Archaic Societies.* Translated by W. D. Halls. London: Routledge.

McWilliam, A. 2011. "Exchange and resilience in Timor-Leste." *Journal of the Royal Anthropological Institute, New Series* 17 (4): 745-763. doi.org/10.1111/j.1467-9655.2011.01717.x.

McWilliam, A. 2020. *Post-Conflict Social and Economic Recovery in Timor-Leste: Redemptive Legacies.* London: Routledge. doi.org/10.4324/9780429347948.

McWilliam, A., L. Palmer, and C. Shepherd. 2014. "*Lulik* encounters and cultural frictions in East Timor: Past and present." *The Australian Journal of Anthropology* 25 (3 [December]): 304-320. doi.org/10.1111/taja.12101.

Meillassoux, C. 1981. *Maidens, Meal and Money: Capitalism and the Domestic Community.* Cambridge: Cambridge University Press.

Mitchell, T. 2002. *Rule of Experts. Egypt, Techno-Politics, Modernity.* Los Angeles: University of California Press. doi.org/10.1525/9780520928251.

Mubyarto, S., H. Loekman, E. Djatmiko, I. Setiawiati, and A. Mawarnlji. 1991. *East Timor: The Impact of Integration (an Indonesian Socio-Anthropological Study).* Northcote, Australia: IRIP (Indonesia Resources and Information Programme).

Oviedo, C. A. 2019. "'De quién es la tierra?'. Prácticas de gobierno y construcciones de Estado en Timor-Leste. Etnografía del levantamiento catastral en el municipio de Ermera." PhD diss., University of Brasilia.

Oxfam International. 2020. *Tempo de cuidar. O trabalho de cuidado não remunerado e mal pago e a crise global da desigualdade.* Oxford: Oxfam. https://wm.org.br/justica-social-e-economica/forum-economico-de-davos/tempo-de-cuidar/ Accessed 10 December 2020. DOI: 10.21201/2020.5419

Palmer, L. 2010. "Enlivening development: Water management in post-conflict Baucau City, Timor-Leste." *Singapore Journal of Tropical Geography* 31 (3): 357-370. doi.org/10.1111/j.1467-9493.2010.00404.x.

Palmer, L. 2015. *Water Politics and Spiritual Ecology: Custom, Environmental Governance and Development.* London: Routledge Explorations in Environmental Studies. doi.org/10.4324/9781315883250.

Palmer, L. 2020. "The cosmopolitics of flow and healing in North-Central Timor-Leste." *The Australian Journal of Anthropology* 31 (2): 224-239. doi.org/10.1111/taja.12359.

Palmer, L. and A. McWilliam. 2019. "Spirit ecologies and customary governance in post-conflict Timor-Leste." *Bijdragen tot de taal-, land- en volkenkunde/Journal of the Humanities and Social Sciences of Southeast Asia* 175 (4): 474-505. doi.org/10.1163/22134379-17504003.

Polanyi. K. (1944) 2000. *A grande transformação. As origens da nossa época.* Rio de Janeiro: Campus.

Polanyi, K. (1944) 1957. *The Great Transformation: The Political and Economic Origins of our Time.* Boston: Beacon Press.

Rodrigues, J., A. C. Santos, and N. Teles. 2016. *A Financeirização do Capitalismo em Portugal.* Lisboa: Actual.

Roll, K. 2018. "Reconsidering Reintegration: Veterans' Benefits as State-Building." In *The Promise of Prosperity*, edited by J. Bovensiepen, 139-153. Canberra: ANU Press. doi.org/10.22459/PP.2018.07.

Sachs, W. 2000. *Dicionário do desenvolvimento: guia para o conhecimento como poder.* Petrópolis: Editora Vozes.

Sahlins, M. 1972. *Stone Age Economics.* London: Tavistock Publications.

Santos, B de S. 2014. *Epistemologies of the South: Justice Against Epistemicide.* London: Paradigm Publishers. doi.org/10.4324/9781315634876.

Santos, B de S. 2018. *The End of the Cognitive Empire: The Coming of Age of Epistemologies of the South.* Durham and London: Duke University Press

Scheiner, C. 2015. "Can the Petroleum Fund Exorcise the Resource Curse from Timor-Leste?" In *A New Era? Timor-Leste after the UN*, edited by S. Ingram, L. Kent, and A. McWilliam, 73-102. Canberra: ANU Press. doi.org/10.22459/NE.09.2015.06.

Shepherd, C. 2013. *Development and Environmental Politics Unmasked: Authority, Participation and Equity in East Timor*. London/Hong Kong: Routledge.

Shepherd, C., and A. McWilliam. 2013. "Cultivating plantations and subjects in East Timor: A genealogy." *Bijdragen Tot De Taal-, Land- En Volkenkunde* 169 (2-3): 326-361. doi.org/10.1163/22134379-12340047.

Silva, K. 2012. *As nações desunidas. Práticas da ONU e a estruturação do Estado em Timor-Leste*. Belo Horizonte: Editora UFMG.

Silva, K. 2014. "O governo da e pela *kultura*. Complexos locais de governança na formação do Estado em Timor-Leste." *Revista Crítica de Ciências Sociais* 104: 123-150. doi.org/10.4000/rccs.5727.

Silva, K. 2016. "Administrando Pessoas, Recursos e Rituais. Pedagogia Econômica Como Tática de Governo Em Timor-Leste." *Horizontes Antropológicos* 22 (45): 127-153. doi.org/10.1590/S0104-71832016000100006.

Silva, K. 2017. "Managing Resources, Persons and Rituals: Economic Pedagogy as Government Tactics." In *Transformations in Independent Timor-Leste: Dynamics of Social and Cultural Cohabitations*, edited by S. M. Viegas and R. G. Feijó, 193-209. New York: Routledge. doi.org/10.4324/9781315535012-11.

Silva, K., A. Ferreira, and L. Gosaves. 2020. "Commerce as 'Total Social Fact': Fair Trade Practices in Dili." In *Performing Modernities: Pedagogies and Technologies in the Making of Contemporary Timor-Leste*, edited by K. Silva, 127-149. Brasília: ABA Publicações. doi.org/10.48006/978-65-87289-07-6.127-149.

Silva, K. and D. S. Simião. 2017. "Pessoa como dívida? Controvérsias sobre dádiva, dívida e redes sociais na construção da pessoa em Timor-Leste: uma aproximação." In *Dádiva, cultura e sociedade*, edited by J. A. Vianna Lopes, P. H. Martins, and A. Lacerda, 105-117. Rio de Janeiro: Casa de Rui de Barbosa.

Streeck, W. 2013. *Tempo comprado: a crise adiada do capitalismo democrático*. Lisboa: Conjuntura Actual Editora.

Thomaz, L. F. F. R. 2002. *De Ceuta a Timor*. Lisboa: Difel.

Traube, E. G. 2007. "Unpaid wages: Local narratives and the imagination of the nation." *The Asia Pacific Journal of Anthropology* 8 (1): 9-26. doi.org/10.1080/14442210601161724.

Trindade, J. and S. Barnes. 2018. "Expressions of the 'Good Life' and Visions of the Future: Reflections from Dili and Uatolari." In *The Promise of Prosperity Visions of the Future in Timor-Leste*, edited by J. Bovensiepen, 157-171. Canberra: ANU Press. doi.org/10.22459/PP.2018.08.

Tsing, A. 2015. *The Mushroom at the End of the World: On the Possibility of Life in Capitalist Ruins*. Princeton, Nova Jersey: Princeton University Press. doi.org/10.2307/j.ctvc77bcc.

Valle, L. de P. 2019. "Ecofeminismo." *Dicionário Alice*, April 01, 2019. alice.ces.uc.pt/dictionary/?id=23838&pag=23918&id_lingua=1&entry=24270. Accessed 5 January 2021

World Bank Group. 2018. *Timor-Leste Economic Report March 2018*. Dili: World Bank Group. documents1.worldbank.org/curated/en/889001521523777495/pdf/124434-WP-P165266-PUBLIC-TLER-MarchFINAL.pdf. Accessed 10 December 2020.

World Bank Group. 2020. *Timor-Leste Economic Report April 2020. A Nation Under Pressure*. Dili: World Bank Group. openknowledge.worldbank.org/bitstream/handle/10986/33749/Timor-Leste-Economic-Report-A-Nation-Under-Pressure.pdf?sequence=1&isAllowed=y. Accessed 10 December 2020.

GLIMPSES OF
THE COLONIAL ECONOMY

CHAPTER 1

The colonial bazaar in 'Portuguese Timor': the taming of the 'savage marketers'

Lúcio Sousa

Abstract

This paper discusses the instrumental role assigned to bazaars by the colonial authorities in Portuguese Timor in the late 19th century until 1930, when Portuguese colonial power was established throughout the territory. We propose that the bazaars were objectified by the colonial authorities as part of the process of imposing the colonial order, a device to implement the effective occupation of the territory, subjugating and incorporating the reluctant Timorese population and other dissidents, such as Chinese merchants who moved almost freely through the territory. This political enterprise was an active tool to control indigenous power structures, standardise the mobility of populations and define the use of space and time in an orderly administrative way.

Keywords: Portuguese Timor; bazaars; colonial power; colonial order

Introduction: on bazaars[1]

At the beginning of the twentieth century, the words *basar* and *mercado* were used interchangeably in Portuguese official records, like the *Boletim Oficial de Timor* (BOT), in Portuguese Timor.[2] In time, *mercado*, the Portuguese word for market, would win official status; however, 'bazaar' (Tetum: *basar*) remained widely applied in the literature and daily life.

The term *mercado* is commonly associated with the marketplace, whereas bazaar refers as much to the site as to the event, either the daily market or the major weekly market.[3] According to Menezes ([1968] 2006, 157), a distinction is drawn between these two events in terms of scope and time: the daily bazaar is known in Tetum as *basar kiik* (the small bazaar) and the weekly event is recognised as *basar boot* (the big bazaar). The daily bazaar is socially and economically restricted to local residents, but the weekly bazaar is a regional multicultural hub, with different regional ethno-linguistic groups attending from nearby villages and regions.

As places, markets/bazaars refer to concrete locations, fixed in space, usually at the centre of villages and generally surrounded by local grocery stores. Commonly, even nowadays, the daily market is at the heart of the 'bazaar', usually located in a building with a tin roof, or a square, with stores surrounding it. In some cases, the bazaar is on the main road or main intersection at the centre of the town. The weekly bazaar stretches from this minor epicentre and occupies the surrounding area, either the square or streets, providing a degree of plasticity to the space. The relationship between the stores and the market is of major significance and, in some cases, it is difficult to distinguish between them.[4] Historically and economically, the existence of stores around the bazaar (most of which are Chinese-owned) is important because there is an interaction between them and the bazaar, especially the weekly one as these stores provide the products to owners of the smaller, peripheric, shops or stalls from neighbourhoods and surrounding small villages.

The bazaar was also, and still is, a parameter of time. Corrêa ([1935] 2009) commented that, in Manatuto, one way of counting the time was according to the days of the bazaar: *basar Maubisse* (for Wednesday), *basar Turiscain* (for Tuesday). The month was accounted for by calculating the weeks since the last bazaar. Today, the routine of the weekly bazaar is still central to the socio-economic life of small and major communities (see Chapter 2, this volume).

Regardless of the name, the *mercado/basar* remains a resilient setting for economic and social interactions between vendors, buyers and onlookers. However, other spheres of social life play a role associated with attending a bazaar. One such dimension is the ludic one, related to the practice of games, the most relevant being the cockfight, a pivotal melodrama depicted by Geertz (1980). The social relevance of the marketplace is expressed by David Hicks (2012, 55): "The space occupied by the weekly emporium offered a forum in which ethnicity, social hierarchy, gender, a pastime (cockfighting), and religious affiliation visually played themselves out and presented a physical replication of social distinctions that defined the character of the town and the sub-district it served."

As Thomaz (1973, 22) declared, the bazaar is a social event. In the colonial context, bazaars were not only an economic activity but also a tool to survey and control economic, political and social actors (Yang 1998). Thus, they can be classified as an instrument of empire—part of the essential tools of colonial imposition and control of an administration and economy (Headrick 1981). As such, they are subject to objectivation, in which the native model is transformed into an object of colonial manipulation. These manipulative purposes subject local social processes to colonial ordering, measurement and standardisation to allow control and order by colonial authorities. Nevertheless, subjectivation can deviate from this process, as different actors can, from within, develop and perform new ideas and roles to counteract the imposition made by outsiders.

This chapter analyses how bazaars were incorporated by Portuguese colonial authorities at the beginning of the twentieth century as, first, a tool of colonial rule to control the native population and the flow of economic exchanges in the territory and, second, to curb and control interactions between the local population and potentially dangerous foreign wanderers. These processes and their long-term effects—including the imposition of the use of cash, replacement of barter with commodity exchange and commodification of certain pervasive assets such as *tais* (local handwoven fabric, used as cloths)—have generated an opportunity to scrutinise colonial power in practice, providing a theatre for the performance of norms by colonial social actors.

The research is based on documentary and archival sources, a literature review as well as ethnographic fieldwork conducted in Timor-Leste.[5]

The chapter has three parts: the first explores the 'native market' and the practices of 'savage marketers' in the nineteenth century, the second analyses the ways these 'savage' practices were tamed by Portuguese colonial authorities through the establishment of *comandos* and the third explores the performance of colonial norms in the bazaars.

The 'savage marketers' at the end of the nineteenth century

The second half of the nineteenth century, up until the first decade of the twentieth century, witnessed a period of recurrent revolts against the Portuguese colonial presence (Pélissier 2007; Kammen 2015) in Timor. During this time of war, it was expected that trade and exchange would be hampered, yet the trade of weapons was among one of the major menaces to Portuguese colonialism. Very little is known about this trade and, particularly, the role of local bazaars in the colony of Portuguese Timor. Castro (1867) and França (1891) hardly comment on them, mentioning only the existence of an economy of exchange between the interior and the coast, with the main action revolving around Dili, that was based on a reduced and limited exchange of goods, particularly those motivated by the needs of war (Castro 1867) or the preparation of weddings (França 1891).

Nevertheless, two little-known eyewitness accounts from the nineteenth century reveal much about the dynamics of bazaars. The naturalist Henry Forbes (1885, 461) visited Portuguese Timor in 1882-1883 and, while travelling in the interior, came across a 'native market' near 'Bibiçuçu' that comprised 'a wild and savage-like crowd':[6]

> There were between two and three hundred people congregated—a wild and savage—like crowd. The men were dressed in little more than the ordinary T-bandage or hakpoliké of native make, about their loins; some, but not all, of them, had a kerchief girt about the

> head, while their hair was twisted into a knot on the top or back of the head, or combed out into a crimped or semi-frizzled mop. Every man wore suspended over his shoulder a tais or plaid, which differed in ornamentation and excellence of manufacture according to the district in which it had been made. From his shoulder-knob depended his coī, or wallet, the cords for whose opening and closing were elaborately strung with circular disks of shells alternating with dice—like beads of bone richly carved. In this is carried a store of betel-leaves and pinang-nut, with tobacco and other chewing necessaries, and the universal bamboo drinking-cup in case in his travels he should meet some friend or acquaintance who has a supply of palm-wine (laru) or of kanipa, as they name the coarse gin imported by thousands of cases every month into the country.
>
> Every man was armed with a spear and a long knife, and if he had not a long Tower flint-lock over his shoulder, he grasped a bow and a handful of arrows, light shafts made of the tall canes that grow everywhere in the island, tipped with poisoned bamboo barbs. Many of them carried besides a buffalo-hide shield to ward off the stones which, suddenly enraged, they are in the habit of discharging—and with wonderful power and accuracy—at each other. Most of the men had round the waist ammunition pouches of thick buffalo-hide, in form much like European cartridge-belts, with compartments for the small bamboo cylinders in which they keep gunpowder, shot, flints, balls of lead or of ruby crystals gathered out of the river beds...
>
> The women wear very few ornaments—a few arm-bands of silver or horn, and occasionally earrings, and, transfixing the knot in which their hair was gathered behind, a high semi-circular comb, elaborately carved in beautiful and complex patterns. These are said to be given by the youths to their sweethearts, and possibly represent a sort of engagement token. Their dress was a simple tunic, the taisfeta, hung from the waist or from the armpits to the knees.
>
> The women did all the selling and buying, while the men strutted about exchanging with each other drinks of palm-wine—to which they are inordinately given. Besides the different food stuffs, there were exposed for sale on the ground, piles of those beautiful cloths, entirely spun and woven by themselves, in which both between themselves and among the surrounding islands a large trade is done, and cigarette and tobacco holders exquisitely woven out of thin shreds of palm-leaf, on which are worked in additional fibres most artistic coloured designs ... I was told that rarely a month passed without once, or oftener, the market being suddenly broken up by a drunken brawl, as few of the men ever leave it sober. (Forbes 1885, 461-464)

Forbes's description of the market and the 'savage marketers' is worth highlighting. The market had a regional dimension, as expressed by the use of the different garments, and its location seems to have been outside the main village, in an open space. The timing is also pertinent as it is mentioned that it took place weekly. The author pays great attention to the attendants' attire, and particularly to the men's weapons, a detail that indicates that Portuguese authority was probably absent. Importantly, he describes the role that men and women performed at the market. Women played the major role in trading—selling and buying—while the men seemed merely to attend, showing their weapons around. The role ascribed to women is similar to the one observed today, and may shed some light on the role of women in managing not only the household economy but also the circulation of goods, both locally and regionally (see Chapters 5 and 8, this volume).

The products mentioned by Forbes (1885, 463), besides food, included "beautiful clothes" and cigarette and tobacco holders displayed on the ground. Reference to an inter-island trade of local garments is significant, as it reveals an autonomous flow of goods in a regional context, uncontrolled by the Portuguese. Also, worth mentioning are Forbes's comments regarding the recurrence of conflicts in the market. These indicate that markets were much more than places of product exchange; they were places of contact between different ethno-linguistic groups from different regions and realms—that is, places of diverse linguistic profiles—and, thus, intercultural arenas of local pride.

José Silva, a Portuguese doctor, provides another account of a bazaar at Bibiçusso (probably the same marketplace). The bazaar he witnessed occurred on a Sunday near the border between three local kingdoms.[7] Local residents attended weekly to barter food and other goods. According to Silva (1892, 27), "it's frequent in these agglomerations, with the rally of armed people and neighbour's kingdoms, that serious disorders erupted by a futile pretext". He recorded that he and his missionary colleagues were the only *malais* (foreigners) present. While he was there, an incident arose between parties of the kingdoms of Allas and Bibiçiusso. As in Forbes's description, both parties had weapons at hand, which would suggest that no Portuguese authorities were present. Silva managed to solve the problem by sending one of the parties away and postponing resolution of the incident to the near future, when no *malai* would be present.

The taming of the 'savage marketers'

The idea that, at the end of the nineteenth century, bazaars took place regularly in relatively isolated parts of Timor without any ostensible control by Portuguese authorities is important because, at the turn of the century, the opposite was purposefully promoted. This fact is inseparable from the process of effective occupation of the territory instigated by Governor José Celestino da Silva (1894-1908). An all new market paradigm would be developed following the establishment of a military-style administrative network called *comandos*—a stronghold of colonial presence with a military outpost.[8] The implementation of these centres followed the

Figure 1.1: A Timorese market (date unknown). Image credit: Source: © Arquivo Histórico Ultramarino. Accessed 22 December 2020. actd.iict.pt/view/actd:AHUD27175.

'pacification' campaigns that, finally, allowed Portuguese authorities to overturn local resistances and claim authority over the territory (Roque 2010; Sousa 2016). The relocation of the site, reconfiguration of place and concentration in settlements controlled by Portuguese were political tools for colonial authorities to assert their power over the population in general, as well as particular groups like wandering Chinese and other foreign merchants, deemed responsible for stemming rebellions as they provided guns to the interior (Figueiredo 2011).

In 1896, Celestino da Silva, in his "Instructions to the military commanders of the district of Timor", affirmed his intention that each *comando* would be a major commercial centre, with regular markets or bazaars. As part of their administrative duties, the commanders should: "i) Propose to the government secretariat the establishment of fairs, markets or bazaars that they deem necessary, and the suppression of others" (Silva 1898, 99). On the subject of 'Relations with the indigenous', the idea of the *comando* as a commercial centre was paramount: "m) To seek by all means to transform the headquarters of the military commander into a commercial centre, establishing periodic markets, making traders establish there and closely watching them not only for the contraband of opium and war material, but preventing them from practicing excesses or steal[ing] from indigenous people and abusing their ignorance" (ibid., 104).

As Figueiredo (2011) explains, these measures were implemented to regulate trade and to ensure the rights of the state. Besides the advantages already mentioned, the governor thought that forcing the 'indigenes' to attend markets would contribute to the abandonment of their, in Forbes's words, 'savage' habits. Thus, markets were imagined as serving multiple enculturation roles, providing for commercial, financial, police and 'civilizational interests' (Figueiredo 2011).

In 1901, Silva complained about the frequency of bazaars, declaring that they did not contribute to economic and commercial development, as they kept the 'indigenes' from their work. Therefore, he scheduled the bazaars, concentrating them on Thursdays and Sundays.[9] In this way, the colonial rule organised the space and time of bazaars, creating new *habitus* that could be spread by edicts or, as there were called locally, *bandos* at the headquarters of the *comandos* (BOT 10 May 1901, 165). The role of the commander-in-chief at each *comando* was crucial: "... he is military, he is a territorial judge, he directs the telephonic-postal service, that of customs posts, collects taxes, watches over trade and markets, opens roads, supervises coffee-growing and agriculture in general, oversees forests and streams, lists the population, pursues loafing and crime, duplicates himself, quadruples himself, appears everywhere, takes care of everything" (quoted in Boavida 2014, 233).

As Silva (1906, 12) remarked: "It was necessary to do everything again, to organise everything, to open roads, to establish markets, to make relations between people's cordial, to give development and security to trade, to encourage progress in agriculture".

Contemporary accounts of these changes can be gleaned. In *Flores de Coral*, published in 1909, Osório de Castro commented that the '*baçar*' or '*feira*'—a Portuguese term for fair—took place at the *comandos* and in 'traditional places', showing the transition that was taking place: "In the military commands, in traditional places, there are periodical fairs, called *baçar* or fair, and to which contributes all the people of surrounding area, usually making up the trade on exchange ..." (Castro 1909, 179).

It is noticeable that the monetarisation of the bazaar was still ongoing. That commerce was mostly by exchange of goods rather than money was also noted by J. G. Montalvão Silva (1910, 38), who explained that coins were valued for other uses: "... this is known and appreciated as material to be used in the manufacture of varied jewellery or used on the combs and belts that bind the hair and the women's flounces."

In 1911, attempts were made to organise 'regional markets' where indigenous goods that could be exported were sold (BOT 16 December 1911, 389-390).[10] The purpose was twofold: 1) to control maverick itinerant merchants (mostly Chinese) who acquired indigenous goods in villages by direct exchange via the imposition of heavy taxes that forced such transactions to be made with cash; 2) to oblige the movement of 'natives' to the administrative headquarters, thereby promoting the development of those villages and "a more regular contact with the Authorities of the province" (BOT 16 December 1911, 389). This last sentence reveals that authorities had a political agenda at work.

Such attempts to control economic activity did not stop clandestine practices, as Anselmo de Lima, a lieutenant and the local commander of Oecussi, observed in 1918:

> I had a complaint that in Nuno-Eno there was a clandestine bazaar every 3rd Tuesday and, having sent the régulo accompanied by two cavalry soldiers and two Europeans, the amanuensis and the soldier posted here, to check what was really going on, they verified that the complaint was true and they arrested some of the people who were in the said bazaar to which this command imposed a 15-day prison sentence and a fine of 10 coconuts to each one and to the chiefs in whose lands the bazaar was held, and which was already coming for some time, a fine of 50 coconuts each, for being the first time, and they declare that they did it for ignoring that it was forbidden, which I do not believe, but I pretended that I conformed to the excuse, and two corporals that were there, I applied a fine of 100 coconuts to them each, because they are the ones who are the guard and police of the sucos, therefore having the obligation to report all the occurrences. (*Boletim do Comércio, Agricultura e Fomento* 1918, 278)

Still, in 1929, the process of sedentarisation of stranded mavericks was far from complete, as Major Lima (1929, 23-24) reports:

> Viewed only from the commercial point of view, it is even more important to adopt the method of concentration of the chinas in the administrative seats. The wandering life they lead today, settling here today, tomorrow there ... is incompatible with the constitution of important settlements, with a definitive character, in the interior ... It is necessary to get out of this primitive phase, which consists in the trader walking with the tent behind the producer, to move to the normal state of establishment and progressive consolidation of the population centres placed in the main lines of trade. ... In conclusion: For political and commercial reasons, the Chinese living in the colony, who almost all dedicate themselves to trade, should be forced to establish themselves at the administrative headquarters of the commandos and constituencies.

As bazaars were a focal point in local society, they were also an index of the political situation. Inso (1939, 24) explained that, in 1911, on the eve of the revolt of Dom Boaventura Sottomayor, "in the Same headquarters, in the *Manufai* kingdom, it was noticeable that many natives abstain themselves to attend the bazaars ...". And, in fact, the Manufahi revolt started on a bazaar day. "Early morning, when the *moradores* were walking around the bazaar, the commander felt the uproar, and as he was still in bed, he got up to see what was going on. A mob invaded the house; they wound him with a spear, he wanted to close the windows and he could not" (Inso 1939, 25).

In 1911, there were 19 recognised regional markets in the 11 *comandos*, as shown in Table 1.1.[11]

Table 1.1: Regional markets in 1911

Comandos	**Markets**	**Day**
Mothael	Ermera	Sunday
	Remexio	Saturday
	Aileu	Thursday
Liquiça	Aipêlo	Sunday
	Boibau	Thursday
	Maubara	Sunday
Hato-Lia	Hato-Lia	Sunday
Batugadé	Balibó	Sunday
Lamakitos	Bobonaro	Sunday
	Suai	Thursday
Manufahi	Same	Sunday
Manatuto	Manatuto	Sunday
	Laclubar	Thursday
Baucau	Baucau	Sunday
	Viqueque	Thursday
Lautém	Lautém	Sunday
	Loré	Thursday
Okusse	Pant Makassar	Sunday
Dilly (county)	Dilly	Sunday

Following the 1911-1912 revolt of Manufahi, the proliferation of policies on bazaars stalled. Nevertheless, the association of markets with the *comandos* was re-established. In 1915, the military administrator of the Lautém district wrote that: "The change of the marketplace near to the *tranqueira* is done, this change brought an increase in the revenue because the number of market stalls on bazaar days are much more than in the old place"[12] (*Boletim do Comércio, Agricultura e Fomento* 1915, 627).

As Felgas (1956, 270) explained, it was thought that markets would "contribute to turning the indigenes more sociable and civilised by the contact with more developed natives and with the Europeans". Thus, the bazaar, like other institutions of colonial rule, became a symbol of development: "In the villages appears schools, infirmaries, and the bazaar buildings" (Braga 1936, 34).

Regional markets continued to be opened until the onset of World War II, including the "Fair or Annual Market of Timor", in Dili in 1925, which displayed "Timorese possibilities" and included representatives from the whole territory (BOT, 18 April 1925, 167-168).[13]

In nearby West Timor, the same politics had been implemented by Dutch authorities since the beginning of the century: "Captain Franssen Herderschee became a Civiel Gezaghebber (Civil Administrator) ... [and] was ordered to introduce new regulations designed to bring rust en orde to the district.[14] These included: abolition of headhunting and slave trading; a prohibition on the possession of firearms; registration of the people; assignation of fixed dwelling places; a pass system for Chinese and other foreigners who wished to enter the interior; establishment of pasars (markets) to introduce competitive trading and end the Chinese-run monopoly barter system ..." (Farram n.d., 106).

Such intercolonial mimicry is not surprising, as it reflects the mirrored political economy and interests of both colonial powers, as well as the global colonial enterprise in general.

The image of a manipulative Chinese tradesman and a passive/indolent 'native' must be reconsidered. In fact, the Timorese had their own economic strategies that often prevailed, as the military commander of Lamaquitos, Cândido Bernardo, observed in 1918: "Some indigenous people bring sandalwood to the market, taking it home again because the price doesn't suit them" (*Boletim do Comércio, Agricultura e Fomento* 1918, 313).[15]

By the end of the 1930s, the bazaar had become a centrepiece of colonial life: "Old bucolic theme of the lands of Timor, symphony of colors and customs, which anesthetises in its strong exoticism, the Timorese indigenous and that has passionate Europeans, the feathers of writers and the eyes of tourists" (Leite 1938, 6).

In the 1940s, in the economic sphere, the outcome of the "protective" measures taken by Portuguese authorities seemed to reflect well on them: "... determining that the transactions take place in daylight, in the regional bazaars, under the protective supervision of the authorities—thus, avoiding the classic exchanges 'en nature' in the nooks and crannies of the Chinese shops under the effects of the *tuaca* ... The money really came into the hands of the natives" (Magro 1947, 25-26).

The colonial performance at the bazaar

Drawing on the lived experience of Portuguese narrators, in this section we analyse how the political measures materialising at bazaars demonstrate different interests, both economic and mundane.

The martial apparatus

The weekly bazaar enabled a display of colonial power via ritualisation and the symbolic use of signs of Portuguese colonial order, namely military attire and the Portuguese flag. On bazaar days people arrived early: "They sit. On his heels, waiting for the commander of the post or the district administrator to signal the opening of the market. And when the signal resounds in the touch of tambour of the *moradores*, a joyful shout rises of the crowd." (Braga 1936, 34)

Trading started after the post-commander or administrator gave a signal; this could be the raising of the Portuguese flag or the playing of drums by the *moradores* (local militia) or the *cipaios* (native police).

This martial performance was also performed at *postos*, lower administrative units in isolated places. For example, at Bázar-Téte:

> At the front of the post, on the square and next to a banyan tree, there is a mast. On Thursdays, as soon as the sun rises, the corporal of the moradores gathers a dozen and a half subordinates in service. He puts simulated rifles in their hands, like those made by children. Then he tells them to march in place, do turn right and left, evolve and march. The drums rumble loudly. And the regiment of Bázar-Téte, with their wooden rifles and lipas, reminding boys playing and remembering Scottish soldiers, goes down the street of the village, to the bottom, turns around and returns to the post. The lábarac and the children of the chinas march in great steps, laughing, with their eyes very open. One cock, two roosters, twenty, thirty roosters, they crow. And the *moradores* line up facing the mast. Then the corporal orders the gun salute. The national flag rises slowly. Hundreds of indigenous rise on their heels and shout. The roosters keep singing.
>
> The bazaar is open, the market. (Braga, n.d., 33-34)

The association between the post or mast and the banyan tree (*ingondoeiro*) juxtaposes the colonial order (post/mast) with the indigenous order (banyan tree): ancient sacred trees where the heads of defeated enemies had been placed.

Bazaar days also provided an opportunity to communicate and receive official information. According to Duarte (1930, 387), the presence of chiefs at bazaars provided an opportunity for authorities to give orders, such as those related to planting, and to receive information about the outcome of rice crops.

The socio-economic dynamics of the bazaar

In addition to the martial rites that opened the bazaar, Braga (1936) vividly described it as a place to see and be seen. For Europeans, according to Braga (1936, 11), it was mostly a place to gaze: "the streets of Dili and the bazaars are like those of Aurea and Augusta streets, Carmo and Garrett, like the Bennard, the Tivoli, the S. Luiz".[16]

The bazaar was a mixed index of development and joy: "At the headquarters of the command, the bazaars have buildings, some monumental. At the *postos*, they take place around banyan trees in a glade in the forest or near a mast where the national flag is swayed, raised on market days. But whether it is the shade of the tin roofs, or in the incidence of strong and aggressive sun, the bazaars are the most typical manifestation of Timorese life, immersed in color and motion." (Braga 1936, 34)

This dual role—economics and 'enjoyment'—is revealed in the former head of the administrative post of Bobonaro, Viriato Vale's (1953, 372) account: "Going to the bazaars (markets) is at the same time work and enjoyment. On horseback and on their backs they take their products to sell to the Europeans and the Chinese, or exchange with other Timorese."

Menezes ([1968] 2006) argues that the bazaar is a "lusotropical institution", due to the products traded and the gathering of a unique intercultural assemblage. However, considering the power relations present, this is something of a benevolent vision.

The motivation for attending bazaars was more than purely economic, as portrayed by Fontoura (1942, 23): "The Timorese are curious to enjoy the bazaars on Sundays, in large towns, where they perform cockfighting, both of his predilection."

The walk to the bazaar demonstrated also the hierarchy of the social order, as depicted by Ribeiro (1939, 104): "We, Europeans, stood at the front, followed by the nona and, at the end, the servants. The auxiliaries had already left, on foot, by impervious shortcuts and only known to them."

Clothing also revealed the social standing or category of the wearers: "Me and two or three other comrades were wearing the classic colonial helmet on our heads, but some were in hair. We all wore khaki shirts and white pants. The nona wore their best and most showy cabaias and dressing gowns... The servants wore lipas and coats and rolled up their heads in the manner of turbans, large, red handkerchiefs" (Ribeiro 1939, 104).

The bazaar facilitated the spread and use of money in the Timorese economy, particularly after the introduction of a head tax in 1908 (Hicks 2012). According to Martinho (1943, 154), the products regularly sold were small baskets of peanuts, areca, rice, sweet potatoes, fruits, salt, tobacco, betel, cotton and small pieces of meat. When tax payments were due, other goods were also traded, such as cloths, jewels, horses, pigs, goats, buffaloes and larger quantities of rice and corn.[17]

In 1947 the need to gather local commodities like coffee, rubber, sisal, copra, beeswax and areca in larger amounts for export led to the creation of 'indigenous markets' in Dili and all the circumscription headquarters (the new administrative organisation). A new ordinance (BOT 1 March 1947, 73-74) stipulated that these bazaars would take place in distinct locations near the coast a couple of weeks before the arrival of certain ships to the territory.[18]

The spatial organisation of products in the bazaar was also a focus of control. Each type of product would be organised in lots, "very tidy, extended in rows to the eyes of buyers, the varied fruits and vegetables, which in Timor exist in abundance" (Leite 1938, 8), and would be displayed either in the open air or inside new buildings. We do not have much data on the interior of these constructions. From the outset, some of the major *comandos* had special buildings for the bazaar, an example of colonial development or '*fomento*'. The best-known is the Mercado of Baucau, considered the "best building in Timor" constructed in the 1930s (Corrêa 1944).

The production of colonial hierarchies notwithstanding, the bazaar was also a levelling moment (in contradiction of its rules), a unique moment of gathering and a reproduction of (part of the) empire. As Paulo Braga observed (1936, 35): "In the bazaar, people are eloquent, animated. Alongside the European, there is the Indian, the Arab, the Chinese, the Timor. The hierarchies disappear. The white, starched suit of the European is mixed with the Chinese persimmons, the kimono or pajamas of the slanted-eyed sloths, the balandraus, and the white flocks of the Arabs, the Cambatis and the Javanese huts and Timores, or, still, with the dusky skin of the Firracos the dark skin of the Mozambicans and Angolans."

The nona and the cockfight: symbolic violence at the bazaar

The bazaar was also an arena of tension in which violence acquired a symbolic dimension (Bourdieu 2012) in two distinct ways: first, in the way it subordinated Timorese women in the mainframe of the 'nona' system; second, in the cockfighting ritual that can be seen, subjectively, as a response by Timorese to the Portuguese colonial control of their mores.

The bazaar was a trading place for the manifestation of desires. Europeans sought more than goods to purchase; they also wanted to look for women. Some young women, hoping to get married, sought to *barlake* with Portuguese and Chinese men.[19] It was for these young women that "Europeans attend the bazaar", Braga (1936, 36) claimed. In Portuguese Timor, many of these women were known as '*nona*' (lover or concubine). This term was used for women who had intercourse with or lived with Portuguese or Chinese men (Costa 2000, 272). In the novel *Caiúru* by Grácio Ribeiro, a relationship between a Portuguese man and a Timorese woman is portraited. Initially, the main character goes to a bazaar in order to 'acquire' a woman.

> "I bring with me all my fortune—fifty patacas—to acquire the most beautiful girl that appears in the bazaar!"
> "With that money you can even afford to get two!"
> "No, I can't. One will do" (Ribeiro 1939, 104-106).

In the end, the protagonist did not 'acquire' a woman, but a horse. He eventually found the woman he wanted. Although, according to Braga (1936, 35), the 'hierarchies disappear[ed]' in such relationships, gender and sexual relations were instrumentalised. The protagonist in Ribeiro's novel obtained a 'nona' after participating in a simulacrum of a feast with her relatives—a corrupt use of a *barlake* practice. The relationship eventually finished when he returned to Portugal. Although there were cases of actual marriages between Portuguese men and Timorese women, most relationships appear to have been based on the *nona* system, particularly for soldiers.

After a morning of economic activity and woman gazing, the bazaar took on a different form at noon, when the spectacle of cockfighting began:

> The bazaar gradually falls apart and the shops of the chinas are filled. Mugs of brandy, of rice alcohol, of cannipa and tuaka are drunk painfully. Bets for cockfights begin to appear and challenges are directed among the different groups of aficionados ... But suddenly the crowd, hallucinating, runs to the square or to the road. They scream, jump, push themselves into an unspeakable enthusiasm. It forms a circle. And the silence then becomes heavy ... And two roosters, hitherto kept at a distance from each other, meet in the middle of the circle. They hit their wings, they dig the ground, they lengthened their necks, with the bristling fuzz. Then they jump, hit each other, stick their beaks and sharp spurs into meat. ... until one of the cock's faints and falls into gasp. Then, in the crowd there are only two expressions: that of those who have won bets and that of those who have lost. The first ones laugh, insult the losing cock, grab it, cut it still throbbing. The second ones walk away, defeated ... The barbarous spectacle ends, the unique barbarous custom that the authorities have not yet been able to forbid and which, with the payment of a license for its realization, is a major source of revenue. (Braga 1936, 38-39)

Here we see the Portuguese authorities' ambiguous position regarding this 'barbaric' practice from which they obtained dividends through taxes. The cockfight and its associated interactions had social and economic relevance for the individuals involved, and these also had structural and symbolic dimensions, as Geertz (1980, 185) stated. Oliveira (1971) claimed that the midday cockfight was functionally equivalent to the economic exchanges that took place in the morning, being a major event at which the community manifested great intensity in an economic and ludic sense: the "set bazaar-cockfight" can be seen as a "unified all and the sign of exchange" (1971, 67). Although incorporated in the tax system, the cockfight constituted a passion—a social drama and performance of life (Geertz 1980), or, as Oliveira (1971, 66) put it, a "a total universe that comes to settle in the relative of everyday life".

As the bazaar started, it also had an end: this was marked by the removal of the Portuguese flag from its pole by the military and the return to home.

The bazaar of the 1930s portrays very different men and women from those depicted by Forbes in 1885.

> The timorese, lean and earthy, squatted around a mound of potatoes or onions that the buyers would pick up. The women gazed at the chickens that surrounded them, trapped by strings, or sold, from time to time, areca or *doet lima* of coarse tobacco.[20] Some carried small pigs on their backs or large bunches of bananas. The Europeans, followed by the *nona* and the servants, discussed and bought everything they needed for the week's expenses. The Chinese, stuck in their kimonos, managed to attract the indigenous people to their shops and there they tricked them with exchanges, almost always disadvantageous to them (Ribeiro 1939, 107).

Ribeiro highlighted the exploitation of the Timorese by the Chinese; however, this position would not have been exclusive. As Ribeiro (1939, 145) acknowledged, many of his Portuguese 'comrades' forced the natives to sell the products to them for an arbitrary and imposed price and many bought horses or had *nonas*, using violence and extortion.

Conclusion

The bazaar is a paramount institution in Timor-Leste. Further research is needed to understand its dynamics in the nineteenth century, a period in which local economies were still controlled indirectly by Portuguese colonial authorities concentrated on the coast, while the interior, often depicted as rebellious, was run by 'proxy' allies—local kingdoms responsible for the collection of indirect taxes.

The effective occupation of the territory and establishment of regional outposts with permanent garrisons (the *comandos*) allowed for the direct taxation of the Timorese. The *comandos* became administrative and economic centres that promoted networks all over the territory, controlling traders and the establishment of marketplaces. The control of transactions and revenues via taxes was associated with the perceived need to 'civilise' the indigenous population and put them in close contact with the colonial authorities, "socialising" them, thereby promoting their integration into the colonial society.

The Portuguese authorities objectified the bazaar and turned it into a mechanism of colonial control by creating routines for acting in a place, like a theatre, and instructing socio-economic relations between the Timorese, the Chinese, and the colonial authorities. A drama was promoted and performed using symbols and signs of colonial authority and power to enhance order so that habit of attendance and participation would be instilled, transforming the 'savage markets' into properly submissive actors. It is worth noting that this practice continued into the 1960s. Commenting on the bazaar at Same, Martins (2008) observed that the ceremony of the flag took place at the headquarters of the administration and that: "The occasion was used to give news, information or to transmit guidance emanated from the Government and to evaluate the state of the plantations or the progress of the harvests" (71).

This was done in the presence of the *liurai* and other chiefs of *suku* who were 'dressed with traditional clothes' (Martins 2008, 169). Martins continued: 'Above the good order the *cipaios* ruled and the business only started after the authorization of the administrator or his substitute' (ibid.).

Further research is needed to understand the dynamics of the bazaar from the perspective of the Timorese and how it evolved during the Portuguese colonial period. The roles of non-economic occurrences such as cockfights and sexual interaction, both charged with highly symbolic violence, as well as the ever present 'violence and extortion' of colonial rule, deserve particular attention.[21] Were these recurrent features across all Timorese social strata or just the poorest ones?

The bazaar should also be analysed as a space for interaction and resistance, not only during the Portuguese colonial period, but also, and particularly, during the period of Indonesian occupation. Among those who arrived on the eve of the bazaar, the exchange of narratives, histories and memories sounds an alternative voice for the Timorese—beyond the colonial one: "The Timorese gathers, huddles in the bazaar, and gives rein to his innate collectivism, smokes with his pipe, tells stories of eras, where there were untamed warriors who cut heads through the mysterious night, queens whom the peoples obey and wonderful hunts through the unexplored jungle. It is a whole world of fantasies arising in his mind that encompasses his unconsciousness" (Leite 1938, 8).

During the Indonesian occupation (1975-1999), the market/bazaar remained an important economic event and also served a social function as a 'meeting place for local people' (Mubyarto et al. 1991, 22). It is possible to argue that bazaars also played a major role in Timorese resistance during this time, as traders arrived from Celebes with the transmigration program. In 1987 a 'mysterious event' occurred that set the Dili market on fire (Arquivo & Museu da Resistência Timorense 2020a, File: 06454.026), and the mobility of some sellers who were also shop owners facilitated the activities of a clandestine front (pers. comm.).[22] So, the bazaar was also a much watched place by authorities with armed personnel (Arquivo & Museu da Resistência Timorense 2020b, File: 05733.036.002).

In contemporary literature, the bazaar or market is associated with notions of local development—roads and marketplaces—as Bicca (2011) shows in his work. Nevertheless, the relationship between local aspirations and state directives can be difficult to manage, reinforcing the need for community involvement in the management of the marketplace. Bicca (2011, 123-125) explains how the marketplace was built, against the advice of local habitants, on a windy site at the intersection of several *suku* (so that it could benefit all), but it was left unattended, while the old marketplace was used.

Bazaars were a focus of tension and places of struggle and control during the violence of 2006, as I witnessed in Dili (Lusa 2006) and Maliana. More recently, they have become places of tension between Timorese and non-Timorese, with locals complaining about foreign traders. As noted, it is felt that the bazaars should be for the East Timorese, and foreigners should be limited to trade in the shops.[23] Hence, the bazaar remains a total social phenomenon, continuing to move beyond its economic dimension.

Notes

1 A preliminary version of this text was presented at the International Symposium on Economic Dynamics and Social Change in the Making of Contemporary Timor-Leste organised by the Institute of Social Studies, which took place at the University of Brasília in 2018, and was published in 2019 in the journal *Plural Pluriel* 19: 138-155. Accessed 21 February 2020. www.pluralpluriel.org/index.php/revue/article/view/184 I am very grateful for the comments and suggestions made by reviewers.

2 I use the term 'Portuguese Timor' as expressed by Gunn (1999, 213).

3 There are also small market stalls, daily, along main roads in the countryside that are sometimes associated with small street restaurants. In some cases, when the main road crosses the village, these are also the venues of the weekly bazaar (e.g., Atabae in Bobonaro district).

4 During the weekly bazaar, shop owners use the veranda or front space of the shop to display products.

5 This includes working as a teacher in Maliana and Bobonaro between 2000 and 2002; Ph.D. fieldwork in August 2003, August 2004 and from September 2005 to August 2006 undertaken with the support of the Calouste Foundation Gulbenkian and the Fundação Oriente; short fieldwork terms in 2010 for the project 'Translation as Culture' (Project FC—PTDC/ANT/81065/2006), in 2012 and 2013 for the project 'The Sciences of Anthropological Classification in "Portuguese Timor" (1894-1975)' (Project FCT—HC/0089/2009) and in 2014 as a consultant for *Sitíos & Formas* in a local market project.

6 Located in today's Manufahi district, sub-district of Fatuberliu.

7 The concept of bazaars on the 'border' or at crossroads of different kingdoms is relevant because it may be seen as a focal point for interaction and communication, verbal and non-verbal, in the multicultural Timorese society.

8 Linked by the main roads and telegraph wire.

9 It is arguable that Sundays were chosen as a way of leading people to attend the morning mass (Hicks 2012).

10 See: Portaria 257.

11 In 1912, a new 'regional market' was allowed in Viqueque on Sundays (BOT 26 October 1912, 221).

12 In Portuguese, *tranqueira* means a wooden fence to fortify. Nevertheless, it is also commonly applied to the stone walls that surround the military headquarters of the *comandos*.

[13] See: 1916, Tualo, Viqueque commando (BOT 22 July 1918, 200); Leto-Fó (Letefo), Hatolia Comando (BOT 22 June 1918, 212); Báâ-Guia (Bagia), Baucau Comando (BOT 13 July 1918, 247); Cova, Batugade Military Command (BOT 12 July 1919, 441); Determination that the Dili bazaar should be held on Wednesdays and Sundays (BOT 18 October 1920, 354); Reorganisation of the days of the market of the regional markets (bazaars) of Hato-Lia, Leto-Fó and Atsabe (BOT 17 April 1920, 85); Fatu-Maquerec, Manatuto (BOT, no. 16, 17 April 1921, 86); Bazar-Tete, Aipelo Civil Post (BOT 13 August 1928, 266); Extinction of the regional market of Fato-Russa (BOT 2 June, 128).

[14] *Rust en orde* means peace and order, in Dutch.

[15] See: 'Boletim do Comércio'.

[16] Lisbon streets.

[17] Particularly in the dry season, a period when socio-ritualistic activities, like marriages, house reconstructions and village rites, occur.

[18] It is difficult to analyse the extent of the success of this measure because of the forthcoming war. The retail trade was practised by local shops, mainly Chinese (Martinho 1943, 154).

[19] *Barlake* is the Tetum term for a marriage contract in which the man's family provides certain goods while the woman's family corresponds with others.

[20] *Doet* lima means *cinco avos*, five 'avos', old currency used in Portuguese Timor.

[21] Some testimonies are critical for certain sexual practices. See: (Carlos. n.d.).

[22] Timorese friend and trader who took part in the clandestine front.

[23] See: Vendedores timorenses tristes pela enorme presença de comerciantes estrangeiros no mercado. 08 de Abril de 2013, 19:07. noticias.sapo.tl/portugues/info/artigo/1310135.html (site discontinued).

References

Arquivo & Museu da Resistência Timorense. 2020a. File: 06454.026. Title: Notícias sobre Timor-Leste referentes a JUL.1987. Subject: Documento de Loikililmau P., membro da Comissão Secreta para a Resistência Nacional dos Estudantes Timorenses na Indonésia, sobre as manifestações dos estudantes timorenses anti-discriminação, o incêndio misterioso no mercado de Dili, e as respectivas mobilizações do exército indonésio. Fundo: Arquivo da Resistência Timorense – TAPOL. Accessed 22 December. casacomum.org/cc/visualizador?pasta=06454.026.

Arquivo & Museu da Resistência Timorense. 2020b. File: 05733.036.002. Subject: Timorenses durante um bazar ao ar livre em Baucau, distinguindo-se um membro das milícias de Team Sera com uma G-3 em serviço de controlo. Legend in the back: Manuscripte: 'Soldier Watching the Market in Baucau the Whole Day Long'. Duas imagens iguais. Negativo/Positivo: Positivo. Fundo: Arquivo da Resistência Timorense – Ramos-Horta. Accessed 22 December. casacomum.org/cc/visualizador?pasta=05733.036.002.

Bicca, A. 2011. "A diferença entre os iguais." PhD diss., Universidade Federal do Rio Grande do Sul. Accessed 18 August 2014. www.lume.ufrgs.br/handle/10183/96159?locale=pt_BR.

Boavida, I. 2014. "Celestino da Silva, a rede de postos militares e a ocupação colonial efetiva de Timor português (1895-1905): Um processo (des)construtivo." *Journal of Asian History* 48 (2-2014): 227-261. doi.org/10.13173/jasiahist.48.2.0227.

Bourdieu, P. 2012. *Sur l'État. Cours au Collège de France (1989-1992)*. Paris: Raisons d'Agir/Seuil.

Braga, P. n.d. "Dili-Bazar Tete (Síntese da vida timorense)." *Cadernos Coloniais* (14). Lisboa: Editorial Cosmos.

Braga, P. 1936. "A terra, as gentes e os costumes de Timor." *Cadernos Coloniais* (7). Lisboa: Editorial Cosmos.

Carlos, R. P. n.d. *Eu Fui ao Fim de Portugal.* Queluz: Literal Editora.

Castro, A. 1867. *As possessões portuguesas na Oceânia.* Lisboa: Imprensa Nacional.

Castro, A. O. 1909. *Flores de Coral.* Díli: Imprensa Nacional.

Corrêa, A. P. (1935) 2009. *Gentio de Timor.* 2nd ed. Ilha da Madeira: Câmara de Lobos.

Corrêa, A. P. 1944. *Timor de Lés a Lés.* Lisboa: Agência Geral das Colónias.

Duarte, T. 1930. *Timor (Ante-Câmara do Inferno!?).* Famalicão: Tip. Minerva.

Farram, S. G. n.d. "From 'Timor Koepan' to 'Timor NTT': A Political History of West Timor, 1901-1967." PhD diss., Northern Territory University.

Felgas, H. E. 1956. *Timor Português.* Lisboa: Agência Geral do Ultramar.

Figueiredo, F. 2011. *Timor: a presença portuguesa (1769-1945).* Lisboa: Centro de Estudos Históricos da Universidade Nova de Lisboa.

Fontoura, A. 1942. *O trabalho dos indígenas de Timor.* Lisboa: Agência Geral das Colónias.

Forbes, H. 1885. *A Naturalist's Wanderings in the Eastern Archipelago: A Narrative of Travel and Exploration from 1878 to 1883.* New York: Harper Brothers. doi.org/10.5962/bhl.title.96922.

França, B. 1891. *Timor.* Lisboa: Companhia Nacional Editora.

Geertz, C. 1980. *A interpretação das Culturas.* Rio de janeiro: LTC – Livros Técnicos e Científicos Editora S.A.

Gunn, G. 1999. *Timor Loro Sae 500 anos.* Macau: Livros do Oriente.

Headrick, D. 1981. *The Tools of Empire: Technology and European Imperialism in The Nineteenth Century.* New York: Oxford University Press.

Hicks, D. 2012. "Indexing social space. A marketplace in Timor-Leste." *Journal of the Humanities and Social Sciences of Southeast Asia* 168 (1): 55-73. doi.org/10.1163/22134379-90003569.

Inso, J. 1939. *Timor – 1912.* Lisboa: Edições Cosmos.

Kammen, D. 2015. *Three Centuries of Conflict in East Timor.* New Brunswick: Rutgers University Press.

Leite, G. 1938. "O Bazar! ... In Timor, Publicação eventual de caráter literário e científico." *Dilly,* 19 de julho de (Ano XIII).

Lima, W. 1929. *Inquérito feito pelo Major Walter Lima (Julho e Agosto de 1929) – III Parte Relatório.* No. 3051-1733. Lisboa: Arquivo Histórico Militar.

Lusa. 2006. "Comoro, o bairro 'da GNR', um grande palco de conflitos." Agência Lusa, March 09, 2006. www.rtp.pt/noticias/pais/comoro-o-bairro-da-gnr-um-grande-palco-de-conflitos_n32251. Accessed 22 December 2020.

Magro, A. J. 1947. *Tropa e Aquartelamentos de Timor*: subsídio para a História das Unidades Militares da Colónia. Separata da Revista Militar. Outubro 1937 a maio De 1940. Lisboa: Tip. da Liga dos Combatentes da Grande Guerra.

Martinho, J. S. 1943. *Timor Quatro Séculos de Colonização Portuguesa.* Porto: Livraria Progredior.

Martins, A. 2008. *Sangue de Crocodilo a saga de Timor-Leste.* Lisboa: Prefácio.

Menezes, F. X. (1968) 2006. *Encontro de Culturas em Timor-Leste (Contribuição para o seu estudo).* Díli: Editora Crocodilo Azul.

Mubyarto, S., H. Loekman, E. Djatmiko, I. Setiawiati, and A. Mawarnlji. 1991. *East Timor: The Impact of Integration (an Indonesian Socio-Anthropological Study).* Northcote, Austrália: IRIP (Indonesia Resources and Information Programme).

Oliveira, C. 1971. "Luta de Galos em Timor." *Geographica – Revista da Sociedade de Geografia de Lisboa* VII (28 [October]): 54-69.

Pélissier, R. 2007. *Timor em Guerra A Conquista Portuguesa 1847-1913.* Lisboa: Editorial Estampa.

Ribeiro, G. 1939. *Caiúru. Romance Timor.* Lisboa: Imprensa Artística.

Roque, R. 2010. *Headhunting and Colonialism: Anthropology and the Circulation of Human Skulls in the Portuguese Empire, 1870-1930*. Hampshire: Palgrave MacMillan.

Silva, J. 1892. *Em Timor*. Macau: Typografia Mercantil.

Silva, J. C. 1898. "Instrucções para os commandantes militares do districto de Timor." *Revista Militar* 50 (4): 97-106.

Silva, J. C. 1906. *Projecto de organização administrativa do districto autonomo de Timor: elaborado no districto em 1906*. Ministério dos Negócios da Marinha e Ultramar. Direcção Geral do Ultramar. Lisboa: Imprensa Nacional.

Silva, J. G. M. 1910. *A mão d'obra em Timor: Breve memória sobre o seu território, clima, produção, usos e costumes indigenas, industria, agricultura e comércio*. Lisboa: Typographia A Editora.

Sousa, L. 2016. "A Revolta de Manufahi de 1911-1912. Testemunhos e a imprensa diária da época." In *Timor-Leste Colonialismo, Descolonização, Lusutopia*, edited by R. Feijó, 93-117. Lisboa: Edições Afrontamento.

Sousa, L. 2019. "O bazar colonial no Timor Português: a submissão dos 'comerciantes selvagens'". *Plural Pluriel*, (19), 138-155. Consulté à l'adresse http://www.pluralpluriel.org/index.php/revue/article/view/184 Accessed on 10 December 2020.

Thomaz, L. F. 1973. "Vida Rural Timorense." *Geographica – Revista da Sociedade de Geografia de Lisboa* IX (33 [January]): 3-29.

Vale, V. L. M. 1953. *Notas Etnográficas sobre Timor Português*. Lisboa: Sociedade de Geografia de Lisboa.

Yang, A. A. 1998. *Bazaar India: Markets, Society, and the Colonial State in Bihar*. Berkeley: University of California Press.

CHAPTER 2

Indexing social space: A marketplace in Timor-Leste

David Hicks

Abstract

Between 1967 and 2007 powerful political, economic, and social events profoundly changed the lives of the people of Timor-Leste. Every *suku* was affected and though some changes were common to all *sukus*, or local communities, each *suku* has its own history to tell. This essay compares changes in the economic lives of the local people in one *suku*, that of Caraubalo, which is located in the municipality of Viqueque, on the southern coast of Timor-Leste during that period.[1]

Keywords: Viqueque; Caraubalo; market; gender

My principal intention here is to show how space and time indexed social identity in the marketplace of one of the larger 'towns' of Timor-Leste (or 'East Timor'), Viqueque, during the years 1966-1967 and to examine their relevance for the social personality and economic character of Viqueque town today.[2] The space occupied by the weekly emporium offered a forum in which ethnicity, social hierarchy, gender, a pastime (cockfighting), and religious affiliation visually played themselves out and presented a physical replication of social distinctions that defined the character of the town and the sub-district it served. The marketplace (*basar*) also provided space enabling persons of different social identity to interact more readily and regularly there than anywhere else.[3] The temporal dimensions of life alternately waxed and waned as six days of relative somnolence were interrupted by a day of excitement filled with commerce, gossip, cockfighting, and—in the case of the few Christians in the locality—celebrating the weekly mass.[4] As was true for other towns in the former Portuguese colony, Viqueque's market contributed substantially to its social life and economy.[5] As such, my comments complement other discussions of the Timorese *bisar* in certain other chapters, e.g., that of Sousa.[6]

A secondary purpose motivates this study. In evaluating the respective merits of the 'Polanyi School' of economic anthropology (Polanyi and Arensberg 1957; see also our editors' remarks in the present volume) whose adherents regarded theories derived from the discipline of economics as inapplicable to primitive and peasant societies, and the 'Formalist School' (Cook 1966), which asserted their relevance, Raymond Firth (1972, 468) roundly declared the dispute to be "largely futile". The issue, he argued, was not "*whether* economic theory could be applied to primitive economics" but "*where, how far, and with what modifications and additions*, economic theory could be found appropriate to interpret 'primitive' systems". In demonstrating how economic values, such as rational calculation, scarcity, and demand, are 'embedded'—as George Dalton (1971), the foremost of Polanyi's followers might put it—in non-economic aspects of communal existence, this study seeks to support Firth's argument.

Focusing on gender, ethnicity, social class, and social identity, and their economic implications, also enables us to gain insight into the process whereby post-colonial nations transform themselves after gaining independence. By comparing the use made of social space at two periods of time separated by four decades during which momentous developments took place in Timor-Leste, we can see in sharper relief the kind of changes urban spaces experience when they are subject to colonial authority, pressures resulting from independence, and—ultimately—the tortuous process of nation-building.

Social identities

The present study is based on a field stay of 15 months in Viqueque town during the aforementioned period, and shorter visits conducted in 1999, 2005, 2007, and 2009.[78] Viqueque town was the largest settlement and commercial hub in the *Posto Sede*, or 'home' sub-district in which it was located, and the sub-district itself consisted of 10 socio-political units known as *suku*, each *suku* consisting of a varying number of villages (*povoações*).[9] Geographically, the town is sited at the edge of what the geographer, Joachim K. Metzner (1977, 22), defined as the "Southern Foothill Zone", where it abuts the "Southern Littoral Plains Zone". Sociologically, Viqueque town was, and remains today, located in the *suku* of Caraubalo and its boundaries overlapped with Cabira Oan, one of the seven villages in that *suku*.[10] Leadership of *suku* was invested in officials known as *xefes de suku*, or *suku* chiefs, who would always be literate Timorese men who possessed a working knowledge of the Portuguese language.

The market nearest Viqueque was that at Ossu, which was about nine miles distant and smaller, while other markets were situated at Lacluta, Uato Carabau, and Uato-Lari. All were held on Sundays only. Viqueque was the largest and most popular market because 1. there were more Chinese Shops in Viqueque; 2. there were more *ema malai* (foreigners, strangers), and educated Timorese families, who needed vegetables and fruits and the Viqueque areas could not provide sufficient supplies to meet their needs;[11] 3. the town and its environs had the highest population density in the district; and 4. the town was conveniently situated near the geographical centre of the district and served by a north-south road that was passable most days even in the wet season. Baucau market rivalled Viqueque's in the number of its participants and its prominence, and was also held twice weekly, on Sundays and Wednesdays. According to Metzner (1977, 213) Baucau's was "undoubtedly" the most important marketplace east of Dili as a result of its strategic location at the crossroads of the entire system of transportation in that region.[12]

The highest order of social classification divided the inhabitants of Viqueque district into two basic categories, *ema timur*, Timorese, and *ema malai*.[13] The former term, *ema timur*, in the Viqueque region at least, incorporated two categories of person, *ema fehan*, or lowlanders—a gloss that included the coastal populace of the southern region—and *ema foho*, or uplanders. *Fehan* denoted Timorese who spoke the indigenous form of the Tetum language (*Tetun Terik*) and resided, for the most part, on the coastal plains of the south.[14] The term *fehan* was a little ambiguous in that some Tetum speakers lived in the uplands, for example, the people of Lacluta sub-district (Viqueque district), while some villages near the coast, especially in the sub-district of Uato-Lari, were home to non-Tetum speakers. But language was privileged over location, upland Tetum speakers being referred to as *ema fehan* and non-Tetum speakers who lived as inhabitants of the plains as *ema foho*.[15] The category *ema foho* included speakers of a number of languages: Makassae, Waimaha, Naueti, Kairui, and Midique.[16] Most *foho* participants in market activities were Makassae or Waimaha, people living in the mountainous sub-districts of Ossu (Viqueque district) and Venilale (Baucau district).[17] Altitude and the availability of water played a major part in determining which crops could be grown as the cooler temperatures and abundance (in some areas) of water were more conducive to the cultivation of fruits such as tangerines (*sabraca-lotuk*), oranges (*sabraca*), lemons (*derok*), and pineapples (*anana*); and green vegetables such as lettuces (*alfase*), cabbages (*repollu*), and spinach (*kankun malai*) than the much hotter area around Viqueque town. The town itself, however, was overwhelmingly *fehan* in its ethnic make-up, such *foho* as there were being members of families which usually provided the incumbents for the position of *xefe de suku*, each of whom (*fehan* and *foho* alike) owned a house in town. Of the 10 chiefly families in the town some were members of the social rank of *liurai*, or royalty, while others belonged to the second social rank, that of *dato*. Administration regulations obliged each *xefe de suku* in the sub-district to have a pied à terre in town, the consequence of this regulation being that nine of the ten chiefs owned two homes, one in the town and the other in their respective *suku*. Unlike the chief of Caraubalo, whose town and *suku* homes were the same, they thus divided their time between two houses.

The exchanges that took place within the category of *ema timur* in the marketplace at Viqueque reflect, to some degree, the widespread Southeast Asian opposition between the produce specialisations of the coastal populations and those of the upland. *Fehan* and *foho* were far more numerous than any other ethnic category participating in the market and most *fehan* who attended the weekly gatherings generally resided in *suku* located no more than a few miles from town, which was surrounded by *suku* whose majority population was *fehan*. Most *foho* resided at greater distances, sometimes dozens of miles away, a circumstance which meant some participants in the market would leave their upland *suku* on Saturday and camp overnight on the way to town or sleep in the market building itself at nightfall. For them the occasion was an event marking an important disjuncture in their daily routines of village life. Apart from the occasional marriage (whose preliminary terms might be negotiated on a market day), relatively little interaction took place between *fehan* and *foho* during the other six days, but once a week in the market they had the opportunity for mutual engagement. Partly owing to the greater distance they had to travel, *foho* would usually only come to market if they had something to sell or a pressing need to buy some specific commodity and would frequently travel as a family. *Fehan*, on the other hand, tended to be more regular buyers and sellers. In contrast to most *foho*, whether as buyers, sellers, observers, or socialisers, *fehan* women and men from the nearby villages would be more likely to come alone or with a couple of relatives and take advantage of the occasion to chat with other *fehan* relatives from other *suku* whom they would not otherwise get a chance to encounter.[18]

Hierarchy, a pervasive feature of Timorese social classification was no less influential a determinant of social identity in Viqueque, and was indeed implicit in the very terms '*fehan*' and '*foho*', in which the former connotes superiority and the latter suggests inferiority, another local expression of a widespread Southeast Asian contrast, that is, the ascription of superiority to coastal cultures and relative inferiority to upland cultures. In Timor-Leste this contrast is reinforced by the superordination accorded to town dwellers over people residing in the countryside and is made verbally explicit in the contrast, *kota/foho*. Hierarchical classification was further contained within each ethnic category since there were four social ranks, which in descending order of prestige comprised *liurai* (royalty), *dato* (aristocrats), *ema reino* (commoners), and *ata* (slaves) (see Chapter 4, this volume).[19] In *suku* Caraubalo five villages were inhabited by *ema reino* while two (Mane Hat and Mamulak) were *dato* communities. Somewhat complicating this allocation of status was the presence of half a dozen or so Timorese, some from other districts, who worked in the colonial bureaucracy. These included policemen (*sapaio*), an interpreter for the administration, a meteorological officer, and a veterinarian nurse (*pecuário*). The policemen played an executive role on market days. Among their duties was walking, baton in hand, among the sellers ready to quell any disturbance or resolve any dispute that might have arisen between patrons. The ability of these officers of the administration to read and speak Portuguese and their prestigious occupations as members of the administration and—more often than not—members of *liurai* or wealthy *dato* families classed them with Timorese of elevated social standing. Educated Timorese, who invariably employed servants to take care of regular purchases for the table, only carried out their own buying when personal judgement was called for, as might be the case in buying a fighting cock (*asuwa'in*), for example, or a piece of cloth of unusual quality (*tais*). Occasionally groups of buyers from the *Segunda Linha* would arrive en masse at the market from their barracks in a military vehicle and descend upon the sellers.[20] Decidedly wealthier than most commoner Timorese, their arrival was met with dismay by the Chinese buyers who knew sellers would be encouraged by the presence of these more liberal spenders to raise prices.

The second basic category, *ema malai*, consisted of the *ema mutin*, the Europeans, and the *ema cina*, the Chinese (including Chinese Timorese), who were for the most part Hakka immigrants from Canton, Fukien, Kwantung, Hong Kong, and Macao. In Viqueque town, where their families owned half a dozen shops (*cantinas*), they numbered several dozens and, as they did throughout the colony, controlled local trade. The Chinese sold very little in the market—they were primarily buyers—but cakes made by one family in the town were sometimes available for purchase, and teenage Chinese boys and girls from that family would walk between the rows of sellers calling out their wares. The European residents were far fewer in number and consisted of a Portuguese schoolteacher and the administrator of the district and their respective wives, and my wife and me.

Religion and gender differences also contributed to the definition of social identity in Viqueque and made their influence apparent in the spatial and temporal dimensions of the market. Although a substantial majority of Timorese in the sub-district comprised non-Christians, the Catholic mission in the town of Ossu had made converts over the years sufficiently numerous for the priest based there to come fairly regularly on Sundays to say mass in the building that arose from the market plaza. Few men attended. Apart from trading and socialising, their interests centred around the weekly cockfighting, an event women never attended. Those men who did partake of the communion were for the most part members of the administration who took advantage of the occasion to consolidate their claims to a Lusitanian identity.[21] During the transactions in the marketplace the activities of men and women could, as we shall see, significantly differ according to context, and although it cannot be said, as happens on the island of Lembata, that "In a crowd of several hundred, women far outnumber the men, making up perhaps ninety percent of those present" (Barnes and Barnes 1989, 405), women were a dominant force in the Viqueque market, especially if one takes into account the Chinese women buyers.

Then there were the itinerant traders, all men of various Timorese ethnicities, who visited Viqueque about four times a year from as far away as Bobonaro and for whom the town was but one stop among several outlets for their non-comestible produce.[22] No space in the marketplace was assigned them. The itinerants would move anywhere there might be prospective buyers for their wares, which included cloth from Bobonaro, Suai, and Atsabe; personal ornaments (such as combs and pins) made from aluminum; and other lightweight items, stopping when accosted.[23]

Market space

The principal watercourse in the region is the river Cuha, which descends from the mountains to the north—Metzner's 'Central Uplands Zone'—and wends its way down the slopes of the Southern Foothill Zone; after a brief crossing of the Southern Littoral Plains Zone, it enters the Timor Sea about 12 miles further on near a place called Be-Asu. As the river reaches the interface between these last two zones its progress is impeded by extensive strata of hard rock that forces it to meander into a half-loop before swinging back into its southerly course for Be-Asu. Inside this half-loop, on the right bank, the town of Viqueque was founded and developed. At certain stretches of the river sedimentary deposits have accumulated to form alluvial terraces, on one of which the Portuguese administration constructed the aforementioned market building for the purpose of accommodating transactions between sellers and buyers.[24] A cruciform white-washed structure topped by a red galvanised roof, the building's main entrance faced south-west and on the three sides around the entrance was a clearing with bare soil interspersed with scattered grasses which formed the plaza that functioned as the principal forum for market commerce (Figure 2.1). From the south-western side of the plaza rose a stone wall several yards high which supported an embankment carrying the road that connected Be-Asu with the towns of Ossu, Venilale, and Baucau to the north. The purpose of the building was to shelter participants in the market during the wet monsoon, which would be expected in November-January and then again from March-July.[25] So when rain was not falling, sellers would sit outside where there was more space for them to display their commodities. With the onset of rain, sellers abandoned the plaza, moved into the building, and returned to their places outside when it ceased. The building was also where mass was celebrated after trading and before the cockfighting started. Access to the plaza was gained by means of a stone ramp descending from the road.

The hand of the colonial administration was also evident in the spatial accommodations made for the sellers, the majority of whom were aggregated into rows extending across the north-western, western, and southern sectors of the plaza.[26]

Although the actual composition of the rows was determined by those occupying them, sellers were expected under administrative fiat to remain in the rows and keep walkways between them uncluttered while the market was in session. In practice, though, almost as soon as trading started rows would begin to disintegrate and walkways would quickly fill in so that the neat order shown in Figure 1 would vanish. The 'L-shaped' rows shown in the figure were occupied by the *foho* and *fehan* and that sector of the plaza they occupied was the central area for trading. Generally speaking, sellers of the same ethnicity sat together. *Fehan* numerically dominated the inner 'Ls', which were situated nearer the building, and *foho* dominated the outer 'Ls' (Figure 2.1). Exceptions, however, occurred.[27] Thus, while *fehan* sold tobacco (*tabako*) and betel (*malus*), some *fehan* sellers would sit in '*fehan* rows' while others would sit with *foho* facing fellow *fehan*.[28] Other commodities also provided a focus for sellers, who would cluster together in a group, and this accounts for the fact that one could never be certain that a '*foho* row' might not harbour some *fehan* sellers, or, of course, vice versa. The number and size of the rows were a function of the number of sellers. In June through August sellers might be packed shoulder to shoulder on some days, but in November (when families were sowing their gardens) or February (when they were harvesting maize [*batar*]) rows would be less compact. Social identity was further indicated in the contrast between the relative immobility exhibited by these sellers, who until they had disposed of their produce remained seated, and the mobility of the *ema cina* or *ema malai* who circulated around the plaza as buyers and the itinerant traders who circulated as sellers.

Although as few as 150 persons might patronise the market, on a busy Sunday the number could rise to as many as 500 especially in the period from June through August. This was the time taxes fell due and households had to raise cash, in the form of the Portuguese escudo. Taxes comprised an annual head tax (*imposto domiciliário* or *imposto de capitação*) of 190 escudos on physically healthy males aged from 18 to 60 and a tax on buffaloes, horses, and Bali cattle at 10 escudos a head (Metzner 1977, 6, 183, 211). Of this sum, 150 escudos went to the provincial government and 30 escudos to the local municipality (*Comissão Municipal*), for example, Viqueque town. The tax had been introduced in 1908 by Governor Eduardo Marquês and replaced a tax called *finta* for which—either in cash or kind—the whole *suku* had been liable. Metzner (1977, 211) points out that since the *finta* was collected by the chiefs of the *suku* and village they were able to skim off a lot of the money and that the head tax was intended to do away with this practice. One result of this innovation was to help nudge the country towards a market-orientated economy since it obliged farmers to raise money either by growing an agricultural surplus—which they were loath to do—or else work for cash. By the mid-1960s, cash had come to replace barter in most economic exchanges in the Viqueque market and it is this form of economic activity that is discussed in this article.[29]

Identities and commodities

Market commerce was mainly determined by the availability of agricultural produce. This, in its turn, depended upon the vagaries of rainfall and constant local variations in such geographic factors as altitude, slope, soil, and groundwater supply as well as various human variables, for example, the decision whether to focus on growing subsistence or cash crops or the need to raise cash.[30][31] Prices responded to scarcity, such bargaining as did occur being effective only when a commodity was abundant, or as the market drew to a close, or in the case of obviously below-par merchandise.[32] They would usually remain firm for about an hour and a half and a buyer who considered a price excessive would simply shift to another seller; but when the most desirable items were gone and Chinese and European buyers (or surrogates) had departed, prices might soften. Thus, whereas the asking price for an average sack of rice could start at around 30 escudos it might eventually fall to six. Or while one escudo might have bought nine tangerines shortly after the drum sounded, the same sum might buy a few more towards closure. Protracted haggling, though, was rare, sellers preferring to take unsold produce home rather than settle for an amount they considered unacceptably low. In any case, bargaining for comestibles was limited to Timorese, since Europeans would not generally haggle, and Chinese buyers would have already decided upon their upper limit, that is, the minimum possible in light of the trading circumstances of a particular Sunday.[33] The determination of the Chinese women not to give more than their predetermined maximum extended to taking advantage of a seller's lack of education by snatching up the selected item, quickly thrusting a pile of small change into the seller's hand, and immediately darting away before the seller—unaccustomed to counting so many coins under pressure—discovered she had been swindled.

Certain vegetables and fruits were sold by both *fehan* and *foho*, but just as the allocation of the different spaces they occupied and the mobility or relative lack of mobility in the market plaza indexed the social identity and gender of the sellers, so did the category of commodity they sold.[34] This was even the case with commodities that belonged to a general class of object, such as ceramics or cloth. Thus, while both categories of *ema timur* sold ceramics, the character and style of their products differed. *Fehan* manufactured undecorated, thin-walled clay pots (*lolon*) in addition to clay plates (*hanek*);[35] *foho* made thicker, decorated pots, but no plates.[36] Likewise with cloth. While both categories of Timorese brought pieces of cloth to sell in the market, and though they were woven from the same raw material, *fehan* cloth and *foho* cloth differed markedly in style.

Commodities can be conveniently listed under the rubrics 'comestibles', 'livestock', and 'non-comestibles' and are displayed in Table 2.1.

The commodities of Caraubalo *suku*

Most *fehan* sellers were residents of Caraubalo villages or those comprising the neighbouring *suku*, of Uma Kik, and their propinquity to the market may have encouraged them to regard the plaza proprietarily. Members of other *suku* would come to the market mainly to trade, and only after their business was concluded, socialise. Villagers in these two *suku* would often come specifically to network. In another respect, Caraubalo held a distinct standing in these commercial activities since its seven villages specialised to some extent in the commodities they sold (see Table 2.1).[37]

Table 2.1: Commodities bought and sold in Viqueque market

Fehan commodities
Comestibles Maize, dry rice (*hare to'os*), cassava (*ai farinha*), a variety of yams (*uhi*), many varieties of banana (*hudi*), breadfruit, melons, papaya (*aidila*), many varieties of pulses (including beans (*fore*) and peanuts (*fore rai*)), cashew nuts, dried pork (*fahi*), eggs (*manu tolu*), pancakes made of unleavened bread.
Livestock Suckling pigs (*fahi*), hens (*manu*), fighting cocks, a fawn (*bibi rusa*) (one occasion), doves (*faluk*), parakeets (*loriku*), cockatoos (*kakatua*), civet cats (*laku*). Non-comestibles Tobacco, areca, betel, lime (*ahu*), cotton (*cabas timur*), a species of vegetable that provides a castor-oil plant termed a*hi oan* ('little fire') and which is used by the Timorese as a lamp, women's cloth (*tais feto*), a variety of items made from palm leaves (baskets, pouches (Lacluta sub-district)), coloured palm-leaf strips, mats, leaf mats, ropework saddles (*sela*), harnesses), black rope (made from the fibrous outer covering of a palm tree), personal ornaments (hairpins, rings, bracelets, and combs), agricultural tools and other products made from iron (*besi*) (knives (*tudik*), machetes (*katana*), digging sticks (*ai suak*), spears (*diman*)), clay pots, clay plates.
Foho commodities
Comestibles Wet rice (*háre natar*) especially from Ossu and Uato Lari, sweet potatoes (*uhi midar*), European potatoes (*fehuk europa*), pumpkins (*lakeruk*) from Ossu and Venilale, 'Japanese' pumpkins (*lakeruk japonese*), lettuce, cabbages, spinach, watercress, tomatoes, cucumbers (*caban*), asparagus (*kamua*), onions (*liis*), garlic (*liis-asu*), oranges, and tangerines sold by Uato Lari people, lemons, pineapples, grapefruits, mangos (*has*), strawberries (*morangu*), sugar cane from Ossu, dried octopus, dried buffalo meat (*na'an carbau*), salt (*masin*). Livestock On occasion a man would bring a fighting cock to sell; but otherwise *foho* rarely brought livestock to market. Non-comestibles Women's cloth from Ossu, Venilale, and Uato Carabau, leaf-woven hats, fishing nets made from palm leaves, conical hats made from palm leaves, personal ornaments (hairpins, rings, bracelets, and combs), clay pots.

Commodities of Caraubalo *suku*
Cabira Oan village: maize, manioc, tobacco.
Vessa village: manioc, clay plates.
Lamaclaran village: manioc, tobacco, iron implements, spears.
Has Abut village: maize, manioc, ropework (rope (*tali*), saddles), iron implements.

Identities, space, time

Trading officially commenced at 9:00 a.m. sharp with the beating of a drum by a uniformed *sapaio*, smartly attired in a cap, khaki tunic, shorts, long socks and soft boots, standing on the road looking down upon the expectant crowd below.[38] Sellers and buyers waited in the building in anticipation of the first roll of the drum and when it came—with an avalanche of Chinese women and their children, baskets in hand in the vanguard—launching themselves upon the sellers in a robust, but targeted, onslaught.[39] In contrast to the Chinese, Timorese never went in for team assaults. On some Sundays, while the sellers quietly chatted in their places below, the administrator, accompanied or unaccompanied by his wife, would be present, checking to see if official protocols were being observed; but in contrast to the Portuguese teacher's wife neither he nor his wife ever made a purchase, what weekly provisions they might require being bought by a servant.[40] The *liurai* families and members of the bureaucracy would from time to time come down into the plaza on a whim or out of curiosity but for regular items, particularly comestibles, like the administrator, they preferred delegating this chore to servants. Especially for men, trading was considered too undignified for someone with an elevated social status to safeguard or self-esteem to uphold.[41]

Among the Timorese themselves, most transactions occurred between the two categories of *ema timur* but so dominant was the *foho* commercial presence that had they shifted their produce to the emporia at Venilale, Ossu, Uato Carabau, or Uato Lari, the result would have been seriously detrimental to the Viqueque economy. Trade between households was not a dominant economic practice among the *suku*, and so trading in the market served to satisfy wants and slough off surpluses. *Foho* traders came to market principally to earn the cash to pay their taxes and buy produce in the *cantinas*, but to a more limited degree they also depended upon *fehan* to supply them with maize, yams, coconuts, the three ingredients for use in betel-chewing (areca, betel, lime), salt, ropework, and metal implements (knives, machetes, spearheads, digging stick heads, arrowheads).[42] *Fehan* traders would purchase wet rice, green vegetables, and fruits from *foho* and maize and root crops from other *fehan*, who because of local agricultural circumstances had a surplus. This was especially important in the wet months of December and

January before the short dry season arrived in February and maize and root crops could be harvested, since by the turn of the year *fehan* stocks would be depleted in a number of *suku* of the sub-district (Hicks 2004, 49). Agricultural possibilities were determined by factors of physical geography and human decisions. As with altitude and climate, soils decisively influenced agricultural potential in the 10 *suku* of the sub-district of Viqueque, and this was reflected in the type of crop and time when it was available for sale. Some soils were predominantly clay; others sandy; and others marl. The soils of Luka *suku* were especially fertile, yielding handsome maize harvests in a good year in contrast to the *suku* of Caraubalo and Balarauain, which cultivated coconut palms as a cash crop instead of subsistence crops. These geographical factors also influenced the times of seeding and harvesting among the *suku*. Because Bibileu was in the northern uplands, the maize harvest in that *suku* came several weeks behind that on the more southerly Balarauain plains, and so in early February the farmers in Balarauain would sell maize to Bibileu buyers while in late March—by which time their supplies were dwindling—the people of Balarauain would purchase maize from Bibileu sellers.

Gender was apparent in the way in which the market operated. As a rough generalisation, most *foho* sellers were men, whereas most *fehan* sellers were woman. In the parallel rows displayed in Figure 2.1, therefore, the *foho* rows had more males than females while the *fehan* rows tended to have more females than males. Various exceptions and nuances modified this broad allocation of gender function. *Fehan* men sold ornaments, metal implements, and ropework, which members of both sexes bought; *fehan* women sold papaya, eggs, maize, pots, cloth, and ceramics. Men and women sold cloth, but while only men sold agricultural tools women sold ceramics for which they were also buyers. *Fehan* men might sometimes sit with their womenfolk as the latter sold their produce, and when the mood struck get up and amble around looking at what was on offer elsewhere in the plaza. For her part, when a woman of either ethnic category was satisfied with what she had sold she might leave what produce that still remained in the care of a relative and take a look around. In social interaction, too, gender distinction was apparent: women generally conversed with women; men with men.

No prescribed ritual closed the market, but after trading ended the marketplace continued to index social identification. Even as the last of the sellers began gathering up their unsold commodities and prepared to depart, members of the Christian community would already have begun preparations for the mass, and some time before the priest arrived they would have taken their places in the building. For an hour or so, refined, yet culturally assertive, liturgical sounds filled the air as the small, almost exclusively female, congregation recited the sacred words while their menfolk—most of whom looked for guidance in the teachings of their ancestors rather than the priests—chatted outside among themselves and anticipated

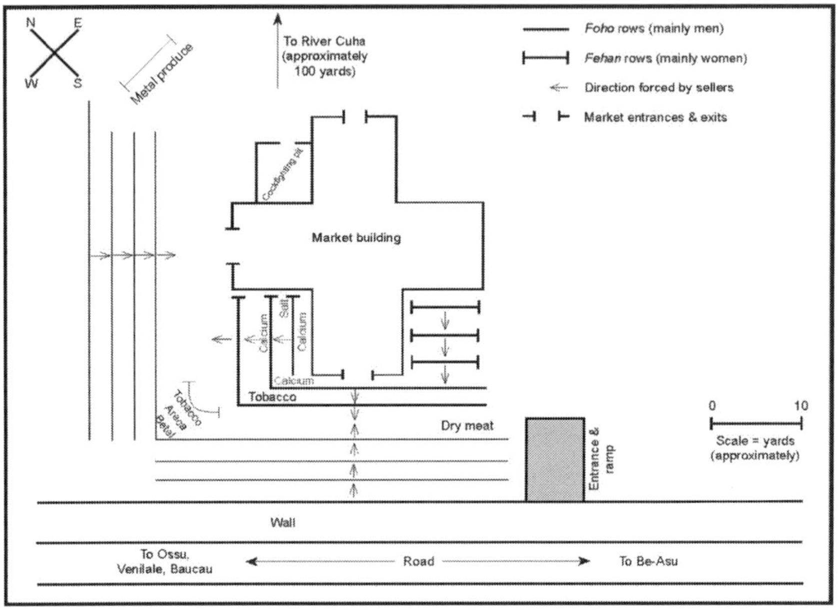

Figure 2.1. Marketplace. Image Credit: David Hicks.

Figure 2.2. Market in 1966 showing selling rows. Image Credit: David Hicks.

the enjoyment soon to be derived from the cockfights. When, finally, the priest dismissed the faithful, the men claimed the plaza for themselves, and at around 3:00 p.m. the weekly avian battles began in an enclosure adjoining an outside wall (Figure 2.1). As men spent the next few hours betting some of the cash the market had brought in, women would look to see what the Chinese *cantinas* offered that day or—on occasion—begin a spontaneous session of dance in the plaza opposite to the place from which the raucous sounds of the cockfight issued.

In contrast to the other six days, then, Sunday was a day dedicated to a dynamic bustle. From the moment of the drummer's signal the little town was abuzz with noise until, with the fall of night, Viqueque's habitual tranquillity returned.

Viqueque 2007

During the period described above, market activities were focused almost entirely on the physical marketplace, and buyers and sellers were still attempting to accustom themselves to the use of cash. Since then, a fully developed system of commerce has evolved while Viqueque's version of itself has undergone a series of avatars.[43] With the incorporation of Timor-Leste into the Republic of Indonesia as its twenty-seventh province, profound changes were unleashed upon the populace. Those Chinese who had not been slaughtered by the armed forces left the country, while huge numbers of *ema timur* were obliged by the Angkatan Bersenjata Republik Indonesia (ABRI, Armed Forces of the Republic of Indonesia) to leave their *suku* and resettle into concentrated settlements. Viqueque town was not spared. Villagers from the nine outlying *suku* were crammed into the town and the excess population overflowed into every available space in Caraubalo *suku*. Almost overnight Viqueque became seriously urbanised and as part of its social transformation came commercial adaptation as Indonesian immigrants established *warung* (small shops or stores) and *kios* (kiosks or stalls) while the rupiah replaced the escudo.[44][45]Although social coordinates of ethnicity and gender contributed to the shape of Viqueque market in the mid-1960s they were complemented by factors of an economic nature. Even as Timorese women and men were cognisant of the cultural context in which they traded, they were also conscious of the necessity of adjusting their expectations to accommodate the supply and demands of the commodities they traded. Goods that were scarce, whether as the consequence of seasonal changes, or unforeseen contingencies, saw their market values rise just as goods in abundance witnessed a decline in their market values. Illiterate though most were, traders deliberately increased or decreased prices accordingly. In today's Timor-Leste, literacy and the level-ling out of cultural differences have served to bring into sharper relief the economic calculations at play in Viqueque commercial life, and the operation of a self-conscious rationality Raymond Firth discerns at work wherever individuals go about satisfying one another's economic needs regardless of the nature of their society is even more evident than at that earlier period.

With Timor-Leste's liberation in 1999 and the Indonesian exodus, changes in Timorese lives took another turn as international agencies (spearheaded by the United Nations, World Bank, and USAID, and supported by a host of NGOs) replaced the ABRI. The *malai* had returned, energised by new directives and propounding new strategies for implementing them.

In Viqueque today the presence of the *ema malai* is unobtrusive. They are no more numerous than in the old days, except at national elections when outside observers descend into the sub-district engaged in the discharge of their various mandates. Now, though, when they do arrive the *ema malai* come as a considerably more ethnically diverse cast of characters as Indians, Japanese, and other nationalities share space with *ema timur*. The district administrator is Timorese, though in 2007 this office had failed to attain the imposing presence it once held during the time of the Portuguese regime. The Chinese have not returned to the town, however, and the marketplace, eviscerated by the accumulation of population under the Indonesian occupation and the shops that Indonesian merchants established to accommodate the increased demand for products, is covered by houses, *warung*, and *kios*. The road from which it once dominated life on Sundays in Viqueque is today crammed on either side by these trading enterprises, many of which are run by Timorese. To these *warung* and *kios*, *fehan* and *foho* men and women bring their surplus garden produce for daily sale. As for the market building itself, its dilapidated space now serves as a handy place for stockpiling firewood and hanging up clothes to dry. Whereas in the past the building was a physically conspicuous representation of European presence and served as a space in which ethnicity, gender, social hierarchy, pastime, and religion were physically marked out, today its barely visible outline merges into those of the buildings adjoining it as though symbolising the changes in social identity that are currently underway.[46] Once clear-cut, identities have grown increasingly diffuse as *fehan* and *foho*, though still discriminable by language, have merged into a more integrated recasting of the category *ema timur* while the distinctions between the ranks of *liurai*, *dato*, and *ema reino* are receding.

In a temporal sense as well, continuum has submerged disjunction. Commerce, formerly characterised by weekly gatherings of social effervescence, has given way to routine. Daily commerce in shops and kiosks and the cycle of six quiet days interspersed by one day of sustained socialising has been superseded by a lineal sequence in which each day follows much like another. The mass no longer visually marks off the faithful as a minority community enclosed once a week within the confines of the multifunctional marketspace. A church has now been built and the town has a resident priest who celebrates daily mass. In a formal sense virtually all Timorese profess to be Catholics and the religion has now been assimilated into the daily lives of both women and men, though to what extent this reflects conviction, particularly on the part of the males, is an altogether different matter.[47] Like the Sunday market itself, cockfights have ceased to provide a focal event for the week and have been displaced from the weekly space they formerly shared with ritual. The cockfighting pit is presently located on the margins of the town where the cocks battle each other every afternoon.[48]

Religion, pastime, ethnic differentiation, social hierarchy, and gender have thus grown more diffuse in their overt manifestations during the last four decades in Viqueque town and their diffusion complicates the ready assaying of cultural identities, a challenge rendered all the more difficult because of the social changes wrought by the dynamism of a developed peasant market that has now become integrated into the national economy. Thus, even were the physical and temporal coordinates still available to mark social and cultural discriminations in today's Viqueque, these would only be of limited value compared with the 1960s, a period when space and time served as plangent indices of social identity.

In conjunction with the United Nations, World Bank, other large international agencies, and the aforementioned cluster of non-governmental organisations, the Timorese populations in the interior of this newly emerged nation-state, like those of Viqueque, are already engaged in advancing along a path that is transforming their identities from that of parochial-minded villagers into nationally conscious citizens. Local governance, as seen more particularly in institutions such as the *suku* council and the executive position of *xefe de suku* (*suku* chief), is now being populated by women, 'youth' (that is, young men and young women over the voting age of 18 years), and persons who previously were debarred because of their subordinate social pedigree in a society dominated by hierarchy (Hicks forthcoming).

Comparison between the two 'time frames' offered by the period 1966-1967 and the contemporary post-colonial nation-state of Timor-Leste suggests that among the consequences of colonisation (whether by other nation-states, international agencies or by non-governmental organisations), invasion, and the process of nation-building itself, is a tendency for ethnicities, social class, social status, gender, and social identity to become much less differentiated in the face of the more assertive demands of state-wide imperatives, the evolution of a sense of national identity, and the values newly assimilated from a world both external and hostile to parochial concerns.[49]

Notes

1 This article was first published at Bijdragen tot de Taal-, Land- en Volkenkunde Vol. 168, No. 1 (2012), pp. 55-73. The editors are grateful to Brill editors for the authorization to republish it in this volume.

2 The term 'town' (*vila* in the Portuguese language and *kota* in the Tetum language) refers to settlements in Timor-Leste which are of much smaller size than the term signifies customarily and one could argue that Viqueque's population of roughly 1000 in the 1960s hardly justifies that characterisation; nevertheless, it is usual to characterise it as such and I do so here. As of the national census year 2004, with a population provisionally set at 5,105, however, the appellation is more defensible; see http://www.citypopulation.de/EastTimor.html (accessed 21 February, 2012).

3 From an analysis of his data from the Bastar district of Madhya Pradesh in India, Alfred Gell (1982) has also suggested that the market can, in effect, serve as a vehicle for delineating social identity and bringing together persons of different identities.

4 A Thursday market was also held, but this was sparsely attended with only *fehan* from local villagers and townsfolk participating. The more intense atmosphere of the Sunday market was absent and officers of the administration did not bother to oversee the proceedings. Few Chinese came and those that did had bought the most desirable comestibles by 9:00 a.m., even though—as on Sundays—buying was not officially permitted until that time. Although some local people might turn up as casual buyers, there were fewer commodities for sale and sellers would tend to keep to the vicinity of the entrance ramp. Such trading as there was terminated by about 11:00 a.m. These Thursday markets tended to be patronised by no more than about 150 persons.

5 Anthony Forge (1991) discusses markets in the *kabupaten* of Timor Tengah Utara and Timor Tengah Selatan in 1989, though his study is not concerned with issues of social identity.

6 I thank the following organisations for their help in funding my research at various times in Timor-Leste: the London Committee of the London-Cornell Project for East and South-East Asian Studies which was supported jointly by the Carnegie Corporation of New York and the Nuffield Foundation; the American Philosophical Society; and J. William Fulbright Foreign Scholarship Board. I wish to express my appreciation to Andrew McWilliam and the two anonymous readers who read the manuscript for their incisive suggestions for its improvement.

7 Then as now Viqueque town was the administrative centre for the district (*concelho*) bearing the same name.

8 My wife and I, who had been working among the Makassae in Baucau since March 1966, when we arrived in Timor, settled down in our Viqueque house in June, and I remained there until early September the following year. Other than the two or three occasions upon which my wife and I paid short visits to Dili, we probably participated in just about every market session during the period we lived in the town. We were thus able to follow the cyclical trade of commodities month by month and record how price fluctuations responded to abundance or scarcity of commodities, an aspect of Viqueque market I hope to describe elsewhere.

9 Also referred to as Viqueque-Sede. The sub-district of Viqueque was made up of 10 *suku*: Caraubalo, Uma Kik, Balarauain, Uma Ua'in Craik, Luca, Uai Mori, Uma Ua'in Leten, Bibileu, Fatu Dere, and Maluro.

10 The other villages were: Mane Hat, Mamulak, Vessa, Lamaclaran, Has Abut, and Sira Lari. All were *fehan* except for Sira Lari, the residents of which were Makassae.

11 The term *ema* itself has as its prime referent 'people' and *malai* derives from Malay or *Malayu*.

12 Compared with such local Indonesian markets as that described for Java's 'Modjokuto' by Alice Dewey (1962), the markets in Timor-Leste before the Indonesian Occupation were simple enough: systems of credit had not been devised, the key market day was on a once-only-in-a-week cycle, and the day on which it was held was not identified with any special designation. On the other hand, we see certain parallels. Dewey's depiction (1962, 69) of the Modjokuto market as "a place to meet people ... sit and watch life go by while gossiping about the latest news and gathering information about crop conditions and prices" holds true for Viqueque and other contemporary Timorese markets as does her allusion to itinerant traders "traveling constantly back and forth between the various markets" spreading news.

13 Alternative renderings: *ema Timor* and *ema Timór* (Hull 2002, 71).

14 *Fehan* = lowlands, southern coastal plains, refined; *foho* = uplands, countryside, unrefined.

15 Andrew McWilliam (pers. comm.) has noted that this opposition is suggestive of another verbal opposition indicating the spatial indexing of others, namely, that of *ema lorosa'e/ema loromonu*, a contrast that received some attention in the press over the course of recent years. Indeed, its interest is so compelling in regard to its relevance for the social classification of identity that I have devoted an article to considering whether it indexes an authentic distinction or is largely specious (Hicks 2009).

16 The *Posto Sede* included both highland and lowland/coastal areas, and certain villages on the lowlands/coastal areas consisted entirely of Makassae and Naueti.

17 If we exclude the itinerant traders, the catchment region for the Viqueque market extended as far as Venilale, Uato Carabau, Uato-Lari, the village of Uma Liurai in *suku* Wai Mori, Lacluta, and Luca.

18 "Since a visit to the market will usually consume an entire day, it is obvious that the cash return and small purchases are not the only consideration. For most, a considerable social dimension is involved. Villagers at markets chat with each other and with Timorese small merchants, but their relationship with other dealers, mainly Bugis and Chinese, is more limited." (Forge 1991, 167)

19 These are the denotations employed in the Tetum language. By the 1960s the category *ata* had been displaced by a category of servant identified by the Portuguese term *criado*. For a lengthier discussion of these ranks in the 1960s, see Hicks, "Unachieved syncretism".

20 The local militia which was composed entirely of conscripted Timorese men.

21 Legally, Timorese were Portuguese citizens.

22 Women were not travelling traders in contrast to Guro Land, in West Africa, where their role as itinerant traders in markets was very useful for communities during periods of warfare since unlike members of the male sex, women "could travel freely ... and continue the trading activities of which they were active agents" (Meillassoux 1962, 283).

23 Unlike in the markets described by Forge, *papalele*, that is, traders who purchased small quantities of produce to resell later, were not present in the Viqueque market.

24 I was unable to discover when the building was erected, but from the evidence of an Australian map it was already standing as early as September 1942.

25 The influence on the market by the European administration is further evinced by the rumour that circulated in 1967 that the administrator was going to compel buyers and sellers to wear trousers and shoes. Two Timorese told me that the policy would result in sellers switching their allegiances to the Uato-Lari market. The logic driving this inspiration remains unclear, but whatever the veracity of the rumour participants continued wearing—or not, as in the majority of instances—their customary footwear.

26 The itinerant sellers did not have any special location on the plaza. After the market commenced they simply wandered about in search of buyers.

27 In the figure I give some indication of a few of the sites where the same produce (salt, calcium, tobacco, and so on) tended to be sold from Sunday to Sunday.

28 I should point out that Figure 1 is a schematic composite of the many Sunday markets we witnessed. Some variation in the seating could and did occur so that individual Timorese, whatever their wares, might, as the need or whim took them, sometimes settle into a row mainly composed of individuals of a different social identity. Most often, however, their seating arrangements accorded with the pattern shown here.

29 A substantive account of barter in the wider region is given in Barnes and Barnes (1989) in their discussion of exchange in Lamalera. They also discern a connection between social groups and the allocation of space (Barnes and Barnes 1989, 405).

30 Metzner (1977, 70-72) considers in some detail this aspect of Viqueque's climate.

31 Copra was a major cash source for the Timorese living near Viqueque town.

32 Bargaining, however, took place with ceramics, metal goods, cloth, fighting cocks, or an unusual luxury item such as a cockatoo or civet cat.

33 On one occasion a Chinese woman friend of ours robustly counselled my wife to demand more than two eggs for her escudo, which up to that time she was content to accept.

34 Ceramic objects were bought only by Timorese. It might be remarked that wet rice was much sought after by the *fehan*, who for the most part cultivated only dry rice in gardens and who lacked the flat fields and terraces of the *foho*. Uato-Lari was a richly productive wet rice subdistrict.

35 *Fehan* pots were made in Macdean village in Uma Kik *suku* and plates in Vessa village in Caraubalo.

36 In Venilale sub-district.

37 In what might be regarded as a kind of sub-set of exchanges between *foho* and *fehan*, in Caraubalo *suku*, Sira Lari *foho* provided wet rice, buffalo meat, fruit, and vegetables and the six *fehan* villages provided maize, coconuts, ceramics, ironwork, and ropework.

38 Chinese buyers, however, would often strike clandestine deals with sellers before the market opened.

39 The rule that buyers must assemble in the market building to await the sound of the drum had been decreed by the then administrator on the grounds that it made the market transactions fairer for everyone. He probably thought this up to militate against the Chinese monopolising buyers.

40 My wife, while occasionally employing a servant, would more often carry out the job of buying herself.

41 For a somewhat similar, though not identical, parallel in a part of the archipelago remote from Timor, see Alexander (1998, 211) in her discussion of the Javanese marketplace. She, too, remarks on "the prominent economic roles of women" in the marketing system (Alexander 1998, 211).

42 Coconuts were not often sold in the market. Most families grew their own.

43 "The primitive world which for so long has dominated the anthropological imagination is inevitably on the wane, being displaced by the world of the peasant and proletarian" (Cook 1966, 338).

44 The term *warung* comes from Javanese.

45 The term *kios* comes from Persian via Turkish and Dutch, as one reader of my manuscript noted.

46 The contrast between the orderliness imposed by the Portuguese and what appears to be—and in many instances is—the disorder evident in Viqueque market activities may, as elsewhere in Timor-Leste, be traced to the Indonesian influence but also to some extent to the prior struggle for power between the contending forces of the *União Democrática Timorense* and those of FRETELIN. The Indonesian army and the Timorese political elite together helped reduce towns, including the capital, to a shambles from which they have yet to recover. Dili, more particularly, bears little resemblance to the Dili of the mid-1960s: dynamism has supplanted tranquillity. But at a price.

47 Indigenous rituals and the ideological attitudes attending them continue to play very important roles in local community life. Hicks, "Afterword", 166-180.

48 Whereas in the 1960s attendance could reach around 100 men, the fights I witnessed in 2007, though well attended enough, were not as large, perhaps because cockfighting had by then become a daily pastime.

49 Or, in the apt terms of one reviewer of a draft of this article, 'homogenised' or 'flattened'.

References

Alexander, J. 1998. "Women traders in Javanese marketplaces: Ethnicity, gender, and the entrepreneurial spirit." In *Market Cultures: Society and Morality in the New Asian Capitalisms*, edited by R. W. Hefner, 203-223. Boulder, CO: Westview Press.

Barnes, R. H. and R. Barnes. 1989. "Barter and money in an Indonesian village economy." *Man (New Series)* 24 (3): 399-418. https://doi.org/10.2307/2802698

City Population. "East Timor: Districts, Subdistricts, Sucos, Cities, Urban areas ..." Accessed at https://www.citypopulation.de/en/timor/ on 21 February, 2012.

Cook, S. 1966. "The obsolete 'anti-market' mentality: A critique of the substantive approach to economic anthropology." *American Anthropologist* 68 (2): 323-345.

Dalton, G. 1971. *Economic Anthropology and Development: Essays on Tribal and Peasant Economics*. New York/London: Basic Books.

Dewey, A. G. 1962. *Peasant Marketing in Java*. New York: Free Press of Glencoe.

Firth, R. 1972. "Methodological issues in economic anthropology (Review Article)." *Man (New Series)* 7 (3): 467-475. https://doi.org/10.2307/2800918

Forge, A. 1991. "Markets in Central Timor" In *Nusa Tenggara Timur: The Challenges of Development*, edited by C. Barlow, A. Bellis, and K. Andrews, 165-177. Canberra: Department of Political and Social Change, Research School of Pacific Studies, Australian National University.

Gell, A. 1982. "The market wheel: Symbolic aspects of an Indian tribal market." *Man (New Series)* 17 (3 [September]): 470-491. https://doi.org/10.2307/2801710

Hicks, D. 1983. "Unachieved syncretism: The local-level political system in Portuguese Timor (1966-1967)." *Anthropos* 78 (1-2): 17-40.

Hicks, D. (1976) 2004. *Tetum Ghosts and Kin: Fertility and Gender in East Timor. Second Edition*. Illinois: Waveland Press.

Hicks, D. 2007. "Community and nation-state in East Timor: A view from the periphery.", *Anthropology Today* 23 (1): 13-16.

Hicks, D. 2008. "Afterword: Glimpses of alternatives; The Uma Lulik of East Timor." *Social analysis* 52 (1): 166-180.

Hicks, D. 2009. "'Ema Lorosa'e', 'Ema Loromonu': identity and politics in Timor-Leste." In *East Timor: How to Build a New Nation in Southeast Asia in the 21st Century?*, edited by C. Cabasset and D. Durand, 81-94. Bangkok: Research Institute on Contemporary Southeast Asia (IRASEC & CASE).

Hicks, D. 2012. "Indexing social space. A marketplace in Timor-Leste." *Bijdragen tot de Taal-, Land- en Volkenkunde* 168 (1): 55-73. doi.org/10.1163/22134379-90003569.

Hicks, D. Forthcoming. "Adat and the nation-state in Timor-Leste: Opposition and synthesis in two political cultures." In *The Politics of Timor-Leste*, edited by M. Leach and D. Kingsbury. Ithaca, NY: Cornell Southeast Asia Program.

Hull, G. 2002. *Standard Tetum-English Dictionary*. Second revised and expanded edition. Sydney: Allen and Unwin. First edition 1999.

Meillassoux, C. 1962. "Social and economic factors affecting markets in Guro Land." In *Markets in Africa*, edited by P. Bohannan and G. Dalton, 279-298. Evanston: Northwestern University Press. [African Studies 9.]

Metzner, J. K. 1977. *Man and environment in Eastern Timor: A geoecological analysis of the Baucau-Viqueque area as a possible basis for regional planning.* Canberra: Development Studies Centre, Australian National University. [Monograph 8.]

Polanyi, K. (1944) 1957. *The Great Transformation*. Reprint. Foreword by Robert M. MacIver. Boston: Beacon Press.

Polanyi, K., and C. M. Arensberg. 1957. *Trade and Market in the Early Empires: Economies in History and Theory.* Glencoe, Illinois: Free Press of Glencoe.

CHAPTER 3

Flirting with Ford, reverting to race? Housing, urban planning and the making of an economic and social order in Portuguese Timor in trans-colonial perspective, 1959-1963

Alex Grainger

Abstract

This chapter examines two transnational ideologies—Fordism and Lusotropicalism—in the context of late-colonial public housing provision in Portuguese Timor. It seeks to understand the extent to which planned housing in the colony was informed either by an economic ideology of mass production or a colonial ideology through which housing was racialised. It highlights the perceptions of Portuguese architects regarding the ability of residents to 'adapt' to indigenous housing. This issue was raised during a housing study tour of Southeast Asia and northern Australia by the architects who wished to investigate possibilities for such housing in Portuguese Timor. The chapter highlights the issues of social conflict which resulted from changes in housing, land use and labour provision in colonial and postcolonial cities; and examines the extent of cooperation among colonial officials to realise shared goals in these contexts.

Keywords: Housing; urban planning; Fordism; Lusotropicalism; Portuguese Timor; Southeast Asia

This chapter examines a housing study tour of Southeast Asia and northern Australia, conducted by two Portuguese architects in the late-1950s. The tour was intended to inform planned indigenous housing in Dili, the capital of Portuguese Timor, which they also later toured and reported on. The two architects, Sousa Mendes and Almeida, were commissioned by the Overseas Ministry's (*Ministério do Ultramar*, formerly the Ministry of Colonies) Directorate-General of Public Works, based in Lisbon, to visit neighbouring colonies and countries where they sought to learn lessons for public housing in Timor.

The architects expressed an apparent preference for 'economic housing' with vernacular features, over mass-produced housing, associated with Fordism, a post-war regime of accumulation intended to ensure economic growth. Apart from Fordism, throughout the chapter I attempt to account for this preference by looking at two further sets of influences. The architects' preferences were informed by Tropical Architecture, a school of architecture that emphasises the role of ethnographic fieldwork and local materials on vernacular house design. Another possible influence addressed throughout is Lusotropicalism, a colonial racial ideology, officially promoted by the Portuguese state throughout the 1950s and early 1960s.

The chapter is structured into three sections. Section one provides an introductory historical sketch, outlining the underlying social and economic objectives of colonial urban planning and housing and also elaborates briefly on Fordism, Tropical Architecture and Lusotropicalism. Section two describes the study tour; and section three assesses the influence of the study tour and ideological influences on attempts to create a socio-economic order via urban planning and 'economic housing' in Dili. Whereas other contributions to this volume examine resistance to colonial attempts to regulate Timor's society (see Chapters 1 and 2, this volume), this chapter emphasises potential convergences and divergences in certain late-colonial societies in the region.

Creating socio-economic orders through late-colonial urban planning

Colonial urban planning and public housing involved deliberate attempts to order socio-economic spaces and to control social reproduction of indigenous households. From the beginning of the twentieth century, colonial cities were increasingly made into places where commodities extracted from rural areas were traded. Despite the increasing importance of consumption in colonial cities, they remained largely un-industrialised and peripheries of the world-economy. In the same period, colonial cities were increasingly designed to absorb labour on a limited scale from rural areas. As part of this process, urban areas were segregated along racial lines, with indigenous populations gradually admitted into circumscribed zones according to labour requirements. This was a relatively common phenomenon in colonial Southeast Asia, it has been argued (McGee 1967 quoted in King 1990, 57) and key to this was the introduction and enforcement of private property rights and the colonial state's ability to appropriate land.

Consistent with these patterns of planning, colonial and some post-colonial governments conceived of socio-economic ordering taking place in terms of the operation of both small- and large-scale dynamics with the following elements in mind: design and construction of public housing and its adaptation to the tropics; urban planning and land-titling; and the mass-production of housing and urbanisation alike which may be partly seen as attempts to produce stable social and economic orders. These were combined with strategies such as "welfare colonialism" (Scott 1998, 97), and the control and reproduction of labour.

Meanwhile, and beyond this colonial context, standardised, mass-produced housing was constructed after 1945 in various settings outside the Portuguese empire. Mass production was also often associated with the term 'Fordism', originally associated with the assembly-line techniques of the Ford Motor Company. Later it came to describe a particular regime of accumulation associated with mass production techniques and its coordination with consumption; a wage policy and urban planning to facilitate communication; and transport between housing, and places of work and consumption (Aglietta [1979] 2000). These conditions had developed in the United States and after 1945 began to expand globally as a capitalist regime of accumulation (Harvey 1989). Fordism entailed coordinating labour and production in the service of producing not only capitalist development but also a social and spatial order allied with these goals (Jessop 1992). In other words, mass-produced housing was a key part of ensuring a stable social and economic order. An example of this integrated approach to economic and social planning was seen in Singapore (see section below).

In contrast, some late-colonial or post-colonial public housing projects were informed by Tropical Architecture, a school of architecture which emphasised that indigenous housing should be subject to ethnographic study to ascertain the practices of its inhabitants. Such housing could be adapted accordingly, so the thinking went, using local materials as far as possible and based on considerations of ventilation, heat and light (Baweja 2007). Tropical Architecture, with its emphasis on ethnographically-informed design, clearly influenced the perspectives of Sousa Mendes and Almeida.

Less clear is the extent to which the two architects were influenced by Lusotropicalism. Lusotropicalism was an official ideology, adopted and implemented throughout the Portuguese empire in the 1950s which posited that the Portuguese colonial relationship with its subject peoples was exceptional. It emphasised fraternisation between coloniser and colonised based on Christianity and, rather than racial segregation, alleged racial mixing (miscegenation) (Castelo 1998).[1] In contrast to the underlying principles of Tropical Architecture, the Portuguese colonial authorities were influenced by a racial perspective that both diluted its relevance to Portuguese territories and also made it a governing concept, albeit to varying degrees in different territories and at different times. For example, some colonial anthropologists of Timor were less influenced by Lusotropicalism's miscegenation thesis rather than set on promoting the exclusive racial origins of Timorese (Roque 2019).

While the ethnographic study of 'tropical' housing as a basis for public housing was not novel in the period, potentially injecting the same study with 'race', in the context of Lusotropicalism, implied Portuguese exceptionalism. But the study tour itself seemed to underscore not exceptionalism, I argue, but rather trans-colonial cooperation. The control and concentration of indigenous labour in colonial cities involved the authorities "... exchang[ing] information on standards, costs, and design [of economical housing] with other European powers ..." (King 1990, 52-53). Portuguese authorities seem to have been no exception to this pattern and engaged in cooperation with other European colonial powers in the field of colonial urban planning (Silva 2016). However, bringing such a trans-colonial perspective to bear in relation to Timor has been a relatively neglected area (Jerónimo and Costa Pinto 2015, 52).

Timor was far-removed from the emergent circuitries of global capital on the periphery of the world's economy (in contrast to, for example, Singapore). It could therefore be viewed as an 'inappropriate' candidate for mass-produced housing. However, when accounting for the choice of more vernacular housing, other factors also need to be considered. For example, did 'Fordist' urban planning and housing seen on the tour influence designs for indigenous housing in Timor? How far did Lusotropicalism provide a restraint on the realisation of this rational model of urban planning and standardised housing? In relation to this, how far did trans-colonial cooperation indicate, in Benedict Anderson's words (2016, 153), a "... typical 'solidarity among whites', which linked colonial rulers from different national metropoles, whatever their internal rivalries and conflicts"? I examine these considerations, along with addressing the extent to which 'indigenous housing' was viewed by colonial authorities as requiring adaptation to house occupants, or, in contrast, whether occupants were viewed as having innate capacities (or otherwise) to adapt to housing.

The study tour

Singapore

By the time of Sousa Mendes and Almeida's visit in 1959, Singapore was in a state of rapid change. Its economy was still fundamentally connected with that of Malaya (which had become independent in 1957) and was based on its 'entrepot' status, of processing primary products for export, especially petroleum and rubber. Before handing over power to the People's Action Party (PAP) government in 1959, the colonial authorities sought to ensure 'stability' through creating manufacturing jobs, welfare reforms, and to attract investment through special concessions to foreign business.

The centrepiece of 'social development' was housing, which was to be integrated with an economic agenda which included increasing manufacturing jobs. After 1945, Singapore became the subject of the largest public housing programme in the British Empire and "one of the largest in the world" (Seng 2013, 7). The Singapore Improvement Trust (SIT) was the authority responsible for alleviating 'overcrowded' central areas of the city. With a new emphasis on planning in the post-war period, rather than housing per se as in the pre-war period (Seng 2013), the SIT began constructing housing on a large scale. Closely modelled on Britain's own post-war state public housing including the establishment of new towns, SIT set about constructing 4,336 houses between 1948-1950 to accommodate a quarter of the population, a target it missed by about 5 percent (Yeung 1973, 45).

Between 1947 and Singapore's independence in 1959, 20,000 houses were constructed by the SIT (Siew-Eng and Savage 1991, 327-328). Most were built in Queenstown and Kallang, planned new towns where Sousa Mendes and Almeida were taken on a tour.[2] As guests of the SIT and Public Works department, they were shown apartments three or four floors high. They noted that there was a great dependence on concrete with no natural materials used. However, they were interested in incorporating design features which provided "good protection against the rain" and the architects saw flats with verandas coated with rubber and synthetic paint to make them impermeable.[3] Prefabricated concrete grillages covered walkways and offered some protection from tropical downpours.[4]

The SIT houses were, the visitors concluded, more likely to make use of "walls rather than spaces". This reflected a taste for European, "even, we would say, English [architecture]", producing "strange" results "for the country and its human content". While this strangeness was partly the result of few concessions to "traditional" styles, incorporating such styles would be complicated, since, they asserted, Singapore was composed of "an amalgam of races".[5] The issue of race was a consideration in the architects' thinking on the question of housing in Singapore where, they believed, "less evolved races"—by which they meant Malay and Indian people, as opposed to the Chinese population—had difficulty adapting to public housing. It is of course possible that the architects had drawn their own conclusions about the existence of such a hierarchy of races from their own brief experiences in Singapore, or from Timor. It is equally likely, however, that they were repeating views put forward by their British official hosts in which the notion of a hierarchy of races originated from the need to assert political and economic dominance, subsequently constructed as "an inevitable reflection of inherent "racial" differences" (Hirschmann 1986, 348; Tajudeen 2011, 229).

The visitors noted the immediate surrounds of the flats they saw, with large lawns between the apartment buildings and a wide extent of forests to the rear and these features seemed to have left a positive impression. However, there was little remaining evidence by the time of their tour of the resultant changes to the surrounding areas to make way for Queenstown. In the previous few years, the area on which it was built contained many 'Attap' (from the Malay for the type of leaves used in roof construction) houses, constructed mainly from wood, with reed walls and grass roofs. The visitors saw examples of Attap houses, but a brief description of the houses' most common location in the city "suburbs" and the local materials used in their construction suggests that they may not have fully comprehended their political, social and cultural significance.

Attap house residents were farmers engaged in agriculture who were referred to by the authorities as "squatters", who comprised about a quarter of the population in 1957.[6] Squatters were defined by the British authorities in Malaya in the post-war period as those living on rural land without title and had fled urban areas during the Japanese occupation (1942-1945). After 1945, pre-war legislation was reintroduced under which wartime settlers were again defined as squatters and were to be moved off land earmarked for development. However, eviction rates were low partly because squatters challenged decisions with the support of unions (Wah 1988, 63, 83, 90). Many such unions were associated with the Malayan Communist Party (MCP) which organised a wave of strikes in order to challenge the legitimacy of the returning colonial authorities. In 1948 the British authorities mounted a counter-insurgency campaign in Malaya, the 'Emergency', moving more than a million rural labourers and squatters to 'New Villages' with the avowed aim of separating the MCP from its base of support among the population (Hack 2012, 212) which was completed by late-1951.

In Singapore, the Emergency's regulations had effectively halted open communist–supported labour movement activity after 1948 (Liu and Wong 2004, 175) but strikes continued.[7] However, squatter claims to land in Singapore were not only connected with the actions of an urban working class, but also agrarian smallholders. Having organised an "Attap Dwellers Association", 266 families resisted removal and by 1954, construction of Queenstown had "come to a standstill". By 1955, the authorities reported that it was "practically impossible to find sites for public buildings that were not encumbered with clusters of Attap dwellings or agricultural settlers" (quoted in Clancey 2004, 39). As Clancey notes, Communist supporters of Attap dwellers could not object to housing reform promoted by the People's Action Party (PAP) government, elected alongside other parties in 1955, since the provision of public housing was a socialist mainstay. Moreover, certain techniques of the 'New Villages' program in Malaya were practiced in Singapore from the early 1950s. Although no New Villages were established in Singapore, colonial administrators that worked on the program were increasingly drafted in to work on housing reform in Singapore.

The construction of new towns required the evictions of Attap dwellers and this served as a formative stage of producing an economic order which was continued after independence in 1959 and which was centred on planned manufacturing industries, foreign capital, social welfare, and relatively high wages. This organisation primarily complemented a global Fordist regime of accumulation by occupying an intermediary position of processing and trading extractive commodities. The visiting architects rejected Singapore-style mass-produced housing for Timor because they viewed it as inappropriate for the tropics, lacking aesthetic value, and believed themselves able to make it more cheaply. And as their report also made clear, these factors had served as obstacles to the 'integration of races' into public housing.

Jakarta

Jakarta was an arena of fluid politics between Indonesia's unilateral declaration of Indonesian independence in 1945 and full recognition of independence in 1949 (Cribb 1991; McVey 1971) and the abode of different classes and several ethnic groups. This pattern of fluid politics continued into the 1950s. In contrast to late-colonial Singapore, in post-colonial Indonesia President Soekarno directed campaigns against 'neo-colonialism'. In 1957 Dutch assets were nationalised and parliament suspended in favour of rule through presidential authority. Under this arrangement, the military gained economic power by taking over Dutch plantations and increased its authority in urban areas and constrained the movements of the Indonesian Communist Party, (*Partai Komunis Indonesia*—PKI), which thereafter worked more closely among the peasantry (Mortimer 1972, 10). Colonial rule had also left a legacy of land 'dualism', whereby most of Jakarta's dwellers were resident on unregistered land and very few houses were built on registered land (Leaf 1994).

The largest planned public housing development was the *Kebayoran Baru* project started by the Dutch. The Indonesian authorities continued this satellite town of modernist inspiration to the southwest of Jakarta, on which 4,630 houses were built between 1950-1953 (Silver 2008) dispossessing about 10,000 fruit growers. *Kebayoran Baru* was originally intended to have a mixture of lower and middle-class inhabitants. However, in the event this intention faded and the development became mostly inhabited by the middle and upper classes (Lubis 2018, 67). Indonesia lacked construction materials and according to some accounts, the houses that were constructed were "ornate ministries..." with "...practically no building of houses for poor people" (Wright [1994] 1956, 109). Instead, the government pursued 'monumental' public buildings.[8] Sukarno intended to clear slums and build Singaporean-style modernist public housing, but difficulties in implementing the plans meant that they were never realised (Abeyasekere 1990, 201).

Other factors contributed to Jakarta's lack of affordable public housing such as the interplay of regional planning, domestic politics and international aid. Jakarta's Master Plan was co-authored by international consultants and US-trained Indonesian planners. In an early iteration in 1952, Bogor, Tangerang and Bekasi (collectively presaging the so-called 'Jabotabek' or greater Jakarta region) were designated as sites of future housing developments but under the plans, the state was to play no role in their construction. Housing co-operatives (*Jajasan Kas Pembangunan*—JKP) were set up but few functioned since household savings had been eroded by inflation preventing further investment in them (Columbijn 2010, 341). 'Self-help housing' was touted by international donors (UN, US) which the JKP was to spearhead, in the manner of "top-down" development aid (ibid., 350); these too failed.

The two-day visit to Jakarta by Sousa Mendes and Almeida was the shortest of all on their tour. It appeared to make the least impression on them which may be explained by the fact that unlike Singapore and Darwin, they were not accompanied by the authorities and were therefore left to locate housing by themselves. For example, they made no reference to *Kebayoran Baru*. Instead, they found single-story houses with large soffits that provided shade and which were "copied from the Dutch", with downpipes and gutters to channel monsoonal rains. Of greatest interest to the visitors was the colonial hill town of Bogor, with landscaped gardens and the presidential palace, some 50 kilometres to the south of the city. They observed that like Singapore's 'green belt', Bogor represented an attempt to integrate a 'natural' aspect which provided respite from heat and crowded conditions but was administratively and geographically separate from the city. As in Singapore, the visitors paid attention to the presumed race of the intended inhabitants. They asserted that Jakarta's society was culturally monolithic with a "unity of people and race". But they also photographed and commented on the roof of a Minangkabau (Sumatran) house. This is significant since Jakarta had been very diverse in character for several centuries (Gelman-Taylor [1983] 2009).

The Portuguese architects undertook a fleeting overview of a limited number of houses. The relative lack of construction of formal public housing in Jakarta after Indonesia's independence may have deterred them from delving more deeply into the matter, but their observations were no less informed by a preoccupation with the suitability of different ethnic groups to public housing as in Singapore and as shown below, in Darwin.

Darwin

After 1945, Australia had a shortage of 300,000 homes (Greig 1995, 1). The government set out extensive plans to stimulate housebuilding in a *Commonwealth Housing Commission Report* (1944) (Bunning et al. 1947, 7). The solution was to use "mass-production" (i.e., Fordist) techniques and local materials. However, rather than taking a direct coordinating role, the government aimed to provide the incentives to large private companies to produce thousands of affordable houses (Greig 1995, 67). The housing shortage was spatially unevenly distributed, with the

Northern Territory less well served by construction companies than southern and eastern states of Australia.

To redress this imbalance, the Federal Government took a larger role in providing housing in Darwin, capital of the Northern Territory, than elsewhere in Australia for two reasons. First, on the back of economic activity, Darwin's population grew by 300% between 1947 and 1957 (Dewar 2010); many 'new' arrivals were also returnees who had no permanent dwelling on their return. Second, the territory was home to a large transient population of bureaucrats and soldiers which required temporary housing. There was a stark contrast between housing policy for this transient population and that of the indigenous population which must be viewed in the context of broader socio-economic dynamics. On the one hand, the departure of many soldiers from Darwin after the war marked a decline in the local pastoral industry, a key part of the economy (Wilson 2015, 186), before mining replaced it by the end of the 1950s (Powell 1981, 220-225).

On the other hand, the pastoral industry relied heavily on Aboriginal labour (Drakakis-Smith 1983, 7). The stations on which Aboriginal people worked encompassed large tracts of land allotted to white settlers or 'grantees'. By law and in practice until 1943, grantees were not required to remunerate Aboriginal labour with money if they "maintained the relatives and dependents" of the worker (Berndt and Berndt 1987, 13). Government policy on Aboriginal housing in Darwin, a hub of a declining pastoral industry, shifted from the 1920s when the main concern was to house cheap indigenous labour in Darwin, to the 1950s, whereby the focus of indigenous housing had shifted to a more ambitious programme of assimilation, partly involving socialising labour in compounds.

The visiting architects did not take into account that there were, in essence, two housing policies, one for European Australians and one for indigenous Australians. Rather, they concentrated on prefabricated ('prefab') housing for European Australians. Prefabs were of great interest to the visitors since they provided uniform sets of houses and architectural styles. The main source of prefab houses in Darwin up to 1956 were 'Hawksleys', built and assembled in Britain and exported to Australia (Dewar 2010, 129). The houses cost 260,000 Portuguese *escudos*, a much higher figure than Singapore, where a SIT apartment cost 50,000 *escudos*. This problem of price could be overcome in Timor, the visiting architects believed, by a "judicious use of [local] materials". Like Singapore's SIT accommodation, the Darwin prefab houses "[left] much to be desired" in terms of aesthetics. In comparing housing in each location, moreover, the visitors also continued to exhibit their pre-occupation with race, believing that Singapore families inhabiting SIT accommodation were of a much 'lower level' than in more racially 'homogeneous' Darwin. Yet here, as in Jakarta, they appear to have misread the local context: Darwin was home, as we have seen, to Aboriginal and Chinese communities who were the main permanent settlers, while those of European origin were most likely to be transient. Indeed, they favoured Darwin's houses above those of Singapore and Jakarta despite what they perceived as its 'racial dissimilarity' to Timor.

The policy on Aboriginal housing in the 1950s must be seen in the context of an official policy of assimilation that was in force in Australia from 1951. Assimilation, it was believed, could be partly achieved through the government's construction of four 'reserves' throughout the 1940s and 1950s including the relocation of an existing reserve (Kahlin, renamed Bagot and relocated in 1938). Bagot had as a central aim the 'detribalisation' of its inhabitants and was aimed to provide employment to inhabitants through 'horticultural production'. Thus, while Kahlin during the 1920s had explicitly economic aims, i.e., to house an Aboriginal workforce who lived segregated from the white population "... outside the town boundary", by the 1950s it was viewed as promoting assimilation (Wells 2000, 73). A centrepiece of assimilation was later the "extensive" welfare provisions beginning in the 1950s which saw Aboriginal people live not in "official settlements" such as Bagot but in "fringe settlements and small towns" (Drakakis-Smith 1981, 41).

The architects admired some aspects of Darwin's urban planning—for example, its botanical gardens. But they harboured doubts about the aesthetic qualities of prefab housing and its high cost. Yet they preferred the possibility for Timor of Darwin's relatively expensive prefab houses to those of Singapore since, they asserted, integrating European Australian occupants had been easier than in Singapore. The architects therefore promised both that cheaper housing could be achieved in Timor with local materials but also that the houses would be better adapted to their indigenous occupants. But as we have seen in the cases examined above, they also perceived barriers to occupants being able to adapt to houses. Affordability and adaptation are addressed together below.

Timor

As we have seen above, what is at issue in the architects' account are two considerations: the planning and provision of housing based on economic factors; and the appropriateness of housing to 'characteristics' of the population. While colonial public housing could be seen as a deliberate effort to ensure social reproduction and control, it must also be seen in the context of urban planning, which had the objective of creating social and economic orders based on spatial organisation. While investment in urbanisation in the late-1940s was very low, the largest aggregate investments in urbanisation in any colony by the Portuguese metropolitan state during the period 1946-1972 were made in Timor and São Tomé e Príncipe (Madeira 2008, 414). The value of these investments was not recouped from the colony: the authorities had hoped for a windfall following oil exploration but by 1963, such hopes had been repeatedly frustrated (Grainger 2018). Hence, in this last section, I show how the project of designing economical dwellings (*moradias econômicas*) must be seen in the context of the allocation of capital and land to urbanisation projects in the 1950s; and in a context of issues that the architects encountered with reconciling the design of economical dwellings to Timor's indigenous population.

Dili was severely damaged during the Japanese occupation of Timor between 1942 and 1945. The returning Portuguese colonial authorities saw reconstruction as an opportunity to conduct urban planning. This was carried out initially under the direction of the *Gabinete de Urbanização Colonial* (GUC, Colonial Urbanization Committee) formed in 1944 and operating until 1947 under the Ministry of Colonies. The GUC (after 1951, GUU or *Gabinete de Urbanização de Ultramar*, Overseas Urbanisation Committee) was highly centralised, meaning that its personnel were largely sent from Lisbon, which consequently restricted its capacity to act in far-flung colonies such as Timor (Vaz Milheiro and Costa Dias 2010, 84). The metropolitan government's priorities also lay elsewhere: the GUC's head, Rogerio Cavaca described plans for the urbanisation of Timor as "unduly vast", and therefore they were subordinated to plans for Portugal's African colonies.[9]

In 1951 the GUU created an urban plan of Dili which contained 13 separate land use zones. Zoning is significant for two reasons: first, it allocated land usage to distinctive areas; and second, it laid claim over land and consequently permitted or circumscribed uses and property claims to it. The centre of Dili was to contain a Civic Centre where commercial activities took place. Outside this central zone, there was a residential zone (for Europeans), a Special residential zone (a superior zone for Europeans based in the present-day Farol neighbourhood); a Natives' residential zone; and a Chinese residential zone.[10] The native zone was in the same area of the city where, it was observed, the indigenous population had already settled. By the early-1950s they constituted an ever-greater number of Dili's population in the east of the city (in present-day Becora and Bidau). Many of their number were "*moradores*" or soldiers (reservists) employed by the state but who also possessed their own means of subsistence in the form of smallholder cultivation and keeping poultry and pigs. In summary, the commercial centre of Dili would see "... individuals of all races and nationalities" admitted, while a series of residential zones were to be circumscribed along the lines of race.[11]

Further plans for economic dwellings emerged again in 1958 when the Dili Municipal Council (*Câmara Municipal de Díli*) discussed commissioning 'showcase' economic dwellings.[12] Reporting on the Municipal Council's discussions, Sousa Mendes favoured only limited production of "standard type" (*projectos-tipos*) houses on a large scale because they would require "careful study". In his view, the priority lay with 'adapting' housing to its inhabitants and it would be better if the metropolitan government, rather than the *Câmara Municipal de Díli*, executed this project.[13] His audience at the Directorate-General of Public Works in Lisbon agreed, because they wanted control over the direction of the projects and land rather than any "future proprietor, or even the *Câmara Municipal de Díli*".[14] The metropolitan state thus played a primary role from the early stages of the 'economical dwelling' project, indicating its importance in securing control over land and consequently an interplay between housing and urban planning, and as we have seen, a study mission to other cities.

The zoning of areas requiring the setting of geographic boundaries closely reflects ethnographic debates surrounding Timor. Such debates saw attempts to attribute racial boundaries based on geography, biology and ethno-linguistic groups which shifted over time and were a matter of dispute (Roque 2010). Mendes-Correa's study (1944) attributed racial and ethno-biological categorisations to the Timorese population partly with reference to ethno-linguistic categorisations. The MAT (*Missão Antropológica de Timor*) study mission in 1953-1954 under the direction of Antonio de Almeida had the "... ultimate aim [of] draw[ing] the Portuguese Timor ethno-linguistic map" (Castelo 2017, 634). Mendes Correa's later work suggested that Timor was a source site of Homo Sapiens who had thereafter mutated without being subject to significant racial mixing—a liberal reinterpretation of Freyre's Lusotropicalism (Roque 2019). These studies point to how professional ethnographic work in Timor developed gradually, and that there was a tradition of considerable 'overlap' between anthropological work and such 'bio-ethnographic' study and, to some extent, colonial policymaking.

This context is significant since Mendes-Correa's study (1944) was referenced by Sousa Mendes and Almeida when writing their report on Timorese house designs. In light of their study tour of Timor, the architects cited in their report four supra-racial categories set out by Mendes-Correa, on top of more numerous linguistic groups, extracted from the study. With both these racial and ethno-linguistic categorisations in mind, the architects then went about assessing indigenous housing. They were directed by the scholar and colonial administrator Rui Cinatti, who had a deep and abiding interest in Timor's flora, fauna, and human societies, and who advised them on what regions to visit to study housing arrangements. Cinatti also had an interest in "study[ing] the main types of 'native housing' and its relationships with the natural and cultural environment", an interest which chimed with that of colonial urban policy as described above (Sousa 2020, 143). The architects set about their task by seeking out archetypal house designs based on each region, insisting on adopting a 'mode of classification' for the populations that they would observe. To provide a typology they observed the ways in which forms of housing changed (or otherwise) "... according to diverse dialects", with the least spoken 'dialects' in the interior and in the east, while the most spoken were on the coast with Tetum having the greatest tendency to spread.

They explained differences in housing by reference to two principal elements: the 'various racial origins' of their inhabitants; and 'climatic conditions'. It became clear, however, that they could not reconcile climate-adapted house design with 'race'. For example, they noted that upland house constructions (where the same cooler climate prevailed) were similar despite being built in different regions of Bobonaro and Maubisse. Likewise, 'raising' native-ancestral housing or *uma lisan* was neither universally practiced, nor exclusive to 'racial origins'. For example, houses in coastal areas which were at opposite ends of the colony—Oecussi, Viqueque and Suai—were all raised off the ground by between one and one-and-a-half metres. In short, they were able to adduce more examples of the practicality of pre-existing house types based on climate, by observing that in upland, cooler climates, roofs extended to the ground to provide more insulation, than with reference to putative commonalities of house design based on occupants' ability to adapt to houses.

The one kind of house in Portuguese Timor that Sousa Mendes and Almeida identified which was observably different from all other houses was that of 'assimilated' Timorese. Such housing, mainly inhabited by *liurais*, was not constructed with wood, bamboo and '*palappa*' (dried leaves of palm trees) but constructed with 'European' materials "using the most economical methods", for example, glass windows and zinc sheet roofs. Where these were unavailable, local materials were fashioned into European styles. Such styles also included housing with a raised ground floor, "definitive walls"—the prevalence of which they had frowned on in Singapore—and sometimes a latrine.[15] The architects did not directly broach the question of how or whether the inhabitants of 'traditional' houses were to become 'assimilated'.

In 1963, Sousa Mendes alone produced plans for two prototype houses for indigenous soldiers in the colonial military. They consisted of two buildings—a main building with an entrance hall and two bedrooms, and an 'outbuilding', with a pantry, kitchen and bathroom. The cost of the houses was 40,000 *escudos*, 10,000 less than Singapore's SIT apartments. The houses were raised 1.15 metres, for unspecified reasons. This was a costly adjustment to previous plans that caused the land area on which the houses were built to be reduced by 10 percent to stay within the total budget. Otherwise, the costs appeared to have been kept to a minimum, as Sousa Mendes and Almeida promised four years earlier by using local materials.

The flooring in the entrance area of the main building was constructed with wood, as were the entrance's ceilings. Elsewhere in the main building, the roof was made from grasses or *palappa* leaves bound with cord and connected to the joists with cane (*cana brava*) and *casuarina* wood. The house was not 'entirely' constructed with local materials as claimed, however. The roof was supported by iron pillars. The second 'outbuilding' had concrete screed floors and wainscots;

and walls made of concrete and a zinc roof. The kitchen was built around a hearth, constructed with three stones, a feature of 'native' houses, Sousa Mendes indicated. Indeed, the division of the house into two buildings seems to have been a Portuguese interpretation of an 'assimilated' Timorese house.[16]

Twenty-eight years after the study tour and 12 years after Indonesia had occupied the territory formerly known as Portuguese Timor, Cinatti, Sousa Mendes and Almeida published *Arquitectura Timorense* (1987), an extensively-illustrated book based on their overview of Timorese housing. Some of the book's chapters expanded on and followed the principle around which the Timor section of their report was structured, i.e., a review of the habitats of the territory's ethno-linguistic groups. However, absent from the work was any reference to their foreign tour but one section briefly detailed city housing of 'assimilated' Timorese and Europeans. On one level, this omission is not surprising since in some respects the foreign tour may have simply served to confirm the architects' existing beliefs that ethnographically-informed housing was preferable to mass-produced housing and deemed unworthy for inclusion. Furthermore, the book's audience, an educated, Lusophone public, may also have found traditional houses a more compelling subject. After all, the publication presents a view of Timor's ethnic groups largely untouched by colonial rule, whereas the project to design and construct economic dwellings involved the colonial state's attempts to create and sustain a social and economic order in an urban environment. The building of economic dwellings continued until decolonisation in 1974, with discrete but small clusters of houses appearing in some of Dili's neighbourhoods.

Conclusion: affordability, adaptation, anxiety

During their study tour, the architects had observed large-scale urban planning and public housing in the service of creating distinct socio-economic orders in late-, settler- and post-colonial contexts. They flirted with this model but ultimately rejected it because they preferred their own hybrid 'economical houses' with vernacular features. Yet in the end, their own model, embedded in a larger urban planning experiment, was not so different. Furthermore, the study tour, the architects' dependence on official hosts, and the zoning of Dili reveal rather colonial cooperation and to some extent, a commonality of approach. This did not stop the architects leaning on a model of Tropical Architecture grounded in pragmatism, albeit one seemingly preoccupied with the 'integration' of occupants. Indeed, while the architects' approach was influenced by questions of affordability, they also made assessments of the perceived ability of occupants to live in houses, thereby relying more on a biologist's view of 'species adaptation' to habitat (cf. Clancey 2006, 86).

At the same time, this perspective appears to have been arrived at largely through contingency rather than based on an unswerving adherence to racial ideology. For example, the architects noted the work of Portuguese anthropologists concerned with demonstrating a view of Timor's 'races' but they did not adopt it to be a predominant criterion for their house designs. The architects' designs of economical houses may have been partially influenced by the colonial ideology of Lusotropicalism, but equally, late-colonial regimes *in general* had begun to emphasise that colonial rule could cede some authority to indigenous elites (whether through French 'associationism' or British 'indirect rule'). In both this broader context and in the context of Timor specifically, the houses and the planned urban socio-economic order in which they were situated may also be a manifestation of colonial anxieties (see Introduction, this volume) as both migration from rural to urban areas and colonial expenditure on urbanisation increased in the years before 1974.

Acknowledgements

Thanks to workshop participants in Brasilia for their questions on an earlier draft of this chapter, and to Kelly Silva, Lisa Palmer, and an anonymous reviewer for their constructive suggestions on later drafts.

Notes

1. These ideas were those of the Brazilian sociologist Gilberto Freyre who also espoused strong views on urbanisation and housing. Like the originators of Tropical Architecture, Freyre had predilections for vernacular architecture, and wanted to "...reconcile international modernity with local tradition" (Burke and Pallares-Burke 2008, 113, 148-149).
2. The SIT houses that they saw "differ[ed] considerably from the normal run of privately-designed houses" (Swee 1956, 62); given their "large average household size, of 5.9. This is no doubt due to the system of allocation of Trust dwellings which gives preference to large households" (ibid., 64).
3. Sousa Mendes, A. and Almeida, L. 'Missão de estudo de Habitat Nativo de Timor. Relatório Síntese das visitas de estudo a Singapura, Djakarta, Darwin, e à provincia de Timor' 4 March 1959, in AHU ICP MU DGOPC DSUH (MU T Cx.22,1), 1.
4. Sousa Mendes, A. and Almeida, L. 'Missão de estudo...', 14.
5. Sousa Mendes, A. and Almeida, L. 'Missão de estudo...' 17.
6. In 1957 the population of Singapore stood at about 1,440,000 (Chua and Singapore Department of Statistics 1964, 43) of which squatters comprised about 360,000 (Kahn 2006, 9).
7. Singapore's ethnic Chinese population was strongly represented in organised labour activity but 'housing poverty' (Aljunied 2009, 237), unresolved by the construction of a planned modernist residential area for Malays (Kahn 2006), had contributed to discontent with colonial rule more widely.

8 For an attempt to "discern concretely" the meaning of such public monuments see Anderson 1990, 174.

9 AHU IPC/MU/T/DGOPC/DSUH (MU/T/ Cx.22,6) 'Projecto de moradias economicas'. Cavaca, 'Informacao no.33 A/46', 6 November 1946.

10 AHU ICP MU CTFC (MU/T) Cx. 22,5 Localização da Colonia de Timor. Aguilar, JA, 'Plano Geral de Urbanização do Ultramar', Localização da Colonia de Timor', 30.

11 AHU ICP MU CTFC (MU/T/ Cx. 22,5) Aguilar, JA, 'Plano Geral…', 9.

12 AHU IPC/MU/T/DGOPC/DSUH (MU/T/ Cx.22,6) 'Projecto de moradias economicas'. Antes de Megré to Director dos Servicos de Urbanismo e Habitacao, 8 July 1958.

13 AHU IPC/MU/T/DGOPC/DSUH (MU/T/ Cx.22,6) 'Projecto de moradias economicas'. Sousa-Mendes to Direcao de Servicos, Obras Publicas, 14 July 1958.

14 AHU IPC/MU/T/DGOPC/DSUH (MU/T/ Cx.22,6) 'Projecto de moradias economicas'. Sanches de Gama 17th July 1958.

15 AHU ICP MU DGOPC DSUH (MU T Cx.22,1). Sousa Mendes, A. and Almeida, L. 'Missão de estudo…', 62.

16 AHU ICP MU DGOPC DSUH (MU T Cx. 4,1) 'Habitações para praças Nativas…'

Archival sources

Arquivo Histórico Ultramarino (AHU), Lisbon, Portugal:
AHU ICP MU DGOPC DSUH (MU/T Cx.22,1) 'Missão de Estudo dos Habitos Nativo de Timor'.
AHU ICP MU CTFC (MU/T/Cx. 22,5) 'Localização da Colonia de Timor'.
AHU IPC/MU/T/DGOPC/DSUH (MU/T/Cx.22,6) 'Projecto de moradias economicas'.
AHU ICP MU DGOPC DSUH (MU/T/Cx. 4,1) 'Habitações para praças Nativas'.

References

Abeyasekere, S. 1990. *Jakarta: A History.* Oxford: Oxford University Press.

Aglietta, M. (1979) 2000. *Theory of Capitalist Regulation: The US Experience.* London/New York: Verso.

Aljunied, S. M. K. 2009. "Hadhramis within Malay Activism: the role of al-Saqqāf(s) in post-war Singapore (1945-1965)." In *The Hadhrami Diaspora in Southeast Asia. Identity Maintenance or Assimilation,* by H. A. Ibrahim, and H. A. Abu Shouk, 225-244. Leiden, The Netherlands: Brill. https://doi.org/10.1163/ej.9789004172319.i-300.77

Anderson, B. (1983) 2016. *Imagined Communities. Reflections on the Origins and Spread of Nationalism.* London/New York: Verso.

Anderson, B. 1990. *Language and Power: Exploring Political Cultures in Indonesia.* Ithaca, NY: Cornell University Press.

Anderson, W., R. Roque, and R. V. Santos. 2019. "Introduction: Luso-tropicalism and its discontents." In *Luso-tropicalism and its Discontents: The Making and Unmaking of Racial Exceptionalism,* edited by W. Anderson, R. Roque, and R. V. Santos, 1-20. New York: Bergahn Books.

Baweja, V. 2007. "The Beginning of a Green Architecture: Otto Koenigsberger at the Department of Tropical Architecture at the Architectural Association (AA) School of Architecture, London, UK."

In *Fresh Air*, edited by C. Veikos, and J. Bing. Paper presented at the 95th ACSA Annual Meeting, Philadelphia, PA, ACSA Press, Washington DC.

Berndt, R. M. and C. H. Berndt. 1987. *End of an Era. Aboriginal Labour in the Northern Territory*. Canberra: Australian Institute of Aboriginal Studies.

Bunning, W., W. H. Ifould, C. R. McKerihan., and S. J. Luker. 1947. "The Housing Problem in Australia." Papers Read at the Winter Forum of the Australian Institute of Political Science, held at Wollongong, June, 1947.

Burke, P., and M. L. G. Pallares-Burke. 2008. *Gilberto Freyre: Social Theory in the Tropics*. Oxford: Peter Lang.

Castelo, C. 1998. *"O modo português de estar no mundo": o luso-tropicalismo e a ideologia colonial portuguesa (1933-1961)*. Porto: Edições Afrontamento.

Castelo, C. 2017. "Ruy Cinatti, the French-Portuguese mission and the construct of East Timor as an ethnographic site." *History and Anthropology* 28 (5): 630-652. https://doi.org/10.1080/02757206.2017.1280672

Chua, S. C., and Singapore Department of Statistics. 1964. *Report on the census of population 1957*. Singapore: Government Printer. Accessed 28 March 2019 at http://eresources.nlb.gov.sg/printheritage/detail/7b306d60-16c1-458d-a9ef-6be4cb6b1821.aspx.

Cinatti, R., L. de Almeida, and S. Mendes. 1987. *Arquitectura Timorense*. Lisboa: Instituto de Investigação Científica Tropical – Museu de Etnologia

Clancey, G. 2004. "Towards a Spatial History of Emergency: Notes from Singapore." In *Beyond Description. Singapore, Space, Historicity*, edited by R. Bishop, J. Phillips, and W. Yeo. London: Routledge. https://doi.org/10.4324/9780203643228

Clancey, G. 2006. *Earthquake Nation. The Cultural Politics of Japanese Seismicity, 1868-1930*. Berkeley: University of California Press.

Columbijn, F. 2010. *Under Construction: The Politics of Urban Space and Housing during the Decolonization of Indonesia 1930-1960*. Leiden, The Netherlands: Brill. https://doi.org/10.1163/9789004263932

Cribb, R. 1991. *Gangsters and Revolutionaries: The Jakarta People's Militia and the Indonesian Revolution 1945-1949*. North Sydney: Asian Studies Association of Australia.

Dewar, M. 2010. *Darwin. No Place like Home: Australia's Northern Capital in the 1950s through a Social History of Housing*. Charles Darwin University Press.

Drakakis-Smith, D. 1981. "Aboriginal access to housing in Alice Springs." *Australian Geographer* 15 (1): 39-51. https://doi.org/10.1080/00049188108702794

Drakakis-Smith, D. 1983. *Towns like Alice: Race and Class in Aboriginal Australia*. Staffordshire: Keele University.

Duguid, C. 1951. *The Aborigines of Darwin and the Tropic North*. Adelaide: Advertiser Printing Office.

Gelman-Taylor, J. (1983) 2009. *The Social World of Batavia: European and Eurasian in Dutch Asia*. University of Wisconsin Press.

Grainger, A. 2018. "The Timor Oil Company's Network, 1956-1968: Interacting internal and external infrastructures." In *The Promise of Prosperity: Visions of the Future in Timor-Leste after Independence*, edited by J. Bovensiepen, 43-60. Canberra: Australian National University Press.

Greig, A. 1995. *The Stuff Dreams are Made Of: Housing Provision in Australia 1945-1960*. Melbourne: Melbourne University Press.

Hack, K. 2012 "Using and abusing the past: The Malayan Emergency as Counterinsurgency Paradigm." In *The British Approach to Counterinsurgency: From Malaya and Northern Ireland to Iraq and Afghanistan*, edited by P. Dixon, 207-242. London: Palgrave Macmillan. https://doi.org/10.1057/9781137284686_7

Harvey, D. 1989. *The Condition of Postmodernity: An Enquiry into the Origins of Cultural Change.* Cambridge/Oxford: Blackwell.

Hirschmann, C. 1986. "The making of race in colonial Malaya. Political economy and racial ideology." *Sociological Forum* 1 (2-Spring-): 330-361.

Jerónimo, M. B., and A. Costa Pinto. 2015. "A Modernizing Empire? Politics, Culture, and Economy in Portuguese Late Colonialism." In *The Ends of European Colonial Empires: Cases and Comparisons*, edited by M. Jerónimo Bandeira, and A. Costa Pinto, 51-80. London: Palgrave. https://doi.org/10.1057/9781137394064_3

Jessop, B. 1992. "Fordism and Post-Fordism: a Critical Reformulation." In *Pathways to Regionalism and Industrial Development*, edited by A. J. Scott and M. K. Storper, 46-69. London: Routledge.

Kahn, J. S. 2006. *Other Malays: Nationalism and Cosmopolitanism in the Modern Malay World.* Singapore: NUS Press.

King, A. 1990. *Urbanism, Colonialism and the World-economy*. London: Routledge.

Leaf, M. 1994. "Legal authority in an extralegal setting. The case of land rights in Jakarta, Indonesia." *Journal of Planning Education and Research* 14 (1): 12-18. https://doi.org/10.1177/0739456x9401400102

Liu, H., and S. K. Wong. 2004. *Singapore Chinese Society in Transition: Business, Politics & Socio-economic Change, 1945-1965*. New York: Peter Lang.

Lubis, F. 2018. *Jakarta 1950-1970*. Jakarta: Masup Jakarta.

Madeira, L. F. 2008. *Les finances publiques, les options budgétaires et les priorités politiques dans l'empire colonial portugais (1946-1974)*. PhD diss., Institut d'études politiques de Bordeaux.

McVey, R. 1971. "The post-revolutionary transformation of the Indonesian army." *Indonesia* (11): 131-176. https://doi.org/10.2307/3350748

Mendes-Correa, A. A. 1944. *Timor Português, contribuições para o seu estudo antropológico*. Lisboa: Imprensa Nacional de Lisboa.

Mortimer, R. 1972. *The Indonesian Communist Party and Land Reform 1959-1965*. Clayton, Victoria: Centre of Southeastern Asian Studies, Monash University.

Powell, A. 1982. *Far Country: A Short History of the Northern Territory*. Melbourne: Melbourne University Press.

Roque, R. 2010. *Headhunting and Colonialism: Anthropology and the Circulation of Human Skulls in the Portuguese Empire, 1870-1930*. London: Palgrave.

Roque, R. 2019. "The Racial Science of Patriotic Primitives: António Mendes Correia in Portuguese Timor." In *Luso-tropicalism and its Discontents: The Making and Unmaking of Racial Exceptionalism*, edited by W. Anderson, R. Roque, and R. V. Santos, 159-183. New York: Bergahn Books.

Scott, J. C. 1998. *Seeing Like a State: How Certain Schemes to Improve the Human Condition Have Failed.* London: Yale University Press.

Seng, L. K. 2013. *Squatters into Citizens: The 1961 Bukit Ho Swee Fire and the Making of Modern Singapore.* Singapore: NUS Press. https://doi.org/10.2307/j.ctv1qv3g0

Silva, C. N. 2016. "Introduction." In *Governing Urban Africa*, edited by C. N. Silva, 1-9. London: Palgrave https://doi.org/10.1057/978-1-349-95109-3

Silver, C., 2008 *Planning the Megacity: Jakarta in the Twentieth Century.* London: Routledge. https://doi.org/10.4324/9780203700013

Swee, G. K. 1956. *Urban Incomes and Housing: A report on the social survey of Singapore 1953-1954.* Singapore: Government Printing Office.

Tajudeen, I. B. 2012. "Beyond Racialized Representation: Architectural linguæ Francæ and Urban Histories in the Kampung Houses and Shophouses of Melaka and Singapore." In *Colonial Frames, Nationalist Histories*, edited by M. Desai and M. Rajagopalan, 213-252. Farnham: Ashgate.

Teo, S. E., and V. R. Savage. 1991 "Singapore Landscape: A Historical Overview of Housing Image." In *A History of Singapore,* by E. C. T. Chew, and E. Lee. Singapore: Oxford University Press.

Vaz Milheiro, A. and E. Costa Dias. 2010. "Arquitectura em Bissau e os Gabinetes de Urbanização colonial (1944-1974)." *Arq. Urb* (2 (January)): 80-114.

Wah, F. L. K. 1988. *Beyond the Tin Mines: Coolies, Squatters and New Villagers in the Kinta Valley, Malaysia, c.1880-1980.* Kuala Lumpur: Oxford University Press.

Wells, S. 2000. "Labour, Control and Protection: the Kahlin Aboriginal Compound, Darwin, 1911-1938." In *Settlement: A History of Australian Indigenous Housing,* edited by P. Read. Canberra: Aboriginal Studies Press 2000.

Wilson, D. 2015. *Different White People: Radical Activism for Aboriginal Rights 1946-1972.* Perth, Western Australia: UWA Press.

Wright, R. (1994) 1956. *The Color Curtain: A report on the Bandung Conference.* Jackson: University Press of Mississippi.

Yeung, Y. M. 1973. *National Development Policy and Urban Transformation in Singapore.* Chicago: Committee on Geographical Studies.

LOCAL ECONOMIC DYNAMICS

CHAPTER 4

On the existence and persistence of the social category of *atan* in contemporary Timor-Leste

Susanna Barnes

Abstract

This paper considers the historical category of *atan* (slave) in Timor-Leste and its significance to contemporary social relations. While Indigenous forms of slavery existed on Timor island before the arrival of the Dutch or Portuguese, distinctions between *liurai* (rulers), *povo* (common people) and *atan* (slave) were produced, reinforced and modified by colonial modes of production and extraction. These categorisations continue to be re-enacted ceremonially, economically and politically in contemporary Timor-Leste. The paper first considers the category of *atan* from a historical perspective. Secondly, gathering traces of evidence in ethnographically grounded research, it examines how the category of *atan* is imagined, resisted and embodied in contemporary East Timorese society. Lastly, it considers the implications of the persistence of this phenomenon.

Keywords: Slavery; dependence; kinship; agency

This paper considers the historical category of *atan* (E: dependent/serf/slave) in Timor-Leste and its significance to contemporary social relations. While Indigenous forms of dependency existed on Timor island before the arrival of the Dutch or Portuguese (Hägerdal 2012), social categories and distinctions between *liurai* (rulers), *ema* or *reino* (common people) and *atan* (dependents/serfs/slave) were produced, reinforced and modified by Portuguese colonial modes of production and extraction as well as Indonesian military occupation. Although the constitution of the Democratic Republic of Timor-Leste upholds the principal of equal rights for all its citizens, these social categorisations continue to be re-enacted ceremonially, economically and politically in contemporary Timor-Leste (RDTL 2001; Kammen 2010; Shepherd and McWilliam 2013). Drawing on historical descriptions and regional comparisons, the paper will first consider the category of *atan* from a historical and linguistic perspective. Secondly, gathering traces of evidence and data collected in ethnographically grounded research in Timor-Leste, it will examine how the category of *atan* is imagined, resisted, embodied and enacted in contemporary East

Timorese society. Lastly, it will consider the implications of the persistence of this phenomenon particularly in relation to kinship and agency.

Slavery and other forms of dependency in historical perspective

Most historians of Southeast Asia agree that 'slavery' existed in the region prior to the expansion of European shipping and trade (Gunn 1999; Ward 2011; Hägerdal 2012). How 'slavery' was understood in the region, however, was complicated by the fact that it included a diversity of forms and practices ranging from chattel slavery and forced labour to debt bondage and other forms of dependency (Ward 2011, 163). Some scholars argue that a distinction should be made between a 'slave' understood as 'a person held to be saleable property, of low social status, and obliged to perform labour and other services for a superior without payment', and other forms of 'bondage' that existed within a broad pattern of social relations based on differential status and mutual obligation (Reid 1983). Demands for labour in expanding regional economies undoubtedly fuelled the trade in slaves across the region. But it is also true that many Southeast Asian societies, including those found on Timor island, were "governed by laws and customs that embedded [these] vertical relations of bondage and reciprocity as the basis of social, economic, and political relations" (Ward 2011, 164).

The scope, motives and forms of slavery and other forms of bondage present on Timor island varied in response to changing socio-economic and political circumstances. While further research is required to understand the extent to which Chinese and Makassarese traders in the region engaged in the slave trade in Timor prior to the arrival of the Europeans, historians suggest that "… after sandalwood, for which the island was famous, slaves were 'the next most profitable commodity' to be found on the island" (Boxer 1968, 189 quoted in Kammen 2010). From as early as the sixteenth century slaves were obtained by both Dutch and Portuguese who engaged in slave raids or collected slaves from the ports of Kupang, Manatuto and Ade (Vemasse) (McWilliam 2007; Hägerdal 2010; Kammen 2010). More commonly however, it was Topasses from Larantuka and Lifau who raided and sold slaves destined for Java and Macau (Kammen 2010). Local rulers were active participants in this trade exchanging beeswax, sandalwood and slaves for counter-gifts of firearms and other manufactured goods (pottery and cloth) (Hägerdal 2010).[1] Stories from older East Timorese suggest that the trade in persons continued well into the late nineteenth century. For example, from Viqueque *atan* were sold as slaves at the port of Beasu in exchange for 'guns and bullets' (T: *kilat no musan*) (Barnes 2017).

While the slave trade became increasingly important in the region following the arrival of European trader/colonisers, Hägerdal has argued that the volume of trade in slaves from Timor island was never very significant (see de Castro 1867, 320; Hägerdal 2010). A lack of evidence in the colonial record, for the trade in slaves, might be explained by the fact that slaves were not prominent in European cargo lists or, the fact that much of the slave-trade was intra-regional carried out by Chinese and Makassarese traders and not directly by the Portuguese or Dutch (Kammen, pers. comm.; Hägerdal 2019). It is also possible that trade in 'persons' or 'slaves' was not a priority for Timorese rulers whose power and wealth was based on the number of people under their immediate control rather than the extent of territory they controlled (Barnes 2017). It is often said that Timorese rulers were 'rich in people' rather than land and a person's worth and social standing is still calculated in terms of their capacity to establish and maintain bonds of reciprocity and mutual obligation (McWilliam 2011; see also Chapter 7, this volume).

Scholars maintain that pre-colonial societies on Timor island were divided into three social categories or ranks commonly described as comprising of chiefs and nobles (*liurai*), commoners (*ema*) and slaves (*atan*) (Gunn 1999; Cinatti 1987; Hicks [1976] 2004). However, given the diversity of forms and practices that have come to be defined in scholarly literature as 'slavery', the categorisation of *atan* as 'slave' requires further consideration.

The Tetum term *atan* is commonly translated as 'slave' in English, and this is also the most common meaning attributed to the word and its variants in Indonesia. However, linguists suggest that locally and regionally *atan*, and its equivalents in other Austronesian languages, has a range of different meanings. For example, in Timor and Flores it may also be used to mean simply 'person' or 'human' (Schaepper, pers. comm.). Blust has also suggested that *atan* could mean 'stranger or outsider' (2013). These linguistic pointers suggest two things; firstly, that those who fell under the category of *atan* may not necessarily have been considered possessions, objects or non-subjects; and secondly, that if they were conceptualised as 'outsiders' or 'others' there were distinctive ways in which persons included in this category could be integrated into local social structure.

I would argue that colonial processes of classification, categorisation and translation established a false equivalency between the notion of *atan* and the category of 'escravo' making it synonymous with Euro-centric notions of 'slave' and 'slavery'. In their book *Slavery in Africa: Anthropological and Historical Perspectives*, Miers and Kopytoff (1977) argued that Euro-centric notions of slavery, and in particular English language scholarship on the topic, were heavily influenced by 'imaginaries' of slavery that drew heavily on the specific experience of plantation slavery in the Americas (Carvalho Ferreira 2019, 51-52). Such notions of slavery presented an image of 'the slave' as a person devoid of any rights, freedoms or capacity for choice. For Miers and Kopytoff, however, the position of 'slaves' in the African cultural context had to be understood in relation to the concept of 'rights-in-persons'

(1977, 7). Rights-in-persons were defined by local laws and the subject of complex transactions. Rights involved 'transactions' between individuals, offices and corporate groups, rights that were mutual but seldom symmetrical, rights that could entail labour and services but also total rights over a person (ibid., 8-9). The concept of 'rights-in-persons' provides a useful framework for conceptualising the position of *atan* in East Timorese societies. Rather than representing a category of persons that would fit Euro-centric definitions of 'slave' described above (p. 2), I would argue that *atan* encompassed a broad category of persons who, as Ward (2011, 64) suggests, found themselves at the bottom of the vertical relations of bondage and reciprocity, a situation which arguably also placed them on the margins and made them vulnerable to forms of extreme exploitation including slavery.

Historically, persons included in the category of *atan* on Timor island were war captives, debtors or serious violators of custom, procured through warfare, as gifts from allies or tribute from vassal kingdoms (Forman 1978; Hägerdal 2010; Kammen 2010; Blust 2013). Historians argue that those persons classified as *atan* generally fell into two categories. Drawing on the terms *ulun-houris* and *lutu-hun* used by Tetum-speaking populations, they suggest that a division existed between what is commonly described as 'chattel' slavery and other forms of more-or-less permanent dependency. *Ulun-houris*, meaning 'living head', was used to denote war-captives, often women and children, who owed their lives to their master. Hägerdal (2010, 270) suggests that *ulun-houris* were 'chattel' slaves, treated as commodities to be bought and sold or even gifted and offered as tribute (see also Kammen 2010). *Lutu-hun*, meaning either the 'dwellers at the bottom of the enclosure' or 'from the bottom of the enclosure', on the other hand, was used to describe those who worked the fields and tended the cattle of the *liurai* (rulers). *Lutu-hun* could not move from their land but neither could they be bought or sold and as such occupied a position similar to that of *serf* (de Castro 1867; Hägerdal 2010). Portuguese anthropologist and public servant, De Menezes (2006, 69) states that *lutu-hun* were considered 'communal' property while *atan* were individual property; a view which was also proposed by De Castro who stated that *lutu-hum* cannot be sold by the king (*rei*) because they belong to the people (*reino*) (de Castro 1867, 320). The extent to which these distinctions were fixed and the degree to which they are applicable across Timor island is debatable. Ethnographic evidence from Viqueque district suggests that chattel slaves could well become serfs, and not only serfs, but also commoners, may have been sold at slave markets. Moreover, not all war captives became slaves. In some cases, they were incorporated into local house-based groups either as allies or vassals (Barnes 2017).[2]

How *atan* were treated by rulers and commoners is a subject that requires more in-depth research. The conditions under which *atan* lived likely depended on time, place and the personality of individuals involved. According to local histories from Viqueque for example, *atan* were at the mercy of the ruler (*liurai*). Elders from Viqueque reported that, in the not so distant past, *atan* were exchanged as gifts and on a ruler's death could be killed and buried with them; they also suggested that during certain rituals such as the planting of house-posts *atan* were sacrificed in lieu of buffalo or pigs (Amaral, pers. comm.; see also Bovensiepen 2015, 113). However, evidence also suggests that over time the descendants of *atan* were given specific tasks and roles associated with ruling (*liurai*) ancestral houses (many would have also been descendants of the men [and also women] of the house) and in some cases incorporated into these ancestral houses albeit without the same entitlements as full-members (Barnes 2017).

The British explorer/anthropologist Forbes, who travelled across Timor in the late 1880s, suggested that *atan* in Timor were relatively well treated and could be freed at any time through the payment of a fixed sum. This is a view shared by Affonso De Castro the Governor of Portuguese Timor (1858-1863) who wrote "the slaves of Timor are not subject to the same ill-treatment found in other countries. If there has been any mistreatment it has been at the hands of the inhabitants of Dili rather than in the kingdoms (*reinos*), where slaves are almost considered family members and do not find any problems in obtaining freedom" (1867, 319).[3] Portuguese poet and ethnographer, Rui Cinatti, wrote, "At the bottom of society lived the slaves, prisoners of war (*lutuhum*). Or people bought (*ata*). Slavery is not very rigid… permitted serfs to become free men" (Cinatti quoted in Kammen 2010). While conditions may have varied depending on circumstances, the category of *atan* clearly does not fit neatly into Euro-centric notions of 'escravo' or 'slave'. However, what also appears to be clear is that persons classified as *atan* had limited freedoms and could be tied to their master's house inter-generationally. It is perhaps the lack of social recognition as members of an independent house-based ancestral group that distinguishes *atan* as 'other' in East Timorese societies.

Although the Portuguese officially abolished 'slavery' in 1869 (Hägerdal 2012), the categorical distinctions of *liurai* (noble, chief), *ema* (commoner) and *atan* (understood broadly as serf/slave/dependant) persisted well into the twentieth, and some would argue the twenty-first, century.[4] Indeed, when in the late 1800s the Portuguese began to establish cash crop plantations (coffee, coconut and candlenut) in an attempt to make the colony more profitable, they benefitted from the 'free' labour 'recruited' by local rulers who were obliged to provide labourers for plantations a certain number of days each month. Local rulers who were 'rich in people' were able to draw on the *atan* class to work on the plantations and expand their own holdings.[5] Free labour on plantations was provided not only by those categorised as *atan* but following the imposition of the head-tax in the early twentieth century, individuals unable to pay their tax (including commoners and some nobles) were forced to work as *auxiliar* (auxiliaries) providing manual labour on plantations or building and road works, or as *ordenança* working as domestic servants for civil servants and local rulers (Clarence-Smith 1992; Kammen 2010; Shepherd and McWilliam 2013). In her ethnography of Funar, in the region of Manatuto, Bovensiepen describes how villagers confided that they had been given as children to the *liurai* because their parents had not been able to pay the taxes the local rulers had collected for the Portuguese colonial government. The children who carried out housework in *liurai* houses were locally known as *ornassa*—a corruption of the term *ordenança* (Bovensiepen 2015, 113). Similarly, in Babulo, Uato-lari, where I undertook my fieldwork, the term *asuliar*, a corruption of the Portuguese 'auxiliar' (Barnes 2017, 66), became part of local vocabularies to denote persons held in debt bondage or positions of servitude.[6]

Kammen has written convincingly of how this history of 'forced labour' fed into nationalist discourses that pitted Portuguese 'masters' and their Timorese elite collaborators against a Timorese mass of 'oppressed', which included both *ema/reino* (commoners) and *atan* (serf/slave/dependants). Collapsing the categories of *ema* and *atan*, Kammen argues, effectively silenced the reality of Indigenous forms of, what he calls, 'slavery' (see analysis of Araujo's "Timorese Elites" in Kammen 2010, 263-264). Kammen suggests that the unspoken legacy of Indigenous forms of dependency and servitude continues to affect contemporary East Timorese social relations. While many East Timorese are reluctant to speak openly about *atan*, and most are quick to state that "We don't have slavery any more", Kammen argues most "[East Timorese] are acutely aware of who is a descendant of a legitimate traditional ruler, who is a descendant of a Portuguese-appointed chief, who obtained positions by collaborating with the Indonesian occupiers. They also know "who was a commoner and who was a slave" (2010, 75). Shame is attached to the fact that East Timorese enslaved other East Timorese, yet *atan* ancestry continues to affect individual and communal aspirations and many descendants of former *atan* remain on the margins. Moreover, a variety of forms of servitude including debt bondage and other subtler forms of temporary and permanent dependency persist (Bovensiepen 2014; Trindade and Barnes 2018).

Atan in contemporary ethnography

Although people were initially reluctant to speak of it during my field work in the *suku* of Babulo, Uato-Lari subdistrict, the topic of *atan* was unavoidable. Babulo is comprised of eight hamlets, each of which broadly correspond to an 'origin' group, a group of families sharing a common ancestor and centred on a common sacred house (*Uma Lulik*). Sometimes referred to by other groups within *suku* as the 'aldeia without land', the hamlet of Roma was established in 2002. Unlike the majority of the *suku* population, the people of Roma hamlet are largely of Makassae rather than Naueti descent. According to one history of the origins of this group, the Roma are descendants of *atan* who served a *liurai* from Babulo who lived in exile near Quelicai. When this *liurai* was invited to return and rule over the people of Babulo it is said he agreed on condition that he could bring his "own people" who "stuck to him like seeds of a long grass" (Trindade, pers. comm.). There are no Roma 'house' structures in Babulo. Historically, members of this group were incorporated into their masters' houses as 'people of the house'. The Roma were not granted specific areas of land on which to farm or settle but were servants to the chiefly houses of Babulo. Their main task was to watch over the herds of buffalo which belonged to their masters. In time, however, the descendants of the Roma started farming near the animal pastures and enclosures they guarded. Now many of this group claim these plots of land as their own based on long-term occupancy rights.

The hamlet of Roma was created after independence by the then Fretilin government in recognition of the Roma people's part in the struggle for independence. There can be no doubt that the aspiration of the people of Roma hamlet resonated with Fretilin's rhetoric concerning putting an end 'to all forms of domination of our people' (Jolliffe 1978, 331). Despite their gains in achieving recognition in the eyes of the state, however, the people of Roma hamlet remain marginalised within the *suku*.

Discussing relations of dependency and *atan* in Babulo is a sensitive issue. For example, at first members of chiefly houses were reluctant to speak to me about the people of Roma hamlet, but as time went past and in more relaxed settings, they would let down their guard. Although there is a general consensus that they should no longer be referred to as such, members of the chiefly houses and main ritual houses continue to identify the people of Roma hamlet as former *atan*. In hushed and embarrassed tones, I was told that they are sometimes pejoratively referred to as *kilat no musan* (guns and bullets) (see above). Some members of chiefly houses told me that during the Indonesian times, education had a levelling effect, and 'people like the Roma' were able to improve their situation through economic activity and employment. A middle-aged member of one of the main ritual houses suggested to me that levelling social relations was not necessarily a good thing and that social tensions were a result of people 'like the Roma' "not knowing their place".[7]

During the course of my fieldwork one incident in particular highlighted the reality and continued social exclusion of some members of Roma hamlet. In 2006, members of the house of Aha Bu'u (the ancestral house of the former *liurai* and *xefe suku* of Babulo) began collecting material to rebuild their ancestral house. In the past, the ancestors of the people of Roma hamlet would have performed this task as servants to the house of Aha Bu'u. In this instance, however, and perhaps as a result of the Roma community organisation to assert their rights in the eyes of the State, the headman of Aha Bu'u had arranged with the new headman of Roma hamlet to recruit members of the hamlet to collect *unu* (T: *tali metan*, Bot: *arenga pinnata*), a type of fibre obtained from black sugar palm, for which they would receive cash in exchange.

One morning, as I made my way to a wake near the secondary school and old-*posto* of Uato-Lari Leten I was stopped by two men, one of whom was a local secondary school teacher. They told me that a murder had just been committed a few hundred metres up the road. A Roma man who had been collecting *unu* for the house at Aha Bu'u had killed the Roma hamlet chief with a machete. Later, I received news that the suspect had handed himself in to local police and was being detained at the sub-district police post in Darabai. In the village, rumours began to spread about the incident. The general agreement was that the suspect had acted out of desperation. A witness to the incident said that the suspect had approached the hamlet chief to discuss the payment for some *unu* he had collected for the house of Aha Bu'u. But the hamlet chief informed him that he was not permitted to collect *unu* and refused to pay him. At this, I was told, the suspect grew agitated threatening the hamlet chief and declaring, "What can I do? I have no land to farm and I cannot collect *unu*? How am I going to feed my family?", He then struck the hamlet chief with his machete and broke down.

The incident prompted much discussion about the predicament of those who do not have access to land or depend on others to gain access to land and other resources within the village. I was told that while the suspect did in fact farm a small piece of land, he had eleven children to clothe, feed and send to school and no means of earning cash. The teacher I had met in the morning suggested that as a citizen of independent Timor-Leste everyone had the same rights to access land and other natural resources; a member of one of the senior ritual houses, however, argued that if the Roma wanted land and other resources they should return to their village of origin.

The nature of social relations between Roma and other groups present in Babulo is more complex than the story above suggests. Descendants of Roma have become 'incorporated' into various 'chiefly' (*liurai*) and 'commoner' (*ema/povo*) ancestral houses including the house of the former *liurai* and *xefe de suku* as well as the houses of the *liurai rai nain* (N: *rea* netana, E: source of the land). Over time, some descendants of former slaves and their former masters have become kin either by birth, or more rarely, through marriage. Yet, unless they are officially adopted by their former masters' house, the descendants of *atan* are commonly considered to be dependents not descendants of the house (see also, Hoskins 2004). While this mechanism of partial or nominal incorporation into a house group is commonly used to cover a range of non-ideal marriage arrangements (see

Fitzpatrick, McWilliam, and Barnes 2012; Barnes 2017), the fact remains that there are no socially recognised *atan* ancestral houses and as such the descendants of *atan* remain on the margins of customary social arrangements.

During my fieldwork in Babulo and elsewhere in Timor-Leste, I also encountered other perhaps more ambiguous yet common forms of servitude and dependency affecting men, women and children. The transfer of people between houses has historically occurred in the context of marriage exchanges between fertility-givers and fertility-takers (Bovensiepen 2015). Bovensiepen has described how marriages between *liurai* in Funar sometimes involved fertility-givers 'giving' slaves or one or two children from a commoner house to their fertility-takers along with other gifts such as cloth and pigs (2015, 113). While expressed in the language of kinship such transfers reveal the stark status inequalities that persist in Timor-Leste, particularly in cases where houses of 'chiefly' status request the payment of debts from their fertility-takers (ibid., 114-115).

In Bobonaro district, for example, men can become bonded labour when debt is owed to their bride's father. In the ritual community of Leosibe, the practice of uxorilocal residence continues whereby a husband must reside in his father-in-law's house and work on his land until marriage debts are repaid either to an agreed amount or in full. During this time any children born of the marriage do not inherit from their father's descent line but the descent group of their mother (Fitzpatrick, McWilliam, and Barnes 2012).

In Babulo, debts between fertility-givers and fertility-takers could (and do) involve the transfer of a person. Depending on the wealth and status of individual families, some households include one or two distant to destitute kin, or individuals who are the descendants of *atan*. Although these household members are not spoken of as servants or *atan* but as 'family,' they are socially inferior and under obligation to serve other members of the household. In exchange for food, shelter and, in some cases an education, these dependent household members are expected to perform a number of tasks including cooking, fetching firewood and water, working the fields and caring for younger children. While other household members also take part in these activities, often the main burden of this work falls on these dependents.

One family in Babulo took on a child as a ward or foster child (*oan hakiak*). Described to me as the child of a 'poor relative', the boys' status was not equal to other children of the immediate family who were also raised as *oan hakiak*. Although he went to school and played with the other children of the family, he was expected to do much of the manual labour of the household. In her ethnography of Funar, Bovensiepen recounts how one young man made explicit the connection between fostering and slavery: "there are two types of foster children (*oan hakiak*): real foster children and slaves. But no one talks about this anymore. Nowadays we just call them all *walin* (younger siblings)" (2015, 113).

The practice of taking orphans or removing children from their parents is complicated by the Indonesian occupation when East Timorese children were taken by Indonesian soldiers. East Timorese children were frequently 'recruited' by the Indonesian military to perform menial tasks and many others were forcibly removed from their families and taken to be raised in Indonesia. The conditions that these children encountered varied greatly, while some were cared for and educated others were not so fortunate (van Klinken 2012; CAVR 2013). Similarly, women were often 'married' (often under coercion) to Indonesian soldiers or kept as sexual slaves (CAVR 2013). The historic reality of the taking of war captives, slavery and servitude, both in Timor-Leste and other parts of Indonesia, may well have provided a precedent for the actions of the Indonesian military and others in this regard.

Beyond the framework of kinship relations there are other cases that blur the boundaries between orphan/domestic, servant/slave, person/possession. For example, in addition to the boy, the family discussed above had also taken in and given shelter to a woman with a history of mental illness who had been abused and accused of witchcraft by her own relatives. Theoretically, she was free to leave but in practice she was indebted to the household and would have found it very difficult to do so. While the living conditions that this woman and the foster child experienced were harsh, they were not as desperate as that of another woman who lived with family of chiefly descent. Although I was never able to speak to her directly, this young woman was clearly the servant of the family. Subjected to verbal and physical abuse by the women of the house, she was tied to the household by status, bonds of personal obligation and fear.

Agency, dependency and kinship

What the descendants of the Roma, the foster-child and female servants described above have in common is that they are all formally denied agency in one way or another; however, they are people with will and desires, who can and do act—even if their actions are heavily constrained by their structural position in society (see Hoskins 2004, 92). Social inequalities express themselves in cultural forms and it is often from within a shared cultural framework that individuals and groups seek to act out their aspirations and desires (see Appadurai 1996; Ortner 2006).

Drawing on Bourdieu's notions of the 'rules and strategies', Hoskins argues that marriage in Sumba is a key arena where the "games of social status are played". In order to be considered full subjects, people of 'slave' descent must find ways of manipulating the 'rules of marriage' to achieve some degree of freedom (Hoskins 2004, 92). In Babulo, descendants of *atan* have sought to manipulate the 'rules' of the game of social incorporation. Not only have they achieved independence and recognition in the eyes of the state following the creation of their own administrative hamlet (see above), they have also re-negotiated their position within the local ritual community.

In the context of political violence that erupted in Uato-Lari sub-district during the Presidential campaign of 2007, the people of Roma hamlet ritually re-affirmed their allegiance to the chiefly houses of their former masters and the houses of the local *liurai rai nain* (N: *rea netana*, E: *source of the land*) by swearing under-oath to protect the domain under the leadership of the former *liurai* (hereditary chief) and *xefe de suku*. Such a move may at first sight appear to be counterproductive to efforts to assert their civil and political rights; however, in renewing their commitment to the chiefly houses of the domain, the people of Roma achieved recognition in the eyes of the ritual community independently of their former masters. During the rice harvest of 2008, for the first time, the people of Roma hamlet were called by name to receive their portion of the ritual meal and ancestral blessings—an acknowledgement of their collective rights to independent group identity.

At an individual level, descendants of slaves can also seek to renegotiate their status by mobilising resources, to improve their condition and achieve social recognition. For example, in 2006 I met a teacher Alberto, who lived in a modest house in the Indonesian-era settlement of Kampung Baru.[8] Alberto, whom everyone referred to as 'Mestre Alberto' is a descendant of former slaves. I was told that Alberto was a messenger, fixer and go-between who served the Source of the Land. The first time I met him he was negotiating the procurement of animals necessary for a ritual sacrifice to be performed by the Source of the Land on behalf of the construction company building the bridge across the Be-Bui river. At the time, he was somewhat flustered finding himself accused of making money from the contractors by members of a subsidiary house of the Source of the Land. Five years later, during another period of fieldwork, I was surprised to find Alberto one afternoon deep in conversation with one of the senior ritual elders of Babulo, the *liurai* Source of the Land (N: *liurai rea netana*, T: *liurai rai nain*). It was immediately apparent to me that his situation had changed from the last time I had been in Babulo. While in the past I had seen him address ritual elders with a degree of humility and servitude, he now sat confidently opposite Source of the Land dressed in new clothes, his fingers adorned with gold rings and a visible thick gold chain around his neck. In the intervening five years I discovered that Alberto had been able to accumulate a small fortune renting out his house to Chinese technicians working on the national electricity grid and had established a few businesses of his own. He still served the Source of the Land as a fixer and negotiator, but his social standing had improved somewhat. When I inquired about his status to members of the Source of the Land's house, I was told that Alberto's ancestors had *always* traditionally served as intermediaries between the Source of the Land and other houses—the suggestion being that Alberto's ancestors had always been 'more than' slaves. Rather than seek status and power from other sources of authority, such as the state for example, Alberto continued to 'serve' the Source of the Land, investing in custom to enhance his status within the ritual community. Following a familiar strategy of incorporation and accommodation of outsiders, the Source of the Land was able to benefit from Alberto's wealth and connections while reaffirming their authority and legitimacy.

Returning to the cases of contemporary forms of dependency and servitude described above, those unable to mobilise individual or collective resources remain marginalised or exert their limited agency by resorting to either clandestine or more visible forms of resistance and rebellion. For example, once he was of age and finished primary school, the foster-child from Babulo ran away to Dili, the capital. The city offered some anonymity, but he could not cut ties completely with the family. Given shelter by a relative, he continued to meet with the sons and daughters of his foster-parents in order to gauge the likelihood of reconciliation or possibility of continued support. The woman with mental health issues, who was taken in by the family I lived with was known to have 'bouts of madness' and disappear for several days. The other of the women of the household confided in me that during this time she usually returned to her husband's house. The young woman, who served a prominent household and was perhaps the person with least agency I encountered, was nevertheless able to rebel in her own way, and on at least one occasion violently. Pushed to the limits while the husband was away in Dili she lashed out at his wife and sister forcing them to seek shelter in the house of my host family for several days until she had calmed down.

Conclusion

In this paper I sought to reconsider the historical category of *atan* in Timor-Leste and its significance to contemporary social relations. By drawing attention to the different meanings of the word *atan* and the way *atan* were historically portrayed in the literature, I called into question understandings of *atan* that tend to reflect Euro-centric notions of 'slave' and 'slavery' based on experience of the Atlantic slave trade (see Miers and Kopytoff 1977). While rejecting these narrow correspondences with the notion of 'slave' and 'slavery', I have illustrated the myriad of ways the social category of *atan* persists today and how individuals and groups seek to transform or resist categorisation. This is by no means an exhaustive survey or analysis—there are modern forms of slavery, servitude and dependency present in Timor-Leste, including those linked to the trafficking of humans, and the conditions of workers, domestic and other. My aim here is to start a conversation and open up avenues for further research.

I have focused in this paper on my own research conducted mainly in the village of Babulo; however, since my initial fieldwork in Timor-Leste the rate of migration from rural to urban centres has increased dramatically, particularly among the 15-35 age group. Often migrants are supported by their parents or relatives already settled in urban centres like Dili. Shame and fear of stigma characterises conversations about *atan* in Timor-Leste. While social categories are well known at village level this is less true of urban settings where the heterogenous population provides a degree of anonymity. Yet, Silva's research on marriage practices in Dili suggests class, family trajectories and education play an important part in shaping urban-based marriage negotiations, and the suspicion of *atan* ancestry feeds into distinctions and prejudices that revolve around the notion of *ema foho* and *ema Dili* (Silva 2018). This raises questions regarding the spatial and social mobility of people on the margins, descendants of *atan* or in positions of servitude, their capacity to access resources through education and employment and/or transcend their social categorisation through strategic alliances.

The question of the persistence of social categories extends more generally to the growing population especially in urban centres, the emergence of a new middle-class and the growth in social and economic inequality. In his discussion of metaphors of slavery in Timor, Kammen raises questions regarding the social origins of East Timorese militia members. In Lautém, militia members tended to be recruited from the descendants of former *atan* (F: *akanu*) while in Liquiçá militia leaders mobilised plantations labourers, former *asuliar* (Portuguese: *auxiliaries*). Kammen speculates that "those at the bottom of the social scale may well have feared that independence would mean the reassertion of *liurai* or landlord power, and hence the revival of internal social stratification" (Kammen 2010, 272). The same questions could be asked in relation to the origins and structure of East Timorese martial-arts groups and other gangs or, in relation to new political movements that seek to represent "the voice of the oppressed" (ibid.).

Across both rural and urban Timor-Leste, the category of *atan* persists and speaks to the reality of unpaid labour not only of women but also vulnerable men and children in contemporary society (see Introduction, this volume, 10-11). It also draws our attention to other entanglements between community-based and market-driven values and arrangements. As observed by McWilliam (see Chapter 13, this volume) and Palmer (2010, 2017), the resurgence of customary or community exchanges that underpin the relations of dependency from which the category of *atan* emerge, is occurring in the context of political and economic transition to a largely neoliberal economy and governance regime (see Introduction, this volume, 19). However, in this context, and perhaps against neoliberal logics, individuals and groups, such as Alberto described above, choose to invest in the community economy seeking social integration and prestige within kin-based networks of gift exchange and alliance (see Chapter 5, this volume). In making these strategic investments they actively seek to re-negotiate and re-define their *atan* status within, and not beyond, the community-based economy.

To conclude, relationships involving *atan* are often presented as an extension of kinship relations. Some argue this strategy has been used as a moral backing for slavery around the world (see Meillassoux 1991). Refocussing on both the nature of gift exchange and dependency in Timor-Leste may shed new light on the boundaries between freedom and disenfranchisement, and just how fragile these boundaries may be (see Hoskins 2004, 90).

Notes

1 Slaves formed part of tribute provided by vassal kingdoms to larger coastal kingdoms who traded with outsiders (Forman 1977).

2 For example, in Babulo a group of war-captives were incorporated into the local house-based social structure. Incorporation involved the exchange of gifts, and the granting of a *rota* (sceptre, rod) from the sacred house of the source of the land to the in-coming group. Slaves may well have been part of these exchanges (Barnes 2017; see also Kammen 2010).

3 Author's translation from original Portuguese.

4 According to Clarence-Smith (1992) "chiefs, headmen, and leading warriors disposed of considerable numbers of slaves long after the export trade in slaves had been stopped, and it was only in the mid-1900s that the Portuguese made hesitant moves to abolish slavery".

5 Clarence-Smith (1992) suggests that local potentates had the right to corvée labour to cultivate their specially demarcated plots or tend to their livestock well into the 1920s. It is possible that individuals entered into arrangements with local rulers and land-owners as a means of avoiding taxation. However, how common or widespread these forms of 'resistance' were, requires further investigation.

6 Of interest here is that the word '*asu*' often used as an insult in a derogatory manner to deprive a person of dignity and personhood, is sometimes used as a form of self-referential humility—much in the same way as the expression '*Atan hau*' is used in Tetum. For example, in a ritual setting in Babulo persons refer to themselves as '*asu*' and not '*ema*' in deference to the ancestors.

7 Underpinning this comment is an understanding of local social organisation predicated on intricate networks of affiliation and alliance within and between ancestral houses that serve to legitimate and confirm the relative standing and entitlements as well as differential social ranking (Fitzpatrick et al. 2012).

8 Alberto is a pseudonym.

References

Appadurai, A. 1996. *Modernity at Large: Cultural Dimensions of Globalization.* Minneapolis: University of Minnesota Press.

Barnes, S. 2017. "Customary renewal and the pursuit of power and prosperity in post-occupation East Timor: a case study from Babulo, Uato-Lari." PhD diss., Monash University.

Blust, R. 2013. *The Austronesian Languages.* Asia-Pacific Linguistics, School of Culture, History and Language, College of Asia and the Pacific, The Australian National University.

Bovensiepen, J. 2015. *The Land of Gold: Cultural Revival and Post-Conflict Reconstruction in Independent Timor-Leste.* Ithaca, NY: Cornell University Press.

Boxer, C. R. 1968. *Fidalgos in the Far East 1550-1770.* Oxford: Oxford University Press.

Carvalho Ferreira, A. 2019. "Sentidos de tráfico e tráfico de sentidos: Dissertação sobre a produção e reprodução social da escravidão no Brasil do século XIX." Master's diss. University of Brasilia.

CAVR (Comissão de Acolhimento, Verdade e Reconciliação). 2013. *Chega! The final report of the Timor-Leste Commission for Reception, Truth and Reconciliation (CAVR).* Jakarta: KPG in cooperation with STP-CAVR.

Clarence-Smith, W. G. 1992. "Planters and smallholders in Portuguese Timor in the nineteenth and twentieth centuries." *Indonesia Circle. School of Oriental & African Studies. Newsletter* 20 (57): 15-30. https://doi.org/10.1080/03062849208729776

de Castro, A. 1867. As possessões portuguesas na Oceania. Lisboa: Imprensa nacional.

Fitzpatrick, D., A. McWilliam, and S. Barnes. 2012. *Property and Social Resilience in Times of Conflict: Land, Custom and Law in East Timor.* Surrey & Burlington: Ashgate.

Forman, S. 1978. "East Timor: Exchange and political hierarchy at the time of the European discoveries." In *Economic Exchange and Social Interaction in Southeast Asia: Perspectives from Prehistory, History, and Ethnography*, edited by K. L. Hutterer, 97-112. Ann Arbor, Michigan: University of Michigan. https://doi.org/10.3998/mpub.19412

Gunn, G. C. 1999. *Timor Loro Sae: 500 years.* Macau: Livros do Oriente.

Hägerdal, H. 2010. "The slaves of Timor: Life and death on the fringes of early colonial society." *Itinerario* 34 (2): 19-44. Cambridge Core. https://doi.org/10.1017/S0165115310000331

Hägerdal, H. 2012. *Lords of the Land, Lords of the Sea: Conflict and Adaptation in Early Colonial Timor, 1600-1800.* Leiden/Boston: Brill. DOI: 10.26530/OAPEN_408241.

Hägerdal, H. 2019. "A world of clothes: Indian textiles and the germination of polities in eastern Indonesia." Paper presented in the 10th EuroSEAS Conference, 10-13 September 2019, Humboldt-Universität, Berlin. Retrieved from http://urn.kb.se/resolve?urn=urn:nbn:se:lnu:-diva-90062 at 20 December 2020.

Hoskins, J. 2004. "Slaves, brides and other 'gifts': Resistance, marriage and rank in Eastern Indonesia." *Slavery & Abolition* 25 (2): 90-107. https://doi.org/10.1080/0144039042000293063

Jolliffe, J. 1978. *East Timor: Nationalism and Colonialism.* St. Lucia, Queensland: University of Queensland Press.

Kammen, D. 2010. "Metaphors of slavery in Timor." In *Parts of Asia*, edited by C. Bastos, 257-280. North Dartmouth, MA: University of Massachusetts Dartmouth.

McWilliam, A. 2007. "Harbouring traditions in East Timor: Marginality in a lowland entrepôt." *Modern Asian Studies* 41 (6): 1113-1143. https://doi.org/10.1017/S0026749X07002843

McWilliam, A. 2011. "Exchange and resilience in Timor-Leste." *Journal of the Royal Anthropological Institute* 17 (4): 745-763. https://doi.org/10.1111/j.1467-9655.2011.01717.x

Meillassoux, C. 1991. *The Anthropology of Slavery: The Womb of Iron and Gold.* Illinois: University of Chicago Press.

Miers, S., and I. Kopytoff. 1977. *Slavery in Africa: Historical and Anthropological Perspectives.* Madison, Wisconsin: University of Wisconsin Press.

Ortner, S. B. 2006. *Anthropology and Social Theory: Culture, Power, and the Acting Subject.* Durham, N.C.: Duke University Press.

Palmer, L. 2010. "Enlivening development: water management in post-conflict Baucau City, Timor-Leste." *Singapore Journal of Tropical Geography* 31 (3): 357-370. doi.org/10.1111/j.1467-9493.2010.00404.x.

Palmer, L. 2015. *Water Politics and Spiritual Ecology: Custom, Environmental Governance and Development.* London: Routledge Explorations in Environmental Studies. doi.org/10.4324/9781315883250.

RDTL (Democratic Republic of Timor-Leste). 2001. *The Constitution of the Democratic Republic of Timor-Leste.* Dili, Timor-Leste: C. Assembly.

Reid, A., and J. Brewster, J. 1983. *Slavery, Bondage, and Dependency in Southeast Asia.* London: Palgrave Macmillan.

Shepherd, C. J. and A. McWilliam. 2013. "Cultivating plantations and subjects in East Timor: A genealogy." *Bijdragen tot de taal-, land- en volkenkunde/Journal of the Humanities and Social Sciences of Southeast Asia* 169 (2-3): 326-361. https://doi.org/10.1163/22134379-12340047

Silva, K. 2018. "Marriage prestations, gift making, and identity in urban East Timor." *Oceania* 88 (1): 127-147. https://doi.org/10.1002/ocea.5185

Trindade, J., and S. Barnes. 2018. "Expressions of the 'good life' and visions of the future: Reflections from Dili and Uatolari." In *The Promise of Prosperity: Visions of the Future in Timor-Leste after Independence*, edited by J. Bovensiepen, 157-172. Canberra: Australian National University Press.

van Klinken, H. 2012. *Making Them Indonesians: Child Transfers Out of East Timor.* Melbourne: Monash University Publishing.

Ward, K. 2011. "Slavery in Southeast Asia, 1420-1804." In *The Cambridge World History of Slavery*, edited by D. Eltis, and S. L. Engerman, 163-185. https://doi.org/10.1017/CHOL9780521840682.009

CHAPTER 5

The *serimónia* network: economic mobilisation through rituals in the hamlet of Faulara, Liquiçá

Alberto Fidalgo-Castro and Enrique Alonso-Población

Abstract

This chapter addresses some economic aspects of the ritual exchange regime in Timor-Leste. Drawing on quantitative data gathered in the village of Faulara (Liquiçá municipality) through a household survey and a qualitative case study on the marriage rituals involving a particular household, we show how ceremonies structured around fertility-giver/fertility-taker (*umane/mane-foun*) relations constitute only a small part of ritual activity in which other types of relationships such as neighbourhood and friendship play a central role as well. Building on that and considering the ritual exchange regime in a broader way, we show how the ritual exchange regime can work as a credit and savings union as well as a safety and solidarity network. In a broader theoretical perspective, we analyse how people use rituals as an economic mechanism and propose that they serve to ensure the economic security and redistribution embedded in kinship and everyday social networks.

Keywords: Timor-Leste; economic anthropology; household economies; ritual exchange regime; ritual revitalisation

Ever since the first social scientists became interested in Timor, the exchange of gifts involved in alliance and mortuary rituals have been a dominant focus, particularly among those working in the last years of the colonial period (Forman 1981; Friedberg 1989; Hicks 1984; Traube 1980a, 1986). Recently, the issue of ritual exchange has gained renewed traction as a topic of interest among social scientists in Timor-Leste, with anthropologists focusing for the most part on mortuary and alliance rituals (Bovensiepen 2014; Hicks 2010; Silva 2018). Other research streams have analysed different ritual aspects, such as linkages with resource management (Alonso-Población et al. 2018; Palmer 2010, 2011; Palmer and Carvalho 2008; Thu, Scott, and van Niel 2007), conflict resolution (Babo-Soares 2004; Simião 2017; Trindade 2008, 2014) and the motivations of people to attend small rituals connected with the *Uma Lulik* (origin house) outside the common ritual cycles (Silva 2019).

Initially, researchers drew attention to the apparent revitalisation of these types of practices (Bovensiepen 2015; McWilliam 2011; Palmer and Carvalho 2008); later, new discourses around ritual practice were identified (Alonso-Población, Pena-Castro, and Fidalgo-Castro 2018; Silva 2017).

Among the first set of researchers, Palmer and Carvalho (2008) explained ritual revitalisation around resource management as an attempt, in part, by communities to play a role in state formation. Bovensiepen (2014) suggested that the expansion of ritual practices enabled communities to deal with past conflicts in a context of post-independence construction and identity formation. In contrast, McWilliam (2011), taking an economic standpoint, suggested that ritual revitalisation arose as a response to the collapse of the market economy after Indonesia's withdrawal from Timor-Leste.

Following this initial focus on ritual revitalisation, other researchers called attention to the emergence of a new discourse that portrayed rituals as a burden for economic development. This issue has been approached from both an interpretive and objectivist viewpoint (Alonso-Población, Fidalgo-Castro, and Pena Castro 2018; Silva 2017). Among objectivist works, policy-oriented development agencies stand out, and, according to Silva and Simião (2012), have played a role in amplifying such discourses. A policy brief published by a local NGO, Belum, and the Center for International Conflict Resolution (CIRC) of Columbia University, have explicitly endorsed the representation of culture as 'burden' (Brandao et al. 2011). Brandao et al. (2011) expressly state that culture is an expense that deprives families of basic resources such as access to education. However, their conclusions are driven by a narrow conceptualisation of 'culture' that focuses solely on rituals in which marriage exchange relations become effective, with special emphasis on ceremonies of alliance (*barlake*) and death.

Based on a case study in the Faulara, we show that ceremonies structured around fertility-giver/fertility-taker (*umane/mane-foun*) relations constitute only a small part of ritual activity (Palmer 2015). However, as we show in this chapter, when seen in a broader temporal perspective, the ritual exchange regime can work as a credit and savings union as well as a safety and solidarity network that goes beyond the *umane/mane-foun* relationship. We highlight this function to discuss some of the hypotheses formulated about the revitalisation of rituals in independent Timor-Leste, specifically McWilliam's (2011) view of rituals as an economic strategy used to mitigate economic uncertainties and grant security after the fall of the market economy at the end of Indonesian occupation.

In a broader way, we also contribute dense ethnographic descriptions to Gibson et al.'s (2018) call for more elucidation of the "community economies of monsoon Asia". This chapter analyses how the people of Faulara mobilise goods and money by mechanisms other than market transactions, specifically by rituals. We propose that rituals serve to ensure the economic security and redistribution embedded in kinship and everyday social networks. By exploring how a particular household deals with their ritual activity, we uncover the ways in which they enable their wellbeing through relations with others (Gibson et al. 2018, 6).

Methodology

This research is based on a case study in the village of Faulara. Information gathering was undertaken through mixed research methods, both quantitative and qualitative.

Quantitative data was gathered through a household survey carried out in June 2011 that aimed to elicit information about the number of rituals a respondent's household attended and/or organised between January 2010 and June 2011. Additionally, the survey was used as a tool to help us understand the economic impact and importance that rituals had on household economies in the hamlet. The questionnaire was developed through an iterative process of test and refinement.[1] It consisted of nine series of open-ended questions, four of which are analysed here:

1. What ceremonies did you attend between January 2010 and June 2011?
2. What assets and animals did you bring to the ceremony?
3. What assets and animals did you bring back from the ceremony?[2]
4. Where did the ceremony take place?[3]

A total of 67 respondents were selected randomly among the 159 domestic units that, according to the *livro de aldeia* (hamlet book), resided in the area.[4] After the data gathering process, responses were codified and classified.

Table 5.1: Name and type of ritual recorded

Name of the ritual	Type	Classification
Ai-funan midar/moruk/rahun (different moments of the mourning ritual)	4/1	1. Funerary
Barlake (marriage)	2	2. Marriage
Kasamento (Catholic marriage)	4/2	3. *Uma Lulik*
Krisma (Catholic confirmation)	4	4. Specifically Catholic
Eskola (school)	5	5. School
Halibur maun-alin/Kumpul (gathering of people)	7	6. Other
Halo rate (construction of a grave)	1	7. Cooperation
Hasai feto (marriage)	2	
Hasai krus (last stage of the construction of a grave)	4/1	
Hatun fatuk-ain (construction of a grave)	1	

Name of the ritual	Type	Classification
Husu misa/Selu misa (pay for a Catholic mass)	4/1	
Kore metan (end of one year of mourning)	1	
Lere dalan (marriage)	2	
Asiste mate (go to a funeral)	1	
Mate ruin (second burial)	1	
Prenda/Bua-malus/Ko'alia feto-foun (first stage of the marriage ritual)	2	
Raut fatuk rahun (construction of a grave)	1	
Riba fatuk-ain (construction of a grave)	1	
Sarani (Catholic baptism)	4	
Sunu metan (end of one year of mourning)	1	
Uma Lulik (sacred house)	3	
Halo koran (blood brotherhood ritual)	7	
Other	6	

Ethnographic research was conducted by the lead author between 2007 and 2013 for 42 months (18 of them in Faulara). For this case study, the lead author followed a particular household through two marriages in which they were a main actor between 2009 and 2011 (both as fertility-givers and fertility-takers). The aim of the case study was to show how a particular domestic unit engages with ritual exchanges and mobilises economic resources through them.

The household in this case study has its roots outside Faulara, in a *suku* (village) called Asumanu, although the house of origin (*Uma Lulik*) is based in Hatuquessi. Both *suku* share borders with Leotelá, the *suku* where Faulara is located.[5]

Julião was born in Asumanu, the place where his parents established their residence, matrilocally, after getting married. Mariana was born in Hatuquessi. They married after the Indonesian invasion and established their temporal residence in the village of Liquiçá, where Juanito, Pepito, Benedita, Leomar, and Josito were born (Pepito and Benedita died young).[6] Afterwards, the family moved to Asumanu where the rest of the children were born at a house they constructed on the land Julião inherited. They decided to move to Faulara in 1997 when the Indonesian administration announced the opening of Faulara's transmigration site. The first one to move there was Julião, along with his sons Juanito and Alsino. Shortly after his arrival he was assassinated and his children were sent back to Asumanu. Even after that, in 1998, Mariana decided to move to Faulara with her children, apart from Juliana, who had been adopted at the age of two by Mariana's elder sister.

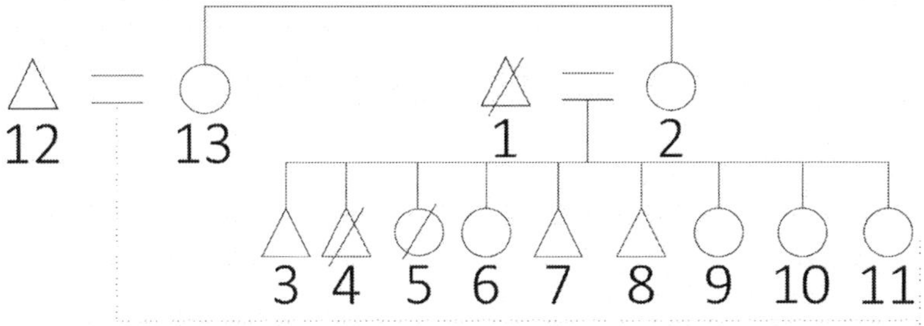

1. Julião Tinto
2. Mariana de Moisés
3. Juanito de Moisés Tinto (Jr.)
4. Pepito de Moisés Tinto
5. Benedita de Moisés Tinto
6. Leomar de Moisés Tinto
7. Josito de Moisés Tinto
8. Alsino de Moisés Tinto
9. Rigoberta de Moisés Tinto
10. Folga de Moisés Tinto
11. Juliana dos Santos
12. José Larreto
13. Berta dos Santos

Figure 5.1: Family tree of the household in 2009. Credit: Alberto Fidalgo-Castro and Enrique Alonso-Población.

In 2009 the household owned one property in Faulara with an approximate total area of 0.45 hectares. Five sons and daughters were permanently living at the house, and two others were living with Mariana's elder sister and husband in the *suku* Lauhata, close to Liquiçá, attending senior and junior secondary school. Juanito Jnr had discontinued his studies and was taking care of the agricultural work along with his mother. Leomar, the woman getting married (see below), was still living in the house after finishing secondary school. Josito had just finished his studies at the Agricultural Technical School of Maliana (Bobonaro district). Folga was finishing her studies at the primary school in Faulara.

The family did not own any rice fields, but they normally planted some each year through agreements with other families (called *lisuk*) who had land titles, or by payments in kind after working in somebody else's fields.[7] They cultivated cassava and corn in the house garden for household consumption, and also used cassava as a cash crop from time to time.[8] Though settled at Faulara, the family kept their land, inherited from Julião, at Asumanu, where they owned 2 hectares of coffee plantations from which they received some money. They had owned two cows, but both had died and the only animals they were raising at that time were two pigs, as well as many chickens. None of the members of the household had a formal job and they carried out different tasks for money. Mariana cooked and sold pastries (*dosi*) during market days.[9] She also had an agreement with two women traders who sold products in the Dili markets. Other economic activities included occasional infrastructure maintenance works carried out by the men of the household.[10]

Results

The relevance of rituals of cooperation

When analysing the frequency of responses regarding the types of rituals attended during the previous six months, three types represented 86.16 per cent of all rituals attended. As can be seen in Figure 5.2, most of the cases (47.5 per cent) corresponded to a ritual called *halibur maun-alin*, which we classified as a 'ritual of cooperation'.

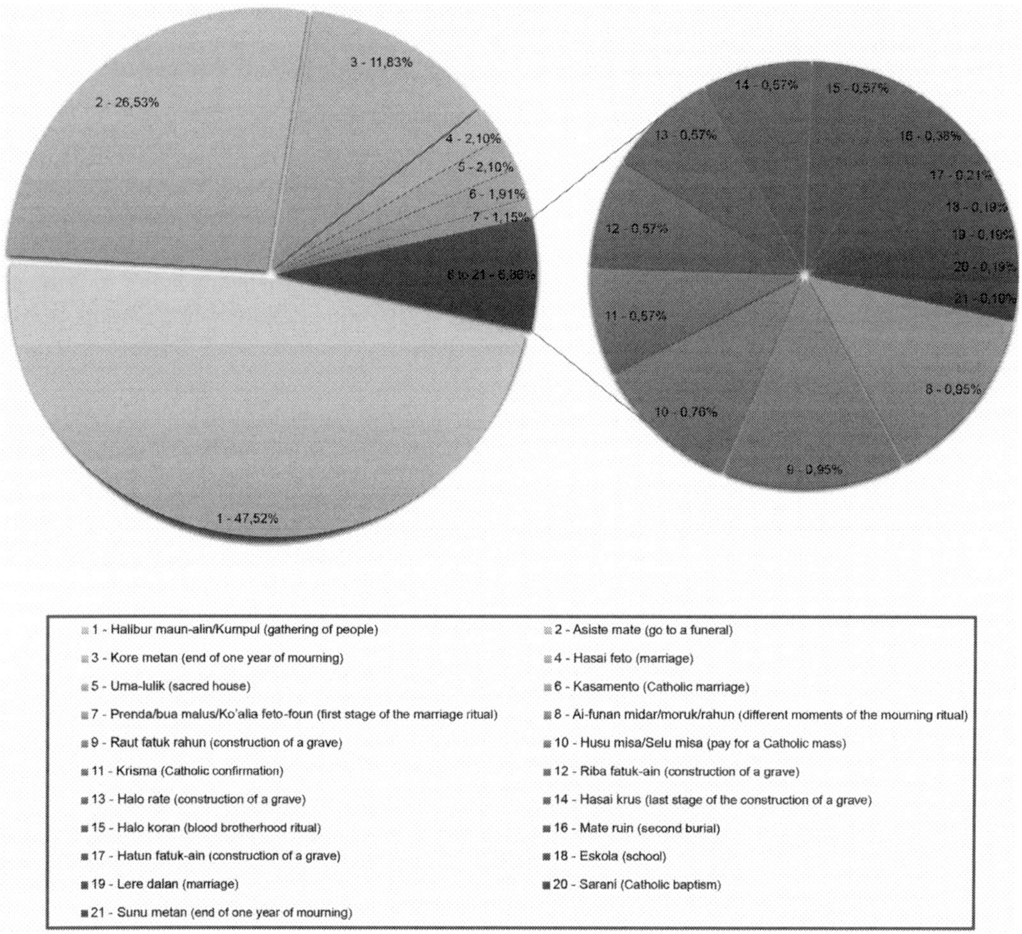

Figure 5.2: Percentage of total ritual movements (names in Tetum) Credit: Alberto Fidalgo-Castro and Enrique Alonso-Población.

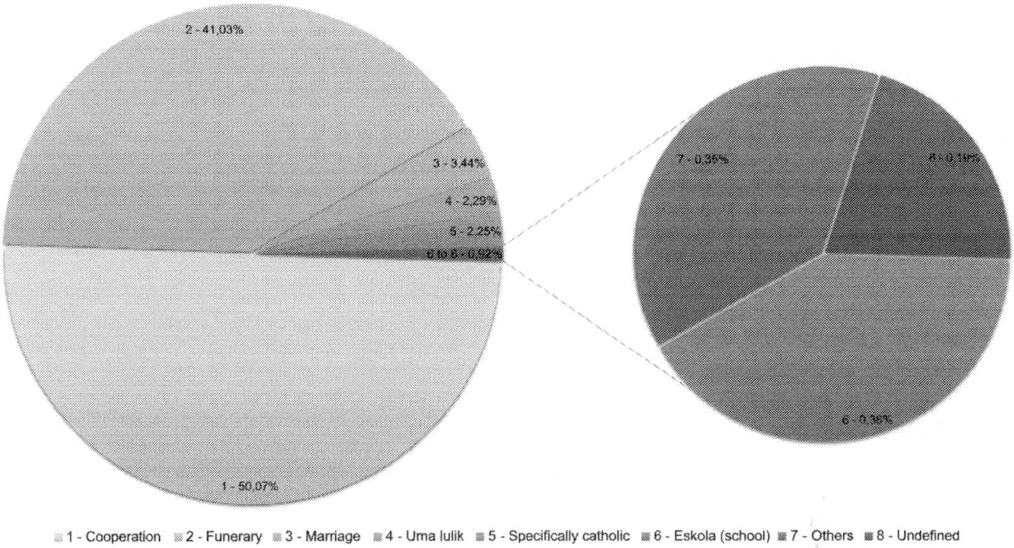

Figure 5.3. Percentage of ritual movements by type (according to Table 5.1). Credit: Alberto Fidalgo-Castro and Enrique Alonso-Población.

Figure 5.3 represents the frequency of rituals mentioned in Table 5.1 sorted by type. The frequencies point to a consistent trend: most of the rituals attended by the participants of the questionnaire were those that we have called 'rituals of cooperation', particularly the ones called *halibur maun-alin* and *kumpul*.

The reason to classify these *serimónia* as rituals of cooperation is because they are usually celebrated for the purpose of gathering the support of neighbours, family and friends in order to acquire a certain amount of money, animals and goods to carry out, or attend, another more expensive ritual (mainly marriage or funerary). These rituals of cooperation are the ones referred to as *halibur maun-alin* rituals (gather the older brothers and the younger brothers), although sometimes they are also referred to as *kumpul* (Indonesian: together) or *kafana* (warm coffee, as it was called in Tokodede according to the accounts of local villagers).

The household that organises or attends a costly ritual (such as a marriage or funeral)—especially as a fertility-taker—usually organises another small ritual in which commensality is the central element and a variable number of animals are sacrificed to offer food to the people attending (among other foodstuffs). Those attending, in turn, make monetary, goods or even animal donations that are carefully registered and kept by the household, for they need to be returned when those attendees organise a ritual of this kind themselves. This monetary exchange is conceptualised as *matak* (raw) or *tasak* (cooked), a classification in which 'raw' is the first of the donations, and 'cooked' refers to the donation that is returned in exchange. It is expected that the monetary refund, called *osan funan* (flowers of money), will be higher than the money received (usually double). The described reciprocity cycle is restarted each time it is completed. Consequently, these rituals could be considered as an investment (with a 100 per cent return rate).

Following the exchange of goods – Part 1: La'o umane—walking the path of the fertility-giver

In August 2009, the household held a marital ritual they referred to as *prenda*. Leomar was getting married to a man from Darulete, a bordering *suku*. The fertility-takers arrived at Faulara the day before the celebration, staying overnight at some of their relatives' houses. After lunch, the fertility-givers started to get ready to receive them. The household's front garden was crowded with people, many of them neighbours. The people who played the central role in the fertility-giver group are shown in Figure 5.4.

The fertility-givers' representatives (*lia-na'in*) for the ceremony were José Larreto, *Siñor* (Mister/Mr) Antonio, *Siñor* Lorenço da Silva and *Siñor* Domingos (12, 14, 15, and 17). Although two of them were not members of the descent group (*uma lisan*), they were asked to act as their representatives because the men of the house

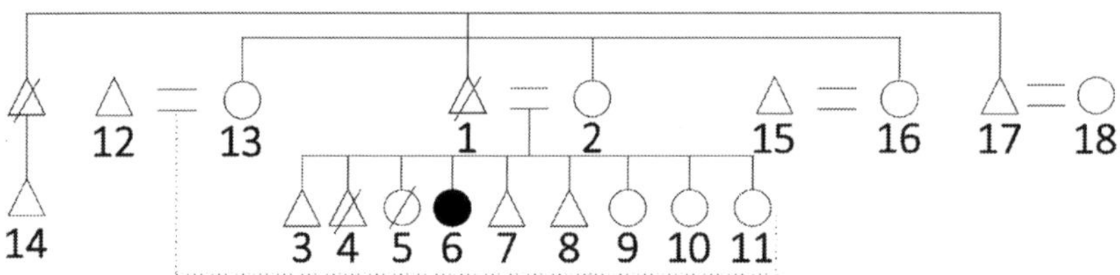

1. Julião Tinto (F)
2. Mariana de Moisés (M)
3. Juanito de Moisés Tinto (eB)
4. Pepito de Moisés Tinto (eB)
5. Benedita de Moisés Tinto (eZ)
6. Leomar de Moisés Tinto (EGO)
7. Josito de Moisés Tinto (yB)
8. Alsino de Moisés Tinto (yB)
9. Rigoberta de Moisés Tinto (yZ)
10. Folga de Moisés Tinto (yZ)
11. Juliana dos Santos (yZ)
12. José Larreto (MeZH)
13. Berta dos Santos (MeZ)
14. Sr Antonio (FeBS)
15. Sr Lorenço da Silva (MyZH)
16. Sra Amelia dos Santos (MeZ)
17. Sr Domingos (FyB)
18. Sra Teresinha (FyBW)

Figure 5.4: Family tree of the fertility-givers' group (*ego* is 6). Credit: Alberto Fidalgo-Castro and Enrique Alonso-Población.

were considered to be too young (*labarik*) to carry out that task. Apart from the people consigned in the diagram, the godparents and the chief of the village and his spouse had important roles during the celebration of the ritual.

The fertility-takers arrived at 6.00 pm. After greeting each other in ritual language, they were received with refreshments in the front garden. After this, the *lia-na'in* of the fertility-taker's group went into a room inside the main house prepared for bridewealth negotiations where they met the representatives of the fertility-givers. There they asked for the blessing of the ancestors from both houses to keep the ceremony going (*hasé matebian*). The fertility-takers handed over US$190, two bottles of *tuak* (wine/liqueur) and a goat—a gift reciprocated with one *tais* and a pig by the fertility-givers. Right after exchanging gifts, the fertility-givers informed the fertility-takers that it was time for them to have a break for dinner. This first contact between both groups was called *tuku odamatan* (knock on the door). Neither the groom nor the bride took part in this first meeting.

Once this first stage of the negotiations was complete, the bride went outside, dressed in a bridal gown, to receive her future in-laws. She offered them betel and areca (*bua-malus*) and kissed their hands (*hola bensa*) as a sign of respect. Then the couple went back inside and paid their respects to the bride's family in a similar fashion. Shortly afterwards, the fertility-givers served dinner, consisting of a banquet of food (rice, pork, noodles, salad and fries) and drinks (beer, soft drinks and bottled water). The next stage of the ceremony was the *kaben* (marriage). Lorenço da Silva acted as the master of ceremonies and some Catholic prayers were offered. After cutting the wedding cake, the groom gave the bride a necklace and they performed the first dance.

Dancing continued until dawn and, while most people took part (particularly the young ones), the representatives of the houses and other adults completed the bridewealth negotiations (which they called *biti ho mama*).[11] The *lia-na'in* of the fertility-givers called the fertility-takers back into the house to present the *bee-manas ai-tukan* (one of the parts of the bridewealth payments). Although they had previously agreed upon an amount of $US500, the fertility-takers presented only $US430, along with betel and areca, some sticks of goat meat, a metal breast plate (*belak*) and one Mexican coin (*pataka*).[12] The fertility-givers rejected these offerings, so the fertility-takers added an *ulsuku* (hairpin made with a Dutch coin). The *lia-na'in* asked Mariana to bring the liver of the pig that had been sacrificed at the beginning of the ceremony; divining its signs (*halo urat*) settled the negotiations.

Once the negotiations were over, both groups wrote a document in which they registered two new deferred bride wealth payments that should be provided before the end of 2011. In the first, the fertility-takers agreed to pay $US250, one metal breast plate (*belak*), one goat and eight bottles of wine/liqueur.[13] In the second, which they considered to be the *barlake* (bridewealth) narrowly speaking, the fertility-takers agreed to provide $US2,500, five goats, one buffalo or cow and 40 bottles of wine/liquor.[14] After writing the document, two of the *lia-na'in* from each group signed it and the fertility-takers were asked to give a dollar as a token representing their commitment to fulfilling it. This marked the end of the negotiations, after which people scattered to rest or continued to party until dawn.

Following breakfast, which was served at around 7.00 am, some participants expressed the intention to leave. Mariana then called a number of people into the house and began redistributing the gifts presented by the fertility-takers. This redistribution was registered, as shown in Table 5.2.

Table 5.2. Redistribution of ritual gains

Person	**Receives**
Marriage godmother	$150
Baptism godmother	$40
Mariana	$100 + 1 *belak* (metal breast plate)
Juanito	$14
Josito	$30
José Larreto	1 *pataka* (Mexican coin)
Berta dos Santos	$50
Antonio	$20 + 1 *belak* (metal breast plate)
Lorenço da Silva	$40
Domingos	$20
Teresinha	1 *ulsuku* (hairpin)
Hamlet chief	$10
Hamlet chief's wife	$20
TOTAL	$494, two *metal breast plates*, one Mexican coin and one hairpin

The redistribution of money and goods was explained as a means of compensating people for their fatigue (*kolen*)—either for their services during the ceremony or because they had helped to raise Leomar.[15] In the case of the hamlet chief (*xefe de aldeia*), this fatigue was conceptualised as governance (*kolen tanba Ita-nia oan feto nia mak ukun*). The rest of the money the household received was redistributed among neighbours and other family members in varying amounts ($10, $5 and $1). This was because of the belief that 'nobody can leave empty handed' (*labele bá ho liman-mamuk*).

Following the exchange of goods – Part 2: La'o mane-foun—walking the path of the fertility-taker

Hamanas kafé – 'Heating the coffee': Problems retrieving the deferred bridewealth
In September 2010 the household was getting ready to attend another marriage. Juanito was going to marry a woman from a neighbouring *suku* in Ermera.[16] He and his bride had already been living together for some months both at his and her families' houses, moving back and forth to help with farming work. The two houses had agreed upon a total bridewealth of US$4,500, and the fertility-givers would allow the couple to establish their residence patrilocally after the 'clearing the path' (*lere dalan*) ceremony. For that ceremony, the household would have to meet the economic requirements of US$500 and a cow.

With the intention of gaining economic support from their familial neighbours (*maun-alin vijiño*) and their fertility-takers (*mane-foun*), the household organised a ritual of cooperation called *hamanas kafé*. They sent a messenger (*manu-ain*) to notify the fertility-takers about the economic requirements. The ceremony took place in October 2010 during the rainy season (*tempu udan*), which is considered to be 'the time of scarcity'. The household's expenditure consisted of a pig (raised by themselves) and US$20 to buy beer, soft drinks and some bottles of palm wine.[17]

When the ceremony started, the people arriving entered a small room in the house where the *lia-na'in* received their contributions. The people who acted as *lia-na'in* were an elder brother of Julião—who could not be a part of the ceremony the year before—and Lorenço da Silva (see Figure 5.4). Josito recorded the contributions in a notebook. The contributions made by the familial neighbours are shown in Table 5.3.

Table 5.3. Neighbours' contributions

Name	Contribution	Note	Name	Contribution	Note
1. Avelina da Costa	$10		22. Jorge Pereira Pinto	$10	
2. Armando Alvis	$5		23. Olandino da Costa	$5	
3. Raimundo Serrão	$5		24. Julião Martins	$5	
4. Umberto da Costa	$5		25. Sezario Alberto	$8	
5. Albino Manekas	$5		26. Tomas Pereira	$9	

Name	Contribution	Note	Name	Contribution	Note
6. Domingos da Costa	$5		27. Valentin da Silva Martins	$10	*Tasak* US$4 *Matak* US$5
7. Antonio Alves	$5		28. Calistro José Marçal	$5	*Tasak*
8. Sonsitançio da Silva	$5		29. Martinho Sampaio	$5	
9. Domingos Babo	$10		30. Alcina da Silva	$5	
10. Moisés	$20		31. Julio Soares	$5	
11. Duarte da Silva	$5		32. Carlos Nunes Correia	$5	
12. Gilberto Pereira	$5		33. Manuel José Manus Marçal	$5	
13. Joanico Aniceto	$10	*Tasak*	34. Alberto Fidalgo	$10	
14. Saturnino da Silva	1 metal breast plate (*belak*)		35. Egido da Costa	$10	
15. Martinho da Costa	$10		36. Agostino Marçal	$5	
16. Francisco da Silva	$5		37. Nelson da Costa	$10	
17. Victor Berrão	$4		38. Gaspar de Jesus	$5	
18. Alberto da Silva	$5		39. Angelino dos Santos	$10	
19. Andino Pereira	$5		40. Loreça da Silva	$5	
20. Manuel Barros	$5		41. Rafael da Silva	$5	
21. Napolião da Silva	$5		42. Julito Alves Ataide	$10	
TOTAL			$281 and one *belak*		

The contributions made by the fertility-takers were recorded separately from those made by familial neighbours. Even though they were informed by the household of the amount of money and goods to bring to the ceremony, they were not able to comply. That day, they brought a small part of the goods and money demanded by the household, and committed to bringing the rest in the dry season (*bailoron*).

Of all the negotiations with the fertility-takers, that with house Betrema took the longest to settle. House Betrema was establishing a second fertility-taking relationship with the household, and the other *mane-foun* were the original ones of the house—the ones that established marriage alliances with them in the 'age of the ancestors'.[18] Consequently, Betrema would carry a heavier burden, as they were asked to present the payment of the *bagi* (see footnote 120), as agreed upon in a document they signed in 2009.

When it was time to make his offering, the spokesman for house Betrema—in this case Leomar's husband—presented US$25, a goat and four bottles of palm wine (*tua*). The *lia-na'in* refused Betrema's offering and mentioned that they had been instructed to bring US$250, a goat and four bottles of palm wine. Leomar's husband replied that the messenger (*manu-ain*) had informed them that they had to deliver *dua puluh dollar* (Indonesian: twenty-five dollars). However, the messenger confirmed that he had asked them to bring *duaratus lima puluh dollar* (Indonesian: two hundred and fifty dollars). One of the *lia-na'in* commented that the fertility-takers may have thought the figure was in rupees, not dollars, since it was not uncommon for some people to refer to ten cents (around 1,000 Indonesian rupees) as *seribu dollar* (1,000 dollars). This comment served to relieve tensions and caused much hilarity among the *mane-foun* and the *umane*.

However, the *lia-na'in* of the house reiterated that they still had to deliver the US$250. The fertility-takers' spokesperson explained that the economic situation of the people on the mountain (*foho*) was very complicated at that time; had they performed the ceremony two months earlier (when the economic returns from the coffee harvest came in), it would have been less difficult to make their contribution. The response of the givers was sharp: when an *umane* calls their *mane-foun* to give what was agreed upon, they have to comply with it whether they are prepared or not. The *umane* repeated that the amount was immovable and warned about the dangers of not delivering what was fixed and, therefore, being 'rejected by the fertility-givers' (*umane la simu*): "*Bele akontese azar oin-oin, ita bele halai soke kareta, dala ruma trabaun la di'ak*" ('Anything can happen, there may be a car accident, the brakes may not work').

The fertility-takers' spokesperson maintained long periods of silence, but did not leave. After a while, he pointed out that the pig the fertility-givers had gifted them the year before at the marriage ceremony had died on the way back to his house, suggesting that they had been given an animal in poor condition. The *umane* replied that it was true that the pig issue was something to talk about, but not on that occasion, since, in his words: "*Buat ne'e iha nia dalan. Ida ohin dalan ida, fahi nian ketak fali*" ('This has its own path. Today is a path, the pig is another'). However, the *umane* immediately proposed a new contribution different from the one originally stipulated: the *mane-foun* could donate US$200 and one cow instead of US$250 and one goat. The fertility-takers' spokesperson did not accept this. A long pause followed during which there was no conversation between the two groups; the silence was only interrupted by the *lia-na'in* of the fertility-giving group who made funny comments and jokes.

After a while, one of the *lia-na'in* asked for a bottle of *anggur merah* (Indonesian: red wine). He opened it and offered its contents to some of those present; he then invited people who were outside the house to come inside and drink a glass. But he did not invite the *mane-foun* to drink. Two hours after the negotiations had started, lunch was called. The representatives of the two lineages were served separately in the place where they were negotiating. Leomar's husband refused to eat, but the *umane* told him that he should not be concerned about breaking any taboo when eating, because the meat was not *lulik*, it was conceptualised as breakfast (*matabixu*).[19] After much convincing, he agreed to eat.

The negotiation continued well into the night. The next morning the lead author returned to the house to ask how it had been resolved; he was told that the parties had agreed to an up-front contribution of US$50, one goat and four bottles of wine and a deferred contribution, in the dry season, of an additional US$150.

Table 5.4: Fertility-takers' contributions

Group name	Contribution (US$)	Deferred contribution (US$)	Goat	Belak	Wine/ liquor
Talibela	10	40	-	-	-
Craeleki Bercoli	5	45	-	-	2
Mau-Meta	5	45	-	1	1
Betrema	50	150	1	-	4
TOTAL	70	280	1	1	7

At the end of the *hamanas kafé*, the domestic unit had gathered a total of US$350 (US$280 from neighbours and friends and US$70 from the fertility-takers), a goat, two metal breast plates (*belak*) and seven bottles of wine/liquor (*tua*). Apart from the expenditure of the goods needed to hold the *hamanas kafé*, the rest of the earnings would be used to present their own offerings for Juanito's *lere dalan*.

Lere dalan: 'Clearing the path': Problems in the accords for the bridewealth payments

One and a half months after the celebration of the *hamanas kafé,* a *lere dalan* (one of the different stages of the marriage, the *barlake*) took place. In that ritual, the people of the domestic unit delivered part of the bridewealth payments they still owed to their own fertility-giver. Mariana sent her son Alsino (see Figure 5.4) to buy a male goat (*bibi aman boot*) from a neighbour, which was going to be handed over in the ritual, since they could not afford a cow, which was what their fertility-givers had stipulated. Not reaching an agreement on the price, the family went to another neighbour to buy a goat on credit. At around four in the afternoon, once everything was ready, we left to go to the house of the fertility-givers, arriving there an hour and a half later.

After asking the fertility-givers for permission to enter, the goat was presented. We were then taken to a house to wait to be called by the *lia-na'in* to begin the ceremony. The initial process that followed was similar to that of the marriage ceremony accounted above. While we waited, two women from the giver group presented us with offerings of betel, areca and tobacco, following the local etiquette. Later on, the woman who was going to marry Juanito, the *feto-foun* (new woman), presented herself to her future in-laws and expressed her respect by kissing each member's hand (*hola bensa*). After this, the first ceremonial exchange took place, in which the *lia-na'in* of both groups carried out the *hasé matebian* (ask permission from the ancestors), presenting the fertility-givers US$50, a bottle of palm wine, betel and areca, which was reciprocated in exchange for a *tais* from the fertility-giver.

After the exchange, we were taken to a space where a snack consisting of pastries, coffee, soft drinks and palm wine was served. Before feasting, some Catholic prayers were conducted and the bride and groom cut the wedding cake and started the dance, which lasted all night.

Later on, the fertility-takers' group was called to attend the *biti ho mama* (the mat and chewing of betel and areca), to which they had to present part of the bridewealth. They presented US$500, a metal breast plate, two bottles of palm wine, betel and areca. The fertility-givers did not accept (*la simu*) the offering, as it had been agreed that a cow (*karau*) and not a goat (*bibi*) should be the item offered. This led to a negotiation of more than an hour; eventually, the fertility-giver agreed to accept the goat if US$50 was added to the total. After this, the fertility-takers were ordered to leave the room where the *lia-na'in* were gathered and were told that they would only be allowed to return when they presented the additional US$50.

Mariana got angry and commented '*umane ne'e explora ita*' ('these fertility-givers take advantage of us'). Nonetheless, they made a new collection from among the family and neighbours who had accompanied them to the ritual—more than 30 people—obtaining the amount asked by their fertility-givers (see Table 5.5).

Table 5.5 Collection made during the negotiation of the bridewealth in Ermera

Name	US$
1. Alberto Fidalgo	10
2. Mãe Meri	5
3. M. Izak	1
4. B [unreadable]	2
5. T. Delfina	2
6. Ama Ensa	4
7. Amatoni	1
8. Azinha	1
9. Ama Teza	2
10. Elvis	1
11. Nona Britis	1
12. T. Dulce	2
13. T. Zito	1
14. T. Samu	1
15. T. Rozita	2
16. Sonistancio	1
17. Pai Joy	5
18. M Maku	2
19. Kera Bel	1
20. Tio Mario	5
TOTAL	50

When the *umane* agreed upon the offerings of the *lere dalan*, the fertility-takers group retired again and was served dinner. Subsequently, a new meeting was held to determine a future date on which the *mane-foun* should deliver the offerings related to the *bee-manas ai-tukan* of the bride. Those negotiations lasted nearly two hours. The fertility-givers intended to set a specific day in August the following year when the fertility-takers would bring the stipulated items for the payment of the bridewealth. However, the fertility-takers refused to agree, arguing that it was impossible to foresee possible shortcomings in the harvest that might prevent them from fulfilling the agreement and, thus, creating a problem between the two houses.

This negotiation was carried out in metaphorical terms in which the delivery of this part of the bride exchange was expressed as the delivery of *isin ho been*.[20] Once the *umane* showed their intention to establish a specific day in August for the payment, and the *lia-na'in* of the *mane-foun* group expressed doubts about their ability to meet that deadline, there was a long period of silence in which the negotiation was halted. Then Mariana intervened, arguing that the fertility-takers were willing to make Juanito reside matrilocally (with the *umane*), working for the family of the bride (bride service) while the payments were not made, and that the fertility-givers had agreed to postpone these negotiations until a year after the celebration of the marriage. Her intervention was answered almost instantly by the elder woman (*ferik*) of the fertility-givers' group, who said: "we won't accept the offerings of the *isin* and the *been* if it takes too long". This warning implied that the failure to comply with the payments of this stage of the *barlake* could have unforeseen and dangerous consequences for the fertility-takers.

This crossing of statements raised tensions that were finally eased by the comical remarks of a *lia-na'in* of the *umane* group. Once the hilarity ceased, the negotiations resumed. Berta dos Santos (Mariana's eZ) intervened, saying that it was irresponsible for the fertility-takers' group to agree on a specific amount with a deadline. They could not anticipate the economic results of the harvest and the production of palm wine (*isin ho been*) and if they arrived in August without the agreed payment, they would be accused of being liars. She proposed to meet again in August and to defer negotiations until then. Her proposal was widely debated for more than an hour by the *lia-na'in* of both groups, who finally agreed that they would meet in August, and would not specify what items had to be delivered on that date. The *ibun ho nanal* (mouth and tongue, spokesperson) of the fertility-givers stated:

La fuik, la leet, mesak umane-mane-foun kedas.
Atu to'o la to'o, aban-bainrua nia sei to'o iha ne'e.
Atu isin la isin, aban-bainrua nia sei isin iha ne'e.
Atu been la been, aban-bainrua nia sei been iha ne'e.
To'o isin ona, isin
Been bá mak been.

Neither savages nor strangers, we are already *umane-manefoun*.
Whether it will be enough or not, tomorrow he will come here.
Whether or not there will be a body, tomorrow he will come to bring it here.
Whether or not there will be juice, tomorrow he will come to bring it here.

When there is a body, there will be a body.
When the juice comes out, there will be juice.

This last intervention put an end to the negotiation. An agreement was reached to postpone the delivery of the *bee-manas ai-tukan* until August of the following year, (2011) at which time it would be stipulated what would be delivered.

In the morning, members of the fertility-takers' group began preparing to return to Faulara, accompanied by the woman whose marriage had been celebrated. The bride and groom dressed in traditional clothes (*tais*) and coral bead necklaces (*morteen*). Before leaving, the *mane-foun* met one last time with the *lia-na'in* of the fertility-givers and gave them US$5 which they referred to as *hiit umane nia ain* (raise the foot of the *umane*). After this, the women from the fertility-takers gave two offerings of US$5 (one for each of the hearth fires used) to the women of the donor group in the kitchen, as a recognition of their work cooking for the ceremony. In exchange, they received half a sack of rice and a *bornal* (backpack) with uncooked pork meat.

Following these last exchanges, the Faulara entourage set off towards the village. When they left the patio of the house, the women from the *umane* started a *halerik* (stylised wail), lamenting the departure of their daughter. Along the way to the river, people cheered for Juanito and for Faulara, calling out "Long live Juanito! Long live Faulara!" When we reached the riverbank, the bride and groom changed their ceremonial clothes so as not to spoil them. On the other side of the river, the entourage stopped at the mechanical gate for the irrigation channel to the rice fields. There, one of the entourages who belonged to the local elite of the village made a speech in which he congratulated Juanito and congratulated himself on Faulara winning (*manan*) a new woman and a new member of the community. This was followed by another round of cheers in honour of Juanito and Faulara, after which the march resumed and people began to disperse in the direction of their houses, bringing the ceremony to a close.

Discussion

Among anthropologists who have focused on the economic dimensions of the exchange regime in Timor-Leste, the work of Andrew McWilliam (2011) is key. He argues that, in the context of post-conflict Timor-Leste, the revitalisation of ritual activity among Fataluku communities is a strategy to mitigate economic uncertainty and reinforce human security following the collapse of the market economy that accompanied the end of the Indonesian occupation. His research emphasises the redistributive character of ritual exchange, a fundamental element that Traube

(1980b, 1980a, 1986) had previously analysed. Yet, 10 years after that economic collapse, and with Timor-Leste increasingly immersed in the market economy, rituals continue to have a strong presence.

We agree with McWilliam's depiction of ritual exchange as an institution that helps to mitigate economic uncertainty. As we have shown, rituals can sometimes involve expenses (especially when attending as fertility-takers), but can give profits too (when attending as fertility-givers). Also, when a household is facing contingent payments for their own ritual activities, they can mobilise neighbours, family members and fertility-takers to redistribute their economic burden (which will always need to be repaid). In this way, the ritual exchange regime as a whole can work as a credit system. In a context in which access to credit is otherwise limited to local moneylenders who impose exploitative clauses (Lundahl and Sjöholm 2019, 222), formal jobs are scarce and few state-sponsored support networks exist, ritual exchange can be seen as a primary practice of local economic life that can be utilised as an economic network and safety mechanism.

Boosted by foreign policy-oriented development agencies (Silva 2017), a discourse that conceptualises rituals as an economic burden has gained prominence. Elsewhere (Alonso-Población, Fidalgo-Castro, and Pena Castro 2018), we have interpreted this phenomenon as a tension between fields, understood as a social space of forces and struggles in Bourdieu's (1991) terms, derived from the interest of certain social groups (e.g., an aspiring consumer class [Alonso-Población, Pena Castro, and Fidalgo-Castro 2018]) in questioning, under certain discursive contexts, the very basis of power acquisition in contemporary Timor-Leste.

Moving to a more grounded discourse, this case study shows that rituals can be both an economic burden—especially when attending them as fertility-takers (e.g., when the household attended a *lere dalan*)—and a profitable venture—when attending as fertility-givers or even as holders of a ritual, as Traube (1986, 204-220) has pointed out. Further, we show that the fulfilment of ritual obligations depends largely upon webs of solidarity that go beyond networks, making household economies strongly reliant on their relationships with neighbours and friends.

We described two sets of rituals performed in 2009 and 2010. In the first set, a domestic unit held a ritual in which one of their female members got married. That ritual established (or renewed) the fertility-giver/fertility-taker relationship between two houses. Once the marriage was consolidated, the household then prepared for the marriage of one of its male members, which we tracked through two ritual moments (October 2010 and December 2010). The first was a cooperation ritual called *hamanas kafé*—a specific type of *halibur maun-alin*—that the domestic unit celebrated with the aim of gathering resources from neighbours, friends and fertility-takers in order to meet the costs of paying for part of the bridewealth of one of its male members. The second ritual was about the marriage event itself; the household travelled to the fertility-givers' house to deliver the *lere dalan* and agree upon future payments of the *barlake*. We suggest that facilitating the marriage of a female member of the house first is a strategy that is used to gain capital (mobilisation of resources and people) and leverage in future negotiations over bridewealth payments for male members' marriages.

By taking a household as the unit of analysis, and by lengthening the time span under consideration, we have been able to widen our view of particular rituals within a gift regime of exchange. The selected household was not a rich landowner household, but a *la'o rai* or newcomer house (Alonso-Población and Fidalgo-Castro 2014) with no property rights in rice producing areas. During the period under review, this household benefitted from their position as fertility-givers and carried the economic burden of being the fertility-takers. By making the strategic decision to marry the woman first, they were able to mobilise the postponed payments of their fertility-takers to pay their *barlake* obligations. Along with everyday economic collaboration with other houses, especially with neighbours, through cooperation rituals, this helped them to cope with their own *barlake* payments. In this way, ritual exchange can be seen less as a 'burden' and more as a savings fund subject to the fluctuations of the life cycle of different houses and households.

Through our analysis of the redistribution of ritual gains and losses, we have shown how, far from simply enriching or impoverishing households, the ritual exchange regime connects people through family and neighbourhood relations (among others), creating a complex, nuanced and wide support web. Unlike previous anthropological works, which have tended to focus on the economics of rituals that engage people through kinship, we have shown, through our focus on what we call 'rituals of cooperation', how relationships of neighbourhood and friendship are essential for social reproduction. This required a methodological approach that did not isolate kinship rituals as discrete units of analysis.

Conceptualisations of the exchange regime as a 'burden' derive mostly from discursive analyses that lead to reductionist understandings of the phenomenon. These not only remove from sight the nuanced complexities and flexibility involved in ritual negotiations (e.g., taking into account the time of the year and the outcomes of the agricultural activity, historical debts between house groups, the patrilocality-matrilocality interplay, etc.) but also neglect the very sources of income that enable the continuous flow of goods and the prevalence of exchange regimes in new contexts (e.g., a market economy).

Conclusion

Several studies have depicted the revitalisation of tradition in Timor-Leste as a mechanism to cope with social and historical change. In present day Timor-Leste, in a context in which access to credit is regulated by exploitative clauses when borrowing from local moneylenders (something that may produce chain debts and thus dependency), opportunities for formal employment are limited and there are few support networks from the state or supra-local entities, ritual practices can be seen as a primary practice of local economic life, as they can function as an economic network and safety mechanism. In this paper, we have shown how, when a household needs to observe their ritual obligations with their fertility-givers, or face some contingency, they can mobilise neighbours and agnatic kin through cooperation rituals, redistributing the burden they are facing. We have also shown how ritual gains are shared back to them. Taking a broader perspective of the economy linked to ritual practice, and avoiding an approach that considers kinship-related rituals as discrete units of analysis, we have been able to tease out some of the hitherto unseen ways in which the ritual exchange regime shapes sociality. In sum, we contend that, from this broader perspective, ritual life can be interpreted as a mechanism that provides a social safety net, ultimately shaping the way the market economy functions and is displayed.

Notes

1 Among the first challenges faced, the selection of words to refer broadly to 'ritual' was crucial. We decided to use the Portuguese-loaned *serimónia* instead of *halo-lia* or *halo-lulik*, among others, as that would narrow the responses. We found that *serimónia* was the word that referred to a wider range of rituals. However, this caused some rituals to remain outside the responses of the participants. Specifically, those related to the annual cycles of the Catholic religion (All Saints' Day—*Loron matebian*) and agricultural-related rituals (*sau-batar*, *nahe-biti*, etc.).

2 For the complete list of items recorded under questions two and three, see Fidalgo-Castro (2015, 230).

3 For the complete questionnaire, see Fidalgo-Castro (2015, 443).

4 The hamlet chief keeps the *livro de aldeia* up to date, registering all the domestic units and people living there.

5 All the names of people have been modified to protect their true identity.

6 During the first years of the invasion and until 1985, the year in which the "pacification campaigns" ended, forced population movements to areas controlled by the Indonesian military were common. The Liquiçá district was "pacified" around 1979.

7 That year they obtained eight sacks of unhusked rice (50 kg each) through one of these arrangements.

8 In Faulara, cassava can be harvested six months after planting. From that year's harvest they got five sacks (35 kg each) of husked corn.
9 The weekly gross profit of this activity was variable but, according to Mariana, it ranged between $7 and $8.
10 During the time the fieldwork was carried out, there was a plan called *serbisu dólar tolu* (three dollar work), promoted by the government and several aid agencies. It was used as a way to create jobs through engaging people in maintenance activities both on the roads and in the irrigation canals for the rice fields.
11 Sitting down on a mat (*biti*) while chewing betel leaves and areca nuts was understood as a metonym of the negotiation.
12 In previous private negotiations that took place a week before the ceremony.
13 This payment was registered under the name of *bagi* in Tokodede, *banin* in Tetum. It was made in honour of Mariana's FZ, which was the woman that 'opened the path'—that is, the one that established the fertility-giver/fertility-taker relation between the two groups.
14 This payment was called *hine-heu* in Tokodede and *feto-foun* in Tetum, meaning 'new woman'.
15 In the case of women's fatigue, this was called 'breastfeeding' (*fó-susun*).
16 The case study was witnessed by Alberto Fidalgo-Castro during his fieldwork. For that reason, in part of the texts, we decided to keep the first-person in the description.
17 Contrary to the ceremony they held the year before, they didn't need to rent an electric generator, because the lead author lent them a small one of his own.
18 This reveals the recent commencement of marriages of choice, as the norm for some houses is to get married within the narrow range of houses with which the house has previous marriage alliances (from the time of the ancestors).
19 The notion of *lulik* meat refers here to meat that can only be consumed by the fertility-givers (goat meat) or fertility-takers (pork) once the ritual exchange has been successfully completed.
20 This expression refers to two productive activities from which the items delivered at the bridewealth were obtained. *Isin* means 'body', both referring to living animals and people as well as crops (in the case of corn, e.g., the cob is called *batar-isin*). In the case of *been*, it refers to the activity of producing palm wine (*ko'a tua*, cutting *tua*), in which *been* (liquid) is consumed.

References

Alonso-Población, E. and A. Fidalgo-Castro. 2014. "Webs of legitimacy and discredit: Narrative capital and politics of ritual in a Timor-Leste community." *Anthropological Forum* 24 (3): 245-266. doi.org/10.1080/00664677.2014.948381.

Alonso-Población, E., A. Fidalgo-Castro, and M. J. Pena-Castro. 2018. "Bargaining kultura: Tensions between principles of power acquisition in contemporary Timor-Leste." *Sociologus* 68 (2): 107-124. doi.org/10.3790/soc.68.2.107.

Alonso-Población, E., M. J. Pena-Castro, and A. Fidalgo-Castro. 2018. "Cambio Social y Cultura: clase, poder y tradición en Timor Oriental'. *Revista Latina de Sociología* 6 (2): 72-84. doi.org/10.17979/relaso.2018.8.2.3352.

Alonso-Población, E., P. Rodrigues, C. Wilson, M. Pereira and R. U. Lee. 2018. "Narrative assemblages for power-balanced coastal and marine governance: Tara bandu as a tool for community-based fisheries co-management in Timor-Leste." *Maritime Studies* 17 (1): 55-67. doi.org/10.1007/s40152-018-0093-9.

Babo-Soares, D. 2004. "*Nahe Biti*: The philosophy and process of grassroots reconciliation (and justice) in East Timor." *The Asia Pacific Journal of Anthropology* 5 (1): 15-33. doi.org/10.1080/144422104200 0201715.

Bourdieu, P. 1991. *El Sentido Práctico*. Madrid: Taurus.

Bovensiepen, J. 2014. "Paying for the dead: On the politics of death in independent Timor-Leste." *The Asia Pacific Journal of Anthropology* 15 (2): 103-122. doi.org/10.1080/14442213.2014.892528.

Bovensiepen, J. 2015. *The Land of Gold. Post-Conflict Recovery and Cultural Revival in Independent Timor-Leste*. Ithaca, New York: Cornell University Press. doi.org/10.7591/9781501725920.

Brandao, C. da C. C. X. E. 2011. "Culture and its impact on social and community life: A case study of Timor-Leste." *Policy Brief* (5). Dili: Belun.

Fidalgo-Castro, A. 2015. "Dinámicas políticas y económicas en el dominio ritual y la vida cotidiana en Timor Oriental. Estudios de caso desde la *aldeia* de Faulara." PhD. diss., Universidade da Coruña.

Forman, S. 1981. "Life paradigms: Makassae (East Timor) views on production, reproductions, and exchange." *Research in Economic Anthropology: An Annual Compilation of Research* 4: 95-110.

Friedberg, C. 1989. "Social relations of territorial management in light of Bunaq farming rituals." *Bijdragen Tot de Taal-, Land- En Volkenkunde* 145 (1989): 548-563. doi.org/10.1163/22134379-90003246.

Gibson, K, R. Astuti, M. Carnegie, A. Chalernphon, K. Dombroski, A. R. Haryani, A. Hill, B. Kehi, L. Law, I. Lyne, A. McGregor, K. McKinnon, A. McWilliam, F. Miller, C. Ngin, D. Occeña-Gutierrez, L. Palmer, P. Placino, M. Rampengan, W. L. L. Than, N. I. Wianti, and S. Wright. 2018. "Community economies in Monsoon Asia: Keywords and key reflections." *Asia Pacific Viewpoint* 59 (1): 3-16. doi.org/10.1111/apv.12186.

Hicks, D. 1984. *A Maternal Religion: The Role of Women in Tetum Myth and Ritual*. Detroit: Center for Southeast Asian Studies, Northern Illinois University.

Hicks, D. 2010. "The barlaque of Timor-Leste." In *Translation, Society and Politic in Timor-Leste*, edited by P. C. Seixas, 115-36. Porto: Universidade Fernando Pessoa.

Lundahl, M. and F. Sjöholm. 2019. *The Creation of the East Timorese Economy. Volume 2: Birth of a Nation*. Cham, Switzerland: Palgrave Macmillan. doi.org/10.1007/978-3-030-22052-5.

McWilliam, A. 2011. "Exchange and resilience in Timor-Leste." *Journal of the Royal Anthropological Institute, New Series* 17: 745-763. doi.org/10.1111/j.1467-9655.2011.01717.x.

Palmer, L. 2010. "Enlivening development: Water management in post-conflict Baucau City, Timor-Leste." *Singapore Journal of Tropical Geography* 31 (3): 357-370. doi.org/10.1111/j.1467-9493.2010.00404.x.

Palmer, L. 2011. "Water Relations: Customary Systems and the Management of Baucau City's Water." In *Land and Life in Timor-Leste: Ethnographic Essays*, edited by A. McWilliam, and E. G. Traube, 141-162. Canberra: ANU Press.

Palmer, L. 2015. *Water Politics and Spiritual Ecology: Custom, Environmental Governance and Development*. New York: Routledge.

Palmer, L., and D. A. de Carvalho. 2008. "Nation building and resource management: The politics of "nature" in Timor-Leste." *Geoforum* 39 (3): 1321-1332. doi.org/10.1016/j.geoforum.2007.09.007.

Silva, K. 2018. "Marriage prestations, gift making, and identity in urban East Timor." *Oceania* 88 (1): 127-147. doi.org/10.1002/ocea.5185.

Silva, K. 2017. "Managing Resources, Persons and Rituals: Economic Pedagogy as Government Tactics." In *Transformations in Independent Timor-Leste: Dynamics of Social and Cultural Cohabitations*, edited by S. M. Viegas and R. G. Feijó, 193-209. New York: Routledge. doi.org/10.4324/9781315535012-11.

Silva, K., and D. S. Simião. 2012. "Coping with 'traditions': The analysis of East-Timorese nation building from the perspective of a certain anthropology made in Brazil." *Vibrant* 9 (1): 360-381. doi.org/10.1590/S1809-43412012000100013.

Silva, R. N. da. 2019. "Tanbasá sa'e foho? Reprodução e transformação da vida social das casas sagradas no Timor-Leste pós-Colonial." PhD diss., Universidade de Brasília.

Simião, D. S. 2017. "Conflict Resolution and the Making of Personhood in Lisadila, Maubara." In *Transformations in Independent Timor-Leste: Dynamics of Social and Cultural Cohabitations*, edited by S. M. Viegas and R. G. Feijó, 246-258. New York: Routledge. doi.org/10.4324/9781315535012-14.

Thu, P. M., S. Scott, and K. P. van Niel. 2007. "Gendered access to customary land in East Timor'. *Geo-Journal* 69: 239-255. doi.org/10.1007/s10708-007-9094-8.

Traube, E. G. 1980a. "Affines and the dead: Mambai rituals of alliance." *Bijdragen Tot de Taal-, Land- En Volkenkunde* 136 (1): 90-115. doi.org/10.1163/22134379-90003539.

Traube, E. G. 1980b. "Mambai Rituals of Black and White." In *The Flow of Life: Essays on Eastern Indonesia*, edited by J. J. Fox, 290-314. Cambridge, MA: Harvard University Press. doi.org/10.4159/harvard.9780674331907.c15.

Traube, E. G. 1986. *Cosmology and Social Life: Ritual Exchange among the Mambai of East Timor*. Illinois: University of Chicago Press.

Trindade, J. 2008. "Reconciling Conflicting Paradigms: An East Timorese Vision of the Ideal State." In *Democratic Governance in Timor-Leste: Reconciling the Local and the National*, edited by D. Mearns, 160-188. Darwin: Charles Darwin University Press.

Trindade, J. 2014. "Réconcilier Les Paradigmes Conflictuels: Une Version Est-Timoraise d'un État Idéal". In *Timor-Leste contemporain. L'Émergence d'une nation*, edited by B. de A. e Corte-Real, C. Cabasset and F. Durand, 143-156. Bangkok: Irasec & Les Indes saventes.

CHAPTER 6

Household decision-making processes and family resources: A case study from Viqueque

Josh Trindade and Ivete de Oliveira

Abstract

Drawing from a place-specific context, this chapter makes explicit a range of local, community and sacred house-based economic values and arrangements which contribute to household decision-making processes. Household (HH) decision making processes in Timor-Leste are an important component in designing the development approaches of government and civil society organisations. Understanding decision-making processes at the household level can enable development practitioners to better design their programs and improve the quality of life for households at the local level. This paper reports on research which has documented gender-based decision-making at household levels across one rural area of Timor-Leste. The primary data for this research was collected from the Municipality of Viqueque, covering 11 *suku* (villages) and four ethno-linguistic groups (Naueti, Makassae, Tetum Terik and Kairui). The research illustrates how rural households make decisions around food preparation, family food gardens (*to'os*) and rice farms (*natar*), livestock (water buffalo, Balinese cows, pigs, and chickens) and household finances.

Keywords: Timor-Leste; rural economy; household decision making

Household (HH) decision making processes in Timor-Leste are an important component in designing the development approaches of government and civil society organisations. Understanding decision-making processes at the household level can enable development practitioners to better design their programs and improve the quality of life for households at the local level. This paper reports on research which has documented gender-based decision-making at household levels across one rural area of Timor-Leste. The primary data for this research was collected from the Municipality of Viqueque, covering 11 *suku* (villages) and four ethno-linguistic groups (Naueti, Makassae, Tetum Terik, and Kairui). The research illustrates how rural households make decisions around food preparation, family food gardens (*to'os*) and rice farms (*natar*), livestock (water buffalo, Balinese cows, pigs, and chickens) and household finances. The data was collected between 2nd-14th of April 2018.

Studies on decision-making processes in Timor-Leste have been largely focused on the public domain (Ospina and Hohe 2001; Niner 2011). The objective of this study is to document and to understand how decisions are made at the household level in relation to family resources. That is, who decides where to farm, what kind of crops to grow, how to use livestock, and how the family money is spent. Drawing from a place-specific context, this chapter makes explicit a range of local, community and sacred house-based economic values and arrangements which contribute to household decision-making processes (see also Chapters 5, 7, and 8, this volume).

Methodology, variables and informants

The data in this study was collected through focus group discussions (FGD) and one-to-one interviews as well as informal discussions and observations. Interviewers used semi structured questions with gender and socio-cultural norms treated as crosscutting issues. The following variables were adopted to understand patterns of the decision-making household:

1. *Household food consumption and family nutrition.* The objectives were to understand patterns of daily food consumption, how daily menus are decided, and the consumption patterns of meals between household members.
2. *Family gardens (to'os) and rice paddies (natar)*: Questions in this section focused on understanding farming practices and the division of labour between men (husbands) and women (wives), decisions around field preparation, seed selection, weeding, harvesting, managing food post-harvest and the consumption of this food in the household.
3. *Livestock (water buffalo, Balinese cattle, pigs, chickens)*: The most commonly reported animals owned by households were water buffalo, Balinese cattle, pigs and chickens. These animals are considered the household's most important livestock resources. Questions explored the types of animals owned by the household, who kept and looked after which animal and decisions around the use of animals.
4. *Household finances:* These questions investigated sources of household cash income; who managed household cash and expenditure choices and decisions.

The total number of informants in the study was 77 (comprising 47 (61%) women and 30 (39%) men). Having a higher number of female informants was an advantage because rural Timorese women are often under-represented in research studies (see Chapter 8, this volume). The education level of the participants was divided into those who were literate (30 (39%)) and those who were illiterate (47 (61%)). Having a higher number of illiterate informants was an advantage for the study because responses from those with little formal education were heavily influenced by the primacy of the socio-cultural norms in the rural setting rather than external sources, namely schools and higher education institutions. For example, while some have reported that urban educated Timorese assume that most Timorese spend their household income on expenses relating to customary rituals and ceremonies (Guterres 2011), this study in Viqueque found otherwise. In this study the most literate participants had completed only a low to mid-level of education, with the majority attending primary school (81%) and a minority also attending junior high school (14%) and high school (5%).

The study included informants from four ethno-linguistic groups in the south-eastern municipality of Viqueque. These included Naueti (18 (23%)), Tetum Terik (27 (35%)), Kairui (10 (13%)) and Makassae (22 (29%)). These comprised 57 (74%) married participants, 5 (6%) widows and 5 (6%) widowers, 8 (11%) boys and 2 (3%) girls. The study was undertaken in 11 *suku* (villages) in four of Viqueque's five Administrative Posts. Two *suku* were in Uatolari (18 (23%)), six *suku* in Viqueque Vila (34 (48%)), two *suku* in Ossu (22 (29%)) and one *suku* in Lakluta (3 (4%)). The Administrative Post of Uatu Carabou was excluded from this study because the two languages (Naueti and Makassae) spoken in this area were covered in other *suku*.

Study findings

Definitions of family and household

The 'household' in this paper describes a physical structure and its usual occupants as a residential unit. A family is taken to be a group consisting of parents and their children living together as a unit. In most cases, many households in rural areas also comprised the elderly parents of either the husband or the wife. This was particularly pronounced as the younger children of the elderly couple were often living outside the village, working or studying in Dili or in other urban areas.

Linked to the idea of household in Timor-Leste is a household's membership of and alliances with other *uma lisan* (ancestral lineages) and associated *Uma Lulik* (sacred houses). To help understand decision making processes at the household level, we briefly discuss the socio-cultural norms linked to these *Uma Lulik* and the ways these are reflected in the meaning and use of public and private spaces in Timor-Leste. Despite their many regional variations, Timorese sacred houses (*Uma Lulik*) are always divided symbolically by a masculine (public) space and feminine (private) space. The feminine space is considered the womb (Hicks 1984), the inner space to nurture life. Meanwhile, the masculine space is considered to be the outer security for the womb. The feminine space occupies roughly 80% of an *Uma Lulik* interior and the masculine space consists of about 20%.

These spaces are not gender exclusive, men and women have access to both spaces. Likewise, the categories of masculine and feminine spaces in no way infers a separation between men and women, rather it is the case that "men and women operate in both" and that "masculine and feminine aspects exist in both sexes" (Trindade 2019, 46). The symbolic classification of the interior/private/feminine space and exterior/public/masculine space is significant in so far as it determines the kinds of activities that take place in these areas. For example, when discussing issues regarding members of a particular house, discussions are likely to take place inside the private spaces of the house. When negotiating relations with others, these interactions will take place in the exterior, public spaces of the house. Gender dynamics within and without these spaces are contingent on numerous intersecting factors including age, rank, degree of affiliation and personality. The social and spatial organisation of these lineages (*uma lisan*) and sacred houses (*Uma Lulik*) nevertheless plays an important role in shaping the organisation of households, especially concerning what is considered appropriate in public and private spaces.

The difference between public and private spaces in the Timor-Leste context

The concepts of private and public spaces in a Timorese context (in this case contextualised in the Viqueque district) is different to that contextualised in western (or global) terms. To analyse the decision-making process at the household level, one needs to understand how the idea of public and private spaces in Timor-Leste also links with cultural ideas bound up with the *Uma Lulik* and how these spaces influence each other and interact when it comes to decision making. There are numerous anthropological studies which have analysed the decision making process in public space in Timor-Leste. For example, Ospina and Hohe (2001, 140) note that, "the decision making process is the domain of the senior male of the existing social groups within the hamlets. Rural women are not supposed to be outspoken and take the floor in public meetings". Furthermore, Niner (2011, 417) has observed that, "in public or political decision-making processes senior men dominate, while women, particularly senior women, have symbolic and ritual power".

Studies like those cited above often lead people to believe that women are excluded from the decision-making process in both public and private spaces because decision-making is the domain of senior males in the hamlet. Secondly, studies on the decision-making process in Timor-Leste have focused heavily on public space while ignoring private space. More recent work on gender and power in Timor-Leste has begun to unpack these characterisations, highlighting the need to take into account questions of age, rank and affiliation (Silva 2017;

see also Chapter 8, this volume). This study finds that, as is often the case with complex ritual events in the *Uma Lulik*, in the private spaces at the household level, men and women have an equal if differently configured say in decision-making processes. Of further significance to this finding is the fact that in most cases any final decisions concluded in public space have already undergone background consultation processes involving both men and women in private spaces. Men have the responsibility to speak about, negotiate and/or convey the final agreement in public meetings. Because this joint male/female consultation process happens in the background and out of public view, there has been a tendency in the literature to conclude that it is only men who make these decisions.

Additionally, we note that one reason why women participate less in decision-making processes in public spaces is because this space has been incrementally colonised by an explicitly patriarchal religious (Catholic) and administrative (Portuguese) system for almost 500 years. As a result, women often feel insecure or unable to speak out in public spaces. Furthermore, when the Portuguese began to administer a census in 1960 (Weatherbee 1966) and register households and families, they usually registered these households under the name of the head of the household, which in most cases meant that the name of the father/husband was recorded. Hence, the unfolding process of colonisation has meant that the role of men has been emphasised and the role of women downplayed in these circumstances. Colonisation has weakened the status of women in Timorese society. In contrast, Niner (2011) describes how in pre-colonial times queens made decisions at the highest levels of society and were politically and diplomatically powerful.

Trindade (2017, 13) notes that, "most research focuses on analysing women's participation in political life and decision-making processes in the formal/public sphere, largely ignoring traditional or localized decision-making processes that occur informally". He further argues that, to comprehend the decision-making process in Timor-Leste, one should expand investigations into the ritual domain (including those that occur in the private spaces of the *Uma Lulik*) because a better understanding of this realm can be used to open the way for enhanced women's participation in the decision-making process in the public realm. This is because while women are actively involved in the decision-making process on informal matters such as traditional rituals and ceremonies, their participation is less obvious or visible in decision-making in the public sphere. As Trindade (2017) argues, even in the private sphere prior to a decision being made, there will be consultation processes occurring between men and women, although the final decision will usually be announced by a man. What is important in these cases is that it is a collective decision-making process. When social outsiders do not have access or understand these background consultation processes, they conclude that the men have made these decisions themselves without consulting women and other community members.

Depending on the situation, it is also difficult for social outsiders to differentiate between public and private spaces in Timor-Leste. This is because these spaces exist in the mind not in the actual space. Even when social outsiders meet with Timorese in literal private spaces, the status and presence of the outsider means that Timorese will respond as though they are in a public space. In this sense, they will only convey some information about decision-making processes and will likely withhold, or not mention, other information. Conversely when Timorese gather in public arenas, if they feel comfortable enough, then they may interact as though they are in a private space. In these situations, they will speak out more openly. Long-term processes of colonisation and foreign control in Timor-Leste has meant that people have often been persecuted for speaking the truth. This has made Timorese feel insecure in public spaces. For this reason, it is extremely important that research encounters take place in friendly and trusted environments. This will enable a better sharing and exchange of ideas and information.

It should also be noted that there are power imbalances between men and women in public space in certain situations. This is particularly the case when men feel they hold more power in comparison to women and this influences the dominance of men in decision-making processes in public space. While some may blame local cultural norms for the dominance of men in these instances, it is important to remember that during the periods of Portuguese and Indonesian colonisation, men had more opportunity to receive formal education than women. Women often did not feel secure to travel to school because of the distance from their home and for security reasons. Yet evidence suggests that, before Portuguese colonisation, Timorese society was more egalitarian. Portuguese archival research reveals that in the 17th century, around one quarter of all political leaders who signed official documents with the Portuguese colonial administration were women (Kammen 2012; Hägerdal and Kammen 2016). From the 18th century onwards, these female political leaders disappeared from the records. Oral evidence suggests that in the pre-colonial period the island of Timor was ruled by a pre-eminent female leader with the title of '*maromak oan*' (child of the creator). This female role was one of ritual leadership and had a higher value and more power than associated male political leadership (Therik 2004). However, women's involvement in public affairs lessened from the 19th century onwards, suggesting that the Portuguese colonial administration preferred to deal with men than women. This is a key reason why in Timor-Leste today we find fewer women active in decision-making processes in public space.

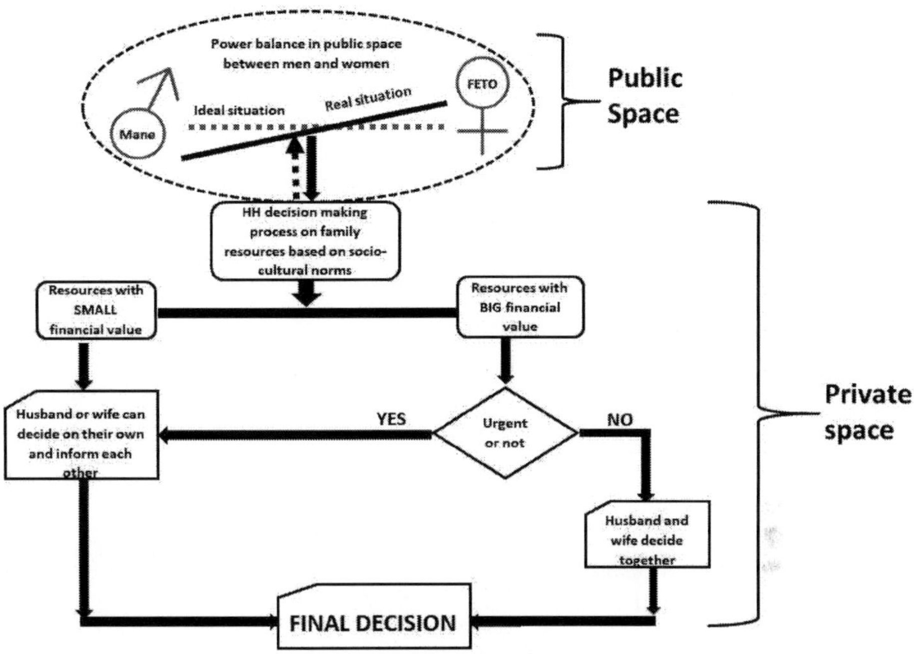

Figure 6.1: Schematic representation of decision making process at household level. The figure depicts the relative weighted power of males and females. Credit: Josh Trindade.

Decision-making processes at the household level in relation to family resources are sketched schematically above (see Figure 6.1). Oral culture in Timor-Leste does not define who should make decisions at household level in regard to resources.

From the diagram above, we can see that, for reasons discussed earlier in the paper, men have more power in public space in comparison to women, yet our findings suggest that women have an equally significant role to play in the private/less visible space of household decision-making.

To make decisions on household resources, husbands and wives must first weigh the economic value of the goods. If the goods have a 'smaller financial value', then either of them can make a decision and the other will be informed later. For items with a 'larger financial value', husbands and wives must make a joint decision to avoid household conflict. The exception to this is in urgent situations such as when children are sick or when there are educational expenses such as school fees.

Different factors influencing household decision-making

There are different factors that influence a household when making decisions about the deployment of resources (see Figure 6.2).

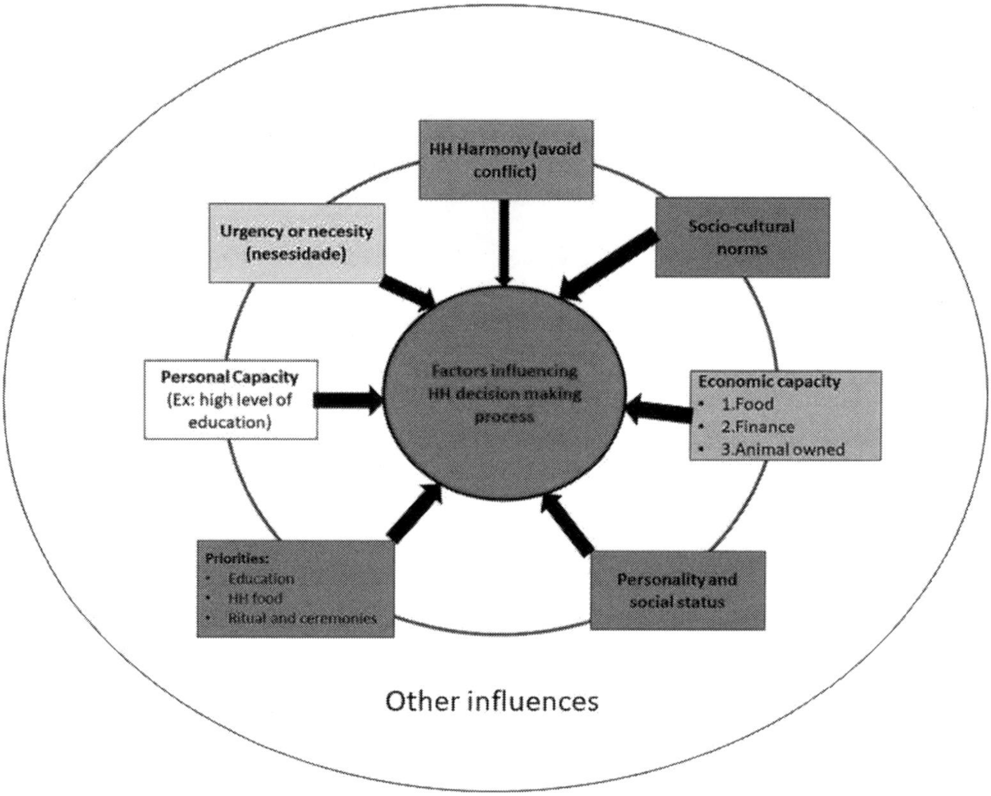

Figure 6.2: Factors influencing household (HH) decision making. Credit: Josh Trindade

- *HH Harmony:* to make a decision in a HH, all HH members should have a high regard for HH harmony. This means that every decision must take into account the interest of all HH members to prevent conflict. To secure this, HH members often undertake informal consultation between parents, children, and other HH members. As a result of this, HH members sometimes sacrifice their personal interests for HH harmony.
- *Socio-Cultural Norms:* Timorese socio-cultural norms that are passed down inter-generationally influence the decision-making process at the HH level whether directly or indirectly.

- *Economic Capacity:* Another key contributing factor to the HH decision making process is economic capacity. Before making decisions, households will consider economic capacity over the long term, especially the availability of stores of food, HH finances, and the amount of livestock owned.
- *Personality and Social Status:* Within a given HH, men or women who have strong personalities and/or come from families of higher social status tend to influence the decision-making process at the HH level.
- *Priority:* HH priorities also influence decision-making processes at HH level.
- *Personal capacity (education level):* The other influencing factor in HH decision making is personal capacity. For example, men or women with higher levels of education or who have access to and control over a large amount of resources, tend to influence decision-making processes at HH level.
- *Urgency:* To make a decision at the HH level, both spouses should consider the urgency of the need. For example, providing for the need of a family member who is sick is more important than providing resources for an unrelated cultural ceremony.

Negotiation processes

This study found that withholding sexual intercourse is sometimes used to negotiate an individual's interest and the outcome of decision-making processes.[1] For example, one participant from a women's group in Viqueque explained that: "If I want to do something but my husband does not allow me to do it, then I can get angry. When this happens, sometimes I throw things around. At night when we sleep, I can turn away from him. But I don't do this for too long, because he can go and find another woman" (FGD with Women Group, Waimori Village).

On some occasions, before decisions are made, there will also be informal negotiation processes occurring between family members in order to secure their interests. There are many ways in which this is done between family members. For example, if a wife wants something from her husband, she will cook nice food and speak softly and nicely to him and vice versa. When men do not get what they want from their wives, they will try to leave the house to cool down and avoid a violent situation in the home. The emotional aspects of household decision-making are thus important to consider. If either the husband or the wife act without first gaining the permission of the other, this can trigger conflict and disharmony in the HH, and often this in turn can lead to domestic violence.

Participants also informed us that sometimes when problems arise between spouses, they do not talk to each other for a while. For some this may be a brief period of up to two hours, but for others it may take one or two days before they acknowledge and repair their rift. Some others informed us that such rifts may continue over the longer term, although a situation such as visitors to the house will mean the spouses make peace temporarily. When their guests leave, they will continue not talking to one another.

Decisions on food, nutrition and household resources

Food in the Household

Cooking is normally carried out by women, but when women are sick or not at home, men cook too. While what food is prepared is primarily a woman's decision, men may request foods that they wish to eat.

Household chores are undertaken by women assisted by the daughters in the household. Men may help when they have time. While two participants in this study explained that in their households domestic tasks were divided equally between men and women, this is not the case for the majority of households. Women generally decide on the allocation of domestic tasks. One participant explained that, because she was breastfeeding, she was not currently doing domestic chores and that she was also asked to eat first when the meals were ready.

When meals are ready, all household members eat together at the table at the same time, but customarily the male head of the household will take his food first. If one of the household members is not at home during mealtime, their food will be set aside for when they return. The now common practice of eating together at a table reinforces the household hierarchy. Timorese meal habits have changed over time and most households now adopt the Portuguese style of eating at tables. Traditionally Timorese ate on a bamboo platform (*hadak leten*) inside the house with food divided into portions on the plates of each household member.

Household Nutrition

Women's decisions about daily food consumption also determine household nutrition. When asked about what they had consumed for the previous evening's meal, the foods listed by the participants were rice and vegetables (cassava leaves, Chinese cabbage, pumpkin leaves), *etu sedok* (a mixture of rice, black beans and vegetables boiled in one pot) and *batar-da'an* (pounded corn boiled with kidney beans, peanuts and vegetables). All respondents (men and women) stated that they had not consumed meat in the previous evening's meal. While a minority of respondents reported that they consumed meat once or twice a month, the majority reported that they eat meat only when there is a traditional ritual and ceremony (*lia mate no lia moris*). Those who have access to money may sometimes buy fish sold on street stalls or by mobile fish sellers.

Young children (under-five) are served each morning with either *sasoro mutin de'it* (just white rice porridge) or rice porridge and vegetables (carrot and pumpkin leaves). For lunch they eat rice and vegetables and at night they are served more porridge. All mothers who participated in this research had breastfed their children for six months or more.

Family swidden gardens (to'os) and wet-rice fields (natar)

Family swidden gardens (*to'os*) are used primarily to grow maize, cassava, black beans and other staple crops. Family gardens and wet-rice fields are considered important family resources and are the basis of the livelihoods of most farmers.

The majority of participants in this study owned swidden gardens (*to'os*), but only some owned or had access to wet-rice fields (*natar*). Those living in the Administrative Post of Uatolari had both *to'os* and *natar*, while those living in Viqueque Villa and Ossu had limited to no access to *natar* and usually had access to *to'os*. Those who only had access to *natar* were able to do so as labourers in the fields belonging to others. In these cases, the harvest would be divided equally between workers and land owners.

When asking about how places are selected for the family swidden garden (*to'os*) most respondents explained that it was the husband who decided where to make the gardens and farm each season. Others described this as a joint decision between the spouses. People explained that they will select a site based on soil fertility and the distance from the family home. *To'os* is planted either on family-owned or community land.

Clearing swidden gardens and rice field preparation is considered men's work, but women also contribute when they have free time. It is considered that men and women contribute equally to field preparation, planting seeds, weeding and harvesting, even though they do not necessarily do the same amount of work. Prescriptive gender relations mean that men and women commonly do different jobs, but these roles are considered to be equal or complementary (Niner 2012; Hicks 2012; Wigglesworth 2010; see also Chapter 8, this volume). For example, respondents from one Focus Group Discussion explained that when men clear the fields or carried out fencing, women would be in charge of preparing food at home to take to the men in the fields at midday. These two tasks are considered equal contributions to household life. One advantage of these prescriptive gender relations is a division of tasks which contributes to household harmony. A disadvantage of these prescriptive gender relations is that women often spend many more hours working on their household and agricultural tasks compared to men.

After crops are harvested, it is the responsibility of the women to manage the harvest storage and consumption. If one of the household members decides to sell a portion of the harvest, they must first consult with other household members in order to avoid conflict.

Livestock

Livestock are considered one of the most valuable assets of a household. Livestock may be sold during emergency situations such as for paying school fees or for healthcare costs when someone gets sick.

The most important livestock for most people are water buffalo or Balinese cattle, pigs, goats or sheep and chickens. The most common animals owned by households are pigs and chickens. Only a small percentage (less than 5% of participants) of household respondents owned water buffalo or Balinese cattle.

In a customary exchange sense, water buffalo and Bali cattle are associated with masculinity or men, therefore it is the men who look after them. Women will look after buffalo when men are not available. Women are customarily associated with pigs because it is considered a female (feminine) animal in marriage exchange. In life cycle (*lia mate no lia moris*) rituals, the fertility-taking group (*fetosan*) gives buffalo to the fertility-giving group (*umane*) who provides a return gift of a pig. Some respondents explained that while women and men can help collect food to feed the pigs, it is women's daily responsibility to feed the pigs. Men will feed pigs when women in the household are sick, giving birth or are not at home.

As livestock have a great economic value for households, except in urgent situations, decisions over animals like a water buffalo, Balinese cattle and pigs need to be made by consultation between spouses and other household members. Decisions about the use of livestock with a lesser economic value, such as chickens, may be made independently by either spouse.

Family Finances

The main sources of cash income for households are selling agricultural produce, selling livestock, contributions from other household members who are employed, and social security payments made to the elderly or veteran's pensions. In some cases, the household heads (one or both spouses) may be employed in the government or non-government sector.

All participants, both men and women, agreed that it is women (the wife) who manages a household's finances. This does not imply that women have autonomy to spend the money however they wish, but rather that men and women usually come to a joint decision about all significant household spending. Both men and women have autonomy over matters involving smaller expenditure.

There are variations between households in terms of what is considered to be of significant economic value. For some households, anything over US$10 is considered significant, while for other households this amount may be over US$50.

All participants agreed that household spending should be first on education, second on food and third on customary activities such as life-cycle rituals. This order of priority contradicts popular beliefs, especially those of educated Dili-based residents, which assert that the majority of rural households spend all of their money on customary activities such as life-cycle rituals.

Conclusions

The objective of this study was to document and to understand how decisions are made at the household level in relation to family resources. That is, who decides where to farm, what kind of crops to grow, how to use livestock, how to allocate food resources and how the family money is spent. While the study identified a tendency toward prescriptive gender relations guiding the allocation of household tasks, it found that these roles were understood to be complementary between men and women. The identified socio-cultural norm for household decision-making was one of collaboration between spouses and where necessary other household members. The necessity for collaborative or joint decisions was especially the case for matters concerning the use or expenditure of significant household resources.

Previous studies on the decision-making process in Timor-Leste have focused heavily on the public sphere with little to no attention to decision-making in private spaces such as households. This household research across four ethno-linguistic groups in the Viqueque Municipality recommends that further study into decision-making in the private sphere be extended to other language groups in Timor-Leste.

Household decision making processes in Timor-Leste are an important component to consider and inform the development approaches of government and civil society organisations. Culturally and context-specific understandings of household decision-making processes are needed to enable development practitioners to better design the programs which aim to improve the quality of life and economy for households at the local level.

Notes

1 This is an area which requires further research.

References

Asia Foundation. 2016. *Understanding Violence against Women and Children in Timor-Leste: Findings from the Nabilan Baseline Study.* Dili: The Asia Foundation.

Guterres, A. 2011. "Kultura Hamate Kapital?" *Building Markets in Timor-Leste*, January 31, https://buildingmarkets.org/blogs/timor/2011/01/31/kultura-hamate-kapital/comment-page-1/. Access 20 November 2020.

Hägerdal, H., and D. Kammen. 2016. "The Lost Queens of Timor." In *Women and the Politics of Gender in Post-Conflict Timor-Leste: Between Heaven and Earth*, edited by S. Niner. London/New York: Routledge, Taylor and Francis Group.

Hicks, D. 1984. *A Maternal Religion: The Role of Women in Tetum Myth and Ritual.* Detroit: Center for Southeast Asian Studies, Northern Illinois University.

Hicks, D. 2012. "Compatibility, resilience and adaptation: The barlake of Timor-Leste." *Local-Global: Identity, Security, Community* 11: 124-137.

Kammen, D. 2012. "Queens of Timor." *Archipel* 84: 149-173

Niner, S. 2011. "Hakat klot, narrow steps: negotiating gender in post-conflict Timor-Leste." *International Feminist Journal of Politics* 13 (3): 413-435

Niner, S. 2012. "Barlake: An exploration of marriage practices and issues of women's status in Timor-Leste." *Local-Global: Identity, Security, Community* 11: 138-153.

Niner, S. 2016. *Women and the Politics of Gender in Post-conflict Timor-Leste: Between Heaven and Earth.* London/New York: Routledge, Taylor and Francis Group.

Ospina, S., and T. Hohe. 2001. "Traditional Power Structures and the Community Empowerment and Local Governance Project – Final Report", Presented to CEP/PMU, ETTA/UNTAET and the World Bank. https://studylib.net/doc/12617616/traditional-power-structures-and-the-community-empowermen... Accessed 10 December 2020.

Silva, K. 2017. "Women, gender and power among indigenous peoples of Portuguese Timor." *Anuário Antropológico* 42 (2): 183-205. https://doi.org/10.4000/aa.2240

Therik, T. 2004. *Wehali: The Female Land – Tradition of a Timorese Ritual Center*. Canberra: Pandanus Books.

Trindade, J. 2017. "Lulik: The Core Values of Timor-Leste." Paper presented at Association for Asian Studies Annual Conference. The Transformation of Religion, Culture and Society in Timor-Leste Panel, Toronto, Ontario, Canada, March 16-19.

Trindade, J. 2019. *Josh Trindade: A Collection of Articles.* Chisinau: LAP – Lambert Academic Publishing.

Weatherbee, D. E. 1966. "Portuguese Timor: An Indonesian dilemma." *Asian Survey* 6 (12): 683-695. https://doi.org/10.2307/2642194. Accessed 30 Nov. 2020.

Wigglesworth, A. 2010. "Becoming citizens: Civil society activism and social change in Timor-Leste." PhD diss., Victoria University.

CHAPTER 7

Gift economy and the acknowledgement of debt: (On) Living and eating with 'mystical' actors in Timorese houses

Renata Nogueira da Silva

Abstract

This essay is based on ethnographic research in a Same community (Manufahi) and it seeks to grasp the ways by which the cohabitation of persons and 'mystical' actors acquires meaning through daily practices of commensality. This essay thus delves into the idea that the stages of making and consuming food are, among other things, moments of communion—with god (*maromak*), with the ancestors (*bei'ala*), and with the sacred house. In light of this idea, the relationship between humans and non-humans is constituted by a constant giving and receiving of food, of which debt and the expectation of reciprocation are a deliberate part.

Keywords: Commensality; cohabitation; sacred house; humans; non-humans; Timor-Leste

Figure 7.1: The preparation of the sacred food offered to *bosok*.[1] *Uma Lulik*, Mau Asu, Sau Batar, 2017. Credit: Renata Nogueira da Silva.

The intention of this essay, which is based on ethnographic research conducted in an East Timorese community (Same, Manufahi) during 2017, is to reflect upon the relationship between food, gift, and debt.[2] The object of this study is the eating practices of my interlocutors (the sons and daughters and also the friends of the Mau Asu Sacred House) and their relationship with different ontological agents, both humans and non-humans (mystical agents).

Before proceeding, some terminology clarification is needed. In this essay, I employ *house*, with a lowercase *h*, to refer to a house, a place where people live. When I am dealing with the ceremonial houses, I employ *sacred house*, a *lulik* and also *House*, with a capital *H*. In this case, I am referring to a House as an entity (even when I do not specify which particular House). I make such distinctions based on Friedberg's (1972, 1989) and Sousa's (2008) suggestions.

I employ the expression mystical actors/entities within this essay to refer to the gathering of non-human entities (which nonetheless have agency in the lives of humans), such as god (*maromak*), ancestors (*bei'ala*) and the sacred house. Throughout the text, the terms ancestors and forefathers are used as synonyms and the expressions non-human entities and mystical actors are related. I have been using the latter since a conversation I had with Professor Kelly Silva, who warned me back then about the risks of not taking into consideration the heterogeneity of the non-human actors (which act upon human lives) in my research field.

For the purposes of this essay, I employ *maromak* as a synonym for god, that is, as another entity amongst the several mystical agents with whom humans interact by means of eating and food.

Moving on now to food, I approach food ingestion as productive consumption (Marx [1859] 1982; Gregory 1982), a phenomenon by means of which life is reproduced (materially and immaterially), in its multiple meanings.

According to Marx ([1859] 1982, 8), "They [the economists] call productive consumption both production that is simultaneously identical with consumption, and consumption which is directly concurrent with production".[3] Such production, analogous to consumption, becomes a second production, for it arises out of the annihilation (consumption) of the product of the first production. That being so, the very act of consuming food and offering it to non-humans allows for the satisfaction of a set of both material and immaterial demands of the productive process (such demands are aimed at the reproduction of life). The material conditions for social reproduction (of existence) are related in a number of ways to certain cosmological representations (which include the mystical realm). The material conditions themselves feed such representations.

Offering food and sacrificing animals to non-human actors is a practice that has long been discussed in the literature on rituals (in Timor-Leste and elsewhere). Tylor (1871) considers sacrifice to be a gift which the 'savage' offers to the gods with whom he or she seeks to have a relationship. Mauss and Hubert ([1899] 2005), in their turn, understand as religious sacrifices everything that includes certain rituals—which are not necessarily actions that cause pain or suffering. Most sacrifices studied by Mauss and Hubert took place by means of rituals which ended with the death or consumption of a victim or an offer (an animal, some food or a human being), which was then taken by the god to whom it had been offered. "Every sacrifice takes place under certain circumstances and for certain ends" (Mauss and Hubert [1899] 2005, 101).

Mauss and Hubert divide rituals into two kinds: occasional sacrifices and constant sacrifices. The former are those which may take place at any given day, whereas the latter always take place on a set day, following a routine. Mauss and Hubert suggest that sacrifice establishes a sort of contract between humans and gods, for if the latter ensure the existence of the former, the reverse is certainly true, also. Gods acquire their food from humans. The flow of gifts remains by means of a deliberate maintenance/nourishment of the debt and it allows for an articulation between the freedom to and the obligation to give and to reciprocate.

At the Urufu *aldeia* or community (in the Same municipality and the HolaRua *suku*), offering food—daily—to the mystical actors at home and having meals—periodically—at the sacred house are essential acts that ensure the harmony between different social groups, the reproduction of life and the balance of the house as a moral entity (Lévi-Strauss 1986).

The non-humans or mystical actors I refer to throughout this essay include: ancestors, the sacred house and *maromak*. Ancestors are not the dead in general but rather those who accumulated several sources of value (be it cultural, emotional, social, religious, economic or political) when alive and had the ability to activate or to access them in different social contexts. Employing an idiom from botany (McWilliam 2009), we could describe an ancestor as a trunk of an origin group (Fox 1996) and its descendants are the branches. Such representation (a trunk and its branches) is the expression of an archetype of precedence (McWilliam 2009, 112) in which the trunk comes before and is superior to the branch, in a temporal sense. The moral authority of the trunk (over its tips, its descendants) is acknowledged, regardless of this particular ancestor being dead or alive.

Authors such as David Hicks ([1976] 2004), Elizabeth G. Traube (1980), Shepard Forman (1980), James Fox (1996), Andrew McWilliam (2009), and Susana Viegas (2016), based on research conducted in different East Timorese contexts, point out the centrality of funerary rites and ancestors' rites in the lives of Timorese men and women. Social life itself depends on the ways by which the connections (between the living and the dead) are nourished during ceremonial occasions (such as funerals). The social life also depends on the ways by which such connections are nourished in daily life. People pay their deference to the dead in ceremonies, such as during the Day of the Dead; tombs are visited by relatives who offer them candles and flowers and the ancestors are fed during those ceremonies. Life is to a large extent ordered by the exchange of gifts and by the acknowledgement of the communications and negotiations with spiritual entities. Certain development programs and projects associate what is considered the country's low economic development to their population engagement with practices and local values. However, when we observe the ways through which the local economic relations are materialised in daily life, we see a different arrangement between different regimes and production, exchange, distribution and consumption relations, amongst which the market and the gift are activated due to life reproduction (i.e., see Introduction, Chapters 5, 8, and 13, this volume).

The aforementioned literature, however, does not explore differences between the scale and the types of ritual practices and specific eating practices. There is also a lack of analysis regarding the daily offering of food within domestic unities (such offerings can be described as a constant sacrifice, as Mauss and Hubert would call it). Hick's ([1976] 2004) work, though, does describe the interior of houses and the events that take place there. Among other things, he suggests that the innermost part of the house, called *labis laran*, is the place of women where food is prepared and where the altar is placed (in which offerings are given to the spirits of the house). The innermost room is used exclusively by women during the daytime.

I highlight here the importance of women in a chain of transformation: food into nutrition, raw food into cooked and nutrition into offer. The raw food may be considered everything out of control from the house and the cooked food as something social, thus allowing the relation and the mixing of things from the world that were eventually separated. Women are fundamental to the physical process of cooking things and also to operating the changes of relation status (see Lévi-Strauss 2004; DaMatta 2004).

Nutrition takes us to family interactions, alliance nets and commitments, to the mystic agents, the house and the sacred houses. On sharing food, we celebrate relations allowing the production and life at its most diverse expression.

Most of the food consumed in the homes I visited in Timor-Leste comes from the commodity regime (the market). When such foods are offered to mystical beings, they change their status and thus begin to circulate in the gift exchange regime. Such regimes are not mutually exclusive but rather coexist in social life and they may be activated (or not) depending on the context. In the case of a gift exchange regime, maintaining the relationship is as important as acknowledging the debt (Silva 2016).

In this essay, I explore how relationships between persons and non-human entities are nourished by, among other things, a constant giving and receiving of foods, in which debt and the expectation of reciprocation are both deliberate. I deal with the distinctions between rituals concerning gifts/sacrifices of foods (conducted inside the sacred houses) and, on the other hand, rituals conducted within the domestic unit. I also propose analogies between the liminality of the food offered to the non-human and the liminality of these very actors, whose actions take place between two worlds—the world of the living and the world of the dead.

Throughout the text, I make it explicit that the foods offered to non-human actors have unique features: they are prepared without seasoning and salt and they are offered half-raw (or half-cooked). Thus, these foods, like their recipients, appear to be in a liminal state (between a natural state and a cultured one, through their cooking).[4]

This essay proceeds in three parts. In the first one, I return to some of the ways by which anthropology has approached the question of food. In the second one, I deal with some of the traits that characterise *fó han* (to feed) in intra-sacred house rituals. These are privileged moments to feed (in the broadest sense of the term) the House, its members, and the very bonds that constitute it. In the third part, in its turn, I analyse the ways in which mystical actors are handled during daily practices of commensality within the home where I was welcomed and stayed for research purposes. Finally, in the fourth section, I explore the nature of the kind of foods offered to non-human actors and I try to derive the analytical implications of it.

Food in anthropology and in East Timorese ritual contexts

Some currents of thought have taken the problem of nourishment as the founding phenomenon of the economy. The capacity of the productive forces to produce more food, beyond the demand for immediate consumption, constitutes in fact the first social surplus; food is thus the fundamental element for the reproduction of a society, at the level which Marx defined as the infrastructure (Carneiro 2003, 22). “Every production, then, immediately becomes consumption, and consumption also immediately becomes production” (Marx [1859] 1982, 218-219). Uniting the realms of consumption and production allows us to highlight some of the subtleties involved in the relationship between human beings and commodities, and thus to reconcile, in some measure, the subject and the object, interiority and exteriority.

In another front of research, Lévi-Strauss ([1962] 1980, 2004) understands food as an analytical unit which allows one to access human thought; as a way to elaborate relationships between groups by means of analogies and metaphors regarding marriages, sexual acts, and alliances. In the wake of this perspective, Leach (1983) and Sahlins (2004) both indicate that food is a symbol which communicates specific messages in social interactions. There is an ongoing discussion on the distinctions between mere nourishment (Portuguese *alimento*) and food. Such discussion sharpens our interpretative horizons. DaMatta (2004), in his study on Brazilian food, states that any nutritious substance is a nourishment (*alimento*), however not every nourishment constitutes *food*. According to him, a nourishment is anything someone ingests to remain alive; food, in its turn, concerns the very constitution of identity. "There are 'nourishments' and there is food. Food is not merely a nourishing substance: it is also a way, a style and a manner of eating" (DaMatta 2004, 56). In a similar perspective, Woortmann (1986) contrasts "food" with nourishment (even though the former derives from the latter), for food is the transformation of provision by means of cooking. For Carneiro (2003, 8), "what one eats is as important as when one eats, where one eats, how one does it and with whom."

Another important contribution to the discussion on commensality and anthropology is Viegas' work (2006) on the historical elaboration of identity among the Tupinambá people of Olivença (state of Bahia, Brazil)—based on the relationship between food and pleasure. In her study, Viegas highlights the importance of "feeding" as a dimension of sociality and of the construction of what it means to be a relative. Throughout this text, I speak of food, nourishment, and food products to approach the different ways of feeding, nourishing and sustaining human beings, non-human entities and the bonds between them.

Persons organised in groups of origin, such as several East Timorese communities, live in mutual dependence—dependence not only on the living but also on those who dwell in another realm of existence. Balancing the most important phenomena that make up the life of the living is conceived as a gift from the non-human entities; such gifts must be reciprocated, so as to ensure the very reproduction of life (Silva 2016).

The vegetable garden, the animals, health, employment and anything which allows the reproduction of human existence are considered to be a gift from the mystical actors. Therefore, people feel in debt to them. Offering food is a way to give thanks for the gifts received and, in a way, to acknowledge a debt which, in fact, can never be paid. Commitment to others, humans or not, ensures the ongoing and permanent nature of the debt. According to Palmer, in this region, sociability is sustained by more than human relationships, involving conscious cooperation and intersubjectivity manifesting and transforming itself through different bodies and things in space and time. This the author calls "inclusive sociality" (Palmer 2015, 42).

Acknowledging the agency of the mystical actors is part of daily life and can be seen in the amount of trouble humans take to feed and take care of such entities. Feeding those non-human entities establishes a system of prestations and counter-prestations, in which food is a vehicle for communication. Feeding the mystical agents is essential to maintain the bonds with those who dwell in different realms of existence.

Intra-sacred house ceremonies

I attended several ceremonies at East Timorese sacred houses, in different municipalities.[5] In each and every one of them, giving food to the non-human entities was a part of the ceremony. Each ceremony has its own scope and dynamics, which involves a certain number of families being together in the vicinity of the sacred house for a certain time, and also involves exchanging respects and goods. The nature and the amount of goods exchanged depend on the position of each family in the context of the ceremony in which persons and goods circulate. Some goods are consumed during the period in which people are staying in the House, while others become relics for the sacred house. And some are distributed according to the rules of precedence among the members of a group of origin called for the ceremony.

In these ceremonies, *bua-malus* is essential: it serves the purpose of enhancing communication between the realm of the living and other realms.[6] It consists in the first offering that is given to the non-human entities. This offering can be placed in different locations, depending on the ceremony. It could be left within the sacred house, at the *bosok*, or on a stone, as the activity taking place prescribes.[7] According to my interlocutors, *bua-malus* opens the *kultura* ceremonies and may also be used to welcome visitors. In other words, *bua-malus* opens paths for both horizontal and vertical relationships, promoting communication between people within the human realm (horizontal) and also communication between human beings and non-human beings (vertical).

Offering, accepting and sharing *bua-malus* is indispensable in communication, exchange and in opening new dialogues. The action of chewing *bua-malus*, on any social occasion, has been described as fundamental to begin and/or to strengthen relationships. This applies equally to isolated encounters as well as to greeting family, friends or newcomers (Sousa 2010). Here we are facing material support of cultural translation (Sousa 2010),[8] capable of ordering the flux of life, by creating a path which connects persons and makes social life possible in the presence of others (Seixas 2009; Sousa 2010; Fidalgo-Castro 2012).

Food prepared for non-human entities in ritual contexts (and here I draw on my experience with the Mau Asu Sacred House as well as other houses in different municipalities) usually is prepared within the sacred house at the *dapkur lulik* (sacred kitchen).[9] It is prepared on stones arranged for this purpose. No salt or other condiments are used. In the Mau Asu sacred house, sacred food is served to the mystical beings in straw baskets (*luhu*). Men who can claim descent from the founders of the house are responsible for conducting the *hamulak* (which could be described as a prayer, if we compare it to the Western classificatory system) and also for sacrificing animals and cooking their meat. Women, in turn, prepare the fire (for cooking rice and also the meat that the men will prepare).

Small baskets with a little rice and some pieces of meat are prepared for offerings to the non-human entities. These baskets are placed on the holiest part of the sacred house (the place where the sacred objects are) and they stay there for some hours. In a separate dish, a mixture of rice and meat is prepared. The meat is shredded or chopped into very small pieces and then mixed with rice. Each corner of the inner part of the house receives a little bit from this mixture. The stones which were used for preparing the meals, the exterior columns that support the house and the *bosok* (also called *fatuk lulik* or *fatin lulik* in other places) also receive it. The ancestors get their food and so does the house—and the human beings. Taking care of the mystical actors ensures the fertility of life in its several manifestations.

Feeding and offering food to the entities implies not only transfers and circulation, but also expenditure and losses. Therefore, it is a kind of productive consumption. For Marx ([1859] 1982), productive consumption is directly associated with capital-labour relations. From this perspective, production is also consumption; firstly, because when an individual produces something, thus developing his or her capabilities, he or she also spends it—consuming it in the very act of production.

Feeding the ancestors within the home

To follow the ritual dynamics of a sacred house implies also getting to know (in a way) the daily life of the people who are a part of the sacred house. It also involves understanding that persons themselves are "produced" through the relationships *between* the homes and the sacred houses. My research took place within such intertwined zones.

In order to research the reproduction and transformation of social life within the sacred houses in post-colonial Timor-Leste, I visited several sacred houses in different municipalities.[10] To get to know the dynamics of a particular sacred house, I focused on the Mau Asu sacred house, located in Same. I was welcomed at Filomena's home. Filomena is the sister of Celeste, who, in turn, is one of my interlocutors, and she is a daughter of the Mau Asu sacred house. Celeste, at that time, was living in Dili. The family who welcomed me had a large home, with several rooms and two kitchens—one of them indoors and the other outdoors. There was also two bathrooms outdoors. In the indoor kitchen there was an electric cooktop, a fridge, a large table and two kitchen cabinets. On the table, one could find household items for daily use. There was a cooktop placed on a chair next to the fridge, which was used mostly to cool water. The fridge was not used to store food such as meat, vegetables, milk or to store cooked food. Rice was the only food which they stored; all other foods (such as sugar, bread, milk, oil, eggs, leaf vegetables, and tuna) were bought daily at kiosks nearby or at the local market, depending on the demand and on the amount of money available at different times.

Meals were prepared in a manner that depended on who was home at the time. When the mother and the father were both home, there was coffee in the morning. When only the children were home, the youngest one had some milk and the others had sweet potato, rice, macaroni, biscuits or bread; *konforme*.[11] Using products stored at home to prepare a meal was rare: going out to buy some ingredients before cooking was part of the house dynamics and its routine.

Filomena (who hosted me) was born in Same. She has a master's degree in Natural Science and she is a political activist, married to Marsal (who comes from a Lospalos family). She has seven children (between 2 and 18 years old) and she spends part of the week away from the family to teach at Betano, which is quite far.[12] When the mother is not home, the father manages the house, with some help from the older daughters and the neighbouring aunts (biological sisters of the mother). Thus, what was cooked (and how and where it was cooked) depended on the presence (or absence) of the mother at home.

Filomena's daughters handled the kitchen utensils, especially the electric pan used to make rice and the electric cooktop. Their chores consisted of boiling water to make coffee, cooking rice, sautéing leaf vegetables from the vegetable garden or from the shop (mustard, watercress, and cassava leaves) and, sometimes, cooking some eggs or tuna. The girls rarely cooked chicken or beef. The siblings took care of each other, so that at lunch time the food was ready, they got everyone bathed and set to go to school.

When Filomena was at home it was common to use the outdoor kitchen. Daughters, female cousins, nieces and daughters of *mana* Mena all gathered to cook their food on the wood stove in the outdoors kitchen. It was quite a feast! The women sang around the fire, laughed, played, listened to music. Cooking food thus became a lengthy process, permeated with affection. By both observing and taking part in the preparation of several kinds of food, sometimes squatting (often almost juggling!) sometimes sitting on a stone with the other women, I slowly learned that the food they cooked was permeated with the affections of those who prepared it. These emotions were passed on to those who would partake of that meal. The food made in that outdoors kitchen assembles values such as sorority and affectivity.

For several months I accompanied my friend Filomena and her daughters in the kitchen (outdoors or indoors) for the preparation of rice, leaf vegetables (*modo*), eggs, meat or tuna for the family meals. In any case, rice was always cooked first. Before it was fully cooked, those who were cooking started preparing plates of food and placing them on the main table.[13] The same procedure applied to the *modo*, eggs or tuna.

When everything was set, there were around five plates of food on a table. Here, for the sake of clarity, I must point out that in the living room, there was always a separate table which was used, among other things, to serve coffee, cookies and other food (to visitors). On this table were also placed the dishes offered to non-human entities. This is the table I am referring to here. Those plates were placed there before the meal for the living is served and remained there afterwards. They were sometimes partially consumed throughout the day by anyone who wanted them, especially the children. Such plates were always served before the two main meals, that is, the non-human entities were always fed first—before the living humans.

Every time we went to eat, the scene described above called my attention, especially because I saw similar things in other homes I visited. We would often eat in front of the table where such plates were laid and that made me slightly uncomfortable. I did not want to ask directly to whom that food was meant, so I kept watching. During the rainy season, however, I spent a lot of time indoors at Filomena's home, not just at night but during daytime also. While helping the girls and Filomena herself cook, I finally started asking about those plates left on the table. Then, Filomena told me something more or less along these lines:[14]

> At my home I offer a plate of food to the spirit of my sacred house (*Uma Malae*), another plate for the spirit of my husband's sacred house (*Uma Yanamli*), yet another plate for *Maromak*, a plate for my husband's family ancestors and also a plate for my family ancestors. I prepare them neat and separately… just like we do in the Sau Batar ceremonies, on the Day of the Dead, when inaugurating something etc—all things within the sacred house. Anything related to *Maromak*, the Sacred House and the ancestors is called *fussu nin* in the Mambae language and *lulik na'in* in the Tetum language. It is part of the East Timorese tradition to leave food for the ancestors—*matebian*—every day before our meals. People usually place it all on a single plate but here I place it separately. (Filomena Nunes, Same, 2017)

Thus, placing plates of food on tables and altars was not just a practice of that particular domestic unit alone. People connect with these mystical actors by means of daily gifts and debts. Everyday food is offered to the mystical actors to thank them for life. Such an offering in a way allows existence to be and at the same time asks for the continuity of this flux of life. It is all about giving and receiving, asking and offering—a constant flux of gifts and debts between the living and the ancestors. It is an extended family (consisting of the living and the dead). Such a family, through food, nourishes and maintains bonds which are thus not interrupted by death (see Chapter 8, this volume).

According to Filomena, in the times of the Biblical Old Testament, the trees, stones, water and everything had a custodian. And people knew that everything had a custodian. Therefore, one needs to give satisfaction to the masters of things.

With the New Testament, there came the time when the ancestors (*bei'ala sira*) started to understand that everything was created by God. To Filomena, one needs to offer food to God (*Maromak*) because he is the creator. One needs to pay respects to the *Matebian* (ancestors) to show them that the living still remember them. Offering food to the sacred house is important because it is the place where people gather to worship the ancestors. At Filomena's home, offering food to the mystical agents happens on a daily basis, no matter who is preparing the meal.

Filomena also told me that the sacred house matters because it is a place where relatives meet each other. The sacred house allows people to locate themselves, to meet and to recognise other people. If there were no sacred house where people gather, then how would the people know where they came from, who is related to whom and thus who they can marry and who they cannot marry?

The quality of nourishments offered to mystical actors

For DaMatta (2004), as mentioned before, food is not just a nourishing substance, but also "a way, a style and a manner of eating". The way one eats something defines not only what was eaten but also defines the very person who eats. Hence, the food on a plate nourishes the body, but it also signals a belonging, and serves the role of a social recognition code (Sobreira, Garavelllo, and Nardoto 2018).

The transformation of raw food into cooked food is interpreted by Lévi-Strauss (2004) (based on his analysis of a set of myths) as the human transition from the biological condition to the social one. The *raw* appears as a metaphor of nature: animals eat raw flesh. Fire, in its turn, is associated with culture; human beings eat cooked meat. It can be said that the kitchen, through women, articulates the categories of nature and culture and interconnects systems of opposition (such as raw/cooked, nature/culture, the dead/the living and so on). For Lévi-Strauss (2004), the invention of the kitchen not only modified and differentiated human eating behaviours, but it also added social functions to meals. The kitchen thus articulates the categories of nature and culture and also expresses a language, for it interconnects systems of opposition. Besides strengthening friendship between equals, eating and drinking together also served to reinforce the relations between unequal (such as a lord and vassals, for instance). Food is made in the kitchen—within this social space, we can observe the sexual division of labour and the organisation of family relations. The elective relations between family, house and home remind us of the concept of fire as both a builder and a driver of the relations of commensality. At the sacred house (in ceremonial contexts) food offered to mystical actors possesses a certain texture. It is only slightly cooked and unseasoned. At home, food offered to non-human entities is the same food humans eat, but not seasoned and not fully cooked.

On the question of spices and condiments, there was something I experienced (outside of any ritual context) which can enrich the interpretative horizon regarding such matters. On one occasion, I was having tea without any sugar and such a choice generated quite a few remarks. The elderly asked me whether I was sick, and the children, in their turn, just laughed a lot. It turns out unseasoned tea was a medicine—a drink for humans who were not at their best human condition. The absence of seasoning on food and beverages is related to certain conditions—the condition of non-human actors who dwell in another realm of existence and also not fully healthy humans. The absence of seasoning, it appears, leads us to a liminal situation.

The liminal condition of these foods offered to mystical actors might indicate the liminal position of these very actors: neither raw no cooked, neither alive nor dead. They are in another dimension of existence and yet they possess agency in the world of the living humans. Perhaps it is precisely their liminal condition that allows them to act in both worlds.

Some substances have the power to connect two kinds of beings. They can gather wishes and desires from humans. Food is a vehicle for mystical power and it works as the unifying force in exchanges between participants in the ceremony. The relationship between human beings and mystical beings at home involves the persons who dwell together there, the ancestors who had an important role in the constitution of that particular family, the spirits from the sacred houses of both the father and the mother, and *maromak*.

The economic participation of women at managing daily life is fundamental. According to what was demonstrated, nutrition is mostly prepared by women; being so, we may say that the mystic aggregating power of relations and people is dominated by women and by them it is agencied. In a context like the East Timorese one in which the accurate development of life is related to the cultivation of relations with the mystic agents, feeding them means guaranteeing life. Women, in turn, feed human beings and mystic agents, allowing life to move on (see also Introduction and Chapter 8, this volume).

Gift and debt: humans, non-human entities, and food

By observing and taking part in acts of commensality (both in ritual and daily moments and both at the sacred house and at home), I learned about the power food possesses to bring people closer and to establish bonds with non-human entities. Based on what I saw, heard and *tried* (especially in the gustative sense) during fieldwork, I suggest we think of food as a vehicle that communicates the recognition of debt between humans and mystical actors. Attending ceremonies at the sacred houses is not enough; one must also feed on everything that is offered—including food offered as sacrifices. In any case, food is a vehicle for mystical forces and it works as a unifier among the different participants of the ceremony (non-human entities included).

The relationship between human beings and mystical actors at home involves, as we have seen, the persons who dwell there, the ancestors who were important in the constitution of that particular family, the sacred houses of both father and mother, and also *maromak*. I have been arguing that the relationship between human beings and non-human entities at the sacred house embraces a greater number of participants and involves a greater quantity and quality of goods offered, and objects as well as relics. In both cases (at home and at the sacred house), however, the mystical actors eat first and the recognition that humans are in a state of debt with non-human entities guides the provision of offerings. To sum up, the sacred house, just like home, allows people to activate their bonds with non-human entities through food, but it happens, in each case, at different scales in terms of groups of persons.

I suggest that there is an elective relation between sacred house, home and the quality of food offered. Unseasoned and not fully cooked food is associated with the sacred house. Seasoned and not fully cooked food, in turn, is associated with home. In short, the type of cooking and the use (or not) of seasoning are associated with the ontology with those who consume it. Finally, I indicate that the transformations which occur in the physical state of food are operated by women and such transformations help us to think over the modalities of relations and actions which allow more-than-human collectives to reproduce themselves in material and immaterial ways.

Notes

1 Also known as *fatin lulik* (sacred stones), a sacred place where offerings to the mystical actors are left.

2 I thank Professor Kelly Silva for her careful reading and comments which much contributed to the development of this essay. I am also grateful to Ana Carolina Oliveira and Alberto Fidalgo-Castro for our fruitful exchanges and their careful listening.

3 For quotations, I used Marxists.org translation (Marx [1857] 1971), available at: <https://www.marxists.org/archive/marx/works/1859/critique-pol-economy/appx1.htm>.

4 Here I work with the premise that, to some degree, the nature-society dichotomy is operative in the context I am studying. I am aware of the fact that such dichotomy has been problematised by a number of authors—see, for instance, Descola (2014) and, of course, MacCormack and Strathern (1980). However, for reasons of space and scope, I shall not delve into this discussion here. For a more in-depth discussion of this, see, for instance, Machado (2006).

5 *Municípios* are the name given to a territorial administrative division that comes from the Portuguese administrative culture (in the “original” Portuguese case, it usually corresponds to a

town). In Timor, a *município* can be a town or a village—it is the administrative headquarters of local (official) authority.

6 *Malus* is a heart-shaped leaf, and *bua* is a nut. Together, they act as material support for the relationships described and they are called, together, *Bua-malus*. In the literature, we recurrently find *betel* (leaves) and *areca* (nuts). Some of my interlocutors defined *bua-malus* as something similar to the catholic host (sacramental bread). For an in-depth look at the relationship between Catholic religion and local practices in Timor-Leste, see Fidalgo-Castro (2012).

7 Such was the term employed by my interlocutors which considered it to be a Tetum word.

8 That is, material elements and items that convey and communicate aspects related to certain cosmological worldviews.

9 Such as my experiences at sacred houses in Baucau, Cova-Lima, and Ermera, for instance.

10 In historiographic terms, I understand 'post-colonial' Timor-Leste here as beginning with the post-Indonesian occupation period and Timor's restoration of independence (post-1999). I feel it is important to explain my definition of 'post-colonial' (here in this context), given the complexity of colonial encounters and mismatches.

11 *Konforme* (similar to Portuguese *conforme*) can mean "accordingly" or "depending on" or even "yes", "precisely" etc. It is one of those catch-all expressions.

12 Betano is 25 kilometers from HolaRua. The trip by motorcycle takes around one hour, due to the road's conditions.

13 In this case, the rice must be removed before the water dries out completely so as to ensure it is not fully cooked.

14 This quotation is not a literal transcription of an interview. It is from a conversation which started in 2017 and was transcribed and (in 2018) submitted (for her appreciation) to my interlocutor, who, in her turn, made some corrections and added some information. I am also grateful for my supervisor's insistence on the need to understand the heterogeneity of the mystical actors which appeared on the horizon of my research. This call, during the writing of my PhD dissertation, took me out of my comfort zone, which made me de-naturalise certain statements.

References

Carneiro, H. 2003. *Comida e Sociedade: uma história da alimentação*. Rio de Janeiro: Editora Elsevier.

DaMatta, R. 2004. *O que faz o Brasil, Brasil?* Rio de Janeiro: Editora Rocco.

Descola, P. 2014. *Beyond Nature and Culture*. Illinois: University of Chicago Press.

Fidalgo-Castro, A. 2012. "A religião em Timor-Leste a partir de uma perspectiva histórico-antropológica" In *Léxico fataluco-português*, edited by A. Fidalgo-Castro, and E. Bouza, 79-118. Díli: Gráfica Pátria.

Forman, S. 1980. "Paradigmas de vida: produção, reprodução e intercâmbio entre os Makassae do Timor Oriental." *Anuário Antropológico* 4 (1): 79-98. Available at: http://www.dan.unb.br/images/pdf/anuario_antropologico/Separatas1979/anuario79_shepardforman.pdf.

Fox, J. J. 1996. "The transformation of progenitor lines of origin: patterns of precedence in Eastern Indonesia." In *Origins, Ancestry and Alliance. Explorations in Austronesian Ethnography*, edited by J. Fox, and C. Sather, 133-156. Canberra: ANU E Press. http://doi.org/10.22459/OAA.10.2006

Friedberg, C. 1972. *Mission Ethnologique chez les Bunaq de Timor Portugais – Exposé sommaire des matériaux recueillis*. Paris: Muséum National d'Histoire Naturelle de Paris (policopiado).

Friedberg, C. 1989. "Social Relations of Territorial Management in Light of Bunaq Farming Rituals." *Bijdragen Tot de Taal-, Land- En Volkenkunde* 145 (1989): 548-563. doi.org/10.1163/22134379-90003246.

Graeber, D. 2016. *Dívida: os primeiros 5.000 anos*. São Paulo: Três Estrelas.

Gregrory, C. A. 1982. *Gifts and Commodities*. London: Academic Press.

Hicks, D. (1976) 2004. *Tetum Ghost & Kin: Fertility and Gender in East Timor*. Long Grove, Illinois: Waveland.

Leach, E. R. 1983. "Aspectos Antropológicos da Linguagem: Categorias Animais e Insulto Verbal." In *Edmund Leach: Coleção grandes cientistas sociais*, organized by R. Da Matta. São Paulo: Ática.

Lévi-Strauss, C. (1962) 1980. *Totemismo hoje*. 2nd ed. São Paulo: Abril Cultural.

Lévi-Strauss, C. 1986. "A noção de casa." In *Minhas palavras*, by C. Lévi-Strauss. São Paulo: Brasiliense.

Lévi-Strauss, C. 2004. *O cru e o cozido. Mitológicas 1*. São Paulo: CosacNaify.

Lody, R. 2004. *Santo Também come*. Rio de Janeiro: Pallas.

MacCormack, C., and M. Strathern. 1980. *Nature, Culture and Gender*. Cambridge: Cambridge University Press.

Machado, I. J. de R. 2006. "Sobre bebês e totemismo." *Mana* 12 (2): 389-418. Available at: https://www.scielo.br/scielo.php?script=sci_arttext&pid=S0104-93132006000200006

Marx, K. (1857) 1971. *A Contribution to the Critique of Political Economy*. Translated by S. W. Ryazanskaya, Lawrence and Wishart. Available at: https://www.marxists.org/archive/marx/works/1859/critique-pol-economy/appx1.htm.

Marx, K. (1859) 1982. "Introdução [À Crítica da Economia Política]." In K. Marx, *Contribuição para a Crítica da Economia Política*. Translated by E. Malagodi. São Paulo: Abril Cultural.

Mauss, M. (1923) 2003. "Ensaio sobre a dádiva." In *Sociologia e Antropologia*, by M. Mauss, 183-314. São Paulo: Cosac Naify.

Mauss, M., and H. Hubert. (1899) 2005. *Sobre o sacrifício*. Translated by P. Neves. São Paulo: Cosac Naify.

McWilliam, A. 2009. "Trunk and Tip in West Timor: Precedence in a botanical idiom." In *Precedence: Social Differentiation in the Austronesian World*, edited by M. P. Vischer, 111-132. Canberra: ANU E press.

Sahlins, M. 2004. *Cultura na Prática*. Rio de Janeiro: Editora UFRJ.

Seixas, P. C. 2009. "Translation in crisis, crisis as translation." In *East-Timor: How to Build a New Nation Southeast Asia 21st Century*, organized by C. Cabasset-Semedo and F. Durand, 65-80. Bangkok: Irase.

Sobreira, L. B., M. E. P. E. Garavello, and G. B. Nardoto. 2018. "Anthropology of food: An essay on food transition and transformations in Brazil." *Journal of Food Nutrition and Population Health* 2 (1): 1-9. DOI: 10.21767/2577-0586.10039.

Silva, K. 2016. "Administrando pessoas, recursos e rituais. Pedagogia econômica como tática de governo em Timor-Leste." *Horizontes Antropológicos* 22 (45): 127-153. http://dx.doi.org/10.1590/S0104-71832016000100006.

Sousa, L. 2008. "As Casas e o mundo: identidade local e Nação no património material/imaterial de Timor-Leste." In *Etnografia (Actas do III Congresso Internacional)*, edited by F. Cruz, 196-227. Póvoa de Varzim: AGIR Available: http://hdl.handle.net/10400.2/2894.

Sousa, L. 2010. "This is the beginning of the relationship: material supports of cultural translation." In *Translation, Society and Politics in Timor-Leste*, edited by P. C. Seixas, 37-59. Porto: Universidade Fernando Pessoa.

Traube, E. G. 1980. "Mambai rituals of black and white." In *The Flow of Life: Essays on Eastern Indonesia*, organized by J. Fox and James J, 290-314. Cambridge, Massachusetts/London, England: Harvard University Press.

Tylor, E. 1871. *Primitive Culture: Researches into the Mythology, Philosophy, Religion, Art, and Custom*. London: John Murray.

Viegas, S. M. 2006. "Nojo, prazer e persistência: beber fermentado entre os Tupinambá de Olivença (Bahia)." *Dossiê História dos Índios – Revista de História* (154): 151-188. https://doi.org/10.11606/issn.2316-9141.v0i154p151-188

Viegas, S. M. 2016. "Territorialidades e ambivalências. A co-habitação dos Fataluku com os missionários em Lautém (1947-1957)." In *Timor-Leste: Colonialismo, Descolonização, Lusutopia*, by R. G. Feijó, 139-157. Porto: Edições Afrontamento.

Woortmann, K. 1986. "A comida, a família e a construção de gênero." *Dados – Revista de Ciênias Sociais* 29 (1): 103-130.

CHAPTER 8

The work of women in Eluli and land economies in Timor-Leste

Teresa Cunha and Mina Bessa

Abstract

As elsewhere, many of the land-associated works in Timor-Leste are the responsibility of women, generating, among other things, fundamental socio-economies for the subsistence of bodies, food for the spirit and the celebration of life that existed, exists and will exist. Having as a theoretical framework a feminist hermeneutics of the epistemologies of the South in this work, we aim to set some theoretical and analytical bases for the co-construction of a post-abyssal feminist knowledge about women's works and economies of land in Timor-Leste. The methodological approach is qualitative based on ethnographic work in the place of Eluli located in the western part of the country in the mountains north of Maubara where the predominant language is Tokodede.

Keywords: Timor-Leste; land; feminist economies; epistemologies of the South

In Timor-Leste, the emplaced and vital relationship between people and the land is constitutive of both the Timorese sociability and their view of themselves and the world. As elsewhere, many of the land-associated works are the responsibility of women, generating, among other things, fundamental socio-economies for the subsistence of bodies, food for the spirit and the celebration of life that existed, exists and will exist (Cunha and Valle 2019; Gudynas 2019; Shiva 2017; Narciso and Henriques 2011; Friedberg 2011; Langton and Palmer 2006; Shiva and Mies 1997).

Having as a theoretical framework a feminist hermeneutics of the epistemologies of the South (Cunha and Sousa 2019), in this work, we aim to set some theoretical and analytical bases for the co-construction of a post-abyssal feminist knowledge about women's works and economies of land in Timor-Leste.[1]

The context of analysis is Eluli, the lands of a family community that descends from *Rainha Dona* Marta (Queen Dona Marta).[2] Eluli is located in the western part of the country in the mountains north of Maubara where the predominant language is Tokodede.

Although Eluli has been governed by women for the past three generations and we can consider that a certain functional matriarchy is acknowledged in the family,

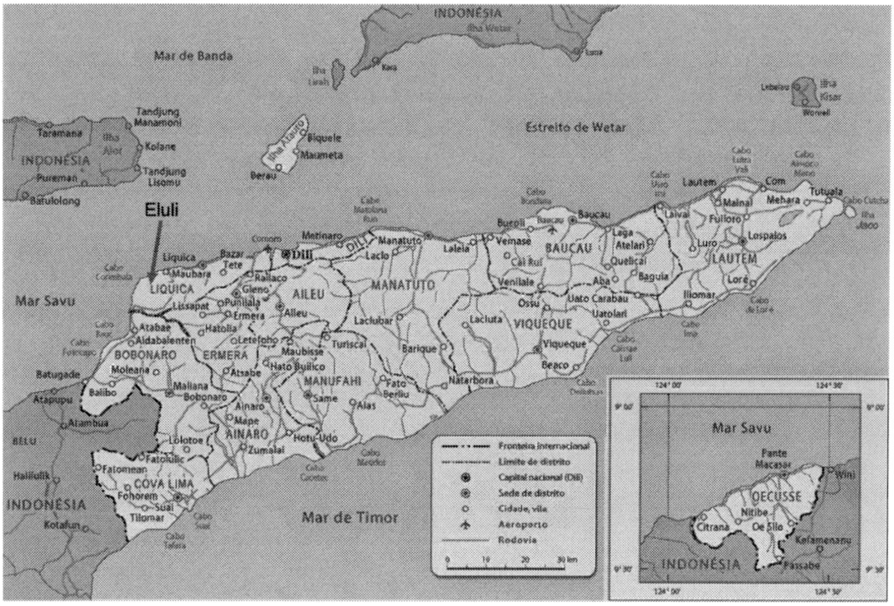

Figure 8.1: Map of Timor-Leste. Available at http://timor-dili.blogspot.com/2015/03/geografia-de-timor-leste.html accessed on 22-10-2020.

this does not mean that there has been a rupture with the customary patrilocal and patrilineal kinship structures of that region of Timor-Leste. We argue that, rather, it is a tactical adaptation to concrete circumstances that has marked, in a very traumatic way, the family and the community in the last seven decades. Several extreme events determined this special rise of women's power in Eluli. The first was the sudden and untimely death of Dona Marta's husband. In the absence of the man, head of the family, it was decided, according to the consultations with the ancestors of the house and after the appropriate rituals were performed, that she should be the one to assume the government of the land and be consecrated *liurai-feto*.[3] The second was the war against the Indonesian occupation that took place between 1975-1999. In addition to the destruction of the territory, it was responsible for the flight and displacement of many people and the death of many others. In the post-war period, the return of surviving people, many of whom were widows and alien to the customary community, the reconstruction and the recovery of non-violent social relations also required exceptional measures. One of the granddaughters, the current matriarch, was married to a Portuguese man (already deceased) and, as a result, he was incorporated in the house of her male ancestors: the Noliku-Nobesi. Therefore, she never left her patrilineal lineage. These events created social and cultural conditions in which the governance of Eluli by women, since the mid-twentieth century until today, became not only possible but accepted. However, the matriarchs of Eluli are aware and affirm their family belonging to the Noliku-Nobesi and secure rituals and rules in conformity to *lisan*.[4] Thus, in customary terms, the three female daughters of the matriarch of Eluli already belong to the houses of their husbands (Silva 2017) and only her male son continues to be linked to the Noliku-Nobesi.[5] However, she affirms that all of her daughters and her son will inherit that land equally (according to the constitutional rights in the country). Moreover, the family has agreed and decided that the next in line responsible for Eluli will be her second daughter. However, it is interesting to bear in mind that none of the female descendants of Dona Marta acquired the status of *liurai-feto* after her. This shows how these processes of authority and legitimacy are instilled with variations and complexities (see Chapters 6 and 7, this volume).

Our methodology includes ethnographic notes, but it is, above all, a co-authorship based on a dialogue with the matriarch *Avó* Mina about the place, the land, her works and those of the women that inhabit Eluli and everything they represent for herself and her family.

We develop two main theses along this chapter. The first is that all the land-work is productive. It produces goods, services, memories, identities, affections, bonds, food, objects. In other words, it produces the abundances that are essential for the endless flow of life. We demonstrate that abundance can be thought of as the power to assess and state what kind of resources and wealth are available and valuable to a community. Ultimately, it is the possibility of exercising subjective and objective sovereignty to decide what kind of resources can never be reduced to commodities. It is also awareness about everything that the community-society-group already possesses to live and live well.

The second is that the socioeconomies with the greatest capacity to resist neoliberal capitalist hegemony are those that define for themselves what abundance is and practice another economy of desire. This other economy of desire that we discuss here points to sobriety as the opposite of neoliberal austerity. Sobriety is a choice in which life, in all its manifestations, is at the centre. In this sense, sobriety is an ecofeminist view of the world (Shiva and Mies 1997; Puleo 2013). Austerity, in contrast, is an imposition to safeguard the wealth of some at the expense of the life and misery of the majority. Sobriety is an alternative to the endless accumulation and extraction of contemporary capitalism because it is the opposite of greed. It is an economy of reciprocities in action and that is why it is the reverse of waste (Gibson et al. 2018). It is to amplify the functional utility of objects and tools; it is the opposite of disposable thinking; it is a rationality that aims at an organic preservation of whom and what takes care of life.

This text is structured in two sections. The first is dedicated to a theoretical reflection that allows us to clarify our feminist approach of the epistemologies of the South (Cunha 2017; Cunha and Sousa 2019). The second is an ethnography carried out in dialogue with *Avó* Mina (Grandma Mina), the matriarch of Eluli, and co-author of this chapter.

Our writing strategy for this second section was based on the artisanal thinking of feminist ecologies of knowledge (Cunha 2017; Cunha and Sousa 2019.). We exercise an inversion of the narrative order that has been naturalised in the social sciences in which the analysis is authorial, and constitutes the main body of the text, and the excerpts from the interviews or ethnographic notes appear as evidence or underlines to reinforce the theoretical and analytical argument. In this logic, even without explicitly stating it, it is considered that on one side lies authorship, meaning the authority of knowledge producers and, on the other, mere information. In our chapter, we consider that the descriptions about Eluli and everything that involves the life that takes place in that territory (Gago 2019) is mediated by subjectivities that think, analyse, and narrate knowledge. In this way, we want to highlight the dialogical construction of this text in which each of the authors, Mina Bessa and I, began to weave our analysis of the same issue on our own terms. It is a record of what we both know about Eluli, the people that inhabit it and the senses they produce with their thinking and daily works with the land. Nonetheless, it is important to state that we are aware of the limits that writing always imposes on us. Our aim is to exercise our epistemological decentre and challenge the limits of canonical textual production and accept *staying with the trouble* (Haraway 2016). We do hope we accomplish the task.

Feminist hermeneutics of the epistemologies of the South

The epistemologies of the South (Santos 2018) are a theoretical field that seems to point to a certain geography of knowledge. For Boaventura de Sousa Santos, this South has the strength of a metaphor of the human sufferings experienced by the violence perpetrated by colonialism, capitalism and heteropatriarchy. However, this South is not solely circumscribed to the victimisation and tragedy that torment inflicts; above all, it represents the strength of knowledge and social practices imagined and created in the struggle against all oppression aiming at paradigmatic and liberating social transformation. The epistemological field is open to think about the diversity of the world in its abundance, without wasting any experience, especially that which has seeped through the exclusionary sieve of modern logocentric science. The challenge is launched: to recognise that there is a South, to go to the South and to learn from the South. In our view, this allows us to break the abyssal line created to separate valid (scientific) from irrelevant (non-scientific) knowledge; it means corrupting the abyssal line that creates a world of beings of which dignity, history, identity, memory, culture and creative power are intrinsic attributes versus a world of ontologically flawed beings where animality, irrationality, repetition, and the incapacity to produce the world as their own are a common feature. It is on these grounds that the concept of the abyssal line is so important for what it reveals, this radically dichotomous way of thinking, along with the indignation it provokes which, in its turn, incites disobedience, divergence, and rupture. Starting from the assumption of incompleteness and imperfection of all knowledge, Boaventura affirms that the western and modern way of knowing the world is only one among many and ignoring or neglecting this cognitive abundance is a tragic waste of experiences (Santos 2002, 2018).

The feminist hermeneutics of the epistemologies of the South that we are proposing allows us to distinguish, with greater clarity, that the abyssal rationality inscribed in the modern logocentric rationality is also androcentric and anthropocentric. In other words, the abyssal separation is also reflected in sexism, understood as a system of disjunction and hierarchy based on the opposition between female and male, reduced to biosocial attributes created and fed by themselves. That is to say, the idea of the 'masculine' (of a certain masculinity or virility) as a measure of all things is central to the abyssal thinking. The proliferation of dichotomies, based on this subordinate opposition between those who represent themselves as women and those who represent themselves as men, has maintained the structurally sexist bias of modern Western thinking.[6]

Far from being blind or negligent in this regard, it is a rationality that takes care, in detail, to maintain the foundations of its power. In this sense, the work of many feminists has been showing how women's strategies are co-opted for the benefit of men (Waterhouse and Vifhuizen 2011). Consecutively, women were invented (Oyewùmí 2017) and as Silvia Federici (2010) warns, women were invented as 'housewives', responsible for the care and infrastructure of life which, in turn, are the necessary conditions for the accumulation of capital; an endless multitude of invisible women, overloaded with subordinate work, who are trying to convince themselves that this is their most natural function to which they cannot and should not aspire to escape. As stated by Amaia Orozco (2014), the promotion of a reactionary ethics of care is at the basis of the modern social contract that continues to maintain the obsession for the conquest of women's knowledge and bodies (Federici 2010; Cunha 2014) reorganising and appropriating their ways of life, their activities, in short, their knowledge and work.

We argue that feminist hermeneutics of epistemologies of the South offers a subversive thinking that questions and confronts any elements or traces of that colonial and cognitive empire that subjugates and discriminates women, their bodies and works (Mcclintok 1995). This has one main consequence which is that the epistemologies of the South have to address two things with equal radicalism:

on the one hand, the ontological, social and cognitive abyssality of sexism that creates women as beings on the side-line, flawed in creative humanity, inferior, empty, whose dignity is derivative and whose existence is subsidiary to the mode of virile domination; on the other hand, the realisation that this abyss is furthermore a colonial one. Women in metropolitan societies may be discriminated but they deal with it with regulative means—laws, conventions, institutions—to emancipate themselves. Otherwise, the women living in the colonial world—the old and new colonial worlds—are conceived as the others-of-others. Their tools for individual and collective emancipation imply a double movement against victimisation: the violence and appropriation of local and global patriarchies.

Although very briefly, it is still important to explore here the anthropocentrism of western modern abyssal thinking and how it is closely related to the idea of 'man' as the measure of all things. In other words, on one side of the line we have human beings, or rather, those beings to whom ontological plenitude is attributed and recognised, even if subsumed in the category of *anthropos* [man]; on the other, all the existences lacking intrinsic dignity and which are designated by nature. Polanyi ([1944] 2001) shows how the commodification of the land, read also as nature, and the capitalist fetishism that followed, implies making the multidimensional and non-market wealth that this entity represented and represents for human societies, critical for the capitalist rationale. The land, instead of being nature understood as a matrix on which the vital conditions of existence are based, is reduced to a landscape or tradable resource (Shiva 2017). This has meant, on the one hand, increasingly violent and larger scale extractive cycles (Svampa 2013) and, on the other hand, that it allows separating life from the economy, work from ways of life and imposes a certain sexual division of labour. As can be seen, androcentrism and anthropocentrism go hand in hand, constituting two sides of the articulation of the three oppressive and constitutive systems of Western modernity: capitalism, colonialism and heteropatriarchy.

The feminist heuristic energy compels us to invoke Mohanty's (1991) ground-breaking questioning about the need to decolonise all feminist thinking that is not deeply humble, situated, concrete and producing real effects in people's lives, especially those of the women. The feminist hermeneutics of the epistemologies of the South represents the continuous rescue of both the narratives of suffering and the struggles inscribed in it as well as the narratives of hope and possibility produced and constructed by the potentially infinite diversity of being a woman (Carty and Mohanty 2014).

This decolonising exercise implies the practice of a feminist ecology of knowledge that puts the diversity of knowledge in the world in dialogical tension and examines the value and meaning that each of them have in every context to solve problems and promote dignity and respect. It involves a pluritopic hermeneutics, rooted in a geography of knowledge that considers the power relations that are established and occupies the epistemological and sociological space to subvert it democratically (Harding 1998). The African philosopher Kwasi Wiredu (2003, 54) stresses that the epistemological dialogue needs open-mindedness, full respect for difference and is not only intended to avoid misunderstandings between the parties. Dialogue needs a cognitive horizon in which other narratives and other unexpected results can be inscribed and take place in other terms than those of the western orthodoxy.

As argued in the introduction to this volume, in Timor-Leste, as in many other places of the world, the diversity of lifestyles and livelihoods is profoundly connected with an ecology of economic relations that exist together in articulation, or/and in tension, one with the other forming a complex and fascinating socioeconomic landscape that has to be understood in order to know how to face and overcome the contemporary challenges (McWilliam and Traube 2011; Palmer 2010, 2015; Silva 2016, 2017; Gibson et al. 2018) and imagine a future of justice for all. The following epistemological exercise is a contribution to the community of knowledge that aims to unveil and problematise the possibilities that exist within the social fabric and constitute micro-politics of another way of organising life, production, consumption and distribution of the welfare.

The economies of the land and the narratives that keep the experiences alive

> One time, in my great-grandmother's day, they saw a turtledove that everyday flew by the huts and landed on the same *ai-dila* (papaya) branch. It was always the same turtledove, always at the same time. The feathers were shiny and her beak was always full of water. The drops could be seen falling on the ground. My great-grandmother then realized that the turtledove spoke with them saying that, right there, next to their huts, was a clean water spring. The turtledove came and went every day until one day, under the stones, the water reached the land in such abundance and was so crystalline that they knew that it was a blessed land where water was born sacred. It was Eluli, sacred water. The turtledove would be, forever and for the entire family, one that would never be touched, injured, imprisoned. Thus, Eluli was born, on the slopes of the mountains of Maubara.
>
> At the peak of the mountain is Guguleu where the *Uma Lulik* (sacred house) is located and all the grandmothers and grandfathers of that region were born. From there, the grandmothers, their daughters and granddaughters continue to stare at Eluli and observe the turtledoves flying over the land and resting on the centuries-old coffee-shade trees spread around, offering immense shadows on the hillsides.

Logocentric knowledge is that which uses instrumental reason to formulate the verifiable explanations that identify, delimit and interpret a certain phenomenon or reality. In this way, knowledge is always a rational act based on concepts that allow extrapolation and, thus, the enunciation of general laws. What feminist epistemologies of the South teach us is that poly-rationality is the condition of possibility for cognitive justice. That is to say, telling the world in its own terms cannot be considered a derivative or metaphorical thought, but a knowledge that cannot be wasted. A post-abyssal thinking, in the wake of the criticisms of post-colonial feminists, has to start from a self-imposed silencing to open mental space for other knowledge, without which we are reduced to the drastic impoverishment that presupposes the pretension of a self-sufficient modern-western thinking. It is assuming a reason, which does not conform with a sole way of knowing and considers emotions, memories and sentiments as an integral part of knowledge production and enunciation.

> Eluli, the land, the water, the coffee plantations, the flights of the turtledoves and the other obligations were attributed to Marta. In Guguleu, at the *Uma Lulik*, all homage and respect were paid and Marta joined the grandmothers as *liurai-feto*. She became known as *Rainha Dona* Marta, as the *malai-mutin* (Portuguese) say. A solemn and respected woman, she was consulted in her Eluli land on the affairs of families spread across these mountains. Her authority and her knowledge to preserve harmony still rests in the memory of those who knew her and call her the Maubara's *liurai-feto*. At a certain point she decided that her youngest son should succeed her in the care of Eluli and later on it should be his eldest daughter who would take care of that place and take over the responsibilities of the family. For grandmother Marta, the *liurai-feto*, Eluli should be transmitted to her granddaughter and her son would only be the intermediary. The other daughters and sons were advised to spread out over the mountains occupying their lands she designated and there raise the children and their descendants.

The androcentrism of modern Western knowledge demonstrates that an authoritative masculinity and its coercive power is capable of imposing himself as the measure of all things. For this reason, the idea of patriarchy, in which the figure of the man-male-father predominates over all social relations, is at the basis of the idea of the existence of a planetary and totalitarian system that victimises and oppresses all women in the world in the same way. In this sense, what vary are some of the patterns and methods of victimisation of women. The second assumption is that women will never be completely free from patriarchal oppression because the system overdetermines their existences.

Postcolonial feminisms have been showing two very important things. The first is that there are several systems of inequality production and some of them should be conceptualised as patriarchy in these terms. In other words, it is necessary to consider the colonial character, the imperial leather to use the words of Anne Mcclintock (1995), that certain concepts, such as patriarchy or gender, have been marking certain feminist narratives of emancipation.[7] The second is that both oppression and liberation are strongly contextual and, therefore, they are always in dynamic articulation between grounds and options.

In this particular case, the exceptional conditions (death, war and marriage) in which these women lived and live opened a rupture in the orthodoxy of customs, providing them with a space of power and legitimacy that they took for themselves and their descendants and exercise despite what was and is established. It is also very interesting to realise that this authority acquired both by circumstances and by the arrival of the modern state with a constitution that enshrines substantive and formal equality between women and men, did not make them forget the origin of their lineage or the obligations to which they are linked through them. These multi-layered and complex realities are, in our view, critical to decolonising any feminist thinking that seeks to see itself as the measure for all women. Therefore, collaborative modes of feminist knowledge and reciprocal learning are needed.

> With the war came the need to escape from destruction and persecution. Exile happened to many and with it the memories of Eluli, the sacred water, the *Uma Lulik* at the peak of Guguleu within the mountains of Maubara, were to be preserved with strength and resilience to somehow maintain our family united over continents, oceans and times. When peace and political independence arrived, we were able to begin the way back to Eluli. Eluli was patiently waiting for someone to arrive to comfort her from years of emptiness and with her recolour the gardens, the coffee plantations and her skies and clouds.
>
> We decided that the family home should be built in the same place where grandmothers and grandfathers had always lived and that had disappeared in the midst of violence, fighting and military persecution. The robusta and arabica coffee plantations had to be cleaned and maintained. The older coffee trees deserved to rest and newer ones should be buried to carry out the renovation of the highland coffee grove. The land suitable for growing gardens had to be cleared and prepared for planting and sowing. The house needed to be built solidly.
>
> We called on men to do their jobs: clearing the coffee plantations and the land, building the house's walls and placing the roof. The women picked, chose, roasted and pillared the coffee cherry, and went to the bazaars to sell the oversupply. It is also the women who plant the gardens, weed, harvest, and make granaries to store corn and beans. They harvest fruits, yams and cassava and prepare food for everyone. They care for chickens and pigs. They dig pits for the hens to lay their eggs away from heat and theft; they collect the eggs and know how to store them in the coolest places in the house. They gather fruits, vegetables and everything they can to give to their pigs by feeding them just as they do

> with their offspring. We organised the house so that we can sleep, eat, live and talk, and do everything else we need.

One of the most recurrent themes in feminist debates is the sexual division of labour as a source and the reason for the inequality of power between women and men. In many cases this is confirmed and all the statistics on the subject usually demonstrate the overload of women doubled by the tasks at work and at home. An assumption is made from there, with good evidence supporting it: this reality results in their subordination, delay in their professional careers, wage discrimination and less decision-making power. Being true in many societies, we need, however, not to colonise the world through the universalisation of this claim. By clearly identifying the jobs of men and the jobs of women in Eluli, we see things that contradict the notion that the sexual division of labour is always a mode of patriarchal oppression. There are three ideas that we want to underline here. The first has to do with the clear adequacy of the work of women and men to their bodies. Women feel protected because they do not have to do things that involve greater physical efforts for which they do not feel prepared. However, when we look closely, we notice that this division of labour is based on the principle of complementarity. This is the second idea: men clear the land with fire, remove the stones and cut the bush, so that later women can plant the gardens. Doing one without the other does not make sense. And the third is that it is up to women to decide on things as important as: what to eat; how food can be preserved; how animals are fed; what to store to stock for times of greatest scarcity and what to sell in order to be able to buy what is missing; what destination is given to the spaces of the house, among other things.

If we manage to silence our Western feminist assumptions what we can see is a system of balanced work and power which, in Eluli's case, gives women greater authority and freedom.

> We throw away things that we can no longer reuse. There are few such things because, if there is any packaging coming from a supermarket, when it is empty, it serves as a cover or as a small container to organise and store whatever is necessary. The life of things is prolonged, new functions are assigned to them, everything is used and reused.

The anthropocentric character of modern-Western rationality has long been identified and is heavily criticised. This radical anthropocentrism of capitalism explains, on the one hand, the intensity of the extraction of everything it can transform into commodities that result in capital gains in favour of profit and the accumulation of a few who control the means of production. On the other hand, capitalism sees the possibility of accumulation as potentially infinite. In this way, nature and all beings, human and non-human, are considered as potentially unlimited, or at least, subjected to endless exploitation.

The commodification of all spheres of life is one of its most brutal manifestations leading to the privatisation of essential goods and the radical separation between humanity and nature. The criticisms carried out by ecofeminists, post-developmentalists, solidarity economies and popular economies, among others, clearly show the limits and the dangers of this extractive and destructive anthropocentrism. We also know that the burden of anthropocentrism, of which the extractive capitalist economy is an utmost expression, is not equally distributed around the world. Environmental conflicts, but also the scarcity of water and the abuse of poisons unequally condemn the populations of the world to lives without security, without dignity and respect. What underlines the knowledge and practices of these Eluli women are two things. On the one hand, the idea that in communities like them, seen as traditional, permaculture and the integrated and holistic view of life that is nowadays conceptualised as a circular economy are known and have been practiced since ageless times. It is neither an ideological option nor a surrender to scientific knowledge. It is ancestral knowledge, proven, tested and assumed as the one that best protects life in all its forms. On the other hand, it shows how women's work, far from being merely reproductive, is what produces, in a real and permanent way, the material and immaterial basis of life. This also is not survival, as development theorists insist on characterising. This is life lived with sobriety because it is based on another economy of desire.

> We are four women who take care of flowers and fruit trees in Eluli and I decide with the others what can be sold in the mountain bazaars in Maubara or what we can take to sell in Dili. I have that authority. The people who live there, in the mountains, also ask me for advice and often my intervention to resolve their disputes or anxieties. I am called *Avó* Mina and I assume this role naturally since I know the value given to older people and their experiences in our community. The example of *liurai-feto* Dona Marta, my grandmother, accompanies me in my role, which, during my exile, first in Indonesia and then in Portugal, I never thought I would inherit and fulfil. But it was not enough to return to Eluli, it was necessary to assume Eluli completely and that means to belong to the land which is much more than to possess the land.

In Kelly Silva's words and analysis, this relationship of belonging to the land and not of possession of the land forces us to think, with another depth, of the relationship between subject and object.[8] As Kelly says, and it is also our argument, along with those of many feminist authors already mentioned in this chapter, one of the main conditions for the commodification of the land was its disenchantment, it was to remove from the land its own agency as a creator of meanings. This relationship of reciprocity with the land, the impossibility of separating, much less ontologically, the land and the beings that inhabit her and are inhabited by her, the practices and experiences of these women in Eluli suggest that, certainly, what characterised economic relations before Western European modernism commodified them to such an extent that only what can be bought and sold is valuable, is beyond life itself.[9]

> I know my responsibilities towards my grandmothers and grandfathers who, on top of the mountain, in Guguleu, continue to be present in many ways. I know that I have to prepare my second daughter to continue to be Eluli's and govern her on her behalf and that of her sisters and brother. I am also preparing my granddaughters and grandson who will succeed me. Life is renewed in each generation, but each one is as outside as it is inside the previous one. This is what I teach the youngest, how to take care of the house, the garden or the coffee plantations; knowing how to harvest, choosing the fruit, where the hens lay their eggs, how to know if they are proper to eat, how to roast coffee, how to ground it; where the graves of grandparents are and what must be done to honour them; knowing the way of the bazaar; knowing how to respect neighbours and families in the community and when and how it is necessary to be present. It is like a school to give meaning to the world where we live and want to live. I am the principal educator of our daughters and granddaughters and grandson and provide all necessary lessons and experiences to them. It is a school without walls and without schedules, but made up of many useful knowledge that can be learned by experiencing everything with the joy of playing or, simply, because we are together and feel that we belong there.

It is known that in Timor-Leste societies are mostly patrilineal and patrilocal. It appears that power and authority within the family and community are patriarchal. Many studies and data prove this (Niner 2017; Silva and Sousa 2011). However, in the case of Eluli, it seems to be more complex and divergent than that normalisation of patriarchal relations.[10] The authority and power seem to be transitive and often, in the last generations, they are expressly feminine. Women were chosen and are given the legitimacy of the power to decide, to teach, to pass on the land and all the connections that it entails and allows. This reality questions in a very clear way that tradition is always being invented and reinvented and how generalisations, even when contextualised, can be inadequate. On the other hand, this situation opens space for other narratives of emancipation of women, endogenous, with strong local meanings and in terms in which they are perceived as a reinforcement of the power and autonomy of women without having to dispense with their view of the world and what makes them feel they belong and have a place in their society.

Final notes

The feminist hermeneutics of epistemologies of the South is an exercise of profound reorganisation of the cognitive agencies with which we have to deal in producing post-abyssal knowledge. Moreover, it is an approach to humbly deal with perplexity in the face of divergent memories, discrepant narratives and stories told otherwise. It is to think beyond the colonial that still binds most of us to Western modernity. It is a constant effort to highlight the ignorance generated by the colonial-capitalist-heteropatriarchal imagination. Visible, invisible, partially exposed and/or still covered by shadows, women and their works narrated by their words teach us several things that we enunciate here very briefly.

Eluli's socioeconomics cannot be reduced to the absence of choices, poverty, ignorance, primitive, backward, obscure, ancestral ways or, in the words of contemporary financial hegemony, as an obstacle to development. It consists of secular practices and struggles for other ways of life, for other paradigms of government of the house, but also with functional adaptations to the monetised world of capitalism or the rules of patrilineality and the powers of men. In these practices, other imaginaries of justice, respectability and authority exist and are recreated. If wealth is more than the accumulation of things and goods, it can be said that they enrich lives and communities by giving them meaning and valuing their skills and knowledge as well as their identities in motion. They are not complete responses and are not thought as such. But they are narratives of dignity and the struggle against vulnerability, violence and its reduction to a secondary or worthless existence.

In Eluli it is easy to understand that women's work is productive. First, all women work, and always have worked. Their works produce countless things, both material and immaterial, at different scales and spheres where they live and perform. Second, questioning and being able to define what abundance is leads us to another economy of desire where there is a sovereignty of its own to define what is important for life to flourish and be lived with respect and joy. In this other economy of desire, in which sobriety is central, what has more value are the fruits of the land but also feelings of belonging and protection, ancestral spirits, goddesses and gods, attention, care, trust, technologies, the knowledge and the wisdom that people throughout the ages and generations have been gathering, keeping and teaching. If the terms of abundance are determined and stated by whom they concern, the constituent power passes from the hands of those who permanently exploit what is scarce and what is abundant to the hands of those who decide on their own lives. This is a paradigmatic shift. Sobriety, as we propose, highlights, on the one hand, the ecology of temporalities in which the past, the present and the future intersect and, on the other hand, the maximisation of justice that such divergent experiences can generate.

Within this collaborative work, we articulated a feminist hermeneutics of the epistemologies of the South with an ethnography about Eluli narrated by Mina Bessa, co-author of this text, about that space-time which is in the mountains of Maubara in Timor-Leste. From this dialogue between different knowledge, we learned several things that we explained in the reflective excerpts. We assume the heterodoxy of the text because we are aware that writing together is, in itself, a form of affirmation and rebellion necessary for the production of post-colonial feminist knowledge.

Notes

1 Santos (2018) argues that the scientific-philosophical apparatus that emerged from the Euro-centric tradition is sustained by the creation of abyssal lines. The abyssal lines are those that create a world of humans and sub-humans and non-humans separated abyssally. Santos adds that the abyssal lines separate people and their worlds through a colonial model that guarantees ontological, social and epistemological inequalities and hierarchies. A post-abyssal thinking is the continuing exercise to radically criticise and overcome this abyssal rationality.

2 As we explain further in the text, Eluli means sacred water.

3 *Liurai-feto* is an expression in the Tetum language that is commonly translated as queen (*rainha* in the Portuguese language). However, the word refers to a position of authority and exceptional recognition in a given community. The expression can be better understood by looking at each literal meaning of its components. *Liu*: form of comparative superiority; *Rai*: earth, ground, world, and *Feto*: female person. See, Costa, *Dicionário de Tétum-Português*.

4 *Lisan* is a Tetum word that means ceremonies, customary rituals, norms and practices. See, Costa, *Dicionário de Tétum-Português*.

5 On this subject of the circulation of fertility and the flow of life in Timor-Leste through marriage and the circulation of women through different houses, it is important to read Silva, “Women, Gender and Power among Indigenous Peoples of Portuguese Timor”.

6 In this chapter we use the word women to refer to all human beings that present themselves as female-women in spite of their biological sex or ascribed sexual identity.

7 Mcclintock, *Imperial Leather: Race, Gender and Sexuality in the Colonial Contest*.

8 These reflections by Kelly Silva occurred when we discussed this chapter. We thank Kelly for her words, generosity and contributions.

9 Here and above, we decided to consider the land as a subject. It is why we are using ‘her’ instead of ‘it’.

10 As the works of Lisa Palmer show, this is occurring across the country where more ambilineal norms and practices remain or emerge in place and shape the daily lives of Timorese people much more than some mainstream views want to acknowledge. We thank Lisa Palmer for the sharing of this knowledge that brought more accuracy to our discussion.

References

Carty, L., and C. T. Mohanty. 2014. "Mapping Transnational Feminist Engagements: Neoliberalism and the Politics of Solidarity." In *The Oxford Handbook of Transnational Feminist Movements*, edited by R. Baksh and W. Harcourt, 82-115. Oxford: Oxford University Press.

Costa, L. 2000. *Dicionário de Tétum-Português*. Lisboa: Edições Colibri.

Cunha, T. 2014. *Never Trust Sindarela. Feminismos, pós-colonialismos, Moçambique e Timor-Leste.* Coimbra: Almedina.

Cunha, T. 2017. "Beyond the Timorense nationalist orthodoxy: The 'Herstory' of Bi Murak." In *Women and the Politics of Gender in Post-conflict Timor-Leste*, edited by S. Niner, 46-64. London/New York: Routledge.

Cunha, T., and V. Sousa. 2019. "Epistemologías del Sur y las Economías de Ellas. La Cooperativa 'Capuchinhas' de la Sierra de Montemuro." *Revista de Antropología Social* 28 (2): 323-344.

Cunha, T., and L. de P. Valle. 2019. "O respeito à economia da vida e as pedagogias ecofeministas. Reflexões sobre a prática da agroecologia e do hamutuk." *Otra Economía* 12 (22): 238-252.

Federici, S. 2010. *Calibán y la bruja: mujeres, cuerpo y acumulación originaria.* Madrid: Traficantes de Sueños.

Friedberg, C. 2011. "O imaginário e as práticas nas relações com os outros seres. Algumas pistas de reflexão com base em dados timorenses." In *Ita maun alin... o livro do irmão mais novo*, edited by K. Silva and L. Sousa, 47-61. Lisboa: Ed. Colibri/Instituto de Estudos de Literatura Tradicional.

Gago, V. 2019. *La potencia feminista o el deseo de cambiarlo todo.* Madrid: Traficantes de Sueños.

Gibson, K., R. Astuti, M. Carnegie, A. Chalernphon, K. Dombroski, A. R. Haryani, A. Hill, B. Kehi, L. Law, I. Lyne, A. McGregor, K. McKinnon, A. McWilliam, F. Miller, C. Ngin, D. Occeña-Gutierrez, L. Palmer, P. Placino, M. Rampengan, W. Lei Lei Than, N. I. Wianti and S. Wright. 2018. "Community economies in Monsoon Asia: Keywords and key reflections." *Asia Pacific Viewpoint* 59 (1): 3-16. doi.org/10.1111/apv.12186.

Gudynas, E. 2019. *Direitos da natureza. Ética biocênctrica e políticas ambientais,* Lisboa: Elefante Editora.

Haraway, D. 2016. *Staying with the Trouble. Making Kin in the Chthulucene.* Durkham/London: Duke University Press.

Harding, S. 1998. *Is Science Multicultural?: Postocolonialisms, Feminisms, and Epistemologies.* Bloomington and Indiana: Indiana University Press.

Langton, M., O. Mazel and L. Palmer. 2006. "The 'spirit' of the thing: The boundaries of Aboriginal economic relations at Australian Common Law." *The Australian Journal of Anthropology* 1 (3): 307-321. doi.org/10.1111/j.1835-9310.2006.tb00066.x.

McWilliam, A., and E. Traube (eds). 2011. *Land and Life in Timor-Leste – Ethnographic Essays.* Canberra: ANU E. Press

Mcclintock, A. 1995. *Imperial Leather: Race, Gender and Sexuality in the Colonial Contest.* New York: Routledge.

Mohanty, C. T. 1991. "Under western eyes: feminist scholarship and colonial discourses." In *Third World Women and the Politics of Feminism,* edited by C. T. Mohanty, Chandra Talpade *et al.* Bloomington: Indiana University Press.

Narciso, V., and P. Henriques. 2011. "Funções da terra para as comunidades rurais do Timor-Leste." In *Ita maun alin... o livro do irmão mais novo,* edited by K. Silva e L. Sousa, 241-256. Lisboa: Ed. Colibri/ Instituto de Estudos de Literatura Tradicional.

Niner, S. (ed) 2017. *Women and Politics of Gender in Post-conflict Timor-Leste.* London: Routledge.

Oyewùmí, O. (1997). *The Invention of Women: Making an African Sense of Western Gender Discourses.* Minneapolis, London: University of Minnesota Press.

Orozco, A. P. 2014. *Subversión feminista de la economía.* Madrid: Traficantes de Sueños.

Polanyi, K. (1944) 2001. *The Great Transformation — The Political Origins of Our Time.* Boston: Beacon Press.

Puleo, A. H. 2013. *Ecofeminismo para otro mundo posible.* Madrid: Cátedra. Colección Feminismos.

Santos, B. de S. 2002. "Para uma sociologia das ausências e uma sociologia das emergências." *Revista Crítica de Ciências Sociais* 63: 237-280. https://doi.org/10.4000/rccs.1285.

Santos, B. de S. 2018. *The End of the Cognitive Empire: The Coming of Age of Epistemologies of the South.* Durham/London: Duke University Press.

Shiva. V. 2017. *Quién Alimenta realmente al mundo?el fracaso de la agricultura industrial y la promesa de la agraecología.* Madrid: Capitán Swing.

Shiva, V., and M. Mies. 1997. *Ecofeminismo*, Lisboa: Instituto Piaget – Epistemologia e Sociedade.

Silva, K. 2016. "Administrando pessoas, recursos e rituais. Pedagogia econômica como tática de governo em Timor-Leste." *Horizontes Antropológicos* 22 (45): 127-153. http://dx.doi.org/10.1590/S0104-71832016000100006.

Silva, K. 2017. "Women, gender and power among indigenous peoples of Portuguese Timor." *Anuário Antropológico* 42 (2): 183-205. https://doi.org/10.4000/aa.2240

Silva, K., and L. Sousa. 2011. *Ita maun alin… o livro do irmão mais novo.* Lisboa: Ed. Colibri/Instituto de Estudos de Literatura Tradicional.

Svampa, M. 2013. "«Consenso de los Commodities» y lenguajes de valoración en América Latina." *Revista Nueva Sociedad* 244: 30-46.

Waterhouse, R., and C. Vifhuizen. 2001. *Estratégias das mulheres, proveito dos homens.* Moçambique: Núcleo de Estudos da Terra.

Wiredu, K. 2003. "L'ancrage de la pensée africaine et les conditions du dialogue interculturel" *Revue Alternatives Sud: Pour une pensée africaine emancipative* 10 (4): 49-60.

ECONOMIC TRANSFORMATIONS

CHAPTER 9

Land and diet under pressure: The impacts of Suai Supply Base in Kamanasa kingdom

Brunna Crespi

Abstract

This chapter discusses impacts of the building of the Suai Supply Base on the economic dynamics of Kamanasa kingdom. It focuses on issues related to land appropriation by the State by exploring phenomena related to diet and increased monetisation. Accelerated by this project, a certain modernity has induced unprecedented changes within the territory and social fabric. To study these changes, I will present a case study of Kamanasa, a Tetum and Bunaq village located on the east coast of Suai.

Keywords: Development; oil project; monetarisation; tradition; Suai

Despite Timor-Leste being considered an independent country since 2002, its territorial integrity was, until recently, under international pressure. In fact, until the middle of March 2018, the maritime borders of this new State were uncertain, given that the neighbouring States, Indonesia and Australia, had long refused to establish a permanent agreement to set the borders between the countries. This conflict has its origin in the fact that the marine subsoil of the zone is rich in oil and gas.

For a long time, the existing off-shore oilfields in the sea of the Timor were explored by an Australian oil company based in Darwin. Timor-Leste expects finally to end this external dependence, with the creation of its own oil company and associated industrial bases, that, according to the government, "will makes possible the consolidation of an independence of the Timor-Leste based on the economic sovereignty" (Program of the VI Constitutional Government Legislature 2015-2017). This affirmation let us glimpse that oil development is an essential condition to reach political sovereignty (Bovensiepen and Nygaard-Christensen 2018), despite the possible impacts of this project on the environment, and the risks of an ecological disaster (Cryan 2015a; La'o Hamutuk 2013a, 2013b, 2014b; Fundasaun Mahein 2013).

It is from the troubled context of a post-conflict country intent on accelerated development that there emerged the idea of a national oil company, Timor Gap, and its oil development project Tasi Mane. This project occupies a large part of the

Timorese south coast and includes terrestrial infrastructure such as a refinery, a petrochemical complex, a gas pipeline, a supply base, a port and an airport.

But this project is a vehicle for change for local society. While modern economic challenges are created by oil, Suai's traditional economy is still based on subsistence farming, with 41% of the Timorese population still living below the poverty line and suffering with a high rate of malnutrition (World Bank 2014). This fragile situation, associated with a strong dependence on oil, creates a sense of insecurity for the local inhabitants. Much of this process is taking place very rapidly and takes little account of the demands and needs of local society (Crespi and Guillaud 2018).

This chapter discusses the impacts of the building of the Suai Supply Base on the economic dynamics of Kamanasa kingdom. It focuses on issues related to land appropriation by the State by exploring phenomena related to diet and increased monetisation, on the basis of information produced during 11 months of fieldwork, divided into several stays between 2015 and 2016, and two other visits in May 2014 and November 2018.[1] The Tasi Mane infrastructure project, implemented by the national oil company Timor Gap, occupies three areas: Beaço (gas processing), Betano (oil refinery) and Suai-Covalima (oil industries and storage). My study focused on the Suai-Covalima, where the project includes a supply base, a new administrative city, an international airport and a highway. More specifically, I observed the transformations brought by the project in two localities: Holbelis, a hamlet affected by the airport extension; and Fatisin, where the Suai Supply Base is to be built. These two localities are part of the kingdom of Kamanasa, the political entity most affected by the mega-project. The kingdom of Kamanasa is an ancient trading kingdom that once controlled the southern coast of Timor-Leste. It corresponds today to a customary territory inhabited by two main ethno-linguistic groups: the Tetum and the Bunaq, the two main communities affected by the project.

Broadly speaking, my article argues that this project is a vehicle for the commodification of important aspects of the economy as feeding and land access, leading to structural changes that affect social systems in place, especially the territoriality, trade and diet. This article is organised in four sections. The first explores local practices and notions of land ownership and use and how the transfer of the land to the project challenged these practices. The second explains the State's plans for the base and the ways in which they have dealt with the expectations and local knowledge related to the land. It also addresses the way in which the State has implemented its compensation practices for land appropriation. The third analyses the tensions emerging among local populations arising from State practices in the region and explores the community's fears and expectations about these matters. Finally, I discuss the economic changes derived from compensation policies and how they have been a major disturbance on the way of life, transforming the local agriculture and diet.

Local practices and notions of land ownership and use

The Tasi Mane project's infrastructure is located over large areas that are essential to the people of the region: it covers land currently used for livelihood purposes, such as farmland (rice fields, maize and other crops of high economic value as teak and tobacco), pasture land, forest areas used for plant and timber collection, and parts of the coast used for fishing and salt harvesting. In addition, many of the sites that will be affected by construction are invested with sacred value, and local people believe that the destruction of these sites could lead to disease, conflict and natural disasters (see Rose 2017; Crespi 2018). This process of land expropriation was financially compensated (starting from 2013 until now, 2019) by the government, affecting people's relationship with their land and existing customary practices.[2]

Most of the inhabitants of the kingdom of Kamanasa have remained food farmers, despite the efforts of the Portuguese government to increase production and the Indonesian regime to develop transmigration as a model of modern, surplus agriculture aimed at developing a market and service economy (Shepherd 2009). Their mode of livelihood is linked to the importance of symbolic relationships with the complex and omnipresent universe of non-humans, spirits and ancestors, which condition the outcome of any human action (Guillaud 2015).

Prior to the arrival of the Tasi Mane project, most of the local lands of Kamanasa, with rare exceptions, were only delimited by customary agreements between the two ethnolinguistic groups in the area, Tetum and Bunaq. It is assumed by this local community that these frontiers had once been delimited by the ancestors and are thus subject to prohibitions and symbolic representations.

In Kamanasa, most of the land has been used collectively: this is obviously the case for forests and springs, grazing lands, and generally sacred sites and cemeteries. On the other hand, the level of the community or the social group concerned with this collective exploitation can vary: lineage, clan, hamlet, village, etc. Community lands are in principle accessible to all members of the community concerned, and there are only a few resources in these areas that are individually appropriate: they concern commercial trees such as sandalwood and teak, the ones present in plantations such as coconut trees, as well as trees bearing hives, domestic animals, etc. Thus, the members of a village have the right to use equitably the lands of the village, but a tree belongs to the one who planted it, even if the land where it is, is cultivated by another (see Chapter 10, this volume). Similarly, when a field is abandoned, other inhabitants of the same hamlet can freely take it back, unless there are perennial trees that indicate the appropriation of the land, such as coconut trees, areca, candlenut, etc. In this system, a field is not necessarily reused by the one who cultivated it previously, which does not mean that users do not take care of these lands.

In this context of a land with multiples users, for the proposed land compensation system, Timor Gap opted for a land registry that followed the national land registry model. This national cadastre is based on the user rights, and does not have the capacity or the purpose to register the various interlocking land rights that form the customary system. However, this register process by Timor Gap was revealing and, moreover, "a catalyst" for the tensions between users, since it exposed the intersection and overlapping of several types of rights that coexist in the customary system (Crespi 2018; Rose 2017; Cryan 2015b; McWilliam 2008), as well as the contradictions in the rules management of resources and spaces between the State and local communities (customary management). More precisely, the transition from an oral system to a written, individual and property title system, was equivalent to moving from a "commons" possession to a private property.[3]

The functioning of the commons is very complex in itself, which is not a problem in a customary system that is regulated on a case-by-case basis, but which returns to its full complexity once we reduce it to a right of individual appropriation, as is the case in the Timor-Leste national land registry. The land belongs in fact to the few original houses which settled the area first, and whose legitimate right to the land is rarely questioned.[4] This initial right to land is branched out into multiple subordinate rights, allotted to allied houses, especially those belonging to the system of matrimonial alliances. These multiple rights of land use are anchored in the memory of "word masters", who in the event of land conflicts are responsible for reconstructing the historical transactions between the different groups in long "sessions" of speech (see more in Crespi 2018).

The symbolic territory

In Suai, the territory is associated with the spiritual control of the place, which is held by the clan having the function of *rai nain*.[5] It is the oldest clan of the place, assimilated to the first arrivals, the only one able to appease and control the evil spirits who protect the land and who also bear the name of *rai nain*; these "land-master" clans, first-comers, therefore have a pre-eminent right over the land and its resources.[6]

According to Friedberg (1982), the oldest clans would be responsible for the integrity of the territory both militarily and in terms of productivity. In Kamanasa, military protection is provided by a clan specialised in war (*kakaluk*) and not by the *rai nain*, the political and military being separated from the spiritual. For Bovensiepen and Rosa (2016), the categories "indigenous" and "sacred" are diametrically opposed to "foreign" and "political". Thus, any new clan arriving in a place must establish a relationship of alliance and precedence with this "land-master" clan, which will then determine the relationship that the new arrivals will establish with the land.

To this first register under customary land law is superimposed another related register, but within the political sphere and guaranteeing the previous rights. In this register, two types of power combine without opposing each other—the first is spiritual power, concentrated in the invisible power exercised by the beings of the afterlife *rai nain*, and controlled by the *rai nain* clan. This is a symbolic mastery since the *rai nain* beings are considered as non-humans, spirits of the earth, present in the forests and owners of the wilderness, as their name implies. They are only present in places considered as *fuik* (= wild) and, considered as evil, are sometimes called "devils", sometimes referred to as *ular* (= giant snakes). The local inhabitants represent them as rather feminine beings. Other researchers (Francillon 1967, 151) consider them to be the spirits of the former occupants of the earth, but this does not seem to be the case in the kingdom of Kamanasa.

The second power is the political power, held by the *liurai*.[7] The *liurai* are responsible for making decisions concerning the territory, such as the management and use of all the lands of the kingdom, and are also involved in legal and important matters, such as those relating to the delimitation of borders between kingdoms. This *liurai* manages land at the *suku* or kingdom level and is responsible for the final decision on the allocation of land.[8] At the time of Portuguese colonisation, the occupants of any land had to pay them a tax, called *rai teen*; this tax went directly to the *liurai* when the clan owned the land, and went to the owning clan when the group only had a right of use.[9]

We can see that these two powers combine and recognise each other, even if at first sight it is the *liurai* that controls the land. Since it is the *liurai* that controls the political decisions related to the territory, the clan of the first arrivals has the power to control the *rai nain* beings and consequently the fertile and productive land as such. These first-comers have no political power over the place, but they continue to have spiritual power. Their rights to the land are inalienable, except in the case of prolonged abandonment.

Concerning the different levels of land ownership (see Figure 9.1), the first one corresponds to the right of ownership over the land and is passed down through generations. The movements of houses observed in this highly mobile society generate rights of appropriation subordinate to the theoretical "initial right" of the first occupant. This is the second level of land control, which includes usage rights, held by the clans who use the land and exploit its resources, but who do not have with it the privileged spiritual relationship of the newcomers. This right is granted by the clans that control the land and is validated by the king (*liurai*) to allies, on the condition that the latter respect the rules put in place by the clan of the first occupants. This category of right itself has several degrees, since a clan that has a right of use on a territory can delegate this right to other allied clans, taking responsibility for them. For example, the forest of Mane Lima belongs to the royal clan of Kamanasa, but rights of use have been granted to clans of Fatisin, who in turn granted the use of the plots to clans of Maneikin, who planted teak stands there.

In the past, before the arrival of the Portuguese according to my informants, when a clan granted the use of its land to another clan it was common practice to exchange it for a service, such as taking part of the harvest of each family cultivating on it, or watching over the land so that others would not come to occupy it. At that time, unoccupied and uncultivated land was the subject of stakes and conflicts, especially when commercially valuable trees such as sandalwood were growing on it.

The multiple rights over the land

In brief, while the *rai nain* clan has an inalienable right of appropriation over its territory, its allied houses as well as those of other clans can also take hold of the territory and even become autonomous after a certain period of land use. This original territorial map and the resources that it may contain thus evolves from a theoretical use of the land of the first-comers clan by its members to a scheme where multiple "borrowers" cultivate the land of another clan over the long term (Figure 9.1). In this complex territory, in which precedence and alliances play an

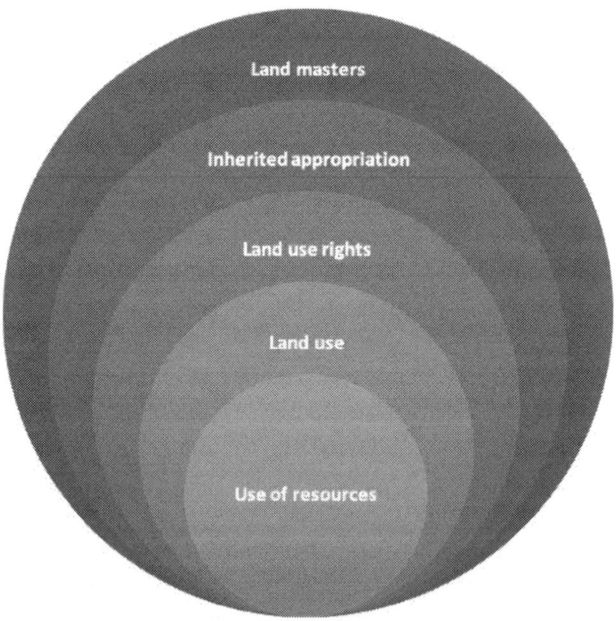

Figure 9.1: The different levels of appropriation of territory in Kamanasa. Credit: Bruna Crespi.

important role, the underlying use rights overlap and may conflict with the original property rights.

But while these multiple use rights may be inextricable, and sometimes contentious, so far, the customary system has demonstrated its ability to resolve land conflicts, relying as a last resort on the ancestors' arbitration. In addition to the customary assemblies established to resolve boundary issues, house renovation ceremonies are crucial moments of sociability and social cohesion during which knowledge about history and territory is expressed and transmitted (Crespi 2018).

Communication between State and local populations

The project schedules and implementation

The government began the preliminary assessments as well as the first discussions with local populations in September 2011, when it made its final investment decision on the Suai Supply Base project. The exchanges officially ended on April 8th 2013, with the official statement from Timor Gap that "land identification, consultations and negotiations with the community have been completed". According to several statements, however, the government did not present to the communities the reality of the project, nor did it specify the potential social and environmental impacts.

These negotiations on the land led in April 2013 to an agreement between the government and the local communities on land transfers and their compensation (Timor Gap 2014; Cryan 2015a; La'o Hamutuk 2016). In this agreement, the entire population of the Kamanasa kingdom agreed to cede a total of 1,113 hectares of land for a duration of 150 years, in return for 10% of the profits of the Suai Supply Base, once the base is active. However, the NGO that accompanied the process, La'o Hamutuk (2014a, 1), denounced the lack of consensus in the community at that moment, the document being signed only by 15 of the 267 families concerned: the opponents to the project as well as women had been excluded from this meeting of agreement between the government and local chiefs. It is necessary here to point out that the society of Kamanasa is matrilineal, and that, consequently, the lands are transmitted to the women; and yet, it was their husbands or brothers who traded in their places. Moreover, the details of the negotiation, as well as the final document, remain secret and are not available, either to the public or to the community itself.

In July 2015, during a government-sponsored "socialisation" meeting with Kamanasa, several villagers revolted against state agents, accusing the project of misleading advertising and neglect of local populations.[10] The local community also accused Timor Gap of unequal treatment among the villages affected by the project, which increases the tension between the different actors in this process: residents complained that other, less affected villages (for example, those with just a few displaced homes and no fields) received the same hiring promises from the government—that is to say, the government promised to hire them on the same basis as those who had completely lost their land and no longer had a way to live from their livelihood—or received money for land belonging to others (for example, villages displaced by the Indonesian government).

Timor Gap mapped and identified the land to be affected by the project, and by 2017, a large proportion of residents of that land had received financial compensation. The compensations proposed by the government for the local inhabitants cover two modalities: the monetary compensation for the monopolised lands, as well as the crops that grow on them; and material compensation for the rituals necessary for the displacement of houses and other sacred elements.

Monetary compensation and property

The land registry proposed by Timor Gap differs, however, from the government's proposals in the *Ita Nia Rai* (Our Land) program regarding land ownership levels: in the national program, individuals are invited to declare only the possession of their lands, and the right of use is not taken into account (Cryan 2015c). The compensation system proposed by the Timor Gap has attempted to approximate local realities and, more specifically, the customary system of land appropriation. Nevertheless, the most visible land use is that which is linked to the present user, who cultivates the land, which leads government officials to register them as "owners" of the land, causing conflicts between the users.[11]

The compensation was determined by the government according to a pay scale that distinguished two types of property: on the one hand the fields (the land itself), and on the other the useful trees and plants that grew on these lands at the time of negotiation. This distinction was made in an attempt to include the local property regime that dissociates the land itself from the crops and trees that are cultivated on it.

Land clearances were planned in two phases, depending on when they would be recovered by the State: land on the immediate perimeter of the highway and the airport were the first to be compensated, while those that would serve the supply base would be compensated only later, during the second construction phase. The first offsets occurred in 2013 with construction commencing at the end of 2014, while compensations for the second phase of the project, which was originally planned for 2015/2016, started at the end of 2016.

The residents of the traditional Kamanasa kingdom transferred a total of 1,113 hectares of land to the Suai Supply Base project. They used the word *fo* ("to give" in Tetum Terik) to describe this transaction, which is different from *faan* ("to sell").

This transaction was seen as a donation to the government, made by signing a register, but none of the research participants were issued documents for such a transaction. Money was transferred to bank accounts that beneficiaries were required to set up for the transaction; most immediately emptied these accounts, preferring the security of cash. Indeed, the Timorese people have low trust in the government and all its structures because of several years of human rights' violations during the Indonesian occupation.

According to information provided by the head of one of the villages affected by the project, Norberto Amaral of the village of Holbelis, the fields were paid at the rate of $3 USD per m^2, i.e. $30,000 USD per hectare. Additionally, productive fruit trees (coconuts, mangoes, jackfruit, etc.) and cultivated plants were compensated. Each fruit tree was estimated at $60 USD per tree, $25 for marungui (Moringa oleifera), and $25 for betel palm (Areca catechu). Moringa leaves and fruits are common vegetables. Betel nut, along with betel leaf and lime, make up the betel quid; it has high customary value due to its use in all ceremonies. Crops like corn, rice and beans were compensated at the rate of 15 cents per plant. Electric poles installed in fields encroaching upon settlements were also compensated at the rate of 50 kg of rice and $250 USD for each pole. The akar palms (*Corypha utan*) which belong to the semi-spontaneous domain were not compensated, nor were the banyan (*Ficus* sp.). Although the Timor Gap paid for the rituals for the displacement of altars, clan houses and sacred places, the displacement of simple family houses was not compensated, either in the form of a payment, of a replacement of materials or in the form of new land. According to the local inhabitants, the government considers that with the land being State-owned in this area, the only exceptions being a private title to the land—and no sacredness being linked to the family houses, compensations are not necessary.

Consulting and participation of the local population

The details of the negotiations conducted by the Timor Gap were never exposed to the public. The local residents indicated that the decisions had been taken by the government and then communicated to the communities, who did not contest the decisions. The NGO La'o Hamutuk (2011) argues that these communities, long lived under the Indonesian dictatorial regime, were legally abandoned (due to a lack of legal assistance) and were not aware of their rights. Moreover, they had no point of reference regarding the market value of their lands and crops, since subsistence farming is predominant in the area.

Consultation meetings with the community revealed in themselves the key problem surrounding land-policy-making methods throughout Timor-Leste: the lack of democracy and of spaces dedicated to discussions during the meetings, or an entire lack of consideration of the opinions of the participants from the local communities by the decision-makers.[12] Moreover, these "consultation" meetings, whose reports and minutes are rare, did not clarify the make-up of communities, nor did they provide protection of community land rights, as they were supposed to do. On the contrary, they even contributed at times to sowing confusion and misinformation among the participants.

I verified that several families who had already received compensation were unable to tell the exact size of their land, which Cryan (2015a) suggests was the result of a lack of information and access to a legal compensation process. The only document made available to the public is the Worley Parsons' Environmental Impact Statement in 2012. Project maps, negotiations and project milestones are not accessible anywhere and Timor Gap officials are not inclined to share them.[13]

The role of popular participation in the process was questioned by Cryan (2015b), as it is unclear to what extent local concerns and recommendations have been taken into account, with state agents using local influence, social pressure and formatting of public opinion—using newsletters and government interlocutors—to allow the implementation of the project (see below).

Indeed, the Timorese government has a very limited tradition of dialogue and engagement with civil society, which for its part is poorly equipped to articulate and communicate the essential messages about public opinion and community aspirations. The government is thus cut off from constructive public feedback and has a weak capacity to understand and respond to public concerns. And as a result, Timorese communities express a low degree of reliability towards the government, accusing it of not establishing a place of effective collaboration between the various sectors of society and of explaining very little about its policies and programs to the citizens (Brady and Timberman 2006; Devant 2008).

State practices leading to local tensions

All aspects of social life, in this period of change, are affected by tensions between groups, but it is especially the land that catalyses most conflicts. We saw that in the context of overlapping rights, which make the question of land inextricable. State-based cartography materialises the borders and the territory, thus, becomes fixed and unchanging, eliminating any possibility of negotiation between the different parties. This cartography also does not take into account the symbolic territory, which is materialised by the places considered as "sacred", and for which a system of private property would be contrary to all that this territory represents in relation to the collective identity, responsible for strengthening and structuring the social relations of a village or clan. The spatial disruption caused by the project underlines how the territorial structure is punctuated by sacred places, which link the groups to their territory and to their past.

Territoriality changes, sacred landscapes and rituals

Furthermore, after the land loss for the Tasi Mane constructions, in Suai, the lands that are still available for forestry and agricultural exploitation for the local inhabitants are a long way from their present villages. As a result, older people fear that young people will abandon cultural practices that require, for example, continuous maize (maize harvest rituals) and harvesting of forest products (for the building of sacred houses). Moreover, traditional practices are often abandoned in such cases, in the expectation of new activities, or in the provision of vacant jobs to the populations. This model represents a danger to the ritual life: the time devoted to ceremonies is shortened, artisanal knowledge is lost with the arrival of objects and industrial materials, and agricultural and forestry activities are gradually forgotten in view of the new facilities offered by a 'modern life'.

But if the older members of the community care about the loss of traditions, the weakening of spiritual sanctions, and the transgression of prohibitions, young people often think differently: attracted by the prospect of new comforts and a better quality of life, young people aspire to modernity without being fully aware of the costs it might require. With these project developments, residents now have to pay for the 'conveniences' of electricity, fuel and education, which drastically reduces their autonomy and increases their need for financial resources. Hence, these villagers who formerly lived by subsistence farming are often confronted with the obligation to pursue professional activities outside of the village, which increasingly alienates them from their former way of life.

Finally, local populations fear that the influence of the State on land will cause a rupture with the current system of collective management of resources ("commons") and a more individualistic behaviour in which exploitation of resources accelerates, with individuals exploiting resources without thinking about the rest of the community or future generations. These fears make us think of the Garrett Hardin (1968) concept of "tragedy of the commons". In the notion of "tragedy of the commons" each individual demonstrates a personal interest in using the common resource in such a way as to maximise his or her individual use, while at the same time distributing operating costs among each user, which would not allow sustainable management of the resource acceptable to society (see also Feeny et al. 1990).

In the past, local communities made the choice of collective management to different degrees in order to manage, value and protect their resources in the long term. In this management regime by commons, characterised by the juxtaposition of different rights of collective appropriation and use, property is not attached to a good, but to its products, which is very different from the modern concept of exclusive, private and indivisible ownership, where the rights of use of land and its resources are attached to land ownership.

Moreover, the lack of state recognition of traditional land management and sharing modes, and the exclusion of local communities from the long-term land management process may weaken customary prohibitions and rights (for example, "*tara bandu*", i.e., to hang the ban, and other "*lisan*", i.e., customs).

As already discussed by other authors (D'Andrea 2003; McWilliam 2001), the abandonment of customary resources management—which evokes the notion of collective use of the territory, or "common good"—can lead to the degradation of local forests and protected areas. When ritual practices (such as a prohibition on cutting trees in the sacred forests) are reduced to simple and meaningless symbolic gestures and when, consequently, spiritual or material sanctions are weakened, the penalties for those who transgress are smaller and may no longer be a deterrent.

But these changes on the territory and in the management of its resources are not the only source of conflict. Different visions of the project and reactions to it between the community also need to be considered. Accelerated due to this project of oil development, the modernisation of infrastructures as well as the important process of monetarisation without precedents in the zone inspires great hope of economic prosperity to the youth of Suai. This image of prosperity carries other prospects: that of a better standard of living although until now these 'novelties' cost more money than they bring (see Bovensiepen 2018).

The expectations of the population: the imagery of a 'New Singapore' versus the fear of misfortune

The inhabitants of the affected area have a double vision of the project: on one hand they expect modernisation and an increase in employment, hoping for a 'better life'; but on the other, they are afraid of losing their lands, forests, livelihoods and, consequently, the traditions and knowledge that constitute the very basis of their identities and livelihoods.[14]

Accelerated by the oil development project, the modernisation of this zone inspires great hope in the Kamanasa youth: the prospect of economic prosperity, more convenient work than their parents, and the access to education are explicit in the imagery of a Timor-Leste that could be the 'New Singapore' of Asia. This view has its roots in the organisation by the Timorese government in September 2013 of a delegation of local power authorities sent to Singapore and other major cities in Indonesia and Malaysia to see for themselves "the benefits of economic development". It is necessary to emphasise that this trip was not perceived by the communities as a "consultation", but as a way of inciting the local inhabitants to abandon their lands, according to the members of this delegation that I was able to interview.

This ambiguous and mitigated attraction for modernisation also gives rise to other hopes, such as the wealth that would allow the inhabitants of the zone to improve their living conditions, although until now, as already mentioned, the measures taken just lead the community to an increasingly important monetary dependence (the monetisation of trade and the increase of life's costs will be discussed below).

Economic changes derived from compensation policies: relationship with money and changes in diets

The economic changes derived from compensation policies brings the community to an increasing monetary dependence, as well as a change in their relationship with money and in the dynamics of non-monetary exchanges. Thus, this situation is a major disturbance to the way of life, transforming the local agriculture and diet.

The monetisation of exchanges, a major disturbance to the way of life

The monetary compensations made by the Timor Gap project led to an important and unprecedented monetisation in the zone, although the last three decades had already been a prelude of this change. During the period of Indonesian occupation, monetary exchanges became slightly more frequent and the arrival of the United Nations in 2000 was followed by an injection of money into the country (aid, wages). In the past, if exchanges linked to long-distance trade could imply a currency—as the old coins now used as ornaments bear witness to—an essential part of exchanges between local populations was on the basis of barter, such as products of the sea being exchanged against mountain products. Even the cockfights ("*futu manu*") that today yield a few exchanges, were originally not monetised: the winner had the right to take the losing rooster to eat it. Consequently, locals were not accustomed to having large sums of money, such as the compensation provided by the project.

This large influx of money into societies where monetary exchanges were limited has only reinforced the illusion of wealth to the inhabitants who do not see money as a resource that must be capitalised and managed but as an excess to be spent quickly (see Chapters 1 and 2, this volume). Thus, several families used almost all of this money in the purchase of consumer goods like motorcycles, mini buses and televisions. Others contracted large debts that they thought would be able to be repaid quickly with the promise of ongoing income from the oil project. Some informants stated that "only a few of them used the money for the children's schooling".

It is also important to remember that the purchase of consumer goods is mostly done by men. Yet, in Kamanasa land belongs to women, who are now losing their property against goods that benefit their husbands the most. This reality poses a problem in the matrilineal transmission system and amplifies the vulnerability of women.

Finally, the traditional houses that were once made from materials collected in the surrounding forests have begun to be rebuilt in bricks. Local clan elders, fearing the environmental degradation of the area, wanted to ensure the durability of their houses. They worried that in the future the wood and palm leaves used for traditional houses would no longer be available.

The transformation of local agriculture and diet

According to the *United Nations World Food Program Report* (2005), households in rural Timor-Leste would have a typical shortage ("the famine season") of 3 to 4 months per year on average. Timor-Leste is located in a region heavily affected by natural disasters, and its vulnerability is aggravated by the threat of climate change, which reinforces food insecurity (WFP 2005). This insecurity is now heightened by the fact that the lands used by the local populations for their livelihoods (agriculture, fishing, harvest) have been abandoned for food production and the community is no longer self-sufficient in their diet, according to my informants. Likewise, based on my own fieldwork observations, most staple products now come from the local market, where most vendors are residents of the surrounding mountains. This context has so far produced two key changes in the region, according to my informants and my own observations.[15]

The first change refers to the products available for consumption (and consequently food). As most products originate in the mountains, this has caused a change in the composition and food diversity of the communities in Kamanasa: maize, sorghum, fruits, and green leaves are less present, giving rise to sweet potatoes and taro, as well as industrial rice and meat.

The second change concerns trade and the cost of living. As demand for commodities increased and supply declined, prices rose sharply. The exchange is also less and less recurrent, since the inhabitants no longer have any fields from which to extract production. The remaining money provided by Timor Gap is thus used to buy basic food products, which has also contributed to the cost of living in the area.

According to the Timor-Leste government, the Tasi Mane project would allow increased employment and education prospects in the area, creating new sectors of economic activity and promoting local products (agriculture, livestock, fishing), as well as creating tourism, catering, transport, business and hospitality sectors. The government have promised local workers will be a priority for the jobs created by the project. The promises of the government thus led many inhabitants to believe that they would get all the jobs, without workers from other areas or even countries being mobilised. However, residents indicate that the rate of job creation so far has been very low and that this has not allowed the communities to secure new livelihoods, with past livelihoods compromised by the use of their land by the oil project. The reason for this is, according to the women of the village, that most local people are now forced to buy their food—which, moreover, is becoming more and more expensive and outside of their usual diet. A reliance on bought food is a result of local lands used by the local populations for their livelihoods (agriculture, fishing, harvest) being evacuated. As a result, the community is no longer self-reliant on food or in control of their diet.

Several NGOs, among them the more active La'o Hamutuk, contest the Tasi Mane's project which, according to them, has so far severely compromised the public budget without the Timorese government having stabilised the unemployment rate, which increases each year.[16] In addition, such funding could have been invested in other sectors such as agriculture and small industries, which would be much more beneficial to local communities (La'o Hamutuk Bulletin 2003).

Moreover, these NGOs accuse the project of lacking economic and technical viability in the national scenario. Fearing a vain sacrifice, they urge the government to create policies that will ensure the long-term economic sustainability and food sovereignty of these impacted communities. But not all families are impacted in the same way. According to Cryan (2015a), family vulnerability is intrinsically linked to status, noble families being less vulnerable than modest households since they "are often already part of the local elite and have greater access to land, business opportunities and political connections" (ibid., 9). Modest households on the other hand are likely to be more dependent on subsistence farming as a source of food.

One last important point is that, with the increase in the search for empty land, the inhabitants of other surrounding villages expect their unused land to be bought by the affected families at the same value as the compensations provided by the State, that is to say $3 USD per m^2, thus leaving very little money available to these families to recommence production on these new lands (Cryan 2015a).

Conclusion

We can observe that this project, so far, is causing more problems than it is helping to improve local living conditions, in addition to causing internal conflicts. Although tangible security, or even comfort (electricity, basic necessities, goods from village grocery stores, opening of telephone networks, highways) is emerging, this new context creates new needs that local production systems and social organisation cannot fully satisfy. New uncertainties are emerging related to the loss of ancestral lands and the conflicts caused by the project, which many elders attribute instead to the disruption of ancient ceremonies.

While elder people resist the adoption of this "modern" way of life and remain intrinsically linked to customary or traditional cultural practices, young people are rapidly integrating change by accepting new convenience goods and the comfort that they offer, even if there is so far no disregard for the culture of their ancestors, which remains an important part of their daily lives by the accomplishment and adaptation of customary rituals—like "blessing" newly acquired motorcycles.

The Timor Gap project has also created problems, even a land crisis, by destabilising the local community and defusing their social dynamics of conflict resolution, which normally follows a peaceful procedure (through a neutral mediation in the customary assemblies and during ceremonies—the stakes of money changing this situation). Other social structures were also committed, such as land use and ownership, and the matrilineal system—by the fact that land, inherited by women, is exchanged for consumer goods that are perceived as more "masculine".

In conclusion, this project has been responsible for radical changes in the local way of life, even if it is important to emphasise that there is a gap between the local populations' vision of these changes and its consequences, stressing their resilience, and ours, anthropologists, archaeologists and geographers, from a comparative and diachronic perspective. And, according to our reading grid, the consequences of this process may lead, in the near future, to the impoverishment, marginalisation and exclusion of this community in the national context, due to the lack of land and work in the area, as well as the possible loss of local practices.

Notes

1 The fieldwork was conducted as part of a doctoral thesis on the impact of the Tasi Mane project on the livelihoods of local communities.

2 For more details, please see Crespi, "Sacralité, rituels et développement chez les Bunaq et Tetun de la région de Suai, Timor oriental", 250.

3 According to Ostrom's (1990) "commons" theory, goods are not considered in themselves as particular goods, but rather in their relation to the social groups that participate in their production or maintenance by relying on them in a complex system of collective property rights and rules.

4 See also Fitzpatrick, D., A. McWilliam and S. Barnes, *Property and Social Resilience in Times of Conflict: Land, Custom and Law in East Timor.*

5 *Rai*= land; *nain*= master. This word that can have several meanings, see more in Crespi 2018.

6 In Timor-Leste each locality has its own territorial organisation. For other cases, please consult: McWilliam, A. and E. Traube (eds.), *Land and Life in Timor-Leste–Ethnographic Essays.*

7 *Liu* = beyond; *rai* = land. This title corresponds to the highest status in Kamanasa, placed at the top of the social hierarchy and politically responsible for the kingdom. Although the explanation most frequently invoked by researchers of the zone (Francillon 1967, 24; McWilliam and Traube

2011, 7; Bovensiepen 2015) translates *liu* as "above" or "superior to", another meaning of this word, "beyond", might be more relevant here, since, according to the accounts, those who originally occupied this function came mostly from outside the island, from "beyond the land."

8 *Suku* is a socio-political unit. Each *suku* has an administrative structure, consisting of a village chief and a council. See also Chapter 2, this volume.

9 *Rai* = land; *teen* = excrement

10 Inspired by the Indonesian "*sosialisasi*", socialisation in this context refers to "efforts made to popularize something that must be known, understood and assimilated by the public" (Kamus Besar Bahasa Indonesia, translation by Dominique Guillaud).

11 As discussed earlier, the question of the land covers two dimensions in Timor: that related to real land, which includes the rights of appropriation and use, and that related to the symbolic territory, which refers to the spiritual and political power, knowing that these dimensions are closely nested. In Kamanasa, land includes property rights and usage rights (which also have several levels), while power is divided into spiritual (*rai nain*) and political (*liurai*) power.

12 See also Scambary, "In Search of White Elephants: Political Economy of Resource Expenditure in East Timor", 283-308.

13 During my fieldwork, I have tried several times to obtain these documents from the representative of Timor Gap in Kamanasa, who promised to send them to me by e-mail each time. However, to date, no e-mail has been received.

14 Based on industrial standards of life, their perception of better life is the availability of goods such as running water, electricity, electrical appliances in the house, transport and other goods and services.

15 Comparing the situation between 2014 and 2018.

16 Note that this only becomes a problem when people become dependent on the market. On the contrary, people always have occupations based on what makes up their livelihood activities.

References

Bovensiepen, J. 2015. *The Land of Gold. Post-Conflict Recovery and Cultural Revival in Independent Timor-Leste*. Ithaca, New York: Cornell University Press. doi.org/10.7591/9781501725920.

Bovensiepen, J. 2018. "The Promise of Prosperity: Visions of the Future in Timor-Leste." In *The Promise of Prosperity. Visions of the Future in Timor-Leste*, edited by J. Bovensiepen, 1-25. Canberra: ANU Press.

Bovensiepen, J. and F. D. Rosa. 2016. "Transformations of the sacred in East Timor." *Comparative Studies in Society and History* 58: 664-693.

Bovensiepen, J., and M. Nygaard-Christensen. 2018. "Petroleum planning as state building in Timor-Leste." *The Asia Pacific Journal of Anthropology* 19 (5): 412-431.

Brady, C. and D. Timberman. 2006. *The Crisis in Timor-Leste – Causes, Consequences and Options for Conflict Management and Mitigation*. Dili: USAID. Disponible: https://apcss.org/core/Library/CSS/CCM/Exercise%201/Timor%20Leste/2006%20Crisis/USAID%20Conflict%20Assessment%20Nov%202006.pdf. Accessed 02 July 2017.

Crespi, B. 2018. "Sacralité, rituels et développement chez les Bunaq et Tetun de la région de Suai, Timor oriental." PhD diss., Muséum national d'Histoire naturelle.

Crespi, B., and D. Guillaud. 2018. "Oil and custom: impacts of the Tasi Mane oil project on local communities in Suai, 2011-2017." *The Asia Pacific Journal of Anthropology* 19 (5): 432-449.

Cryan, M. 2015a. "Dispossession and Impoverishment in Timor-Leste: Potential Impacts of the Suai Supply Base." Discussion Paper presented SSGM 2015/15, Canberra. Available at http://www.laohamutuk.org/Oil/TasiMane/SSB/2015/DP-2015-15-Cryan.pdf.

Cryan, M. 2015b. "Empty Land? The Politics of Land in Timor-Leste." In *A New Era? Timor-Leste after the UN,* edited by S. Ingram, L. Kent and A. McWilliam, 141-151. Canberra: ANU Press.

Cryan, M. 2015c. "The Long Haul: Citizen Participation in Timor-Leste Land Policy.", Discussion Paper presented SSGM 2015/13, Canberra. Available at http://dpa.bellschool.anu.edu.au/sites/default/files/publications/attachments/2016-07/dp_2015_13-cryan.pdf.

D'Andrea, C. 2003. "The Customary Use of Natural Resources in Timor-Leste" Paper presented at Regional Workshop on Land Policy Administration for pro-Poor Rural Growth, [n. p.], 1-35.

Devant, S. G. 2008. "Displacement in the 2006 Dili Crisis: Dynamics of an Ongoing Conflict." Refugee Studies Centre, Working Paper no. 45, Oxford University Press.

Feeny, D., F. Berkes, B. J. McCay, and J. M. Achason. 1990. "The tragedy of the commons: Twenty-two years later." *Human Ecology* 18 (1): 1-19.

Fitzpatrick, D., A. McWilliam, and S. Barnes. 2012. *Property and Social Resilience in Times of Conflict: Land, Custom and Law in East Timor.* Surrey & Burlington: Ashgate.

Francillon, G. 1967. "Some matriarchic aspects of the social structure of the Southern Tetun of Middle Timor". PhD diss., The Australian National University.

Friedberg, C. 1982, *Muk gubul nor, 'la chevelure de la terre': Les Bunaq de Timor et les plantes.* PhD diss., Université Paris V.

Fundasaun Mahein. 2013. "Suai Supply Base: Dezenvolvimentu ka Ameasa?' [Suai Supply Base: Development or Danger?]." *Mahein Nia Lian* (57). Disponible at http://www.laohamutuk.org/Oil/TasiMane/2013/MNL57SSB29Aug2013te.pdf.

Hardin, G. 1968. "The tragedy of the commons". *Science* 162: 1243-1248.

Guillaud, D. 2015. "Le vivrier et le sacré. Systèmes agricoles, rituels et territoires dans l'Est indonésien et à Timor-Leste." *Archipel* 90: 245-274.

La'o Hamutuk. 2003. "Double issue foci: Timor Gap oil and Brazilian aid to East Timor." *The La'o Hamutuk Bulletin,* 4 (3-4-August). Available at https://www.laohamutuk.org/Bulletin/2003/Aug/bulletinv4n34b.html.

La'o Hamutuk. 2011. "South Coast Petroleum Infrastructure Project." Updated, 02 April, 2019. Available at: http://www.laohamutuk.org/Oil/TasiMane/11TasiMane.htm. Accessed 02 July 2017.

La'o Hamutuk. 2013a. "South Coast Petroleum Infrastructure Project." Updated, 02 April, 2019. Available at: http://www.Laohamutuk.org/Oil/TasiMane/11TasiMane.htm. Accessed 02 July 2017.

La'o Hamutuk. 2013b. "Suai Supply Base: Benefit or Boondoggle?" La'o Hamutuk Blogspot, May 1. Available at: http://Laohamutuk.blogspot.de/2013/05/suai-supply-base-boon-or-boondoggle.html Accessed 20 October 2017.

La'o Hamutuk. 2014a. *Submisaun Ba Prezidente da Repúblika Timor-Leste Husi La'o Hamutuk relasiona ho Esbosu Dekretu Lei Transmissão de Direitos sobre Bens Imoveis no projecto Suai Supply Base.* Dili: Timor-Leste. Available at: http://www.laohamutuk.org/Oil/TasiMane/SSB/2014/LHsubPres-SuaiLand21Oct2014te.pdf Accessed 23 October 2017.

La'o Hamutuk. 2014b. "Timor-Leste's Petroleum Fund/Fundo Petroliferu." Report by La'o Hamutuk, The Timor-Leste Institute for Development Monitoring and Analysis." Updated, 11 October 2021. Available at: http://www.Laohamutuk.org/Oil/PetFund/05PFIndex.htm Accessed 23 October 2017.

La'o Hamutuk. 2016. *Relatóriu peskiza hosi La'o Hamutuk Kona-ba Impaktu hosi Konstrusaun Aero-Portu Suai ba komunidade sira iha Aldeia Lohorai, Suku Matai, Posto Administrativu Maukatar, Munisipiu Covalima.* Dili: La'o Hamutuk. Available at: http://www.laohamutuk.org/Oil/TasiMane/SSB/PeskizaSuaiOct2016.pdf Accessed 25 October 2017.

McWilliam, A. 2001. "Prospects for the sacred grove." *The Asia Pacific Journal of Anthropology* 2 (2): 89-113.

McWilliam, A. 2008. "Fataluku healing and cultural resilience in East Timor." *Ethnos* 73 (2): 217-240. https://doi.org/10.1080/00141840802180371.

McWilliam, A., and E. Traube (eds). 2011. *Land and Life in Timor-Leste – Ethnographic Essays*. Canberra: ANU E. Press

Ostrom, E. 1990. *Governing the Commons: The Evolution of Institutions for Collective Action*. Cambridge: Cambridge University Press.

Rose, M. 2017. "Development, resistance and the geographies of affect in Oecussi: Timor-Leste's Special Economic Zone (ZEESM)." *Singapore Journal of Tropical Geography* 38 (2): 201-215. https://doi.org/10.1111/sjtg.12190.

Scambary, J. 2015. "In search of white elephants: The political economy of resource income expenditure in East Timor". *Critical Asian Studies* 47 (2): 283-308. https://doi.org/10.1080/14672715.2015.1041281

Shepherd, C. 2009. "Participation, authority, and distributive equity in East Timorese development." *East Asian Science, Technology and Society: An International Journal* 3, (2-3): 315-342. https://doi.org/10.1007/s12280-009-9098-1.

WFP (United Nations World Food Program). 2005. *Food Insecurity and Vulnerability Analysis*. Rome: WFP.

Timor Gap. 2014. *Relatório Anual 2014*. Dili: Timor Gap. Available at: http://timor-leste.gov.tl/wp-content/uploads/2015/08/AnnualReport_TIMORGAP_PT.pdf Accessed 25 October 2017

CHAPTER 10

The socio-cultural benefits of emerging market-based instruments for carbon in Timor-Leste

Lisa Palmer and Sue Jackson

Abstract

Climate change mitigation and adaptation are pressing societal challenges necessitating new approaches to the management and governance of nature-society relations. Market-based instruments under the ecosystem services framework have emerged as innovations in conservation policy and practice. Yet the ways in which these neoliberal projects intersect with, build on or disrupt a range of other diverse economic projects and logics are underexplored. This chapter examines the entangled market and non-market interactions and values of a reforestation program in the Matebian mountain range of the Baucau Municipality, a project financed by a voluntary carbon offset program. It highlights the opportunities and tensions faced by farmers and their extended kin networks in relation to the carbon values of their fields and forests.

Keywords: Carbon offsets; community forestry; ecosystem services; markets; customary governance

Climate change mitigation and adaptation, biodiversity conservation and water management are pressing societal challenges necessitating new approaches to the management and governance of nature-society relations. Market-based instruments under the ecosystem services framework have emerged as innovations in conservation policy and practice. Yet the ways in which these neoliberal projects intersect with, build on or disrupt a range of other diverse economic projects and logics are underexplored. Through a brief engagement with selected literature and preliminary empirical work, this paper begins the task of examining the entangled market and non-market interactions and values of a reforestation program in the Matebian mountain range of the Baucau Municipality, a project financed by a voluntary carbon offset program (WithOneSeed/CarbonSocial). Program documentation asserts that it provides viable and environmentally sustainable livelihoods by restoring watershed services, enhancing farm productivity, improving access to cultural resources, and contributing to more diversified local economic markets, skills and participation.[1] The long-term objective is to leverage the ongoing sale of the country's carbon offsets and ultimately assist Timor-Leste in becoming carbon neutral. In this paper we inquire into the ways in which the CarbonSocial reafforestation program is framed and understood locally, as well as the ways in which it may or may not be intersecting with localised processes of customary environmental governance.

The paper is part of a broader comparative project which is studying the diverse social relations bound up in the production of two emerging 'commodities', namely carbon and water (Tsing 2013; Bakker and Bridge 2006; Bakker 2009).[2] Drawing on longstanding geographical and anthropological critiques of the conception of markets as apolitical or non-cultural (Appadurai 1988; Gibson-Graham 2006), we are exploring, in an open-ended way, the points of social and political change emerging in new water and carbon commodity contexts, examining the factors driving their generation and any sociocultural benefits. Throughout we are paying particular attention to two factors: how people shape the "commoditisation, and sometimes decommoditisation and recommoditisation, of things" (Langton et al. 2006) and the ways in which, especially across cultural units, "what is apparently transacted or communicated is not necessarily what is received or understood" (Kapferer 1976, 11). As geographers we are particularly attuned to the socio-spatial dynamics that drive global exchanges of carbon credits in voluntary markets, creating spaces through which carbon and their local valuations travel. Our aim is to explore how these differing cultural logics exceed (or not) the influence and rationality of the neoliberal policy measures which are ostensibly enabling these new markets and are, in much of the critical literature, considered to always and inevitably inflict harm on unwilling recipients (Upton 2019) and reinforce the cycle of poverty and environmental degradation. The implications of this coexistence of cultural and economic logics (see Chapters 1, 5, and 8, this volume) for emerging environmental markets in the diverse economic context of contemporary Timor-Leste will then be considered.

Carbon trading: 'cultures of carbon'

Now considered as mainstream climate mitigation options, carbon emissions trading and offsetting have created new forms of exchangeable property which become commodities when traded (Corbera and Martin 2015). According to Corbera and Brown (2010, 1792) carbon becomes a commodity "when property rights over [forest] offsets are defined and the results are economically valuable and tradable through an institutional market-based framework, as well as alienable from its ecological context as a standardized good".

This largely voluntary offsetting market is governed by the private sector and NGOs. Proponents of such projects often advance the claim that they are reducing poverty as well as carbon emissions. Since 2005, hundreds of companies have employed a range of approaches and practices to source projects, generate carbon credits and sell them (Lovell 2010). Many of these projects fall within the remit of payment for ecosystem services (PES), which is an increasingly dominant global model for environmental policy and management. Ecosystem services include provisioning services such as food, water, timber, and fibre; regulating services that affect climate, floods, disease, wastes, and water quality; cultural services that provide recreational, aesthetic, and spiritual benefits; and supporting services such as soil formation, photosynthesis, and nutrient cycling (MEA 2005, v). Through these PES processes, the 'stock' of nature and its value are comprehensively measured and the services that 'nature' provides to humans are commodified, appropriated and commercialised under the rubric of ecosystem services.

Elsewhere we have analysed these emerging trends toward PES and have argued that it may indeed be better to value instead actual human and non-human interrelations and practices associated with these 'services', especially in the context of indigenous and local peoples (Jackson and Palmer 2015). In this way, we argued, we might usefully reconfigure not the reified 'stock of nature' or things but diverse socio-cultural *relations* between people and nature as the valued 'stock'. Drawing insights from the trajectory of indigenous environmental management experience in Australia and elsewhere we explored how valuing 'nature' may be reconfigured as a way of enabling the valuation of alternative or non-capitalocentric (Gibson-Graham 2006) ways of being in, knowing and doing nature. The challenge of reconfiguration we argued is to think through the ways in which these PES value fields can make visible the significance and worth of communicative reciprocity within and across human and non-human realms (Jackson et al. 2017). In understanding the value of ecosystem services in this way, we prioritised attention to the efforts of indigenous groups and others to preserve, extend, adapt and benefit their lifeways in rapidly changing global and local contexts. By opening up spaces to explore the pragmatic possibilities emerging from this now dominant form of environmental governance, we resisted the urge to only see the conceptual alienation of relationships between humans and nature through these processes. We also highlighted the ways the 'local' is always actively engaged in creating the 'global' (Nielson and Serjesen 2013; Head and Gibson 2012).

In a subsequent paper focussed on carbon, carbon offset trading and what we termed 'carbon cultures' (Jackson et al. 2017), we further argued that "[c]limate change and the associated need to decarbonise poses not just risks to cultures but potential opportunities for cultural experimentation, renewal and economic dynamism [... and that for indigenous peoples this often involves] a very distinct conceptualization of payment for ecosystem services, one that values the labour and reciprocal relationships and logic of care required to abate or sequester carbon" (2017, 878).

In their attempts to carry out a diverse range of often novel carbon projects, we argued that indigenous and local peoples, their advocates, policy-makers and NGOs in Australia are exploring and discursively shaping both carbon policy initiatives and private willingness to pay for indigenous carbon abatement and sequestration schemes. We argued that such 'carbon work', including the work done to define, promote and market carbon products and attendant services, also acts to reconfigure relations between people and nature. Rather than alienating and abstracting human-nature relations, this reconfiguration we argued might also enable a cross-scalar deepening of relations imbuing the local with the global as well as vice versa. For this reason, we suggested that such emerging 'cultures of carbon' might be considered for their potential to enrich human life including people's place-based connections to 'nature' and each other. These arguments are supported by similar research carried out in indigenous contexts elsewhere (Shapiro-Gaza 2013; Osborne 2015; see more recently Shapiro-Garza et al. 2019; Upton 2019).

At the same time, we reviewed the torrent of academic and popular criticism against offsets, including global schemes such as REDD+ (Reduced Emissions Through Avoided Deforestation and Forest Degradation) (see Roth and Dressler 2012; Fletcher et al. 2016). We stated that:

> "[a] body of literature on the process of carbon commodification has developed in parallel with interventions from transnational activists and civil society organizations [...] A key conclusion from this critical literature is that carbon offsetting is implicated in commodification and financialisation processes that in places dispossess and de-territorialises vulnerable groups from carbon rights and/or land resource (by producing a standard fungible commodity that infuses spaces of carbon in the global South with flows of capital) (Corbera and Martin 2015; Wang and Corson 2015)" (Jackson et al. 2017, 4).

Alongside this critique, we noted that other scholars of market-based conservation have shown how social movements and local communities have (sometimes) been able to beneficially "hybridise" the market-based ideal type of payments for ecosystem services, including carbon mitigation (Shapiro-Garza 2013, 5; Singh 2015; Jackson and Palmer 2015; Diaz et al. 2018). We argued that incorporating community perspectives and investigating the potential for qualitative data found in narrative accounts to contribute to carbon offset monitoring, evaluation and verification functions is essential to a more nuanced understanding of the emerging nature-society relationships. It contributes to a more rounded understanding of the wider processes enrolled in and shaping the commodification. These often expansive and locally generated qualitative accounts, or 'back stories', are, we argued, also often attractive to those investors interested in supporting and potentially sustaining the socio-cultural benefits associated with particular forms of carbon offsetting (Jackson et al. 2017).

In the remainder of this paper we seek, in a preliminary way, to build on this alternate body of scholarship and provide an initial account of some of the (potential) socio-cultural benefits associated with carbon commodification and governance in Timor-Leste. Our aim here, as before (Jackson and Palmer 2015; Jackson et al. 2017), is not to refute the critique of these neoliberal processes, but to begin an alternate reading, which, while acknowledging the dangers of (capitalist) domination, reification and alienation (Dunlap and Sullivan 2019), is attuned to alternative possibilities present or latent within capitalist social formations and relations (cf. Gibson-Graham 2012). Inspired by the work of Gibson et al. (2018) we are also attuned to the ways in which practices of caring might be woven through this carbon program, how a diversity of understandings of labour and property might be deployed, and the ways in which these things and relations are being recognised and exchanged as they are continuously brought into being through these new arrangements.

In the following section we provide an overview of the WithOneSeed Program and offer some preliminary thoughts on the way in which the Program is received and construed locally, as well as briefly elaborating on some of the Program's challenges and opportunities. We then turn to an examination of the way a range of customary processes are subtly implicated in the production of carbon offsets under the Program.

WithOneSeed: Program overview

The WithOneSeed carbon offset program involves over 800 small-holder farmers in the Baguia sub-district in the Municipality of Baucau, Timor-Leste. In this region, remote highland forests have been decimated during decades of conflict with Indonesia and through subsequent land clearing activities. The Indonesian military settled permanently in the region around 1978 and, concerned about potential attacks from Timorese resistance forces, ordered the local population to clear the forest. The felled timber was then taken by the Indonesian forces and sold on for use in construction. Since national independence was achieved in 1999, population growth (mainly from an increased post-war birth rate) has led to further forest felling for house construction, swidden gardens and timber sales.

The WithOneSeed Program is asserted to provide viable and environmentally sustainable livelihoods by restoring watershed services (through the establishment of an interconnected mosaic of forests from the mountains to the coast), enhancing farm productivity (e.g., via increased soil fertility and crop yields), improving access to cultural resources and wellbeing (i.e., through the reforestation of particular trees, associated forest products, restoration of the forest canopy and locally significant springs, as well as forest and indigenous knowledge based school educational programs), and contributing to more diversified local economic markets, skills and

Figure 10.1. Baguia forestscape. Image Credit: Lisa Palmer

participation. The latter is to be realised through annual cash benefits accruing to each participating farmer from carbon offset sales, increased local sales of the agricultural surplus resulting from enhanced soil productivity, and associated livelihood initiatives including 13 plant nurseries and a community-based tourism and trekking program.

One of Timor-Leste's most prominent politicians states that "[t]he program is helping to build the local economy, boost education and training, and increase social and economic participation [adding that] while it is a small program today, we aim for its expansion nationwide" (Horta 2018). The Program is Timor-Leste's first (and currently only) Gold Standard certified community forestry program (https://carbonsocial.global).[3] Actors involved in the program include small landholder farmers, NGOs, government and international donors and agencies, consumers of social carbon credits (marketed and sold to a range of Australian and other international corporations and individuals with ethical commitments to the new nation of Timor-Leste) and scientific experts.

Preliminary field research

In May 2018, Palmer made a preliminary visit to Baguia to meet with WithOneSeed program staff. She was hosted during this time by Leopoldina Guterres, a local Baguia woman and the Country Program Director for WithOneSeed. WithOneSeed (Tetum: *Ho Musan Ida*) has been an entity in Baguia since 2010. It was founded by Australian Andrew Mahar representing the xpand Foundation (an Australian based social enterprise funded by philanthropic organisations) who worked to set up the initiative in Baguia in collaboration with Leopoldina and her late husband, Joao. The program now employs eight full-time staff and five assistants. Their work revolves around the management of three main seed nurseries (all propagating with the use of local manures) and the co-ordination of more than 800 farmers who have planted over 150,000 trees. Some of these farmers have had trees in production for nearly 10 years. Each farmer receives 50 cents per year for each tree they have planted (after the tree has survived the first year of planting). Many of these farmers have now planted around 800 trees, some have up to 1200 or more trees. Hence farmers are able to earn around US$600 per year from their tree plantations, a significant sum of money in this region where most farm production is for household consumption. Most will use this money to assist with the long distance educational expenses of their children and grandchildren. The maximum number of trees each farmer can plant under the program is normally 1200 (so as to allow resources to be shared, or 'tree justice' as the Program calls it, allowing new farmers to join). To accommodate early adopter farmers who have already reached plantings of 1200 trees, farmers with 1200 trees may now augment their crop by planting an additional 100 trees per year. A key aim of the Program is to distribute wealth rather than see it concentrated (Andrew Mahar, pers. comm.).

Aside from these restrictions, the number of trees each participating farmer has planted depends on the length of time they have been participating in the

Program and/or on the amount of land they have available for planting. The trees are planted on individually (or family) owned land. Ownership of this land is recognised through customary processes. In common with much of rural Timor-Leste, there are no formal land titles issued by the state for farmland in the Baguia region. Customary landowners formalise an agreement with the Program, receive (for free) their trees and register them as soon as they are planted. The agreement is that the trees must be grown to sequester carbon for 30 years. At the end of this period, tree owners can do as they wish with them. It is hoped that any felling of mature stands at that point will be offset by ongoing plantings.

In 2010 the Program began by focussing exclusively on mahogany (*ai-mahoni*) production (*Swietenia macrophylla* is a naturalised tree in Timor-Leste and international studies had identified that this tree sequesters a high amount of carbon). However, over the years it has become clear that mahogany will not grow well at the higher altitudes in the region and, in 2016, the program diversified the type of trees which can be propagated and included. Additional species currently endorsed are eucalyptus (*ai-bubur*), casuarina (*ai-kakeu*), rosewood (*ai-naa*), sandalwood (*ai-kameli*) and wild almond (*ai-nitas*). Cacao is also now propagated under the program (although for its fruit resources, not for carbon sequestration).

In 2018 the program had sequestered over 40,000 tonnes of carbon and the investor price paid per tonne for carbon offsetting was US$10 (https://carbonsocial.global/about/).[4] In order to explain the rationale behind the global trade in carbon credits, WithOneSeed Program staff have developed their own ways of explaining the idea of payment for carbon offsets to farmers. They frame the Program's external economic rationale and appeal to investors about the need to counter the global problem of *ar foer* (dirty air). These explanations, adapted to people's experiences of the local economy, focus on Baguia forests' potential contribution to decreasing the polluting effects of the smoke from household fires, electricity use, land-use burning, car exhausts and tobacco smoke. While some farmers want to know more about the specific details of the Program (such as the price paid per tonne of carbon sequestered etc), most appear happy with only a basic explanation of the complex Program mechanics. Program staff are now trained in basic GPS (Global Position System) data collection and annually collect data on the area and extent of plantings as well as tree diameters (the latter used as an indicator of the amount of carbon being sequestered by each tree) so as to validate the Program's carbon reductions.

The program has four main objectives:

1. To improve the local environment including increasing the stock and quality of forest, water, and agricultural plants.
2. To diversify the local economy.
3. Education.

4. Collaboration and networking to build beneficial linkages locally, nationally and internationally.

While the promotion of a tree monoculture at the expense of a diversity of food crops is an often expressed concern for similar carbon offsetting initiatives (Spash 2010), in this Timor-Leste case agroforestry diversification is central to the program's grow/eat/buy local initiative. Program staff have identified at least 41 food types which can be planted alongside tree stands, depending on the age and type of trees in the stand. A lot of these food types are no longer cultivated by farmers due to the widespread availability of cheap imported rice and noodles. In the understorey of young mahogany trees, people are encouraged to grow corn and many other of these 41 foods. Even older shady stands of mahogany can also still host a range of food crops. Additional crops planted include turmeric, ginger, sweet potato, kidney beans, wild beans (*lehe*), *kontas*, wild yams, wild banana, and pineapple. Such diversity contrasts markedly with teak plantations (encouraged during Portuguese colonial times) that can only host wild yams. In many cases, farmers elect to plant Program trees around the edges of existing fields.

At least once a year, Program staff gather together at one site with all the local school children from the Baguia region's ten or so schools. They invite the children's parents and elders (most of whom are farmers) to come and talk about the benefits of the forest. Discussion during these gatherings frequently revolves around the medicinal use of forest products (something local farmers know a lot about) and the benefits of forest conservation (a priority for the WithOneSeed program). The latter discussions around forest conservation are an attempt by the NGO to address a perceived local tendency to consider that the 'forest grows itself', that it does not need active cultivation or care (Leopoldina Guterres, pers. comm.).

The Program is also opening up fresh conversations about trees that were once used frequently by local people but which are now no longer widely available. For example, a tree known in the Makassae language as *kokoreli* is favoured by both colonies of wild bees and by local people who prize it for its suitability for coffins. Its moist wood enables the body of the deceased to be embalmed in coffins and laid in the home for the often long periods of time needed for people to gather and negotiate complicated funerary proceedings. This tree is now scarce and the potential for it to be a part of the WithOneSeed program is an idea that at least some people are considering (Abel Guterres, pers. comm.).

Alongside their medicinal and other local uses, trees are quite simply valuable property. Trees which are planted (and hence owned) are frequently gifted by parents to their children as a part of their inheritance (and these rights may or may not be linked to property rights in the land where they are grown). Hence under the Program, farmers value the trees they are planting both for the current annual payment they receive, and for the economic windfall that will be available to them (or their descendants) once they are harvested. For this reason, farmers often choose to plant their tree stands in areas accessible to vehicles, so that when they are eventually felled the trees can be more easily transported.

Across Timor-Leste, trees are both property and markers of property (and property boundaries). Communally and even individually owned land can be at least partially alienated by tree plantings, and people pay close attention to the tree planting histories and activities on particular lands. While in Baguia all farmers participating in the Program claim ownership of *both* the land and their planted trees, it is important to recognise that these claims are social tenures, recognised through local customary processes and activated in-common with other farmers. Given this localised and socially embedded recognition of tenure (and the social fact that tree plantings can open the path to later claims over land) there was some concern about the implications of outsiders providing trees for the farmers to plant. Indeed, when the Program first began in Baguia, many farmers were concerned that by planting these trees the organisation supplying the trees would become the de facto owners of the trees and so (partially) alienate the landowners from their own land. It was not until a Memorandum of Understanding (MOU) was signed between WithOneSeed and the Timorese Government that these farmers felt secure enough to participate in the program. This MOU was also one way of meeting the Gold Standard international certification process requirement that the Program guarantee the legitimacy of tenure arrangements of all participating tree farmers and secure their free and prior informed consent to participate in the Program. The Program also has a range of agreements with farmers that are based on western legal frameworks. Yet in a context where social tenures and resource management practices are negotiated in-common as always to be determined by social facts and outcomes, the efficacy of these western frameworks for meeting Program objectives is uncertain.

Intersection with customary practices

In this study, we are also interested in the potential for the CarbonSocial and reafforestation program to intersect with the concomitant renewed Timorese focus on cultural and customary environmental governance. In particular, we are interested in the relevance (or not) for the program of a geographically widespread form of ritual resource prohibition known in Tetum as *tara bandu*. These ostensibly similar, but always locally enacted customary practices of ritualised prohibitions, are given their moral force through forms of human communication and negotiation with the ancestral realm. Across the country, this comprises a suite of highly locally contextualised practices that regulate a range of social and environmental relationships. Since early in the independence era, a resurgence of such customary practices has been linked to community initiatives aimed at controlling natural resource exploitation, enabling and controlling resource access for housing reconstruction and restoring social cohesion (D'Andrea et al. 2003; Carvalho and Correa 2011; Meitzner Yoder 2007; Palmer 2016). As an agglomeration of practices used to regulate place-based *social and environmental* relationships, it is as practice with obvious resonance and relevance to the new environmental and social interactions, as well as local governance processes, which comprise the WithOneSeed initiative.

While susceptible to state and development industry co-option (Meitzner Yoder 2007; McWilliam et al. 2014; Silva 2016), such *tara bandu* like processes also have their own logics. It is our conjecture that such logics are capable of both building on and exceeding the influence and rationality of the neoliberal policy measures being rolled out to enable these new carbon markets. Based on research carried out elsewhere in the country, it is clear that customary communities in Timor-Leste are well aware that they must draw together and pull apart these kinds of often divergent and conflicting logics (Palmer and McWilliam 2019). Over time we hope to explore the intersection of these diverse economic processes in Baguia, drawing out the range of understandings, strategies, disbenefits and benefits with which the various Program participants engage and respond.

In contrast to other major crops (such as rice and corn), there are no rituals required when the trees under the Program are planted, rather they are treated in the same way as crops of other types of commonly grown fruits and vegetables.[5] The oldest trees counted under the Program (all of which are mahogany) are now 10 years old. The trees have been planted under the volition of individual farmers and are grown largely outside of the influence of more communal customary regulation. However, the need for some kind of communal regulation is now a topic of local discussion. There are a number of reasons for this. Within the next five years these older trees will become valuable, fungible timber resources (mahogany is particularly good for furniture), and it is anticipated that farmers may start to feel the urge to monetise the value of these trees and abandon the program. The 50 cents per year per tree offered through the sequestration program will start to seem somewhat less attractive than the windfall available to farmers from a wholesale harvest of the now valuable timber. A further complication for the Program is that mahogany tree stands, although good for co-planting with food crops, are known by farmers to be less fire resistant. As such they are susceptible to escaped burns from nearby swidden fields or even incendiary attacks from jealous passers-by (in contrast to teak which is largely fire resistant). For this reason, some farmers worry about investing in this crop over large areas of land and for long periods.

To address such possible threats to the Program's viability and individual returns, Program staff have initiated community level discussions about ways in which the

Baguia community might work to diversify and protect tree stands and ensure compliance with the agreement to not harvest for 30 years. Discussions have included the idea of fines to dissuade early harvesting and a regime whereby any early harvested trees must be replaced with two new saplings. Other ideas have centred on the reinvigoration of *tara bandu*, the customary domain of ritual resource regulation discussed above. However, the latter is especially complicated. As discussed below, it would involve bringing together and finding common agreement between all the various ritual leaders, village heads and farmers of Baguia's ten villages.

Tara bandu was carried out regularly, and widely upheld, in Baguia in Portuguese times, mainly to protect valuable tree plantations such as teak. It was not done at all in Indonesian times, nor in contrast to other areas of the country has it been done since independence. In contrast to some other areas of Timor-Leste where a large amount of conflict and post-conflict related in-migration has occurred, outside of Baguia township itself there is little dispute over land ownership or issues with people stealing each other's crops and other resources. In these small mountain villages everyone knows one another and the histories and stories which connect people to land and other property. People do carry out their own individual rituals, known in Tetum as *tara horok* (hanging the talisman) to protect particularly valuable fruit trees from the interest of passing foot traffic. Ignoring such ritual signage is a serious misdemeanour, the spiritual repercussions of which can include illness and eventual death. While *tara bandu* is in many ways a community level extension of this individualised *tara horok* practice (see Palmer and McWilliam 2019), a recent *tara bandu* (not specifically related to forest products) in a more distant village has not been successful. This was due, it is said, to the fact that the process was driven by outside actors rather than originating as an idea and process from within the community.

In contrast, in Baguia, the idea of a *tara bandu* like process has been under discussion with Program farmers for four years now. Program staff are adamant that the community needs to have ownership of any process which transpires. This means the conversations and initiatives must start from within the community and include the various ritual and political leaders from each of the 10 villages, along with, eventually, the sub-district head, local clergy and police. Ensuring all these actors are mobilised and working together towards the same goal would take considerable time, economic, social and cultural capital. In addition, each village would need to carry out their own specific *tara bandu* ritual to draw on and respect their own specific ancestral traditions. While, as noted above, in contrast to some other areas of the country, issues of land and resource disputes are not a driving force behind the desire to reinstate communal customary processes, there are other areas of community governance which the community do consider are in urgent need of addressing. These include a high incidence of adultery and divorce, domestic violence, and youth related violence. Any proposal to use *tara bandu* to ritually protect the tree plantings would need also to address and include these other community concerns.

While background discussions around the efficacy and need for *tara bandu* continue at the Program level, other factors which regulate and enable social tenures and exchanges are already present in the region's quotidian customary economies. When Palmer visited the region in 2018, Leopoldina Guterres took her to several of the tree planting areas in the region. Along with trees, the food crops growing in a given area's fields and in the understorey of its newly emerging canopy was a focus of our attention. As we walked the muddy tracks up and down the valleys, Leopoldina pointed out each food source we came across and explained its use in careful detail. She took great pride in identifying the ones that had slipped out of local diets, but which the Program was working to bring back into dietary 'fashion'. '*Kontas*' a red lily like plant with a long white tuber and which grew seemingly wild, was explained as "something that kept us alive when we were hiding out in the jungle during the early years of the invasion. It is good food. We need to keep using it". During the early years of the Indonesian occupation, Leopoldina who was still a child had sheltered for years in these remote mountain terrains. It was during these terrible years that her family and much of the regional population who had fled to the mountains, learnt how to live from the forest. Even as people were continually on the run from Indonesian guns and encirclement, they also somehow managed to clear and tend to remote forest gardens. Likewise, they learnt to survive by encouraging the more random cultivation of wild tubers and fruits. They learnt too about using the bark of particular trees for clothing and to rely on forest foliage for bedding and shelter. Given the hardships of their new forest lives, they built too on the medicinal knowledge handed down from their forebears. Many became medical specialists, trialling and testing a range of forest medicines on themselves and their families and then spreading these plants and knowledge to others. When it was possible these plants were cultivated, expanding their ecological range through careful, if deliberately opaque, processes of human attention. This knowledge, which kept people alive in desperate circumstances, remains deeply embedded and valued in rural Timorese households into the present (Palmer 2020).

These stories of people's dynamic connections to their forest and each other, resonate with the work in other indigenous contexts. In Northern Brazil, Manuela Carneiro Da Cunha (2012) has documented the ways in which the huge diversity of plants are cultivated and brought into being. Focussing on cassava seedlings and their cultivation as prized objects of gift exchange, Cunha argues that these exchanges are facilitated primarily between women (mothers and their daughters-in-law) in the context of rotational swidden farming. She notes however that these seedlings are also frequently exchanged between more geographically dispersed groups of people as they come together for cultural and religious events. These exchanges, she argues, are highly dynamic, producing extraordinary biological diversity that is embedded and activated through nuanced cultural and communicative processes involving people, plants and soil. This biodiversity is made visible through the naming practices attached to each new cassava seedling type (in some cases numbering in the hundreds). The pride of the often female cultivators of these cassava types ensures pride and careful attention to the history and necessity of ongoing exchanges. It also encourages constant seedling type innovation.

Likewise, in Baguia it is fruitful to think further about the ways in which food and tree plantings are embedded in histories and exchange networks which activate and enable botanical flourishing, as much as they link as well to people's ideas of property, of sharing and of interconnection. Such intergenerational processes of botanical exchange are discernible in the highland valley farmed by Leopoldina's parents. Leopoldina's father is a farmer and early adopter in the WithOneSeed program. While he and his wife once tended many gardens and rice fields, they now have only two swidden fields active in the valley at any one time. Leo's mother's ill health means she is no longer able to be as active in the fields and the couple's terraced rice fields have been dysfunctional since the 1980s (due to landslides damaging the irrigation canals). These terraces and retired swidden fields have now been turned by Leopoldina's father and brother into sites for various tree plantings (mahogany, casuarina and wild almond). In recent years, Leopoldina's father has been able to make up to US$1000 a year from these trees. He makes another US$1000 a year or so from the local sale of betel leaf and areca nut sourced from his spring groves. He might also make up to US$1000 from the sale of the peanuts which he cultivates in his active swidden fields. He also receives a biannual retirement pension of US$180 from the government which he uses to purchase rice, oil and other basic items. The range of other food crops he grows in his mixed-use fields, foods like pineapple, long beans, cassava and corn, are for his extended family to consume. Indeed, Leo's large household of twenty or so mainly adopted children rely on the weekly harvest of these foodstuffs. The money the old man makes is also a 'bank' for Leo and her other siblings who would otherwise struggle to meet the needs of their households for items such as children's schooling expenses.

Many of Leo's household, including her daughter Enny who is the WithOneSeed Program secretary, trek the long journey from their house to this forested valley each Saturday. They collect the food growing in the fields and in the understorey of the valley's newly planted forest, along with any fallen wood for their cooking fires. Returning home with all they can carry on their backs, these items they collect will be enough to feed their own large household for the week. This kind of embodied knowledge about tree plantings and the possibility for understorey and adjacent crop plantings are then exchanged through Program meetings which bring together households from across the region's 10 remote villages. In this account too, we can see that women, their knowledge and cultivation of foodstuffs and firewood, are critical to this emerging biodiversity and the carbon it stores.

Conclusion

These emerging entanglements between farmers, their extended kin networks and their fields and forests are clearly an important facet of Baguia's emergent post-conflict local economy. Clearly as well, the market-driven underpinnings of the Program are having effects on both the commons and practices of communing. Many questions arise and need to be investigated further. How are these new practices intersecting with and/or challenging local understandings of communal and private agro-forestry resources? Are these new approaches to tree planting creating the risk of a narrowing of both agricultural practices and the values embedded within these practices? What tensions will emerge between customary land managed in-private, or in-common, as ancestral bequeath? What changes will occur as these new forest resources are increasingly standardised and co-produced with outside actors? We do not yet know the answers to these questions. Below we summarise what we do know.

In Baguia, as well as elsewhere in Timor-Leste, the planting of trees is linked to the establishment and maintenance of property and property rights. The WithOneSeed program encourages farmers to plant trees on their own land and hence affirms and augments their claims to particular areas. As with other tree plantings, these trees are valued primarily for their (always diverse) economic values including the co-production of agro-diversity and wellbeing. Contrary to the critical literature on the dangers of environmental market-based instruments commodifying 'nature' and alienating people from its production, in this setting 'nature' to some extent already has a 'price' (although its value is always contextually determined). In this way, the WithOneSeed program fits within, rather than creates anew, already existing property rights within an existing agro-forestry logic. However, potential problems might arise if the aims of the program (a 30 year sequestration of carbon per tree) contradicts desires on the part of the farmers to benefit more quickly from this 'stock of nature' in other more lucrative ways.

The ways to address this latter issue are as yet unresolved. What is clear is that a fully indigenous regime of *private* property—not common property—in planted trees has provided the basis for a successful reforestation program to date. Farmers may one day be tempted to sell for timber the trees they have planted under the thirty-year reforestation scheme. Whether this should be prevented by coercive means, whether farmers should be provided with new monetary incentives not to do it, or to plant new trees in the place of the ones they fell is a matter still under discussion. In this suite of discussions, recourse to customary ritual regulations such as *tara bandu* is another possibility to add to the WithOneSeed program response. While post-independence *tara bandu* processes have not been successful in other parts of the Baguia valley, they are successful as a community governance mechanism in some other parts of the country (see Palmer and McWilliam 2019).

Along with a diversity of understandings of labour and property in Baguia, we have glimpsed how a range of practices of care are already woven through this carbon program and the ways in which these things and relations are being exchanged and brought into being.[6] What is being actively reworked in such contexts are the ways in which particular relations between people and nature and between people and people are recognised, enabled and valued. Customary processes repurposed in this way to include the aims of a carbon trading scheme could, as we have seen above, trigger a range of other social and cultural benefits as well as biodiversity exchanges. Program leaders are aware that there is also the potential (un-explored in this chapter) for these additional 'co-benefits' to be recognised in the carbon tonnage price offered to investors/consumers in the voluntary carbon market. These important human-nature social relations and practices of care may well become a valued quality of the carbon credits produced for the global market from Baguia.

People in Timor-Leste are adept at reworking external logics to fit in with their own. In this case, what we can see is that a number of externally derived conceptual frameworks, namely sustainability, poverty reduction, and climate mitigation, are actively infusing local people's concerns and practices. Yet from a preliminary analysis of local framings and understandings of this Program, it is clear that a number of key endogenous principles underpin the ways in which these external frameworks are being reworked. These principles (which are broadly similar across the country) include a commitment to locally instantiated inheritable land and property rights, including those concerning the cultivation of land and planting of trees, and a commitment to intergenerational wellbeing and exchange. The idea of ameliorating *ar foer* (dirty air) and generating Carbon-social credits are simply an added bonus for this already established set of land use practices (one that is also contributing to the diversity of trees/crops being planted). As we have seen above, Program staff are focussed on carrying out GPS data collection of trees stands, tree diameters and sequestration rates. Farmers in Baguia do not necessarily understand the details or the need for this data collection, but they are happy to enable and support this process if this is what is needed to be known and measured, even if the staff show a stronger desire to participate directly in calculation and evaluation exercises.

Planted trees are property with or without the WithOneSeed program. This is a basic fact of life in Timor-Leste—trees are linked to a range of property rights and exchange processes all of which are contextually activated by the histories and stories of who, when and why these trees were planted, and what is known about their use. In the West, where the investors in carbon offsets largely live, people are hungry for stories that, in meaningful ways, link people with place and nature. Stories like the need to reafforest the *kokoreli* 'coffin' tree or the potential for a tree planting program to reinvigorate local diets, medicinal knowledge and customary governance are just the sort of 'back stories' that investors in carbon social credits desire (see Jackson et al. 2017). In Baguia, and Timor-Leste more broadly, where there are so many such stories, the idea that they might be beneficially framed, of interest and capitalised to external others is still taking hold.

Funding acknowledgement

This research was supported by an Australian Research Council Grant (DP190100875).

Notes

1 See https://carbonsocial.global/about/ Accessed 9 April 2020.

2 A collaboration with geographers Lesley Head, Noel Castree, Morgan Robertson, and Marie Stenseke.

3 "Gold Standard was established in 2003 by World Wildlife Fund and other international NGOs to ensure projects that reduced carbon emissions featured the highest levels of environmental integrity and also contributed to sustainable development. With the adoption of the Paris Climate Agreement and the Sustainable Development Goals, we launched a best practice standard for climate and sustainable development interventions, Gold Standard for the Global Goals, to maximise impact, creating value for people around the world and the planet we share". See: https://www.goldstandard.org/about-us/vision-and-mission, Website Accessed 9 April, 2020).

4 By October 2021 the *Ho Musan Ida* program in Baguia had increased to 1000 participating farmers, 20 full time staff, four central plant nurseries, 250,000 trees sequestering 106.000tCO2 with the investor price paid per tonne US$30.

5 As well as the cosmological context in which staples such as rice and corn are grown and exchanged with the ancestral realm, a further reason for the close and often communal ritual attention to planting and harvesting periods is the higher susceptibility of these crops to pests (Palmer 2015).

6 The ways in which these exchanges might be understood relationally by carbon credit consumers is beyond the scope of this chapter.

References

Appadurai, A. 1988. *The Social Life of Things: Commodities in Cultural Perspective.* Cambridge: Cambridge University Press.

Bakker, K. 2009. "Neoliberal natures, ecological fixes, and the pitfalls of comparative research." *Environment and Planning A* 41: 1781-1787. https://doi.org/10.1068/a4277

Bakker, K., and G. Bridge. 2006. "Material worlds? Resource geographies and the 'matter of nature." *Progress In Human Geography* 30 (1): 5-27.

Carvalho, D., and J. Coreia, J. 2011. "Tara Bandu nudar: Matenek ekologia tradicional." In *Matenek Lokal Timor Nian,* edited by D. Carvalho, 52-67. Jakarta: UNESCO.

Comissao Justica e Paz Paroquia Viqueque. 2005. *Ukun Fuan Rai Laran Kona Ba Lia Moris, Lia Mate no ba Tara Bandu iha Paroquia Viqueque.* Viqueque: Paroquia Viqueque.

Cunha, M. C. da. 2012. "Cassava in the Amazon" Presented at *Traditional Knowledge: Nature, Objects and Methods Lecture Series,* College de France, Paris. Available at https://www.college-de-france.fr/site/en-manuela-carneiro-da-cunha/course-2012-05-24-14h30.htm.

D'Andrea, C., O. da Silva, and L. Meitzner Yoder. 2003. *The Customary Use and Management of Natural Resources in Timor-Leste.* Dili: Oxfam, GTZ & DTP, TL.

Corbera, E., and K. Brown. 2010. "Offsetting benefits? Analyzing access to forest carbon." *Environment and Planning A: Economy and Space* 42 (7): 1739-1761.

Corbera, E., and A. Martin. 2015. "Carbon offsets: Accommodation or resistance?" *Environment and Planning A: Economy and Space* 47 (10): 2023-2030.

Diaz, S., U. Pascual, M. Stenseke, B. Martín-López, R. T. Watson, Z. Molnár, R. Hill, K. M. A. Chan, I. A. Baste, K. A. Brauman, S. Polasky, A. Church, M. Lonsdale, A. Larigauderie, P. W. Leadley, A. P. E. van Oudenhoven, F. van der Plaat, M. Schroter, S. Lavorel, Y. Aumeeruddy-Thomas, E. Bukvareva, S. Demissew, G. Erpul, P. Failler, C. A. Guerra, C. L. Hewitt, H. Keune, S. Lindley, and Y. Shirayama. 2018. "Assessing nature's contributions to people." *Science* 359 (6373): 270-272.

Dunlap, A., and S. Sullivan. 2019. "A faultline in neoliberal environmental governance scholarship? Or, why accumulation-by-alienation matters". *Environment and Planning: Nature and Space*: 1–28.

Fletcher, R., W. Dressler, B. Bruscher, and Z. R. Anderson. 2016. "Questioning REDD+ and the future of market-based conservation." *Conservation Biology* 00 (0): 1-3.

Gibson-Graham, J. K. 2006. *A Postcapitalist Politics.* Minneapolis: University of Minnesota Press.

Gibson-Graham, J. K. 2012. "Diverse Economies: Performative practices for 'other worlds.'" In *The Wiley-Blackwell Companion to Economic Geography*, edited by T. J. Barnes, J Peck, and E. Sheppard. Oxford: Blackwell.

Gibson, K., R. Astuti, M. Carnegie, A. Chalernphon, K. Dombroski, A. R. Haryani, A. Hill, B. Kehi, L. Law, I. Lyne, A. McGregor, K. McKinnon, A. McWilliam, F. Miller, C. Ngin, D. Occeña-Gutierrez, L. Palmer, P. Placino, M. Rampengan, W. Lei Lei Than, N. I. Wianti and S. Wright. 2018. "Community economies in Monsoon Asia: Keywords and key reflections." *Asia Pacific Viewpoint* 59 (1): 3-16. doi.org/10.1111/apv.12186.

Head, L., and C. Gibson. 2012. Becoming differently modern: Geographic contributions to a generative climate politics. *Progress in Human Geography* 36: 699-714.

Horta, J. R. 2018. "In the Mountains of Timor-Leste, A Small Success On Climate Change." *The Huffington Post,* 3 Jan. Available at https://www.huffingtonpost.com/jose-ramoshorta/in-the-mountains-of-timor_b_12976624.html?ncid=engmodushpmg00000003 Accessed 20 May 2020.

Jackson S., and L. Palmer. 2015. "Reconceptualising ecosystem services: Possibilities for cultivating and valuing the ethics and practices of care." *Progress In Human Geography* 39 (2): 122-145.

Jackson, S., L. Palmer, F. McDonald, and A. Bumpus. 2017. "Cultures of carbon and the logic of care: The possibilities for carbon enrichment and its cultural signature." *Annals of the American Association of Geographers* 107 (4): 867-882.

Kapferer, B. 1976. "Introduction: transactional models reconsidered." In *Transaction and Meaning: Directions in the Anthropology of Exchange and Symbolic Behaviour*, edited B. Kapferer, 1-22. Philadelphia: Institute for Study on Human Issues: Philadelphia.

Langton, M., O. Mazel, and L. Palmer. 2006. "The 'spirit' of the thing: The boundaries of Aboriginal economic relations at Australian Common Law." *Australian Journal of Anthropology* 17 (3): 307-321.

Lovell, H. 2010. "Governing the carbon offset market." *Wires Climate Change* 1 (3): 353-362.

McWilliam, A., L. Palmer, and C. Shepherd. 2014. "Lulik encounters and cultural frictions in Timor-Leste: Past and present." *The Australian Journal of Anthropology* 25 (3): 300-320.

Meitzner Yoder, L. S. 2007. "Hybridising justice: State-customary interactions over forest crime and punishment in Oecusse, Timor-Leste." *The Asia Pacific Journal of Anthropology* 8 (1): 43-57.

MEA (Millennium Ecosystem Assessment). 2005. *Ecosystems and Human Well-being: Synthesis.* Washington, DC: Island Press.

Nielsen, J., and Serjesen F. 2013. "Earth system science, the IPCC and the problem of downward causation in human geographies of global climate change". *Geografisk Tidsskrift-Danish Journal of Geography* 112 (2): 194-202.

Osborne, T. 2015. "Tradeoffs in carbon commodification: A political ecology of common property forest governance." *Geoforum* 67: 64-77.

Palmer, L. 2015. *Water Politics and Spiritual Ecology: Custom, Environmental Governance and Development.* London: Routledge

Palmer, L. 2016. "The 'environment' in Timor-Leste." In *Routledge Handbook of the Environment in Southeast Asia*, edited by P. Hirsch, 483-495. London: Routledge.

Palmer, L. 2020. "The cosmopolitics of flow and healing in North-Central Timor-Leste." *The Australian Journal of Anthropology* 31 (2): 224-239. doi.org/10.1111/taja.12359.

Palmer, L., and A. McWilliam, A. 2019. "Spirit ecologies and customary governance in post-conflict Timor-Leste." *Bijdragen tot de taal-, land- en volkenkunde/Journal of the Humanities and Social Sciences of Southeast Asia* 175 (4): 474-505. DOI: 10.1163/22134379-17504003

Roth, R., and W. Dressler. 2012. "Market-oriented conservation governance: The particularities of place." *Geoforum* 43: 363-366.

Shapiro-Garza, E. 2013. "Contesting the market-based nature of Mexico's national payments for ecosystem services programs: Four sites of articulation and hybridization." *Geoforum* 46: 5-15.

Shapiro-Garza, E., P. McElwee, G. Van Hecken, and E Corbera. 2019. "Beyond market logics: Payments for ecosystem services as alternative development practices in the global south." *Development and Change* 51 (1): 3-25.

Silva, K. 2016. "Administrando Pessoas, Recursos e Rituais. Pedagogia econômica como tática de governo em Timor-Leste." *Horizontes Antropológicos* 22 (45): 127-153.

Singh, N. M. 2015. "Payments for ecosystem services and the gift paradigm: Sharing the burden and joy of environmental care." *Ecological Economics* 117 (C): 53-61.

Spash, C. 2010. "The brave new world of carbon trading." *New Political Economy* 15 (2): 169-195.

Tsing, A. 2013. "Sorting out commodities: How capitalist value is made through gifts". *HAU: Journal of Ethnographic Theory* 3 (1): 21-43.

Upton, C. 2019. "Conserving natures? Co-producing payments for ecosystem services in Mongolian rangelands." *Development and Change* 51 (1): 224-252.

Wang, Y., and C. Corson. 2015. "The making of a 'charismatic' carbon credit: clean cookstoves and 'uncooperative' women in western Kenya." *Environment and Planning A: Economy and Space* 47 (10): 2064-2079.

CHAPTER 11

China's engagement in Timor-Leste's economy

Laurentina 'Mica' Barreto Soares

Abstract

Chinese nationals have been playing a dominant role in China's engagement in Timor-Leste's economy. The Chinese are known for their entrepreneurial spirit and business acumen. They possess great commercial skills, financial capital and wide business networks. They have become important economic intermediaries between China and other countries through various economic activities. Since Timor-Leste's independence, the presence of Chinese nationals has been on the rise. Their increased presence, coupled with the return of local Timorese-Chinese, has significantly changed Timor-Leste's economic landscape. This chapter argues that their particular economic activities can be considered as new forms of economic and settler colonialism. Notable evidence is seen in the influx of Chinese migrants and their occupation of strategic locations as well as domination in local economic activities.

Keywords: Chinese nationals; economic activities; business networks; economic intermediary

This chapter examines China's economic activities in Timor-Leste post-independence. The analysis focuses on China's state and non-state actors' immersion in Timor-Leste's economy over the past two decades. China's non-state actors refer in particular to the overseas Chinese community in Timor-Leste. The term overseas Chinese refers to the *Huaqiao* and *Huaren* groups. The *Huaqiao(s)* are those overseas Chinese who reside outside of China and have obtained permanent residency abroad but still maintain their Chinese nationality, while the *Huaren(s)* are defined as those ethnic Chinese who reside and become nationals of foreign countries (Tan 2013, 2-3). In this case, the analysis of the Chinese community in Timor-Leste focuses on Chinese nationals or Chinese newcomers and Timorese-Chinese and their different economic activities in the country.[12] In-depth accounts concerning the history of Timorese-Chinese communities can be found in Douglas Kammen and Jonathan Chen's 2019 book *China Timor: Baba, Hakka, and Cantonese in the Making of Timor-Leste* and Juliette Huber's 2021 chapter "At the Periphery of Nanyang: The Hakka Community of Timor-Leste" in Caroline Chia and Toom Hoogervorst's edited volume on overseas Chinese in Southeast Asia. This study, carried out between 2014 and 2018, is based on extensive analysis of documentary sources and fieldwork interviews with relevant state and non-state Chinese actors, including independent scholars from China and Timor-Leste.

The presence and economic activities of China have significantly changed Timor-Leste's economic landscape. Overseas Chinese, particularly the Chinese newcomers, and to some extent the Timorese-Chinese community and their particular economic practices can arguably be considered a new wave of economic and settler colonialism. This claim is evidenced by the influx over the last two decades of Chinese nationals and their settlement in strategic locations as key players in a range of economic activities in the country.

Over the past two decades, enhancing its strategic influence and economic objectives has arguably become China's primary consideration in its engagement with Timor-Leste. Nonetheless, China is not the leading player in Timor-Leste in major capital investment and major economic activities such as oil and gas industries. These areas have been dominated by the Australian, United States, Italian, and Japanese firms.[3] However, its interactions are significant and on the rise. In the past five years or more, China's economic interactions have become increasingly noticeable at both the state and non-state level. At the non-state level, there is a proliferation of Chinese nationals present and carrying out economic activities in the country. At the state level, there are an increasingly amplified number of cooperation agreements which emphasise economic development. These include invitations for Timor-Leste to participate in different economic forums in China including the Boao Forum for Asia. China has also expressed great interest in investing in Timor-Leste in the future in the areas of petroleum, the Tasi Mane Project along the south coast, ZEEMS in Oecussi and the agricultural industry (Sampaio 2015). This makes China a significant player in Timor-Leste's economic landscape along with Indonesia, Singapore, Australia, the United States, Portugal, Malaysia, and others. The Timor-Leste government's annual trade statistic report in 2019 indicates that China is the fourth most important country from which Timor-Leste imports goods and services and that 14% of Timor-Leste's exports go to China (RDTL 2019).

Overseas Chinese are known for their entrepreneurial spirit and business acumen. They are well-equipped not only with high-level commercial skills but also with financial capital and wide business networks. Chinese leaders as well as Chinese scholars attach great importance to overseas Chinese and consider them a great asset for China's economic development (see Zhu Rongji 2001 quoted in Liu 2005, 302; Guoto 2017). Overseas Chinese are seen as a 'secret economic weapon' to advance China's desire for national rejuvenation. China uses economic power to reclaim its past identity as a great power within the international system.

In 2014, it was estimated that between 7,500 to 8,000 people identifying as overseas Chinese resided throughout Timor-Leste. Among them, the number of Chinese nationals and overseas Chinese from other countries in the region was predicted to be between 3,000 to 4,000 people, with Timorese-Chinese around 4,000 people.[4] Newcomers and other overseas Chinese from the region come to Timor-Leste for different economic reasons. Chinese citizens come predominantly from the southern coast of China, particularly from Guangdong and Fujian provinces. The latter area has been well known as China's great source of internal and overseas migration for centuries (Liang and Morooka 2004, 145).

In the independence era, overseas Chinese have been key players in Timor-Leste's local economic activities ranging from small to medium and large-scale enterprises. Chinese state-owned and non-state-owned enterprises are involved in various infrastructure and non-infrastructure projects and benefit from Timor-Leste's public funds, particularly those that involve infrastructure projects.

This discussion on China's engagement in Timor-Leste's economy begins by presenting an overview of China as state actors and their economic relations with Timor-Leste between 2002-2018. Subsequently, it outlines China's economic activities through trade and investment. It then examines overseas Chinese engagement in Timor-Leste's economy by highlighting Chinese state and non-state owned companies and overseas Chinese economic activities between 2002-2018. Prior to the conclusion, it discusses the ramifications of China's increased economic engagement in Timor-Leste.

China's economic diplomacy with Timor-Leste

China's early economic interactions with Timor-Leste can be traced through the arrival of Chinese traders on Timor Island in the 13th century (Kammen and Chen 2019; Durand 2016; Gunn 2016, 1999; Pinto 2014; Fox 2003). Chinese traders were among the early arrivals prior to the Portuguese spice traders in 1511 and the Dutch a century later in 1613.[5] This early economic contact was marked with sporadic trading in various Timorese commodities such as sandalwood, beeswax and honey. However, the Chinese trade-network appeared more effective with the arrival of the Europeans in the 16th century (Gunn 2016; Fox 2003). The Europeans eventually colonised and divided Timor Island into two parts, Dutch to the West and Portuguese to the East.[6] For centuries, Chinese settlers focused on commercial activities and established communities across the island (Kammen and Chan 2019). Chinese merchants dominated and took charge of the trading markets—they controlled the trade of both local and foreign produced products (Roque 2010, 315).

In contemporary Timor-Leste, China began to establish significant economic links with the country as early as 2000 whilst Timor-Leste was still under the United Nations transitional administration. A Chinese delegation visited Dili and met with Timorese leaders and expressed their willingness to engage in Timor-Leste's economy.[7] In an effort to further strengthen its presence in the country, in 2003 China signed a cooperation agreement with Timor-Leste in which China outlined aspirations to be involved in rebuilding Timor-Leste (Storey 2011, 279). The agreement indicated China also aspired to explore economic and trade cooperation with Timor-Leste and it was this cooperation agreement which provided a window of opportunity for China's public and private business enterprises to engage in Timor-Leste's economy.

In April 2014, China and Timor-Leste signed another cooperation agreement. Both countries agreed upon a number of areas for cooperation and named the cooperation an "all-round cooperative partnership" (Dan 2014). These partnerships included, among others, a plan to expand bilateral economic relations through trade and investment, to deepen cooperation in security, to make an agreement on visa exemption for holders of diplomatic and service passports, to enhance relationships between the two countries through people-to-people relations such as cultural and sports exchange, and reciprocal visits of state and non-state actors and tourism (RDTL 2014). Following this agreement, Beijing has been actively intensifying its economic diplomacy with Dili.

It is observed that apart from bilateral arrangements, China's economic relations with Timor-Leste are also organised regionally within the framework of Timor-Leste's engagement with the Macau Forum and the Community of Portuguese-speaking Countries (CPLP). While the existence of the Forum and Timor-Leste's active participation is a positive development for the country, overall, the country has yet to see significant benefits from its involvement in the Macau Forum.

China attaches great importance to Timor-Leste's geographical location within the Southeast Asia region. In his welcome message to Timor-Leste in 2015, Chinese Ambassador Liu Hongyang stated, "Timor-Leste is one of China's neighbours in Southeast Asia, which is of great importance in the neighbourhood policy of the Chinese Government" (Hongyang 2015). Such neighbourhood policy considerations incentivise Beijing to consider Timor-Leste as part of its grand strategy for global economic connectivity through the 21st Century Maritime Silk Road (MSR) proposal. The MSR is part of the One Belt One Road (OBOR) or the Belt and Road Initiative that was introduced by Chinese President Xi Jinping in 2013 to boost infrastructure connectivity throughout Southeast Asia, Oceania, and East Africa. The MSR focus on maritime trade complements the Silk Road Economic Belt that also focuses on infrastructure development over land through Central Asia (Green 2018, 1).

In China's view, the Belt and Road Initiative aims to promote connectivity through land and seas between China and Asian, European and African countries. While Beijing argues that the Initiative focuses largely on economic development, some observers argue that the Initiative also involves a geopolitical component wherein Beijing aims to enhance its influence in the world and challenge the world order (Green 2018; Sagi and Engelberth 2018; Cau 2018). This issue is beyond the scope of this chapter, but it is important to note that for China, the Initiative is not a new approach but a revival of its ancient trade road known as the Silk Road from 2000 years ago (Sagi and Engelberth 2018, 13-14). Thus, China considers Timor-Leste's participation in the Initiatives as a revival of its old trading link from the 13th century before the arrival of Europeans on Timor Island.

Since the MSR proposal was introduced to Timor-Leste in 2014, China has framed its relationship with the country as part of its overall cooperation under the initiative of building the 21st Century MSR. Like other Southeast Asian countries, Timor-Leste welcomes this proposal and has been willing to cooperate with China under the proposed initiative. In his visit to Macau in May 2019, former president of Timor-Leste, Jose Ramos-Horta, reiterated Timor-Leste's eagerness to boost the country's cooperation with China in order to develop its economy and expressed his full support of the OBOR proposal.[8] Speaking to Lusa News Agency, the former president at that time said that for the purpose of Timor-Leste's national development, the country could benefit from partnerships with China, as well as other partnerships (MacauHub 2019).

Timor-Leste is now among the 64 member countries which officially takes part in China's OBOR project. In 2017, the OBOR Bank's Board of Governors approved Dili's application to become the institution's "Regional Prospective Member". As such, Timor-Leste now joins more than 60 other countries as the Bank's members with its first capital investment around US$16 million. In Timor-Leste's view, its participation in the Bank aims to "improve economic and social development in Asia by investing in high quality, financially viable and environmentally friendly infrastructure projects" (RDTL 2017).

Despite the proposal's ambition, the ways in which this initiative is mutually beneficial for both China and Timor-Leste remain unclear. While China considers that the proposal has been effected through the involvement of its nationals in different infrastructure projects and other economic activities, Timor-Leste remains unclear on how exactly the proposal will be implemented and how it will benefit. In September 2015, in my fieldwork interview with a senior official of Timor-Leste's Ministry of Foreign Affairs, it was apparent that, although Timor-Leste had officially welcomed the initiative, the country was still far from ready to properly make use of the opportunity in order to benefit from it. Between 2015-2018, Timor-Leste made unsuccessful attempts to mobilise finance mechanisms under the OBOR framework.

Trade and investment

It has yet to be seen how China's economic initiatives and investment will impact Timor-Leste's development plans. Nonetheless, China has been investing in strategic areas of Timor-Leste's government infrastructure: Chinese has helped to build the presidential palace, the ministry of foreign affairs and its diplomatic training center, and the ministry of defence. Similar investment exercises are carried out by China in other developing countries, including Portuguese-speaking countries. The Chinese Ministry of Commerce reported that China's general foreign direct investment to Timor-Leste between 2010-2014 soared from US$7.5 million to US$15.8 million (HKTDC Research 2016, 2). In 2018, this increased significantly to over US$45 million (HKTDC Research 2019, 8). In 2014, the Macau Forum media reported that three Chinese companies had indicated strong interest in investing in Timor-Leste's US$400 million ZEEMS project (Sampaio 2014). It is important to note that the majority of Chinese companies operating in Timor-Leste are state owned companies. While at the time of writing, none of these Chinese companies have become involved in ZEEMS projects in Timor-Leste's enclave of Oecussi, some Chinese companies have put forward concrete proposals for investment in agricultural production. For example, one proposal involved 400 acres of land to plant bananas to be exported to China. Another proposal involved 100 acres to plant pineapples for export (Sampaio 2015). A Chinese state-owned company called China Civil Engineering Construction Corporation has also signed a contract with Timor-Leste's national oil company Timor Gap to construct a port in Beaco, Viqueque district. The estimated cost of the Beaco port construction is US$943 million dollars (MacauHub 2019). Beaco is expected to become the destination for the oil pipeline from the Timor Sea connecting to other sites along the south coast designated for processing natural gas as well as a port facility for the export of liquefied natural gas (Timor Gap 2019). A Chinese airline company has expressed interest in investing in aero-connectivity between Dili and Hong Kong (Plataforma Media 2019).

However, given their active involvement in the oil and gas sector, Australia, the United States and Italy are the major investment players in Timor-Leste. Along with Portugal and Indonesia, Australia is also involved in financial investment. Nevertheless, China and Indonesia have higher numbers of registered companies and business enterprises in Timor-Leste. A lack of statistics on foreign business enterprises in Timor-Leste makes it difficult to provide an exact figure for Chinese and Indonesian business properties. However, with the increased number of Chinese newcomers present in the country, it can be said around 300 business enterprises belong to Chinese merchants. In his 2015 interview with the Jakarta Post Newspaper, former Prime Minister Rui Maria de Araújo stated there are over

20 Indonesian state-owned companies and up to 400 Indonesian private companies operating in Timor-Leste (Aritonang 2015).

The volume of China's bilateral trade with Timor-Leste has also increased steadily over the past years. China is now one of the major import trading partners in Timor-Leste. Indonesia is the source of Timor-Leste's largest imports—almost 90% of goods circulating in Timor-Leste's market are from Indonesia. Other major trading partners include the United States, Australia, Hong Kong, Malaysia, Portugal, Thailand, South Korea and Japan. Timor-Leste also has direct trade relations with Taiwan—an activity mostly revived from Timor-Leste through Timorese-Chinese and in which the main export commodities have been coffee and some other organic agriculture products. Taiwan's exports to Timor-Leste include foods, diesel and vehicle parts, and accessories.

In general, as a small country, Timor-Leste is highly dependent on imports due to its limited domestic industry. Statistics on China's trade with Timor-Leste as recorded by the Forum for Economic Cooperation and Trade between China and Portuguese-speaking Countries revealed that from 2013 to 2019 China's total export to Timor-Leste is over US$79.5 million and its total imports from Timor-Leste is over US$3 million. Table 11.1 below indicates China's trade relations with Timor-Leste as reported by the Forum for Economic Cooperation and Trade between China and Portuguese-speaking Countries from 2013 to 2019.

Table 11.1: Statistics on China's trade with Timor-Leste from 2013-2019 (US$'000)

Year	Import	Export
2019	2,456.09	14,357.88
2018	300.59	13,294.56
2017	156.21	13,327.37
2016	29.97	17,188.29
2015	72.49	10,595.44
2014	9.99	6,034.79
2013	39.7	4,730.67
Total	3,065.04	79,529.00

Source: This public document was extracted from the Permanent Secretariat of the Forum for Economic Cooperation and Trade between China and Portuguese-speaking Countries. See http://www.forumchinaplp.org.mo/category/news/trade-data/?lang=pt

Meanwhile, data from the Timor-Leste government revealed that from 2004 to 2019, with the exception of 2007 due to the 2006 political crisis, total imports of both merchandise and non-merchandise items from China increased exponentially. See

Table 11.2 below regarding Timor-Leste government's statistics on Timor-Leste's exports to and imports from China from 2004 to 2019. The statistics reveal a massive trade imbalance between China and Timor-Leste. China's main imported goods to Timor-Leste include pre-fabricated building materials, vehicles, cigarettes, uncooked pasta, uncooked rice, tractors, mounting fittings for building of base metal, apparatus for carrier-current or for digital system and medical treatment, and household and sanitary products. Timor-Leste's exports goods to China are mainly coffee and a few other organic agriculture products such as vanilla, candlenuts and turmeric.

Table 11.2: Statistics on Timor-Leste's export (including re-export) to and import from China between 2004 and 2019 (US$'000)

Year	Imports	Export & Re-Exports	Coffee Exports*
2004	1,321	10	0
2005	1,684	13	0
2006	2,209	126	0
2007	0	0	0
2008	5,363	0	0
2009	11,572	57	28,110
2010	21,531	295	103,197
2011	55,913	13,911	111,360
2012	43,603	559	82,800
2013	39,787	309	0
2014	41,335	77	0
2015	53,151	81	0
2016	97,775	674	304,504
2017	83,457	2,062	58.464
2018	65,157	2,599	66,528
2019	69,243	20,005	361,351
Total	593,101	40,778	1,057,908.46

* The nominal from coffee export is expressed as it is
Source: This statistic is extracted from Timor-Leste government's public document on external trade annual statistic report with modification from the author. See http://www.statistics.gov.tl/tl/category/survey-indicators/external-trade-statistics/anual-reports/

In 2008, the Chinese government offered zero-tariff treatment to Timor-Leste's merchandise exports to China (Chinese Embassy in Timor-Leste 2011). Such treatment is arguably part of China's soft power approach to gain Timor-Leste's attention in strengthening its trading activities. While Timor-Leste welcomed China's offer, due to Timor-Leste's limited merchandise exports, the opportunity has not been fully utilised by the country. Timor-Leste most likely will not be able to reduce its trade imbalance with China for obvious reasons relating to its geography, demography and economic capacity. See Table 3 below regarding Timor-Leste's trade balance. It indicates from 2004 to 2019, Timor-Leste's total trade deficit is over US$5.2 billion.

Table 11.3. Statistics on Timor-Leste's Trade Deficit 2004-2019 (US$'000)

Year	Export	Import	Trade Balance
2004	105,654	164,108	-58,454
2005	43,451	109,127	-65,676
2006	60,685	100,802	-40,117
2007*	19,179	206,133	-186,954
2008	49,207	268,584	-219,377
2009	34,512	295,096	-260,584
2010	41,660	298,091	-256,431
2011	53,253	339,630	-286,377
2012	76,893	670,121	-593,228
2013	53,278	528,824	-475,546
2014	39,065	553,658	-514,594
2015	38,415	491,230	-452815
2016	161,800	511,703	-349,903
2017	24,857	588,217	-563,360
2018	48,302	565,246	-518,944
2019	153,741	596,989	-443,248
Total	1,003,952	6,287,559	-5,258,608

* Statistics recorded for 2007 were based on trend estimates for missing months
Source: This is extracted from Timor-Leste government's public document on external trade annual statistic report with modification from the author. See http://www.statistics.gov.tl/tl/category/survey-indicators/external-trade-statistics/anual-reports

Overseas Chinese involvement in Timor-Leste's economy

Despite the early origins of China's involvement in Timor-Leste's economy (Kammen and Chen 2019; see also Chapter 1, this volume), its economic presence rose steadily following Timor-Leste's internal political crisis in 2006. As the economy steadily recovered from this period, there was a massive influx of Chinese private and state-owned companies and business enterprises to the country. However, the absence of formal statistics on international foreign business enterprises makes it difficult to present accurate figures of overseas 'Chinese' business in the country.

The visibly increased presence of these entities in the Timor-Leste business landscape was on the one hand a part of China's 'going out strategy' policy that was introduced in the 1990s. This strategy encourages not only Chinese citizens who are interested in better economic conditions to leave China, but also Chinese business enterprises, both state and non-state owned enterprises, to venture and operate overseas in the form of outward foreign direct investment (Abeliansky and Martínes-Zarzoso 2019; Wang 2016; Nash 2012). For some, migration was facilitated by the Chinese government, notably the Ministry of Foreign Affairs, Ministry of Public Security, and Overseas Affairs Office of the State Council, in the form of financial capital and other related administrative arrangements. While others, particularly the private-owned companies and business enterprises, develop their own arrangements through family and friendship network connections (Fieldwork interview with representative of Chinese newcomers—Dili, 6 September 2015).

On the other hand, the increased presence of Chinese business enterprises and companies and other international economic players in the country can be read as an outcome of incentives offered by Timor-Leste's strategic development plan. Its 2030 Strategic Plan and related investment laws encourage a diversification of foreign direct investment in the country.[9] Since its restoration of independence in 2002, whilst trying to improve the nation's quality of life, health and education, the government of Timor-Leste has also been focusing on infrastructure development aimed at laying groundwork for its economic development. This includes building and improving roads, bridges, waterways, power plants, expansion of airports and seaports and telecommunications. The government has allocated over US$1.2 billion specifically for infrastructure development. Such an enabling environment opens up a window of opportunity for international economic players from different parts of the world to come to Timor-Leste.

From 2008 to 2019, Chinese companies received over US$450 million of Timor-Leste public funds through a public bidding process. For example, China Overseas Engineering Group Co. Ltd and China Railway First Group Co. Ltd won public bids for building the first highway construction on the south coast of Timor-Leste. 30 km of a 151 km highway was completed in late 2018. The road is expected to connect Suai and Viqueque districts and facilitate road transport between the aforementioned south coast Tasi Mane oil and gas industrial hubs. China regards the completion of the project as a sign of Chinese companies' great accomplishment and the news was widely reported by different Chinese state media outlets in China. The China Harbour Engineering Co. Ltd was subcontracted by a French transport company called Bolloré Ports who was contracted by the Timor-Leste Government to build the new Tibar port and harbour (Macau Forum 2017a). The Tibar harbour project is by far the biggest public construction project to be built on the outskirts of Dili with an estimated cost of around US$490 million. It will be funded through a public-private partnership arrangement, in this case, private partners, the Timor-Leste government and Bollore Ports (ibid.).

In 2008, the Chinese Nuclear Industry 22nd (CNI22) was awarded over US$350 million via public tender, the highest amount ever awarded in Timor-Leste's history, to build a power plant in Timor-Leste. According to La'o Hamutuk NGO, CNI22 was also awarded another government contract totalling over US$1 million for school table and chair supplies (La'o Hamutuk 2013). This has made CNI22 the biggest beneficiary of Timor-Leste government funds among Chinese companies, its dominance prompting criticism from local non-governmental organisations. In 2013, La'o Hamutuk wrote a formal protest letter to the Government Procurement Office but received no formal response (ibid., 2013).

China sees its companies' engagement in Timor-Leste as an opportunity to expand its Maritime Silk Road influence through infrastructure development. In his remarks to journalists in a media gathering in Dili in April 2019, Chinese ambassador Xiao Jianguo named the projects as 'one grid', 'one road' and 'one port'—a play on Beijing's narrative with regards to the networks of the One Belt One Road Initiative (Chinese Embassy in Timor-Leste 2019). Chinese firms have not only competed and received funds through Timor-Leste's direct public funding, they have also competed for and received loans provided by the World Bank, Japan and the Asian Development Bank for public infrastructure projects, particularly road construction.

It is important to note that Timor-Leste's Service for Business Registration (SERVE) has also registered companies from Indonesia, Portugal, Australia, Japan, Malaysia, South Korea and Spain to be involved in large infrastructure projects in Timor-Leste (Fieldwork interview with head of SERVE—Dili, 2 September 2015). Indonesian companies have significantly benefited from Timor-Leste's public funds. Indonesian Ambassador to Timor-Leste, Sahat Sitorus, in his interview with Indonesian online Detik Finance news on 19 September 2017, confirmed the dominant presence of Indonesian state owned companies in Timor-Leste's development projects:

> Pembangunan di sini memang didominasi sama BUMN Indonesia. Kita berperan penting terhadap pembangunan yang terjadi di Timor-Leste. Bisa dilihat BUMN Indonesia ini

> komplit ada di sini, Hutama Karya, Waskita, WIKA, PT PP, Adhi Karya. Bikin jalan, perumahan, gedung sampai bioskop pun ada di sini (Simorangkir 2017).
> Development in Timor-Leste is indeed dominated by Indonesian state-owned enterprises. We play an important role in Timor-Leste's development. You can see many Indonesian state-owned companies that are here such as Hutama Karya, Waskita, WIKA, PT PP and Adhi Karya. They construct roads, houses, buildings as well as cinemas.

At the level of small to medium scale businesses in Timor-Leste, overseas Chinese and Timorese-Chinese are also important players. Prominent enterprises among Chinese-Timorese include AKAM (the owner of Leader, Lita Store, and Toyota dealer), Jape family of Timor-Plaza and Star King. These business enterprisers are located in Dili and considered the top three players among the Timorese-Chinese community. During the Portuguese colonial regime, ethnic Chinese monopolised the territory's market economy—they controlled 95% of some 400 wholesale and retail commerce in the territory (Dunn 2003, 38). They also cultivated and exported Timor coffee. It was reported that out of the twenty-five largest firms in the territory under Portuguese administration, only two of them were Portuguese firms, namely SAPT and SOTA.[10] The most vibrant and largest business owner among the ethnic Chinese at the time was the two brothers of the Sang Tai Hoo family (Dunn 2003, 38-39). This family business managed to extend their commercial network to other parts of Asia predominantly occupied by ethnic Chinese such as Hong Kong, Singapore and Macau.

Post-independence, most Chinese newcomers involved in trading activities settled in the capital Dili, as it is the centre of economic activities. They are involved in various economic activities from trading and retailing of cheap goods to wholesale construction materials, business in hotels, gas stations, restaurants, internet cafes and brothels. Interestingly, most of the goods and materials sold by the Chinese new merchants are directly imported from Indonesia. This shows how overseas Chinese economic activities in Timor-Leste have also indirectly contributed to Indonesia's economic development.

Many of these Chinese merchants occupy strategic locations along the main roads of Dili. The neighbourhood around Hudi-Laran Road and Fatuhada Road in Dili is now populated mainly by the new Chinese traders from Fujian province. The new Chinese traders rent the land and properties from the Timor-Leste government and private individuals for a minimum of 10 to 20 years. Land and property rents cost between US$300 to more than US$1,000 per month (Fieldwork interview with a Chinese new merchant, Zhen Jiang—Dili, 3 September 2014). Similar localised patterns of occupying most strategic places and involvement in various types of business are found in the economic activities of Chinese migrants in Africa (Park 2009, 7-9) and small-island developing Pacific countries.

Implications of China's increased economic engagement in Timor-Leste

China and Timor-Leste's economic relations are asymmetric in many ways. While undeniably China's engagement has contributed to diversifying Timor-Leste's economy, its increasing economic presence has ramifications at both state and non-state level in the country and to some extent beyond Timor-Leste's border. Its dynamic interactions, particularly through its overseas community's engagement in different economic activities, prompts conflicting views among Timorese locals, including the Timorese-Chinese community and government officials (Barreto Soares 2019, 323). Some locals are critical of China's economic engagement strategy as advanced through Chinese newcomers' increased presence and economic activities in the country. Others, including Timorese officials, have raised no concerns about it (Fieldwork interviews 2014-2018). These official views largely asserted that the presence of Chinese newcomers and their economic activities was an important contribution to the country's social and economic development as well as helping to address local needs. In the interview with former chief of staff of the president's office it was stated that:

> I think, like many countries in other parts of the world, the influx of new immigrants such as newly arrived Chinese and other foreign workers could recreate and create opportunity for parts of the local economy to grow. Having a rather criminalizing immigration is not a solution, or having utterly and strongly xenophobic policy is not a solution either...rather than criminalizing that, we have to make sure that our people become more competitive and be more prepared (Fieldwork interview with Fidelis Magalhaes—Dili, 2 September 2014).

Evidence also suggests that the presence and economic activities of newcomer Chinese traders provide employment to locals, improve local skills and knowledge in business development particularly for young Timorese, generate income for Timorese families and the state by leasing private and state land and properties, paying tax to the government and creating competition in the market by making the price of goods affordable for many ordinary Timorese (Barreto Soares 2019, 323). Furthermore, the Chinese newcomers are seen as risk-takers, willing to expand their economic activities to remote villages where other traders, including locals, are hesitant to undertake business activity (Barreto Soares 2019, 323).

On the other hand, the increased presence and economic practices of Chinese newcomers, and to a certain extent some Timorese-Chinese returnees, can be considered new forms of colonialism. Their occupation of strategic economic sectors and also domination of some key economic activities is evidence of this and resembles what Ogunrotifa Ayodeji Bayo refers to as the neo-colonial processes bound up in Africa's recent experience with the arrival of Chinese economic migrants (Bayo 2011, 228).

Such practices generate concern over the long-term social, cultural, economic and political consequences for the country. As one Timorese economics scholar observed:

> With many Chinese newcomers coming into Timor-Leste, their relationship with Timorese is also full of risk—they will influence Timorese's social and cultural domain through inter-marriage ... I see this phenomenon as natural but it is not normal. It is natural because we see interracial marriage is everywhere but it is not normal because it does not follow Timor-Leste's cultural norms and as a result, things that are supposedly natural become not natural. This will bring risk to Timor-Leste in the future (Fieldwork interview with Lucas da Costa—Dili, 2 September 2014).

Chinese migrants' involvement in various economic opportunities, particularly in local economies have created a sense of tension among both Timorese-Chinese and Timorese locals. Timorese-Chinese feel threatened that newcomer Chinese merchants and other ethnic Chinese are taking over their historically privileged role as major economic players in Timor-Leste's economy. Chinese newcomers' intrusion into local markets has also impacted the demographic of traditional market development, which so far has been dominated by locals (see Chapter 2, this volume). In an interview with a representative of the Dili-based Chinese-Timorese Association, the respondent stated that Chinese newcomers are greedy and very aggressive in doing business and that their increased presence has destroyed local market development and impacted property rental prices (Fieldwork interview—Dili, 8 October 2014).

Interestingly, while the Timorese-Chinese community raise concerns over Chinese newcomers' economic practices, many Timorese have been disturbed by some of the Timorese-Chinese community's economic engagement. Of most concern is the Jape Kong Su family, who has been accused of 'land grabbing'.[11] The family was accused of evicting Timorese families to build its large commercial property known as Timor-Plaza creating tension between the Timor-Plaza owners, local landowners and a local NGO Matadalan ba Rai, which advocated for the evicted families (Barreto Soares 2019, 325). Being a key player in the property market amongst the Timorese-Chinese community, the Jape family also reportedly purchased cheaply over 50 acres of land over the hills in eastern Dili for different economic purposes, including renting out land to other business developers (ibid., 2019). At the time of writing, some construction works on this land include land demarcation and road construction, sparking much criticism by local NGOs regarding the issue of environmental degradation in the area.

Remittances of funds generated by overseas Chinese business interests is another significant issue. The absence of official statistics makes it difficult to present the actual figure. However, as profit-takers, it is believed that most Chinese migrants sent their remittances back to China or other countries. This is consistent with past practices. During the Portuguese administration, most ethnic Chinese sent their remittances to Taiwan and Macau, including some to sustain the revolutionary wars of Ciang Kai-sek and the nationalists. This is a similar remittance pattern to overseas Chinese in other Southeast Asian countries (Yong and McKenna 1990 quoted in Cheok et al. 2013, 76).

The increased presence and engagement of Chinese migrants has also brought with it urban environmental and safety concerns. For example, their increased presence has increased the capital Dili's density and land and property rentals have become expensive. This has forced some Timorese families to relocate further inland or move to other more remote areas in search of affordable accommodation. Nonetheless, to date, there have not been incidents of public hatred or public expressions of anti-Chinese sentiment. However, there are some isolated cases which have prompted localised tensions and some read these incidents as expressing racially motivated sentiments against Chinese newcomers. There are also reports of isolated incidents of fighting between locals and Chinese newcomer shopowners in some neighbourhoods in Dili and in the Municipalities due to social jealousies. Some of these tensions have been brought to the attention of the Chinese Embassy in Timor-Leste who have been asked to intervene to assure the safety and security of Chinese newcomers (Fieldwork observations between 2014 and 2018).

It is also asserted that some Chinese newcomers have been involved in illegal practices including gambling, money laundering and human trafficking. A number of brothels in Dili are owned by Chinese newcomers and the women who work there have been brought from China and other Southeast Asian countries. Some Chinese migrants are also involved in supporting black market money lending directed not only at new Chinese migrants but also to some locals (Interview with UN police officer Jose Brito—Dili, 13 October 2014). In 2017, the activities of a Chinese company named Fuzhou Hoo Long Ocean Fishing Co. Ltd, which was licenced by the Timorese Government to fish in Timor-Leste seas, prompted public protests over its alleged involvement in illegal fishing of protected sharks in Timor-Leste waters. The company's fleet of 15 vessels was held but then released without charge after paying a considerably small bail of US$100,000 (Sea Shepherd 2018).

Conclusion

Any consideration of economic diversity and community-based economic acitivites in contemporary Timor-Leste must consider the long-standing, active and ever changing participation of Chinese state and non-state actors in Timor-Leste's economy.

Beijing's judicious economic diplomacy has turned China into one of the significant economic players in Timor-Leste. Having observed Beijing's active economic diplomacy and its non-state actors' considerable activities over the past two decades, it can be concluded that China has profound interest in Timor-Leste's economy. Overseas Chinese community involvement in Timor-Leste's economy has gone beyond state level—the newcomers in particular have encroached into the local economy. Their active engagement has brought certain ramifications for Timor-Leste and others beyond its borders where China's economic bolster is turning Timor-Leste into a battle ground for competing economic and geopolitical interests of major powers.

On the other hand, the Chinese are not alone—Indonesian and other non-Timorese owned business companies and enterprises have increasingly intruded in the local economy. They have benefitted significantly from both public and private funds, although the latter is less significant compared to the relative availability of public funds in Timor-Leste.

China's engagement is expected to increase over time. Its Belt and Road Initiative will serve as its strategy for further connectivity with Timor-Leste's economy in the years to come. Meanwhile, Timor-Leste's national development plan has created an enabling environment for China and other countries to take up various economic opportunities in the country.

The ramifications of this for the national and local community economies require both the Chinese and Timor-Leste governments' attention in order to avoid the potential for increased negative impacts at the state and society level.

Notes

1 The term Timorese-Chinese is commonly expressed in reverse order in Tetum (the national language of Timor-Leste) as Xina-Timor.

2 In this paper, the term Chinese newcomers is used interchangeably with Chinese migrants.

3 However, recently, a United States' firm has withdrawn from one of the oil and gas project deals in the Greater Sunrise project.

4 According to a research report conducted by the Office of President in 2014, in that year around 1,000 new Chinese migrants arrived in Timor-Leste. The Immigration Office reported around 3,000 to 4,000 new Chinese migrants arrived in Timor-Leste between 2002 and 2014. Some of them left the country after their contracts terminated with the Chinese companies. However, the number of new arrivals continues to increase every year. In a fieldwork interview with a representative of a Chinese newcomers' association by the author in March 2022, it was reported that as of December 2021 there are around 5,000 Chinese nationals residing in Timor-Leste.

5 Apart from Chinese traders, there were Malay, Javanese, Arab, Indian and Gujarati merchants who frequently visited Timor Island for trading of beeswax and sandalwood (Lea and Milward 2001, 42).

6 It is important to note that despite Portugal's initial contact in 1511, its official colonial rule did not begin until 1702.

7 This is based on personal observations since 2000 and an informal conversation with a Timorese leader in Dili during my fieldwork in 2017.

8 At the time of writing, Jose Ramos Horta sworn in for second time as president of Timor-Leste for the period of 2022 to 2027.

9 While the exact number of Chinese firms in Timor-Leste is unknown due to the absence of official statistics, those that operate on the ground include China Overseas Engineering Group Co. Ltd, China Railway First Group Co. Ltd, China Harbour Engineering Co. Ltd, China Railway International Group, Shanghai Construction Group Co. Ltd, China WuYi Construction no Guang Sha Co. Ltd. Other Chinese enterprises currently working in Timor-Leste include China International Construction Cooperation (CICO), Fujian International Cooperation, Guangxi International Construction Engineering, China Shandong International Economic and Technical Cooperation Group Co. Ltd and Shun International Economical and Technical Corporation Group Company. Most of these establishments are state-owned.

10 SAPT (*Sociedade Agricola Patria e Trabalho*, also known as the Sociedade) was a state-owned firm that was established by Portuguese Governor Celestino da Silva towards the end of the 1800s. Meanwhile, SOTA (*Sociedade Orientale do Transportes e Armazens*) was an investment company controlled by the Japanese before the Portuguese took over after Japanese's occupation during WWII. It was a successor to the pre-war Asia Investment Company. These two companies were involved largely in coffee plantations and export/import activities (Dunn 2003, 38).

11 The Jape Kong Su family are Timorese-Chinese who returned to Timor-Leste after Timor-Leste's independence. The Jape family is a well-established business group in Australia's Northern Territory.

References

Abeliansky, A. L., and I. Martínez-Zarzoso. 2019. "The relationship between the Chinese 'going out' strategy and international trade." *Economics: The Open-Access, Open-Assessment E-Journal* 13 (1): 1-18. doi: 10.5018/economics-ejournal.ja.2019-21

Aritonang, M. 2015. "Discourse: Indonesia, Timor-Leste have developed a mature relationship: PM Rui Maria De Araujo." *The Jakarta Post*, August 31. Retrieved 27 June 2017, from http://www.thejakartapost.com/news/2015/08/31/discourse-indonesiatimor-leste-have-developed-a-mature-relationship-pm.html.

Barreto Soares, L. 2019. "Overseas Chinese, soft power and China's people-to-people diplomacy in Timor-Leste." In *Routledge Handbook of Contemporary Timor-Leste*, edited by A. McWilliam, and M. Leach, 314-330. London: Routledge.

Bayo, O. A. 2011. "The Chinese in Africa: New colonialism is not a New Deal." *Botswana Journal of African Studies* 25 (2): 228-245.

Berlie, J. A. 2015. "Chinese in East Timor: Identity, society and economy." *HumaNetten* 35 (Autumn): 35-49. Doi: 10.15626/hn.20153503.

Cau, E. 2018. "Geopolitical implications of the Belt and Road Initiative: The backbone for a new world order?." *Contemporary Chinese Political Economy and Strategic Relations: An International Journal* 4 (1): 38-105.

Cheok, C. K., L. K. Hing, and P. P. Lee. 2013. Chinese overseas remittances to China: The perspective from Southeast Asia. *Journal of Contemporary Asia* 43 (1): 75-101. Doi:10.1080/00472336.2012.735918.

Chinese Embassy in Timor-Leste. 2010. "Bilateral relations." Press release. Retrieved 18 August 2016, from http://tl.chineseembassy.org/eng/sbjx/.

Chinese Embassy in Timor-Leste. 2011. "Long standing relationship between China and Timor-Leste." Press release. Retrieved 18 August 2016, from http://tl.chineseembassy.org/eng/is/t784186.htm

Chinese Embassy in Timor-Leste. 2019. "Remarks of H.E. Dr. Xiao Jianguo, Ambassador of the People's Republic of China to the Democratic Republic of Timor-Leste at the Media Gathering." [Press release]. Retrieved 4 May 2019, from http://tl.chineseembassy.org/eng/zdgx/t1656250.htm.

Dan, Z. 2014. "China, Timor-Leste announce all-round cooperative partnership." *Xinhua* Abril 08. Retrieved 9 March 2016, from https://www.chinadaily.com.cn/china/2014-04/08/content_17415420.htm.

Dunn, J. 2003. *East Timor: A Rough Passage to Independence.* 3rd ed. Double Bay, NSW: Longueville Books.

Durand, F. B. 2016. *History of Timor-Leste.* Chiang Mai: Silkworm Books.

Fox, J. J. 2003. "Tracing the path, recounting the past: historical perspectives on Timor." In *Out of the Ashes: Destruction and Reconstruction of East Timor*, edited by J. J. Fox, and D. Babu, 1-27. Canberra: ANU Press.

Green, M. J. 2018. "Foreword." In *China's Maritime Silk Road: Strategic and Economic Implications for the Indo-Pacific Region*, edited by N. Szechenyi, 1-3. Washington DC: Center for Strategic and International Studies.

Gunn, G. C. 1999. *Timor Lorosae 500 anos.* Translated by J. Aguiar. 1st ed. Porto: Tipografia Greca.

Gunn, G. C. 2016. "The Timor-Macao sandalwood trade and the Asian discovery of the great South Land?" *Review of Culture* 53: 125-148.

Guoto, Z. 2017. "Xi's secret economic weapon: Overseas Chinese." *Nikkei Asian Review*, April 03. Retrieved 8 March 2018, from https://asia.nikkei.com/Economy/Xi-s-secret-economic-weapon-Overseas-Chinese2.

HKTDC (Hong Kong Trade Development Council) Research. 2016. Timor-Leste: Market profile. Retrieved 29 June 2017 from http://china-trade-research.hktdc.com/business-news/article/The-Belt-and-Road-Initiative/Timor-Leste-Market-Profile/obor/en/1/1X000000/1X0A3NDQ.htm

HKTDC (Hong Kong Trade Development Council) Research. 2019. "Timor-Leste: Market profile." Retrieved 21 July 2019, from file:///Users/micabarretosoares/Downloads/hktdc_MzU3OTg5ODg5_en.pdf

Hongyang, L. 2015. "Welcome message of Ambassador Extraordinary and Plenipotentiary of the People's Republic of China to the Democratic Republic of Timor-Leste." Press release. Retrieved 18 August 2016, from http://tl.chineseembassy.org/eng/dszc/t1281688.htm

Huber, J. 2021. "At the periphery of Nanyang: The Hakka community of Timor-Leste", In *Sinophone Southeast Asia: Sinitic Voices across the Southern Seas,* edited by C. China, and T. Hoogervorst, 52-90. Boston: Brill.

Kammen, D. and J. Chen. 2019. *China Timor: Baba, Hakka, and Cantonese in the Making of Timor-Leste.* Connecticut: Yale Univ Southeast Asia Studies.

La'o Hamutuk. 2013. "LH protests contract award to CNI22." Press release. Retrieved 14 July 2017 from http://laohamutuk.blogspot.com/2013/10/lh-protests-contract-award-to-cni22.html.

Lea, D., and C. Milward, C. 2001. *A Political Chronology of Southeast Asia and Oceania* (1st ed.). London: Routledge/Taylor & Francis Group.

Liang, Z., and H. Morooka. 2004. "Recent trends of emigration from China: 1982-2000." *International Migration 42* (3): 145-164. Doi: 10.1111/j.0020-7985.2004.00292.x.

Liu, H. 2005. "New migrants and the revival of overseas Chinese nationalism." *Journal of Contemporary China, 14* (43): 291-316. Doi: 10.1080/10670560500065611.

Macau Forum. 2017a. "Chinese company bags contract to build East Timor harbour." *Macau Forum*, December 13. Retrieved 7 March 2018, from http://www.forumchinaplp.org.mo/portugues-empresa-chinesa-escolhida-para-construir-novo-porto-em-timor-leste/

Macau Forum. 2017b. "Chinese contractors build road to remote East Timorese town." *Macau Forum*, January 8. Retrieved 29 December 2018, from http://www.forumchinaplp.org.mo/portugues-chineses-constroem-primeira-auto-estrada-em-timor-leste/

MacauHub. 2014. "China wants to set up partnership with Timor-Leste." MacauHub, April 09. Retrieved 9 April 2014, from http://www.macauhub.com.mo/en/2014/04/09/china-wants-to-set-up-partnership-with-timor-leste/

MacauHub. 2019. "Chinese company builds a port in southern Timor-Leste." *MacauHub*, April 29. Retrieved 29 April 2019, from https://macauhub.com.mo/2019/04/29/pt-empresa-da-china-constroi-porto-no-sul-de-timor-leste/

Nash, P. 2012. "China's 'going out' strategy." *Diplomatic Courier*, May 10. Retrieved 20 August 2017, from http://www.diplomaticourier.com/china-s-going-out-strategy/

Park, Y. J. 2009. "Chinese migration in Africa." *SAIIA Occasional Paper* (24): 1-17.

Pinto, P. J. d. S. 2014. "Visitors and settlers: Notes on Timor and the Chinese as cultural and economic brokers (Sixteenth to Nineteenth Centuries)." *Journal of Asian History* 48 (2): 139-164. Doi:10.13173/jasiahist.48.2.0139.

Plataforma Media. 2019. "Chinese company builds a port in southern Timor-Leste." *Plataforma Media*, April 29. Retrieved 8 May 2019, from https://www.plataformamedia.com/en-uk/news/society/interior/chinese-company-builds-a-port-in-southern-timor-leste-10843656.html

Rahman, R. 2019. "After Oecusse Airport, Wika eyes more in Timor-Leste." *The Jakarta Post,* June 21. Retrieved 21 June 2019, from https://www.thejakartapost.com/news/2019/06/21/after-oecusse-airport-wika-eyes-more-timor-leste.html

RDTL (Democratic Republic of Timor-Leste Government). 2014. "Joint statement between the People's Republic of China and The Democratic Republic of Timor-Leste on establishing comprehensive partnership of good-neighbourly friendship, mutual trust and mutual benefit." [Press release]. Retrieved 15 April 2014, from http://timor-leste.gov.tl/?p=9967&lang=en.

RDTL (Democratic Republic of Timor-Leste Government). 2015. "High level official of the People's Republic of China meets with Prime Minister." [Press release]. Retrieved 18 August 2016, from http://timor-leste.gov.tl/?p=11581&lang=en

RDTL (Democratic Republic of Timor-Leste Government). 2017. "Timor-Leste's application for membership of AIIB approved." [Press release]. Retrieved 28 March 2017, from http://timor-leste.gov.tl/?p=17618&lang=en

RDTL (Democratic Republic of Timor-Leste Government). 2019. Timor-Leste annual trade statistics 2019. Retrieved 2 January 2020, from https://www.statistics.gov.tl/wp-content/uploads/2020/07/Publication-Trade-2019.pdf

Roque, R. 2010. "The unruly island: Colonialism's predicament in late nineteenth-century East Timor." *Portuguese Literary & Cultural Studies* 17 (18): 303-330.

Sági, J., and I. Engelberth. 2018. "The Belt and Road Initiative: A way forward to China's expansion." *Contemporary Chinese Political Economy and Strategic Relations: An International Journal* 4 (1): 9-37.

Sampaio, A. 2014. "Chineses querem comprar todo o projeto de Oecussi." *Plataforma Media,* June 23. Retrieved 20 August 2017, from http://www.plataformamacau.com/lusofonia/timor-leste/chineses-querem-comprar-todo-o-projeto-de-oecussi/.

Sampaio, A. 2015. "China disponível para reforçar cooperação com Timor-Leste." *Portal SAPO.PT/ LUSA*, April 02. Retrieved 27 August 2017, from http://24.sapo.pt/noticias/internacional/artigo/china-disponivel-para-reforcar-cooperacao-com-timor-leste_19056869.html.

Scott, J. 2019. "Australia Vows to Upgrade Timor-Leste Naval Base as China Hovers." *Bloomberg*, August 29. Retrieved 31 August 2019, from https://www.bloomberg.com/news/articles/2019-08-29/australia-vows-upgrade-of-timor-leste-naval-base-as-china-hovers.

Sea Shepherd. 2018. "Fleet Targeting Sharks in Timor-Leste Released Without Charge." *Sea Shepherd Global*, July 04. Retrieved 5 July 2018, from https://www.seashepherdglobal.org/latest-news/timor-leste-follow-up/.

Simorangkir, E. 2017. "BUMN RI dominasi pembangunan di Timor-Leste." *Detik Finance*, September 25. Retrieved 25 September 2017, from https://finance.detik.com/berita-ekonomi-bisnis/3650588/bumn-ri-dominasi-pembangunan-di-timor-leste

Storey, I. 2011. "East Timor and China: Beijing look to secure long-term interests." In *Southeast Asia and the Rise of China: The Search for Security*, edited by I. Storey, 274-284. New York: Routledge.

Tan, C. B. 2013. *Routledge Handbook of the Chinese Diaspora*. New York: Routledge.

Timor Gap. 2019. Beaço LNG–Plant. Retrieved 25 May 2019, from https://www.timorgap.com/databases/website.nsf/vwAll/Bea%C3%A7o%20LNG%20%E2%80%93%20Plant

Wang, H. 2016. "A deeper look at China's 'going out' policy." *Centre for International Governance Innovation*, March 8, Canada. https://www.cigionline.org/publications/deeper-look-chinas-going-out-policy/.

Interviews

1. Fieldwork interview with Fidelis Magalhaes, former Chief of Staff of the Presidency—Dili, 2 September 2014.
2. Fieldwork interview with Rita dos Santos, former General Secretary of the Macau Forum—Macau, 23 June 2015.
3. Fieldwork interview with former Director of the Multilateral Division of Timor-Leste's Ministry of Foreign Affairs—Dili, 25 September 2015.
4. Fieldwork interview with representative of the Chinese Newcomers Association—Dili, 6 September 2015.
5. Fieldwork interview with Senior Official of Timor-Leste's Ministry of Public Infrastructure—Dili, 15 August 2015.
6. Fieldwork interview with Senior Official of SERVE—Dili, 2 September 2015.
7. Fieldwork interview with a new Chinese merchant—Dili, 3 September 2014.
8. Fieldwork interview with representative of Chinese Timorese Association—Dili, 8 October 2014.

CHAPTER 12

Migrant work and homecoming: Experiences of Timorese seasonal workers

Ann Wigglesworth and Abel Boavida dos Santos

Abstract

Most of Timor-Leste's population is dependent on subsistence agriculture and young people flock to the capital in search of further education or work in the capital. With the lack of work opportunities in Timor-Leste, the government sought to send young Timorese overseas as temporary migrant workers. Two official programs for temporary workers were established in South Korea and Australia, but a greater number travel to the UK (United Kingdom) through informal migration channels. This paper focusses on the development outcomes of migration programs, seeking to understand how migrant work impacts the family economy and wellbeing. It draws on the case study of Timorese workers in Australia's Seasonal Workers Program, their experiences as migrant workers, their use of remittances and how migration contributes to their potential to support their family on return to Timor-Leste.

Keywords: Timor-Leste; labour mobility; work; remittances; family economy

Labour mobility is driven by social inequalities in the global marketplace, evident by the gap between the poor rural agricultural producers and the middle classes in the 'modernising' urban areas. The exploitation of migrant labour in low grade jobs making cheap goods for the consuming middle classes has become the face of stark global inequalities. Meanwhile in the locations of poverty, rural-urban migration has become a strategy to reduce poverty by families around the world, often as a first step leading to international migration. It provides vulnerable households a way to engage in asset accumulation that can provide families with exit routes from poverty (Ellis 2003).

Labour mobility is a relatively new phenomenon in Timor-Leste. There are thousands of Timorese working overseas as a means to support their families, in three major destinations: Australia, Korea and the UK. The conditions they face overseas are diverse, but the reasons they go are similar. This paper is focussed on understanding how migration opportunities are taken up by young Timorese, drawing on an in-depth study of the Australian Seasonal Worker Program (SWP) to identify the short to medium-term impacts for workers participating in the SWP. It also situates this research in the broader context of Timorese migrant experiences in Korea and the UK. This research finds that these migrants see themselves as contributors to their families and communities through their financial contribution (see Chapter 14, this volume). At the same time, a broadening of their horizons has supported criticism of some traditional practices, resulting in their desire to challenge local customs that are inequitable.

Labour mobility in Timor-Leste

The movement of people from their place of origin is often influenced by diverse factors such as poverty, war or conflict. Labour migration is driven by expected improvements in the life of a migrant's family which might include higher wages, employment, health and education. International migration generally is beneficial for most of those involved, resulting in higher Gross Domestic Product (GDP) growth for countries of destination and increased wages for migrants (ESCAP 2016, 10-11). Remittances sent by migrants have positive effects not only for their families, but also for communities and their country in general. Potentially, countries of origin can benefit when migrants return with new skills that are useful to the national economy.

The theory of New Economics of Labour Migration recognises that migration decisions (who goes, where to go, for how long, to do what etc.) are not individual decisions but joint decisions taken within the ambit of the household, and for different members of the household (King 2012). This is particularly the case in communitarian societies such as in Timor-Leste where the extended family plays a central role in decision making.

Economic inequalities between urban and rural Timor-Leste are increasingly evident, with the wealthier residing in urban areas, while the vulnerable poor are predominantly in the rural areas (McWilliam 2015). This wealth contrast is a driver of rural-urban migration. Internal migration to the urban centres also resulted from people fleeing the conflict in 1999. Since 2000, the economic opportunities from aid and development resources have been concentrated in the capital, leading to rapid population increases in Dili.

The mobility of young people to access education and work opportunities starts with school students moving to their district town (municipal centre) and then often onto the capital Dili to attend secondary school. Most of them do not return to the rural areas to live but remain in the urban areas seeking further education or work opportunities. During the Indonesian occupation, students were told that they should go to school so that they could get a job in the government. Now this is every student's aspiration. As Ego Lemos, Timor-Leste's premier permaculturalist stated, "Young people were not interested in agriculture. Once they had some education they assume agriculture is not a good source of employment" (quoted in Wigglesworth 2016, 108).

In 2009, around 22% of the total working age population living in Dili were migrants and close to 39% of the working-age population moved to Dili for economic or educational reasons (ILO 2016, 11). Permanent jobs remain elusive for most young people. The number of available jobs has been small relative to the large size of the cohort of youth leaving formal education in search of work each year (UNDP 2018, 58).

McWilliam and Monteiro (2019, 48) observe that continued poor employment conditions and a persistent lack of work opportunities in the Timor-Leste economy, especially in rural areas, resulted in migration. Their research in Lautém district found that high school graduates who failed to secure places at a university or employment in town, and whose parents were not in a position to support further education, often elected to work in the UK as a way to build savings and gain experience prior to pursuing studies in later years.

A political crisis in 2006 saw youth gangs take to the streets in violent communal conflict, which triggered some concern about the disaffection and social marginalisation of youth as a result of lack of employment opportunities. Following this, the government of Timor-Leste sought to enhance work opportunities through labour migration, initially through the South Korea Temporary Workers Program pilot from 2006.

The second official labour migration program to be established was the Australian Seasonal Workers Program (SWP), which started in Timor-Leste in 2012. The SWP is an Australian government initiative which allows workers from the Pacific and Timor-Leste to work for up to nine months (previously six months) to fill low-skill seasonal vacancies in Australia.[1] It is supported by the Labour Mobility Assistance Program (LMAP) which provides in-country support to the in-country labour supplier. In Timor-Leste this is the Department of Overseas Workers at the Secretariat of State for Vocational Training and Employment Policy (SEFOPE).

Timor-Leste was the fifteenth Asian country to join the South Korean Employment Permit System (EPS), which regulates labour migration. The EPS allows young Timorese to work in South Korea for three to five years. Potential migrants must learn Korean to be eligible. Of 8,638 participants in the Korean language course between 2009-2015, 40% passed and 60% failed the test (Wigglesworth and Fonseca 2016). Like the SWP, this program is run by SEFOPE. This small study of Timorese workers who had returned from South Korea was carried out by Ann Wigglesworth and Zulmira Fonseca in 2015.[2]

A much larger number of Timorese migrant workers travel as undocumented migrant workers to the UK. Since the first Timorese found work in Northern Ireland in 2000, thousands have travelled a well-trodden path to join family or friends working in the UK. This is possible because Timorese born before 2002 have the right to a Portuguese passport which gives them access to European Union (EU) countries. There are now an estimated 16,000-19,000 Timorese resident in UK, on Portuguese passports and without official support, predominantly working in meat factories, warehouses and cleaning jobs. A small qualitative independent study of Timorese working in the UK was undertaken by Ann Wigglesworth and Lionel Boxer in 2016.[3] In the research the workers had spent from one to fourteen years in the UK. New arrivals are assisted by family members or friends who are already there and these networks are disproportionately linked to the eastern districts of Timor (Wigglesworth and Boxer 2019). Migrants who had worked in the UK, South Korea and Australia all said that the lack of job opportunities at home was their reason for engaging in overseas work. The scale of this migration reflects a strong unmet demand for paid work in Timor-Leste. Andrew McWilliam, in the following chapter, provides more insight into the cultural and social impacts of UK migration in one of the eastern districts.

The numbers of Timorese migrants that have worked in the two official overseas work programs in Korea and Australia are relatively small, with less than 2,000 migrants having been placed in the EPS from 2009-2015 (when the research was undertaken) and 1,400 by the SWP from 2012-2017. The program was growing quickly with thousands waiting in the Work Ready Pool (with equal numbers of men and women) for a placement. COVID has had a profound impact with border restrictions curtailing movement over two years.

Remittances are now Timor-Leste's largest source of foreign revenue after oil and aid, overtaking coffee, the major export. An estimated US$44 million was remitted in 2017, US$27.1m from the UK, US$9.6m from Korea and US$5m from Australia (Curtain 2018).

This paper draws on the three research projects on Timorese migration as mentioned above. The Korea and UK surveys used a similar simple questionnaire to gather quantitative and qualitative data. Thirty returnees from Korea were interviewed. For the UK study some interviews were conducted with migrants in Northern Ireland or England and others with returnees from the UK in Dili. A total of 21 interviews were held, a cohort too small for quantitative analysis.

The SWP questionnaire was much more comprehensive, particularly about working conditions, the use of remittances and post-SWP activities on return home. As with the Korea study, all interviews were conducted with returnees in Timor-Leste. This comprehensive survey also reached fifty respondents in the first phase and 39 of these same workers in the second phase. The data interrogates the terms and conditions of the migration experience, the rationale for becoming a migrant, the purposes for which remittances were used and migrants' aspirations for their future.

While the experiences of working in different countries were different, it was found that the motivations, expenditure of remittances and future aspirations of the migrant workers were similar across all three programs. Due to the more comprehensive data from the SWP research, this paper will use SWP data on the experiences of Timorese migrant workers, their motivations and aspirations for the future.

Timorese seasonal workers in Australia research

The Labour Mobility Assistance Program (LMAP) is funded by the Department of Foreign Affairs and Trade (Australia's foreign aid program) with the specific purpose of supporting SWP partner countries to increase the number and quality of workers participating in the programme, and to support targeted activities that will increase the benefits (financial and other) for workers and their communities resulting from their participation.

A study of Timorese seasonal workers was commissioned by Cardno as part of the LMAP in 2016-2017.[4] The research team for the SWP study was led by Dr Ann Wigglesworth with Mr Abel Boavida dos Santos and a team of three women and two men who were recruited and trained as data collectors. The first phase of research involved interviewing 50 returned workers shortly after their return. In the second phase these same workers were interviewed after five or six months at home and before they returned for another season of work.[5]

The SWP is a complex program with multiple stakeholders in Australia and has operated in Timor-Leste since 2012. After a slow start, the program recruitment has built up. At the time of the research in 2016 almost 600 workers had been sent since 2012. By late 2017 this had more than doubled to 1,400 workers and the annual participation is said to have continued to increase.

Table 12.1. Numbers of Timorese SWP workers per year up to 2017

Year	Male	Female	Hospitality	Horticulture	Total
2012	7	5	12	0	12
2013	25	10	21	14	35
2014	100	31	46	85	131
2015	115	46	41	120	161
2016	227	71	34	264	298
2017	556	225	42	739	781
Total	1,030	388	196	1,222	1,418
%	73%	27%	14%	86%	100%

Table developed from data from LMAP reintegration and tracer survey and updated on 2017 annual data via personal communication with LMAP.

In Australia the registration of SWP employers is managed by the Department of Jobs and Small Business. Its purpose is to meet seasonal labour shortages in Australia in the horticulture and accommodation sectors.

The LMAP support the in-country labour supplier, SEPFOPE, particularly in relation to pre-departure briefings and reintegration briefings. Seasonal workers brought into Australia by employers are subject to the same workplace relations and work health and safety safeguards as Australian workers.

Of the 50 workers interviewed, 10 were women and 40 were men, the majority between 26-35 years old with an average age of 30. Of workers interviewed, 70% had just secondary school education and 22% had a university degree. In this largely Catholic country, 98% were Catholic, 58% were married and 36% had never married including four of the ten women in the sample.

Gender disaggregated data indicates that 27% of Timorese SWP workers are women, a higher proportion than any Pacific country participating in the SWP. This compares with women making up only 5% of Timorese workers who go to South Korea and probably not more than 10% who go to the UK. This is in part due to the gender equality policy of DFAT (Department of Foreing Affairs and Trade) paying attention to the gender balance of participation. They also provide an orientation on gender equality and norms in Australia prior to departure.

When asked which district they are from, every district of the country was represented. However, 45 of the returned workers were recruited in Dili and continue to be resident in Dili. This is because large numbers of young people migrate to Dili for education, training or work opportunities which are greater in Dili, generally staying with extended family members. Typically, when asked what district they are from, Timorese will respond with the origin of their family, often also their place of birth, even if they are no longer living there.

Initially, the Korean EPS and the Australian SWP were both seen by the government as a way of resolving the issue of high youth unemployment in Dili in order to reduce youth on the streets, so recruitment from the urban areas was intended, even though most of the SWP work was in horticulture. The consequences of this will be discussed later.

Research findings

The work

The two types of work in the SWP are horticulture, the largest category, and hospitality in Northern Australia during the cooler winter tourism season. At the time of the research in 2016, most men work in horticulture (72%) while the women interviewed were more evenly split between the two categories (60% horticulture and 40% hospitality). This imbalance is influenced by perceived gender roles in Timor-Leste where housekeeping is seen as women's work and hard labour as men's work.

The decision to send a family member to work overseas is often based on decision making within the extended family (see Chapter 6, this volume). Where the migrant is a woman, and often a wife and a mother and the major provider through food production, child care and other domestic tasks, women migrants make personal sacrifices in leaving their children for the benefit of her family. However, she can also make an increased economic contribution to her family and often gain an increased status within the family. Sometimes women also gain new perspectives on gender roles which enables her to challenge those local customs that lead to inequality.

A higher proportion of women in hospitality than horticulture is partly due to the fact that some Australian farmers are reported to consider size and strength as a factor in worker selection and thus prefer to recruit men, just as some labour recruiters choose to recruit Tonga men rather than the smaller Timorese. However, others have reported that Timorese workers are more reliable than some of the Pacific Islanders. On the other hand, employers tend to see women as more suitable to kitchen and housekeeping services in hotels in the hospitality sector and many women workers prefer this type of work.

When workers return to Australia for a second (or more) time, the workers are often invited to return to the same employer. In this research, all hospitality workers returned to the same workplace. However, there was a significant reduction in horticulture workers returning to the program. Horticultural work was found to be hard, and in Victoria and Tasmania workers suffered from very cold working conditions. A number of workers, particularly women, chose to change their workplace from horticulture to hospitality in the north of Australia as their preferred option.

Within the two broad sectors of work there is a considerable variety of tasks. Some workers named just a single task they were doing every day while others named a variety of tasks. Crop work made up 68% of horticultural work, the largest number in fruit picking and others in land clearing, preparation, planting, weeding, driving or a combination of these. In hospitality, housekeeping involved making up bedrooms and laundry work, while some simply said 'hotel work' implying more varied tasks within the hotel.

Most workers worked six days a week (68%) with some 12% of workers working only five days and 20% of workers working 7 days a week. The hours worked was more variable. Most hospitality workers averaged eight hours a day, while 85% of horticulture workers worked either eight or nine hour days. Some of the horticulture workers were paid on a piece rate basis and could work longer hours to get more money. Of those interviewed, 36% received piece rates for some or all of their work, while the majority (64% of workers) were paid by regular wages.

There were a few workers who were unhappy about the hours they worked. This included workers who said the hours of work were insufficient, due to limited fruit available to pick, and others who did not like having to work into the night (i.e., asparagus pickers). Some workers had been sent too early in the year and incurred accommodation and living costs several weeks before the fruit was ready for picking and they could start earning. The majority, however, became accustomed to the working hours and the hard work, and appreciated the work they had, well paid by Timorese standards, that enabled them to adequately support their families at home.

Working conditions and life in Australia

A pre-departure briefing provided by LMAP is important for workers to have a thorough understanding of the work and living conditions that they will have, and the rights and responsibilities of themselves and their employers.

More than 80% understood what their working and living conditions, rights and responsibilities would be. Weaker understanding was evident for the questions on Australian Law about which less than half the respondents had a good understanding, and Australian culture and gender issues. The UK study illustrated the importance of migrant workers understanding the laws of the country, for instance in Northern Ireland several workers got into trouble for inadvertent illegal activities and unacceptable behaviour (Wigglesworth and Boxer 2019, 10.1).

In relation to accommodation, 42 workers (84%) rated the quality good or very good and 38 workers (76%) rated the value for money good or very good and also accepting the rules imposed at the accommodation. This was in spite of the fact that acceptable accommodation is a major area of complaint within the SWP in general.

Elsewhere, SWP workers have had excessive rent deducted from their salaries for a shared bedroom. For example, one employer charged A$195 a week each from six workers who were living in a shipping container.[6] Where such exploitation comes to the attention of organisations or trade unions, they can advocate on behalf of the workers, and by doing so assist SWP in weeding out unfair practices by employers.

In contrast, Northern Ireland workers are free to make their own arrangements, resulting in a considerable variation in their preferred accommodation arrangements. Some shared between many workers, for example a dozen people sharing a three or four bedroom house to reduce outgoing expenditure and maximise their remittances home. Others chose to rent a house alone or with a friend or partner at greater cost, wanting to better connect with the neighbours and local community.

Thus, workers may accept basic accommodation to save money, but this is very different from paying high rent for substandard accommodation as can occur in the SWP.

In many worksites, transport was made available for workers to go shopping (36%) and for recreation (24%) but it was charged to the worker as a deduction. Access to banks, medical services and religious centres was acceptable for the majority. Church attendance has been a major source of connection with the host community in rural towns. Those who attended a local Catholic Church had a greater opportunity to associate with local people outside of their workplace. In some cases, it has been an important source of support and advice for migrant workers as well as opening possibilities of engagement with the host community. For instance, some Timorese have joined the local church choir and others have been invited to participate in local community activities through church connections.

Access to the internet in Australia was available to only 30% of workers. Some workers were in such remote locations that they could not make calls home by either phone or internet except on weekend shopping trips to town. In Northern Ireland, where many workers do not return home for many years, workers often speak to their family on a daily basis through Skype, Facebook or other social media sites. This shows how important communication with the family back home is. Some SWP workers pointed out that where contact with their family is lacking there is a risk that doubts, jealousies and uncertainties can interfere with harmonious family life.

Worker's skill development and job satisfaction

The vast majority of workers felt that they had benefited significantly from the SWP experience, not only for the money they earned but also workers believed that they had gained useful skills which they could put to use when they return home. High on the list was English speaking, Occupational Health and Safety, working in groups, using household appliances and punctuality. Many also mentioned horticultural skills, however the second phase of research showed that skills gained in Australia that were used included hospitality skills, English skills and general work skills. None of them had used horticultural skills.

Across Timor-Leste, subsistence farming is associated with poverty, so returning to the land is considered a backward step, not only by youth but by their family. Skills to enhance agricultural practices to make them more productive and marketable are much needed which will require the young generation to be educated in a way that both changes their negative beliefs about agriculture and enables them to make improvements in local production, preservation and marketing of food.

Most of the returning workers do not own or have access to land because they are urban residents. An important recommendation by SWP workers was that youth from the rural areas, who were accustomed to agricultural work, should be recruited in order that their skills development can contribute to development in Timor-Leste. Some workers criticised young urbanised team members citing that they did not pull their weight in horticultural work in Australia which impacted negatively on their team's work to meet productivity targets. As a result of the findings of this research, LMAP have trialled recruitment of SWP workers in rural areas.

When asked how satisfied they were with their recent SWP experience, 96% of workers said they were satisfied with 68% being 'very satisfied', which is an extraordinarily high satisfaction rate. It may have been influenced by their desire to return to Australia. However, wanting to return is also an indication of satisfaction with the overall experience.

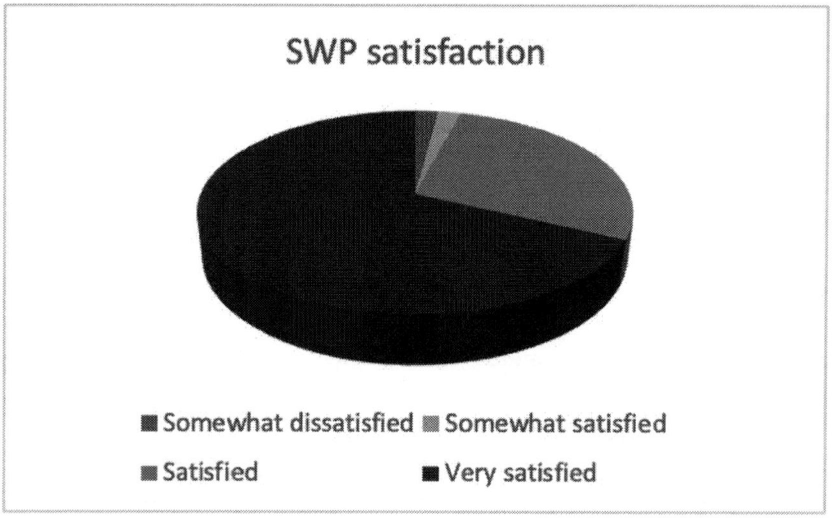

Figure 12.1: Satisfaction with SWP experience. Source: LMAP Data Base Q7 (this graph was prepared by LMAP).

For levels of satisfaction, the Australian SWP compares favourably with the Korean EPS. Of the returnees interviewed from Korea, 30% had not completed their contract and returned home early. Many struggled with the demands to work 'fast, strongly and diligently' for long hours. Some only received two Sundays off a month. Some lived on a boat at sea for extended periods, others were in isolated locations. Many tried to change their employment, in the process breaking their contract which resulted in them being deported. Two interviewees faced serious injury and were expected to return to work more quickly than they felt was reasonable.

The challenges faced by Timorese workers in Korea are considerably greater than those that SWP respondents presented in the course of this research. However, the longer period of work contract (3 years, with possible extension to 5 years) gave workers greater levels of skill development than is available to SWP workers. Many also worked on small family farms and at fisheries in contrast to the large-scale farming in Australia, thus offering more suitable models of productivity to replicate at home. The placements were mostly family businesses, for instance 10 (33%) workers were in a company with four or less workers and another 10 (33%) in a company with 5-10 workers. While many male workers in the fishing industry did not complete their contracts, the most successful category of workers were female agriculture workers. They were most likely to complete their contracts in a single company and spoke positively of their experiences (Wigglesworth and Fonseca 2016).

Impacts and remittances

The benefits to the family of labour migration are substantial. SWP horticultural workers saved on average AUD 6,000-10,000, while hospitality workers had more varied (higher and lower) savings. Some workers have the opportunity to work overtime to increase their income if they wish.

In Korea, average earnings were USD1000-2000 per month, and more than half of the workers in Korea would send back more than USD 6,000 a year to their families (Wigglesworth and Fonseca 2016). In the UK, many workers were living on, or near to, the minimum wage (£950 per month), which is locally considered a hardship. However, Timorese workers worked overtime or sometimes two jobs to send money home. Unlike the Korea and SWP programs, workers can stay for the long term in UK and some settled down there. If a Timorese couple had children in the UK, then the bulk of their earnings would be spent on their family in the UK and remittances would be reduced. They would also receive UK government benefits for their children. A few of the interviewees sent £6,000 a year (USD8,000), others sent half that amount and some families with children at school in the UK sent little or nothing (Wigglesworth and Boxer 2019).

The average remittance sent by SWP workers during six months was AUD3,200. The most common use of remittances is for daily living expenses (78%), house renovations or building (54%), educational expenses (50%) and customary obligations (44%), followed by household purchases and health related expenses.

Customary obligations arise from the communitarian social structures in which the family takes priority over the individual. Further discussion on this is found in the following chapters by McWilliam and Rose.

Research with Fataluku migrants in Lautém district and Dili by McWilliam and Monteiro (2019) shows the remittances were spent principally on consumption, house building, education 22% and cultural gifts 28%. They note that construction of houses amongst migrant households is a clear indicator of their improved circumstances. The comparatively high spending in obligatory gift exchange suggests that migrants remain closely engaged and connected to the daily rhythms and events of everyday family life in Timor-Leste (McWilliam and Monteiro 2019, 52). In this volume, McWilliam has shown how the flow of remittances to both Dili and Lospalos has been important to support both immediate household priorities but also cultural obligations and activities, thus investing in the ancestral traditions in Timor-Leste.

Many SWP workers referred to customary gifts as a part of their obligations. However, young people sometimes criticised the high level of expenditure in customary ceremonies, believing that it prejudices the health and education of family members by prioritising family expenditure in such ceremonies over sending the children to school and other basic needs. One worker lamented he had nothing to show for three years of work in Korea because all the money was spent on a funeral. Some SWP workers claimed to have set up a secret bank account to quietly save for a future business to protect the money from family demands.

An average of AUD 1,242 per worker was spent in Australia on goods to carry home, mostly mobile phones, computers, and clothes, shoes and educational materials. These items are visible signs of economic wellbeing.

Returning home

The second phase of the survey took place in November 2017. On returning to Timor-Leste, after six months at home, 75% of male workers lived off their savings, with 18% involved in house building or renovation activities. Of the 20% who had wanted to look for a new job only 13% actually did so and all but two failed to find one. Many young Timorese earn money through informal work such as selling goods on the street, driving taxis or running minibuses but it is not considered exactly 'employment', but as temporary, transitional work whilst awaiting a 'proper' job in an office (Wigglesworth 2016, 76). Some SWP workers decided not to look for a job because they wanted to return to Australia and would not want to give up a job they had recently acquired.

Of half the returned male workers who had wanted to start a business, less than half of these achieved this. Many reasons were given for the difference between the planned and actual activities. Some 20% said that they changed their plans because they had to spend their money on supporting relatives and paying school fees. One had to spend all the money on a funeral and another had to spend most for customary obligations for a wedding, so they did not have the start-up capital. Others who wanted to start a business failed to find a suitable premises, changed their ideas on the type of business to establish, built or renovated a house or spent the capital on other items instead.

Half of the women also wanted to start a business and one worker previously had a job in a restaurant and returned to that job. No women planned to live off their savings rather than work. All the women who wanted to start a business achieved this.

Of the 10 interviewed male and female workers who started a business, all involved other family members, mostly 2-4 other members. They established businesses using their own financial resources, including a guest house, a restaurant, three shops, sale of processed food and transport businesses. The majority either had no training or advice or they learnt skills from a family member (including a sister, a father and a husband). One mentioned they developed the required skills in Australia. Only one had formal training from the Institute of Business Support (IADE) in Dili to develop a business plan. This is one of a range of business support and market access programs in Timor-Leste that could offer support to returning workers on their return home, if appropriate linkages were made to better assist the workers on their return.

Workers were asked if they had difficulty adjusting to life when they returned to Timor. Their major concern was that it is difficult to come back to where there was no work, and the only possibility was to wait until they could go to Australia on SWP again. Some men expressed a sense of demoralisation or being 'in limbo' because there were few options to contribute to the family in Timor. This is another reason for maximising the opportunities of returning workers to use their new skills in the Timorese economy. However, many Australian employers are opposed to limiting the number of times that SWP workers can return, because they want to build a reliable workforce where trained and effective workers return year after year.

SWP's role in meeting livelihood needs of the family varies over time. Initially much money is spent on improving home infrastructure, buying material goods and paying education fees for family members. After these expenses have been met, workers start to consider longer term investments in their future, often looking to set up a business. Most married workers see SWP work as a means to an end, to earn enough money to meet their family's needs and to establish a better life for their family in Timor-Leste. For this to occur they need to look for ways to leverage their SWP skills and capital to establish a business or to find work in the Timorese economy. It is a sacrifice to be away from their families and while the children are young, they say this is not a problem, but many want to be at home while their children are growing up and at school. Married workers do not want to be a permanently absent parent. Some workers reported that their children were proud that their parent was working overseas, as it is a source of status.

Single workers said they sent remittances to support their parent, to purchase equipment for disabled members of their family and to support the education of their siblings.

The physical expression of improved circumstances is evident by the newly renovated or built houses which are springing up in communities that migrants come from. Workers spoke sometimes of building a house for themselves as well as for their parents in the village, or if they lived in Dili they might have to buy land first before they can build a house.

Cultural-gender impacts

When a family member is away overseas for a prolonged period there are domestic adjustments to be made. The family may call on older daughters, grandparents and nieces to help in the home. Women who had worked in Australia or the UK spoke of their husbands and other family members taking a bigger role in household activities and looking after the children while she was away. This was accepted within the context of the wellbeing of the extended family and indeed it is common for children to be sent to live with extended family members in Timor-Leste in a range of circumstances.

Disadvantages to migrant work that were highlighted included distrust between couples, particularly of female workers by their husband or boyfriend while they are overseas. Concern about how the money is spent was sometimes an issue, particularly by female workers who fear their husband might gamble the money away.

Before going to Australia, SWP workers received training in gender and cultural differences and how in Australia men and women should be treated equally. They also observed that in Australia they learnt that women can play many diverse roles in society, such as driving trucks and may also be a boss or supervisor. These new experiences opened their minds about the roles of women and had an influence on how they thought about gender issues.

Asked whether their views on gender had changed since returning from Australia, workers gave a surprising response. In the November survey, 62% of men and 60% of women said they had significantly changed their perspective about their own role in their family. By the second research phase, all the women and 82% of the men said their views had changed, indicating that the change in attitude had consolidated with time in Timor-Leste.

A number of male workers said that before going to Australia they had forbidden their wife, younger sister or daughter to continue her education. It is commonly believed that it is a waste to educate girls because they will be married into another family and only do domestic duties, which include the double burden of food production and marketing, as well as household duties. A number of workers explained that after they returned from Australia, they assisted female family members to enrol and pay to attend school. They realised that they had been wrong to limit the potential of women and girls in their household.

Women workers spoke of the experience of being treated as an equal in the workplace, not having to defer to men that they worked alongside. This gave them more confidence. They took this experience home and shared it with their families, sometimes finding voice in place of formerly subservient behaviour. One described how previously she had to obey her drunkard husband, but in Australia she learned that women and men are equal which gave her confidence to make decisions for herself. Other women workers expressed pride and confidence from making a greater contribution and economic responsibility for the household.

The rate of domestic violence in Timor-Leste is very high, as it is in Australia, and in both countries it is illegal. In Australia the principles of equality of women are more accepted (although still under-implemented) in many spheres of work. In contrast entrenched ideas of patriarchy in Timor-Leste result in male leadership and decision making still considered normal in Timor-Leste. Women are raised to keep their opinions to themselves and defer to their husband's decision making. Consequently, there is a very low representation of women in rural village councils.

In 2010 a Law against Domestic Violence was passed in Timor-Leste. The law refers to the term *Violência doméstica* (domestic violence), a phrase imported from Portuguese and entirely new to the Tetum vocabulary. Research into violence within the family revealed that this allowed it to be associated with new meanings. Rural leaders appeared to have re-interpreted the national law so that it is more consistent with customary law that considers intimate partner violence in the family as normal. They considered 'domestic violence' to be only when a woman suffered serious injury such as drawing blood or requiring hospital treatment, contrary to the broad definition in the Law against Domestic Violence (dos Santos and Wigglesworth 2016, 63).

This shows the importance of changing attitudes. New social values can be established through exposure to new ideas such as the workers were exposed to in SWP. Amongst the workers interviewed, the majority of men said that they had changed their attitudes toward the women in their families and are now more supportive of women getting an education and of helping with domestic duties than they were before. Women workers have strengthened their resolve to take greater control over their lives. These workers provide important insights into their experience of different cultural attitudes to male and female roles.

Analysis of the impacts of migrant work

Labour migration offers higher wages that are generally paid regularly and on time, typically earning more in a week than what they could earn in a month in Timor-Leste (if they could get a job). The three studies (Korea, UK and SWP) cannot be directly compared because of different methodologies, however some common themes emerge.

Whether earning in Korea, the UK or Australia, most remittances were used to fund their family's daily living expenses, pay school and university fees for siblings or other family members and invest in home improvements. The pattern of expenditure changes over time. Firstly, workers meet immediate family needs for housing, equipment and transport. When workers come towards the end of their contract in Korea or have worked for a number of consecutive years with SWP they look at how they can use their work skills and cash to establish a livelihood in Timor-Leste. For many workers, the technical work they had been doing was a source of inspiration to establish a business back home, and they started to save money, looking to the future. For some workers, customary obligations may unexpectedly require large proportions of their earnings to be spent on family ceremonies such as funerals or weddings, which put on hold other plans. Many educated and aware young people disagree with excessive spending on traditional ceremonies which have no productive value. Also, the strong paternalistic nature of Timorese society makes the voices of educated young men and women undervalued, leading to a kind of covert protest by some of them. While all workers saw it as a duty to contribute to the extended family wellbeing, they did not agree when expenditures were perceived as jeopardising the family's ability to meet their basic needs of consumption, education and wellbeing.

Temporary workers in Korea had been away for 3-5 years but when they returned home, they received minimal support for their reintegration. A number of returnees from Korea had worked in small family agriculture or fisheries businesses and mentioned wanting to establish a horticultural or aquaculture business similar to the one in which they worked. Although they had a very useful experience for the Timorese context, they felt isolated on return from a long time overseas and did not know how to go about getting the support they needed, and were not assisted in any way by the sending agency, nor was there any debriefing process for returnees.

The UK workers have no support to assist departure or reintegration, yet most of the ten returnees interviewed in Dili had successfully established a business or got a job on the basis of their English skills. These migrants had not waited for support but had worked off their own initiative since going to the UK, and this continued when they returned home. Also they were in general more mature than the average SWP and Korea workers, because there was no age limit to go to the UK and many had stayed many years and had worked toward planned activities they would do on return.

The SWP holds re-integration briefings which includes sharing information about the various business support programs in Timor-Leste, but follow-up support is needed to help workers access these services. SEPFOPE needs to make suitable arrangements for support of returning workers in order to facilitate both the SWP and the Korean EPS returnees to find a livelihood at home, as workers from both programs express the same difficulties in economic integration at home.

Younger Timorese are often lacking confidence to approach government officials and others perceived as 'senior' to them. Thus, opening the door for them to feel welcome in such settings is important. Commentary from workers returning from both SWP and South Korea showed that they felt they needed such technical support to be able to establish themselves in the local economy, particularly given the government's notoriously difficult process to register a business.

Of particular note was that returned workers from all three destinations were proud of being able to improve the lifestyle and wellbeing of their families which was their main objective in going overseas for work. Visible improvements in the economic wellbeing of their families have a positive impact on people's perceptions of their family, increasing their social status in the community.

A highly significant and remarkable finding of the SWP research was the degree to which workers claimed to have changed their behaviour with respect to gender attitudes since working in Australia. The requirement to attend gender equality training in the LMAP program, followed by experiencing women working as equals in a range of traditional male work roles, opened their minds to new ways of thinking. Timorese society is a transitional society where the cultural context and old values still have a strong influence. But younger generation Timorese are also keen for change. With their new experiences and knowledge there has been greater recognition of the need for greater fairness and equality in relation to the right of all family members to adequate food, housing, education and health care.

As Jose Ramos Horta stated days after his inauguration as President in May 2022 regarding Timorese people going abroad to work: "They make much more money than we will ever be able to pay them and they send money home. They learn new skills and they come back changed. It's a bit like going to university but instead they go to work."[7]

Conclusions

Timorese workers are appreciative of the opportunity to support their families through migrant work. Overall, they contributed a large part of their time and money in Timor-Leste towards house improvements and daily living expenses. Labour migration has become the most important source of income for many families. The government of Timor-Leste sees these programs as reducing the numbers of unemployed youth and building work skills.

The experience and work skills that were acquired through migrant work motivated many workers to establish business activities at home. Long term development outcomes is a stated objective of the Timorese government in promoting labour migration, so more attention should be paid to supporting the reintegration of the returnees. Then the national development impact would be much greater.

In Timor-Leste the younger Timorese have a high degree of respect for their elders and cultural values, but there are also two areas of social change being called for. One is a women's lobby aiming to achieve equality for women, particularly the political participation of women in local and national government, and an end to the high rate of domestic violence that exists. The second is a concern about the monetisation and commodification of customary ceremonies which introduces a competitive status-seeking approach to spending large amounts of money, replacing the traditional practice of exchange of goods (dos Santos and Wigglesworth 2016, 62). Many young people see this as being to the detriment of family wellbeing.

Globally, migration has become a widespread strategy by poor families to gain the resources they need to improve the wellbeing of their family. In Timor-Leste, it is an opportunity to lift families in the subsistence economy out of poverty. As well as the benefits that remittances bring, the impact of migration on social change in Timor can also arise from new perspectives on how to respond to immediate economic needs of families. New international experiences can accelerate the process of social change which has been taking place in the country since independence. So far, migration appears to have brought benefits to poor rural communities that have seen little in the way of economic opportunities since independence.

Notes

1 The SWP is led by the Department of Jobs and Small Business (formerly department of Employment), supported by the Department of Immigration and Border Protection (DIBP), Fair Work Ombudsman (FWO) and Department of Foreign Affairs and Trade (DFAT). Operating since 2009 in the Pacific, SWP is available to nine Pacific countries: Fiji, Kiribati, Papua New Guinea, Nauru, Samoa, Solomon Islands, Tonga, Tuvalu, Vanuatu as well as Timor-Leste.

2 Wigglesworth and Fonseca, "Experiences of young Timorese as migrant workers in Korea" presented at the Australasian Aid Conference 2016, Development Policy Centre (DPC). The research was commissioned by the 'Labour Mobility in the Pacific Project' at the DPC at the Crawford School of Public Policy, Australian National University (ANU).

3 Wigglesworth and Boxer, 2017, "Transitional livelihoods: Timorese migrant workers in the UK." Presented at the Australasian Aid Conference 2017. The original research involved 19 participants, ten in Northern Ireland and nine interviewed after returning to Dili. A second visit included revisiting some earlier participants about the implications of Brexit and interviewing two new migrants in UK, bringing the participant number to 21. A revised and updated version of the paper was published as Wigglesworth and Boxer 2019, "Positioning for their future: Timorese migrant workers in the UK."

4 A change of management of the SWP since the research resulted in Palladium taking over from Cardno as the managing contractor, referred to by Rose in chapter 14 of this volume.

5 Wigglesworth and dos Santos, 2018, "Timorese migrant workers in the Seasonal Workers Program." Presented at the Australasian Aid Conference 2018, Development Policy Centre (DPC).

6 Conversation with a Colombian priest and member of Australian Catholic Religious Against Trafficking in Humans (ACRATH) in Victoria. As a member of the Seasonal Worker's Program Advisory Group, ACRATH plays an active role in bringing issues of exploitation or unfairness to the attention of the SWP team (Interview, Peter O'Neil, Melbourne, 11/11/2019).

7 Allegra Mendelson interview with Jose Ramos Horta, "East Timor's president to focus on economy, political stability", *Al Jezeera*, 24 May 2022.

References

Curtain, R. 2018. "Timor-Leste remittances update." *Devpolicy Blog*, Development Policy Centre, March 27, ANU. http://www.devpolicy.org/timor-leste-remittances-update-20180327/

da Costa, S., and M. Rose. 2020. "Young entrepreneurship in Timor-Leste." *Devpolicy Blog*, Development Policy Centre, January 23, ANU. tps://devpolicy.org/young-entrepreneurship-in-timor-leste-20200123/

dos Santos, A. B., and M. Guterres. 2020. "Developing sustainable agriculture and communities in Ermera." *Voz Timor* (1): 26-29. Victoria University, Melbourne.

dos Santos, A. B. and A. Wigglesworth. 2016. "Valóres konsuetudináriu no influénsia globál iha atitude foinsa'e sira konaba jéneru no violénsia iha Timor-Leste [Customary values and global influences in youth attitudes to gender and violence in Timor-Leste]." In *Timor-Leste: the Local, the Regional, the Global*, edited by S. Smith et al., 59-64. Hawthorn: Swinburne Press.

ESCAP (Economic and Social Commission for Asia and the Pacific). 2016. *Asia-Pacific Migration Report 2015 – Migrants' contribution to development.* Bangkok: United Nations' Economic and Social Commission for Asia and the Pacific.

Ellis, F. 2003. *A Livelihoods Approach to Migration and Poverty Reduction,* Paper Commissioned by the Department for International Development (DFID), accessed 4 February 2020. Available at https://www.researchgate.net/profile/Frank_Ellis/publication/228593669_A_Livelihoods_Approach_to_Migration_and_Poverty_Reduction/links/00b49524a93a66592c000000/A-Livelihoods-Approach-to-Migration-and-Poverty-Reduction.pdf.

ILO (International Labour Organization). 2016. *Structural Transformation and Jobs in Timor-Leste.* Dili: International Labour Organization. ISBN 978-92-2-131322-9 https://www.ilo.org/jakarta/whatwedo/publications/WCMS_536580/lang--en/index.htm

King, R. 2013. "Theories and Typologies of Migration: An Overview and a Primer." Willy Brandt Series of Working Papers in International Migration and Ethnic Relations 3/12, Malmo University, Malmo. ISSN 1650-5743. Online publication http://sro.sussex.ac.uk/id/eprint/69108

McWilliam, A. 2015. "Rural-Urban Inequalities and Migration in Timor-Leste." In: *A New Era: Timor-Leste after the UN,* edited by S. Ingram, L. Kent, and A. McWilliam. Canberra: Australian National University Press. http://dx.doi.org/10.22459/NE.09.2015.

McWilliam, A., and C. dos S. Monteiro. 2019. "Fataluku labor migration and transnational care in Timor-Leste." *Indonesia* 107: 41-54.

Mendelson, A. 2022. "East Timor's president to focus on economy, political stability". *Al Jazeera*, May 2022. Accessed at https://www.aljazeera.com/news/2022/5/24/east-timors-president-to-focus-on-economy-political-stability?taid=628c5bc99c851e00019ddf12&utm_campaign=trueAnthem%3A+Trending+Content&utm_medium=trueAnthem&utm_source=twitter on 10 June, 2022.

UNDP (United Nations Development Programme). 2018. *National Human Development Report 2018: Planning the opportunities for a youthful population.* Dili: UNDP. http://hdr.undp.org/en/content/national-human-development-report-2018-timor-leste

Wigglesworth, A. 2016. *Activism and Aid: Young Citizens' Experiences of Development and Democracy in Timor-Leste.* Clayton: Monash University Publishing.

Wigglesworth, A., and A. B. dos Santos. 2018. "Timorese workers in Australia: Seasonal work experiences, skills and future options." Paper for presentation presented at Australasian Aid Conference, February 2018, ANU, Canberra. http://devpolicy.org/2018-Australasian-Aid-Conference/Papers/Timorese.migrant.workers.in.SWP-Wigglesworth&dosSantos.pdf

Wigglesworth, A., and L. Boxer. 2017. "Transitional Livelihoods: Timorese Migrant Workers in the UK." Discussion paper for the Development Policy Centre. Accessed at https://devpolicy.org/2017-Australasian-Aid-Conference/Papers/Wigglesworth-Boxer_Transitional-livelihoods-Timorese-migrant-workers-UK.pdf on 29 April 2020.

Wigglesworth, A., and L. Boxer. 2019. "Positioning for their future: Timorese migrant workers in the UK." *Papers on Social Representation* 29 (1): 10.1-10.20. http://psr.iscte-iul.pt/index.php/PSR/article/view/498.

Wigglesworth, A., and Z. Fonseca. 2016. "Experiences of young Timorese as migrant workers in Korea." Paper for presentation at Australasian Aid Conference, February 2016, ANU, Canberra. http://devpolicy.org/2016-Australasian-aid-conference/Papers/Wigglesworth-Fonseca-Experiences-of-young-Timorese-workers-in-Korea.pdf

CHAPTER 13

Refashioning Fataluku origin houses

Andrew McWilliam

Abstract

A prominent feature of post-independence Timor-Leste has been a sustained 'return to custom' across the country. This includes the phased rebuilding of clan origin houses (*Uma Lulik*: 'sacred house'), many of which were destroyed during the Indonesian occupation. As economic conditions improve, *Uma Lulik* are once again becoming architectural features of the rural landscape. In this paper, I reflect on the delayed re-emergence of the Fataluku equivalent of the *Uma Lulik* and the innovative changes that have been made to traditional construction in recent years. The changes speak to shared expressions of a characteristic pragmatism that epitomises Fataluku cultural adaptation to changing circumstances and the embrace of modernity. It also highlights what is arguably, following Gudeman (2016), a successful economic accommodation between mutuality and the market.

Keywords: Fataluku houses; economy; innovation; ancestors

One of the striking features of the post-independence landscape of Timor-Leste has been the sustained revival of Timorese customary practices. Susanna Barnes (2017) has described this trend as a 'return to custom' as the response reflected the limited choices that village communities faced in the immediate aftermath of the Indonesian occupation and the absence of functioning government and limited provision of support services (Hicks 2004, McWilliam 2008). Faced with few viable alternatives, a majority of Timorese households have stayed in place and embarked on the arduous task of economic recovery and re-building their shattered communities. They have done so by drawing on their own reserves of customary resilience, local resources and the enduring inter-generational relations of reciprocal exchange and obligation that have long shaped the sociality of their settlements and familial alliances (Barnes 2011; McWilliam 2007). Drawing on the language of Stephen Gudeman, we might see this choice as one of supporting the community base and economic relations 'kept for their own sake', in the absence of a supportive market economy (2001). Gudeman refers to these customary contexts as, 'high relationship economies,' where motives of mutuality, namely the meaning people seek in community relations and reciprocity, play a vital role in guiding collective action (Gudeman 2016). In the context of the immediate post-conflict landscape of Lautém, practices of mutuality were especially prominent in the absence of operating banks, market trading and commodity supply chains (see Introduction, this volume).

Among the array of activities and household level projects that supported the recovery has been the well-observed rebuilding of 'origin' or 'sacred' houses, *Uma Lulik* in the Tetum vernacular, that have mushroomed across the landscape (Barnes 2011). Each House represents the focus of an extended kin group, originating from a revered founding ancestor (male or female depending on the mode of reckoning) and expresses simultaneously a social construction and a ritualised focus for the articulation of social relations and exchange among 'house' members' (see McWilliam 2005, 28).

In a diversity of architectural variations around shared symbolic themes, the re-emergence of these origin houses asserts in striking material and public form, a kin group's commitment to ancestral clan communities and the revitalised spiritual protection of its agnatic membership. An example of the intensity of these rebuilding projects, following decades of neglect and wilful destruction during the Indonesian occupation, is provided by Loch (2009, 99). He recorded roughly two hundred *Uma Lulik* under construction in the Baucau district over the two years of his residence during the early post-occupation period. The scale and extent of these efforts demanded considerable economic sacrifice on the part of the agnatic membership, to generate the resources required for both the construction and the demanding ritual costs that accompany the process. This commitment has been even more impressive, given the widespread economic impoverishment of the people at the time. Comparable efforts to reinstate *Uma Lulik* are occurring across the country with a similar kind of prioritising of scarce resources that underpins the deeply held esteem accorded these structures and their lasting significance (see Barnes 2017; Bovensiepen 2014).

Uma Lulik, 'Houses of origin' in Timor-Leste reflect local variations on a broadly shared Austronesian heritage of built structures where the particular configuration of posts, beams, platforms and thatched roofs provide what Fox (1993, 23) has termed, 'a theatre of memories' for the encoding and storing of cultural knowledge. Over generations, different language communities across Timor-Leste have developed their own distinctive styles of construction and decorative forms of *Uma Lulik* designs. Each provides a focus for the life cycle rituals of its clan membership and serves as a repository of ancestral sacra and other revered objects of venerated power (McWilliam 2005). The intense focus on *Uma Lulik* as a central structure for social identity and inter-generational, familial performance creates what Sandra Pannell has described as an "imaginative arena for living that signposts forms of social behaviour, rights, responsibilities and relations" (Pannell 1997, 165). Their complex symbolic and relational qualities speak to long histories of residence and authoritative assertions of claim and entitlement over local resource domains. However, the process can also re-ignite old disputes and tensions over status and recognition among the agnatic group. Judith Bovensiepen for example, shows how Funar rebuilding of origin houses "led not only to the reproduction of previous modes of sociality but also to their reconstitution" (2014, 291).

The rebuilding of sacred houses across the settled landscapes of Timor-Leste has been a widespread feature of post-Independence and provides an important anchoring point and undoubtedly a psychological comfort for so many households whose lives were blighted during the struggle for liberation. But the process has unfolded unevenly across the country and not all customary communities have exhibited the same urgency to revitalise their *Uma Lulik* structures. One region of Timor-Leste where the rebuilding of 'origin houses' has arguably been slow and apparently not accorded the same level of attention as elsewhere, is the far eastern municipality of Lautém. Here among resident Fataluku language communities, whose distinctive and iconic house structures have long been viewed as the archetypal model of the *Uma Lulik* in Timor-Leste (McWilliam 2005, 31), redevelopment has been muted. For many years during the post-independence period of recovery and restitution, apart from a few externally funded project 'houses' built in the traditional style for heritage or perhaps tourism purposes, there were few new traditional style houses constructed. A scattered number of still impressive old style stilted, Fataluku houses remained intact and preserved, but they represented largely remnant structures that had survived the destructive rampage of the local pro-integration militia group (*Tim Alfa*) and the Indonesian withdrawal.

As elsewhere, the road to recovery in Lautém has been a slow and difficult one. Most families elected to repair their damaged houses to a habitable condition with whatever materials came to hand and then gradually improved the quality of construction as resources came available. Others constructed more rudimentary, one room, rectangular stilt houses (*lalu cu)* with split bamboo cladding and palm thatch or re-used corrugated iron roofs. Fataluku house designs of this type are still widely observed across the landscape of Lautém. However, they are mainly interim structures or stop gap measures while their owners generate the means to build in the now aspirational style of rendered rectangular cinder block houses, (known as *le varaca* or *le pitine* [white house]) with corrugated iron roofing (*kalen*) and tiled floors (*keramik*). It is only in recent years that a revitalised commitment to re-constructing the highly stylised and decorated family based ritual houses known generically as *le ia valu* (lit: House with legs/stilts) has emerged and with it, concerted efforts among growing numbers of lineage groups to publicly express their commitment to the built tradition.

In this paper, I reflect on the delayed revival of the iconic Fataluku origin houses highlighting a suite of factors that have influenced their re-emergence.

These include impacts of historical displacement and a gradual improvement in economic conditions; growing population numbers and the continuing vitality of ancestral religion, and not least, the advent of certain innovative changes that kin groups have made to traditional forms of construction in recent years. The changes speak to shared expressions of what I see as a characteristic pragmatism that epitomises Fataluku cultural adaptation to changing circumstances and their enthusiastic accommodation to modernity (McWilliam 2008, 2020). They also highlight the complexity of choices that confront contemporary Timorese households and economic ecologies as they strive to build prosperity and material well-being, while retaining their intense social obligations to customary relationships including ancestral ones. Finally, there is also the possibility that in terms of the politics of group identity, the delay in Fataluku origin house reconstruction may have more to do with prioritising the central role of the sacrificial hearth (*acakaka* or *lafuru tei*), than the material structure in which it is desirably housed. These are matters of interpretation and go to the definitional scope of terms like *Uma Lulik*.

Fataluku origin houses: Archives of memory

In her landmark study of the traditional houses of Lorehe village (Lautém), Maria O. Lameiras-Campagnolo (1975) charted in meticulous detail the range of residential structures that comprised Fataluku built heritage. Her study, undertaken during the late Portuguese period in the years before the Indonesian occupation, offers compelling insights into a time before the widespread destruction of traditional settlements and their residential dwellings, all of which were sourced from locally procured materials and laboriously, shaped, notched, fitted, thatched and tied together. From the humble and seasonal garden huts (*cu* and *mo*) to the grandly decorated and symbolically gendered, double houses with linked walkways (*le amarua*—'twin houses'), each structure expressed in a variety of condensed forms the cultural heritage of Fataluku emplaced traditions and their rich symbolic associations.[1] To understand something of the significance of these structures into contemporary times, this chapter focuses on Fataluku customary ideas and practices associated with the house as a ritual and familial centre.

Fataluku refer to their four posted stilt houses with steep sided thatched roof and elevated living quarters as the *le ia valu*. This model follows a consistent architectural pattern and core structural features, but the finer details, arrangements of panels and decorative elements vary with house design (see Lameiras-Campagnolo 1975). They are typically specific to different origin group architectural heritage and ancestral histories. One of the largest and most impressive of these architectural styles are the imposing high peaked houses known as the *fia le*. The *fia le* house takes its name from the distinctive black thatch roofing derived from the fibrous webbing that grows around the trunk of the Areng, 'black sugar palm' (*Arenga saccharifera:* F: *ma'arau*), a key resource for Fataluku households and one that is deeply implicated in the very constitution of Fataluku society (McWilliam, 2022b). The black fibre thatch has for generations, provided a vital element in the lasting integrity of the house roof. Four sheets of the thatch (80cm x 40cm x 3cm deep) are bundled together to form a large panel (*fia lafai ukani*) and dozens of panels are then layered over the roof battens and fixed with handmade *areng* and jungle rope ties (*taru*) to create a dense watertight covering that can last for decades with regular maintenance.

Historically and into contemporary times these tall, timber and black thatch structures that fade to grey over time, with their singular decorated rooves rising 6 metres and more above the base, are striking symbols of high-status households and the provenance of senior agnatic, land-owning lineages (*mua ocawa ratu*—lord of the land) within a settlement. The capacity to build in the *fia le, sei-mecen le* or *le lohai* (tall house) style was the privilege of high rank lineages (*ratu*). Conventionally built on the customary lands of the owners, each house has unique features and a bespoke ritual name that distinguishes its ancestral heritage and references the mythic origins of the ownership group (*ratu*) itself. The following example is the long form name of the *fia le* (house) of the Konu Ratu origin group:

Le lafai, Le pokala
Fia le, Taru le
Asi Renu ara, Ao Renu ara
O'o lo Kon ara, Moi lulur ara
Sepe li ara, Kai ron ara.[2]

Lesser status or subsidiary lineages typically did not aspire to constructing these structures, and consequently housing styles historically gave general, public expression to the ranking of social status between households (Lameiras-Camapagnolo 1975). A subsidiary house form was known as *Vata'asa le* (lit: coconut frond house) or with lesser status again, as a *Ver'asa le* (referencing their use of long grass thatch (*imperata*) gathered in open fields to create the thatching).[3] Historically, these material distinctions reflected inherited caste-like status differences between the three main groupings in Fataluku society; namely *ratu, paca* and *akanu* families. The latter group is a 'slave', category with ancient origins across the region (see Chapter 4, this volume). During colonial times, war captives or households that became indebted and then indentured to more powerful patrons due to punitive colonial tax regimes have subsequently inherited that status. In the past, the *le ia valu* was a form to which most people aspired, but only the senior *ratu* status groups had the rank and means to build the *fia le*. In present day democratic

Figure 13.1: Image of twin houses (*le amarua*). Image credit: Andrew McWilliam.

Timor-Leste these distinctions are much more muted, but they remain important social categories with sensitive dimensions of difference between groups in a variety of arenas especially marriage and origin house structures.[4]

The size and expense of construction is one of the constraining aspects of rebuilding *fia le*, with their massive ironwood posts and beams, intricately carved timber panelling and roof structures sheathed in tightly fixed layers of black thatch. On the apex of the roof are attached elaborate comb fans (*leu loporu*) with decorated shell strings and large nautilus shells (*liliru*), and depending on the history of the group, carved wooden figurines or birds adorning the apex.[56] Each house expresses the public signature of agnatic group identities and, by inference, the networks of affinal households that coalesce around them in long-term relationships of reciprocal exchange and obligation. *Fia le* (houses) represent one of the crowning artistic and architectural achievements of Fataluku living heritage and remain richly symbolic and evocative structural expressions of their shared material culture. Many elements of the house, its verticality and orientation, as well as the architectural and stylistic aspects of construction convey multiple cultural meanings and significance. For this reason, it has long represented a key ritual arena for the conduct of performative life cycle transitions of the agnatic group and its constituent related households.

The construction of the origin house conventionally involves a collaborative project between the agnatic and affinal household networks involving reciprocal exchanges that mirror the pattern seen in marriage or funeral gifting and feasts (McWilliam 2011).[7] The first structural element that initiates the construction of a new house is the planting of the primary house post (the 'elder sibling post': *tutu kaka*), traditionally a redwood or ironwood post (*ete materia*, or *fara*) harvested and carried from the forest, shaped and positioned facing the favoured eastern direction (*mua cao*—the head of the land). The process also initiates a series of sacrificial offerings and invocations to 'strengthen the house' and ensure the well-being of those who dwell and are protected within it. The following prayer is an example:

House and 'nest'	*Le ho vari*
to cleanse,	*em varis em pai*
to strengthen	*em kesim pai*
to sacralise (protect)	*em tei pai*
so that illness and sickness are warded off	*nawar potina hara tana acone*
so that there is vitality	*nawar huhu meren ane*
there is life	*pupuk ane*
there is abundant growth	*lao-he ane*
there is increase.	*tune ane*

The ritual includes an offering of rice and distilled liquor (*tua harak*) in the conventional manner of presenting a series of small portions of food (rice and meat and small amounts of liquor laid out in a double row [7 x 2]). The offering is directed to the first 14 origin ancestors and the main house post is circled seven times before a chicken (*aca*) is torn open (to inspect its liver) and its blood is sprinkled over the offerings. A commensal meal accompanies the work on the construction.

Completion and inauguration of the new house also requires a celebratory commensal feast, with sacrificial offerings and ritual feeding (*fané*) along with the requisite divinations (*mu'u-fuka totole* and *lonia*) to confirm that all is in order and there are no lingering, unfulfilled obligations or errors of omission that might attract retributive spiritual measures.[8] As a final stage, a house cooling ritual is undertaken that includes commensality for the participants and the splashing of coconut water mixed with blood (*vata ira*) on the walls of the structure and intended residents.[9] Other protective measures include the placement of ritually charged invocations accompanying offerings of a whole egg placed over small forked sticks (*saka/aca*) fixed at strategic openings to the house. Known as *le o'o utu-natana* (guarding the door of the house) these devices are designed to ward off any unwanted malevolent forces (human or spirit in form) entering the domestic space.

Traditionally the origin house served as both a living space for senior households as well as symbolically charged repositories for ancestral sacra and protective regalia of the lineage.[10] The most important element, however, was and remains the installation of the sacred hearth (*lafuru tei* or *acakaka*), which is always secured opposite the hatchway (*wai hula*) in the corner above the eastern facing support pillar (*tutu kaka*). Fataluku have commented to me that the principal role of the ritual house was and remains to provide a secure repository for the sacred hearth (*acakaka*). The reality is that the 'sacrificial hearth' is the primary focus for most households, more so in practice than the structure in which it is installed. It follows that it is possible to maintain the integrity of the sacrificial relation to the collective spirit world without the need to maintain an origin house (*le ia valu*). This has been the reality for most households since liberation.

The sacred hearth has the singular purpose of cooking sacrificial food and presenting prayers and offerings to house and origin ancestors, while enjoying commensality with immediate male agnatic kin (see Chapter 7, this volume). Sacrificial meat is referred to in parallel speech as *leura tei // ipilu tei* and may not be consumed by female members of the *ratu* lineages or non-kin.[11] Traditionally a separate boxed hearth (*lafuru*) is utilised in the house to prepare daily meals for family consumption.

In Fataluku cultural practice, the establishment of an *acakaka* is a gift from a father to his sons on the occasion of their marriage and the establishment of a separate household.[12] The process of initiating a new *acakaka* requires the passing of a burning piece of firewood (*acakaka nana kafu*) from the father's ritual hearth to that of his sons to ignite the new hearth.[13] The transfer is one replicated over generations of practice and means that conceptually and ritually all *acakaka* are ultimately connected to the original hearth of the founding ancestor of the origin group (*acakaka i irinu*). In this respect the idea of sacred hearth (*lafuru tei*) in Fataluku culture may be thought of as a conceptually distributed but ultimately indivisible protective and interactive field that extends across the living members of the *ratu* clan and encompasses group ancestors who maintain a watchful presence over their living descendants.

Over time, the development of extended families within the origin (*ratu*) group generates a disbursed but closely interrelated set of households with their own sacrificial hearths, shared family histories and a common identity within the group. In these circumstances, the *acakaka* of the grandfather (*calu*) or father (*palu*) of the group becomes a site where the sons and grandsons will gather (*acakaka na cuaré*) to seek blessings and protection through sacrifice and divination on special occasions, usually when there are matters arising that affect the wider group. These issues include concerns over illness, disputes and misfortunes affecting the extended family, as well as annual celebratory gatherings to renew familial commitments to one another.

The point to highlight here is that historically the preferred installation site of a sacrificial hearth was in its rightful place in the eastern corner of the elevated *le ia valu*, ancestral or origin house. For this reason, another name used for this style of house was and remains *le tein*, 'a sacred house', or an *Uma Lulik* in the Tetum vernacular, because it holds the sacrificial hearth. The apparent linguistic equivalence here holds even though it is evident that the Fataluku ritual house does not share the same attributes and centrality of the stand-alone origin group, *Uma Lulik* found elsewhere in Timor-Leste, often with specific named functions within a ranked ritual community (see Clamagirand 1975; Traube 1986).[14] At the same time, its historical and functional role in social life remains strongly resonant.

The integral role of the *le tein(u)* in the conduct of Fataluku ceremonial life and religious practice came under intense pressure during the Indonesian military occupation (from 1976 in Lautém). Many houses were simply destroyed, or damaged beyond repair during the initial years of active warfare and the mass dislocation of local populations (1976-1978). This period was followed by highly restrictive movement and resettlement regimes, implemented as part of a sustained program to eradicate armed resistance and to separate the local populations from their Falintil relatives and *combatentes* operating in the forested uplands of Lautém district (1979-1999). In this protracted context of mutual suspicion and repressive control, one that included the promotion of Catholicism (over ancestral sacrifice) as the preferred religion of a modern Indonesian Timor-Leste, the capacity of

Fataluku agnatic communities to publicly perform their traditional practices at sites of ancestral veneration was severely curtailed. In the shared Indonesian view, any obvious continued attachment to tradition and customary practice was regarded with suspicion and people faced the real risk of being targeted as a 'communist' sympathiser of the resistance against Indonesian rule. In the face of persistent military repression and surveillance, for many extended families a focus on maintaining or rebuilding ritual houses was simply not a priority, nor one that was readily condoned by the authorities.

Ironically, however, even during those difficult times as the iconic Fataluku, *fia le* houses were disappearing from view, the occupying Indonesian government in a celebratory gesture promoting a generic Timorese customary identity was adopting the stylised images of the same structures.[15] The distinctive architectural forms gracing the covers of government reports, tourist brochures and various public relations events reflect an unspoken appeal to an inclusive East Timorese integration within the Indonesian nation-state.[16]

Changing patterns of practice

The liberation of Timor-Leste when it finally arrived in the wake of the destructive withdrawal of Indonesian troops and personnel in 1999 ushered in a wholly new phase of independent governance and economic uncertainty. With the end of travel restrictions and intrusive surveillance, the achievement of independence brought with it a strong desire across the country to rebuild shattered lives and the familiar relationships of customary exchange that inform the conduct of community life.

Over the course of my field work and ethnographic writing about Fataluku communities, which has now covered over 20 years of regular, if intermittent field visits, I have written extensively about processes of social and economic recovery that have transformed social life in Lospalos and Lautém. Over that time, I had come to the view that Fataluku agnatic kin groups had reconciled themselves to the idea of no longer reconstructing their large and finely crafted origin houses. Their priorities simply lay elsewhere focusing on conserving the ritual hearth (*acakaka*) for ancestral protection. It is true that a small number of impressive new houses were built in selected locations in the years following independence, but the great majority of these were funded by external projects to encourage the preservation of Fataluku architectural heritage.

For most residents who needed to gather local resources for the task, there were simply too many impediments for such projects to proceed. These included the emotional difficulties of reaching consensus within the kin group about when and even whether to embark on the joint project at all. There is a strong Fataluku convention that you should not declare your intentions to pursue a particular venture or activity if you do not subsequently intend to carry it out. Such actions attract spiritual sanction and misfortune especially in relation to activities that would arouse ancestral interest. There were also inevitable tensions over the shared costs associated with its construction at a time when general economic resources were limited. The costs included both sourcing the appropriate materials and a weighty ritual loading in sacrificial animals for different phases of the construction. At the same time there was a growing scarcity (and cost) associated with securing quality supplies of the heavy hardwood support posts (*tutu*). A key issue in this respect was the establishment of the Nino Konis Santana National Park covering extensive forest reserves in the region with regulatory restrictions on extractive timber activities (see McWilliam 2013). The desired fibre (*fia*) of the black sugar palm for roof thatching is available at a price, but the technical skills required to create a high quality steeply sloping thatched roof are in short supply. Finally, the commitment to honouring ancestral traditions also had to be weighed against the competing demands on scarce family resources and their aspirations for improved material well-being and quality of life. These tensions are a growing feature of contemporary social life across Timor-Leste where the expectations to meet customary obligations such as bridewealth exchanges (F: *valahana*, T: *barlake*) and elaborate funeral gifts, challenge the aspirational desire among Timorese families for self-provisioning and enjoyment of consumer goods and other markers of economic distinction (see Hicks 2012; Niner 2012; Silva 2018). In Lautém these confounding issues appeared to outweigh the customary imperative to install the sacred hearth (*lafuru tei*) of the *ratu* lineage in a finely crafted and symbolically charged, traditional stilt house.

However, as it turns out I was premature in my judgement on this matter, and over the past few years of travelling around Lautém, there has evidently been a growing number of the striking Fataluku stilt houses (re)-appearing in villages across the municipality. Their visibility is made more apparent with new constructions in relocated villages that line the main roads. The elegantly shaped buildings are immediately recognisable but often with a striking (purists would say, scandalous), modification of the traditional structure. In place of the thick black *fia* roof thatch are sheets of variably blackened corrugated iron roofing (*kalen*); and instead of the massive, hand carved support posts (*tutu*) with their encircling rectangular, carved wooden disks (*sala fuka*) and heavy timber cross beams (*fatu, pokala*), the whole base structure is at times fashioned out of moulded concrete.[17] The effect is striking in its strong resemblance to the general appearance of the original timber and thatch models, especially as many of the new versions incorporate the older decorated panels and timber beams, reclaimed from the superstructures of previous traditional houses that had fallen into disrepair. This work of reclamation and reinstating

Figure 13.2 and 13.3. New style *Le ia valu* houses. Image credits: Andrew McWilliam.

original elements of the former ritual house into the new structure is a vital element of continuity and the symbolic transfer of protective ancestral authority.

In observing the emergence of this contemporary interpretation of the customary house, it was apparent that Fataluku agnatic groups may have resolved a series of long-standing concerns that have impeded its (re)appearance. The first concern was a practical one, given the propensity of the original building style to deteriorate over time in the tropical monsoon climate, especially without careful and costly maintenance. Thatched rooves rot and lose their waterproof qualities over time, as do support pillars, driven into the ground they gradually succumb to processes of decay and borer attack. The lack of alternative options may have constrained any enthusiastic prioritising of construction. But the recent appearance of relatively cheap corrugated iron sheeting available through an influx of Chinese traders in the markets of Lospalos and the now wide availability of imported cement and steel reinforcing from Indonesia, offered the prospect of a cheaper and more durable solution to the problem. These market developments were evidently not lost on many attentive Fataluku families, who were seeking to re-constitute their ancestrally authorised ritual centres for the celebration of agnatic solidarity and the social prestige and recognition that accompanies their restoration.

The next important requirement for ritual house reconstruction was the need to assemble sufficient resources and labour commitments from within the local kin group. The general absence of paid work opportunities in the local economy and a reliance on near-subsistence agriculture to provide sufficient food stocks and resources to participate in obligatory social exchanges, may have all contributed to lengthy delays in the building of new origin house forms. But here again, two significant developments in Fataluku household domestic economies changed their fortunes. The first was a decision by the National government to pay old age pensions and cash compensation to the families of former resistance fighters (*veteranus*) who died fighting for national independence (Wallis 2015; Roll 2018). Many Fataluku families in Lautém and Dili benefitted from these direct social transfers and allowed them to cover household consumption costs. But of much greater financial benefit has been the dramatic expansion of informal labour migration to the United Kingdom (Britain) where some thousands of aspiring young Fataluku have been working in Britain on Portuguese passports, across a range of comparatively well paid, unskilled factory and services sector jobs. The savings generated from this work has seen a regular and very welcome flow of US dollars remitted to grateful family members in Dili and Lospalos (see Chapter 12, this volume; also McWilliam 2012; McWilliam and Monteiro 2019, McWilliam 2022a).

Much of this income has been allocated to immediate household priorities (especially consumption, education support for siblings, residential house repair and construction). There have also been funds available for cultural obligations and ceremonial activities (marriages, funerals, grave construction) that include the restoration of lineage based ritual houses. Putting this another way, the fruits of labour generated in the market economy of the United Kingdom have contributed the means to re-invest in the mutuality of ancestral traditions in Timor-Leste.

Overcoming financial constraints to construction may have changed the equation in relation to reinstating Fataluku origin houses, but there remained a third important dimension and challenge to finalise traditional house construction projects. This was the question of whether the ancestors (*kaka ho pal* // *calu ho papu*) would approve of the adaptive departure from the traditional building forms and techniques of the Fataluku ritual house. These structures are after all, culturally infused archives of human habitation and ritual knowledge. They serve as vital centres of protective ritual blessings for the agnatic community and via the transformative power of the sacred hearth (*lafuru tei*), a focus for the sacrificial feeding (*fané*) of house ancestors. Errors of omission or transgression of customary forms and ritual practice, risk spiritual retribution or misfortune in varying ways. Furthermore, most people are naturally cautious about changing well-established conventions, particularly the canonical stylistic features of named and ancestrally protected structures. Elsewhere in Timor-Leste, the idea of building *Uma Lulik* with concrete and corrugated iron is strongly resisted out of fear of retribution from angry ancestors.[18] There are similarly Fataluku cultural advocates and general observers of these developments who remain uncomfortable and unconvinced about the new trend, considering the innovation a risky practice that may yet rebound on those involved in the form of illness, misfortune and loss. One of the people I canvassed on this issue dismissed the trend as a form of household display of financial capacity and group aggrandisement. "But it makes no difference", he added, "because everyone knows who they are", referring to their existing social status.

However, in what I take to be an openness on the part of Fataluku culture for adaptive accommodation to contingent events and embracing new opportunities, the 'modern' style of construction appears to be readily accepted by many household groups, and so far at least without mishap. The use of the new materials still requires ancestral permission or at least their acquiescence via divinatory signs, for the integration of the new materials. But in the cases where I have sought confirmation on this point, there have been no outright refusals. One house member offered the insight that when they sought guidance through divination (*ari toto*—liver divination) about the use of the corrugated iron roofing, the initial red and white coloured sheets were rejected. Subsequently the idea of painting the roofing sheets black to mimic the *fia* thatch was accepted. Others appear more sanguine on these matters, such as my Fataluku colleague who explained that 'we don't mention the changes in the house [to the ancestors], we just refer to the *le tein* and invite their assistance'. Another interlocutor suggested that there was likely an element of prestige, pride and public signalling in being able to display a fine new *le ia valu*. At this point then, it seems that an innovation to a long-established set of customary procedures and protocols has been realised and provisionally accepted. It announces in a modified but celebratory way, the revival of the uniquely styled, Fataluku origin house.

Balancing pragmatism and preservation

The quiet reappearance of Fataluku *le ia valu* across the settled landscapes of Lautém, albeit in modified form that seeks to emulate traditional structural features and aesthetics while utilising new technologies and materials, signals a new phase in the process of post-conflict recovery. The changes to traditional structures arguably speak to a cultural pragmatism that epitomises Fataluku historical accommodations to processes of change and modernity. Having reached a point where immediate household needs and aspirations were now adequately realised, attention has focused on a renewed commitment to revitalising ancestral traditions as part of the age-old Fataluku concerns with health and well-being (McWilliam 2008). In this process, 'modern' technology has played a crucial role.

I have focused in this chapter on the re-emergence of the agnatic, origin group ritual house (*le ia valu*) as the obligatory repository for the sacrificial hearth (*acakaka*) and other sacra. It forms a key site for offerings and prayers directed to the health of family members secured through the protective agency of ancestral blessings. The process of restoration has required a significant commitment on the part of related households and familial networks, providing household and group resources to projects for the common good. In Gudeman's terms, the interactive dialectic between mutuality and the market has found common ground in a shared commitment to reinstate the sacred house and with it, a public (re)affirmation of group identities and the ancestral spiritual commons on which they depend. The result is the re-creation of ritually potent and materially striking built structures for the celebration of life cycle transitions, especially the public formalisation of marriage alliances and the commemoration of death including the ritual curation of deceased souls (*i huma'ara*) into the ancestral collective (*calu ho papu*).[1920] But I would go further than this and suggest that the recent enthusiasm for re-instating origin houses as a focal feature for ceremonial life is but one aspect of an extended process of restoring Fataluku ancestral spirit ecologies into mainstream social and economic life (Palmer 2015). Fataluku have always directed significant resources to funerals and the commemoration of the death of loved ones, given the importance placed on their continuing protective agency as ancestral spirit guardians. The renewed desire to construct ritual houses has been accompanied by a gradual but marked increase in the scale and elaboration of a family member's grave. As household incomes and discretionary resources have improved, so too has the desire to honour the dead through investments in expensive graves and richly decorated memorials that highlight in a very public way, both the heartfelt expression of the family's loss but also the extent of resources assembled to honour their passing. Similar kinds of private commemorative projects have been extended to the remains of relatives and loved ones who suffered and died in the struggle for independence; their former simple graves constructed in a time of deprivation and shortage are now subject to expensive renovations and refurbishment in projects of redemption and care. But rites of death are also constitutive of social life (Grenfell 2012, 86), bringing together networks of kin and their affinal connections in obligatory gift exchange and commensality that extends to the ancestors of the house.

It is also worth noting here that the sustained revival of customary practices need not be seen as a turning away from the doctrines and ideologies of Catholicism towards a more animistic embrace of ritual sacrifice. Fataluku, like many Timorese communities (Grenfell 2012; Rosa 2019) have been able to accommodate both forms of religious practice as complementary and mutually reinforcing expressions of protective power, despite misgivings among the Catholic priesthood (Viegas and Feijó 2019; Bovensiepen and Rosa 2016). One only needs to witness the enthusiastic support offered by Fataluku families during the periodic overnight visits of saintly effigies and statues (*Nossa Senora* or *Kristu Rei*) when they make their much anticipated rounds of the district. In the all-night vigils and prayers of the faithful culminating in a thanksgiving service (*Missa agradesimentu*) for the forgiveness of sins and the healing of the sick and infirm, the Fataluku embrace of Catholicism is clearly and genuinely felt. It provides a now familiar and comforting set of practices in the social life of village communities that cohabit (Viegas and Feijó 2017) with the ancestral presence and the interactive benefits and mutual obligations that the enlivened spirit world confers.

Across Timor-Leste, customary communities continue their engagement with the rebuilding and restoration of their ancestral house traditions, especially the built form referred to as the *Uma Lulik* or 'sacred house.' The range and material expression of these structures of sociality are highly variable and reflect the specific ethno-linguistic traditions of their source communities. Their progressive re-appearance across the landscape highlights the high esteem and value attributed to their symbolic status as both a source and reflection of social identity, and the readiness of origin groups to commit limited resources to their reconstruction. I have argued that Fataluku origin houses share a range of attributes with the *Uma Lulik* traditions of Timor-Leste, but also significant differences, particularly with the central focus accorded to the sacred hearth (*lafuru tei* or *acakaka*) that instantiates the house as a *le tein* (*Uma Lulik*). In the end however, for Fataluku it is not so much the structural form sheltering the sacrificial hearth that matters, but rather the communicative value of the sacred hearth as a medium for invocation to and intercession of group ancestors.

Acknowledgements

Research for this chapter was supported by the Australian Research Council [DP160104519]. The interpretation presented has benefitted from numerous conversations with Fataluku colleagues over the years. I thank in particular, Almeida Fernandes Xavier, Edmundo da Cruz, Robella Mendez, Fernando Santana and Olivio Marques. Thanks also to Kelly Silva, Carmen dos Santos Monteiro, Susana de Matos Viegas and Lisa Palmer for their helpful comments.

Notes

1 Structures known as *cu* and *mo* are associated with simpler built forms made of timber and bamboo frames with loosely tied thatch. A *cu* is a basic residential structure within a settlement (*lata*) and may also be elevated on timber poles (*lalu cu*). The *mo* is usually associated with seasonal dwellings erected outside or on the edge of the settled areas. Garden huts (*pala mo*) or camps associated with the distillation of palm liquor (*tua mo*) are examples (see McWilliam 2022b).

2 The *pokala* refer to the two large round 'head beams' that form the major structural cross beams and rest on the *fata* timber beams above the four supporting house columns. The term *taru le* means 'the tied house' and refers to the strong *areng* palm twisted black rope that secures the structural features in place.

3 There is some variation across Lautém on this matter, in drier areas where areng palm is not abundant, the use of coconut or lontar palm thatch was substituted.

4 These distinctions are not formally observed in contemporary housing styles, although relative wealth differences between *ratu*, *paca* and *akanu* households can be reflected in the scale and style of their respective housing choices.

5 The term *leu loporu* refers to a flowering plant in the forest with large cup-like flowers, that resemble the cone style structures that cap the roof.

6 In former times of endemic and internecine warfare, reportedly bleached human skulls (*cao hafa*), the result of victorious, headhunting raids sometimes were used to decorate the roof thatch (F. Santana, pers. comm.).

7 They comprise the agnatic 'brothers and fathers' (*kaka ho pale*), friends and acquaintances (*lan ho tava*) of the sponsoring house, and the affinal, 'sisters and children' (*leren ho moco*) and 'brothers-in-law and uncles' (*vain ho paien*[u]). The groups exchange reciprocal gifts with one another—pigs and textiles flow from the sponsoring house to their daughters and husbands (*tupurmoko*) and buffalo and gold/money are reciprocated to the woman's natal house of origin (*omara/ ara ho pata*).

8 These and other forms of divination remain important diagnostic techniques for ensuring the safety or appropriateness of courses of action (see McWilliam 2008).

9 The action mimics the use of Catholic holy water for religious blessings of new houses highlighting the historical influence of Catholic practices and expressive forms that by association have been integrated into the ritual techniques of the ancestral religion (see Rosa 2019 for discussion).

10 The traditional large *fia le* style house could also include an inbuilt, boxed framed storage structure under the main floor of the building with access from above via a trap door.

11 Sacrificial meat is taken from the thorax and internal organs of the animal—boiled and roasted and cut into smaller portions to be served on shallow plaited trays (*neru moko*) to the male members of the ratu group.

12 Unmarried sons will make use of their father's or older brother's sacrificial hearth.

13 It is conventional for the youngest son (*moco vehula*) to inherit the house and *acakaka* of his father upon the latter's death. If a man has no sons, his *acakaka* will be closed down and laid to rest on his grave following death.

14 I note that Fataluku also use the phrase *le tein(u)* (sacred house) in reference to a Catholic Church and its priests as *ma'a tei*, loosely translated as 'man of the *lulik*'. Similarly, a very old ritual house which contains the sacred objects and other potent symbols of power, may be referred to as the 'sacred house' (*le tein*) for a dispersed clan group.

15 In the early 1980s in a demonstration of defiance by the armed Falintil resistance, many of the iconic Fataluku *le ia valu* were torched in strategic raids on Fataluku settlements to demonstrate to the Indonesians that their resolve and capacity for resistance was undiminished.

16 The same gestural reflex is observable in contemporary, post-Independence, Timor-Leste where the state has adopted a similar appropriation of Fataluku *fia le* images for their own promotional purposes.

17 A structure to stop rats climbing into the house and despoiling stored food and grain.

18 Changing times however, can prompt a rethink of older practices as in the recent trend among Mambai *Uma Lulik* (*fad luli*) in Ainaru to install reinforced concrete support pillars in their otherwise intricately worked traditional timber and thatch houses. The thinking here is that the

innovation will guarantee structural integrity and facilitate easier maintenance of the overall structure in the years to come.

19 Ceremonial activities focused on the origin house combine the ritual language of marriage exchange and agreement with various aspects of the architectural qualities of the house itself. A series of bridewealth gifts for example are linked in ritual verse to the steps of the house ladder (*ke'eru*) that permits the groom access to his bride in the platform above.

20 In Tetum these key elements are summarised as *lia moris* and *lia maten*.

References

Acciaioli, G. 1985. "Culture as art: From practice to spectacle in Indonesia." *Canberra Anthropology* 8 (1-2): 148-172. doi.org/10.1080/03149098509508575

Barnes, S. 2011. "Origins, Precedence and Social Order in the Domain of Ina Ama Beli Darlari." In *Land and Life in Timor-Leste: Ethnographic Essays*, edited by A. McWilliam and E. G. Traube, 23-46. Canberra: ANU Press. doi.org/10.22459/LLTL.12.2011.

Barnes, S. 2017. "Customary renewal and the pursuit of power and prosperity in post- occupation East Timor: a case study from Babulo, Uato-Lari." PhD diss., Monash University.

Bovensiepen, J. 2014. "Installing the insider 'outside': House reconstruction and binary ideologies in independent Timor-Leste." *American Ethnologist* 41 (2): 290-304. doi.org/10.1111/amet.12076

Bovensiepen, J., and F. D. Rosa. 2016. "Transformations of the sacred in East Timor." *Comparative Studies in Society and History* 58 (3): 664-693. doi.org/10.1017/s0010417516000311.

Clamagirand, B. 1975. "La maison Ema (Timor Portugais)." *Asie du Sud-Est et Monde Insulindien* 6: 35-60.

Fox, J. J. 1993. Comparative perspectives on Austronesian houses: An introductory essay. In *Inside Austronesian Houses: Perspectives on Domestic Designs for Living*, edited by J. J. Fox, 1-28. Canberra: Department of Anthropology, Comparative Austronesian Project, Research School of Pacific Studies, The Australian National University.

Grenfell, D. 2012. "Remembering the dead from the customary to the modern in Timor-Leste." *Global Local: Identity Security Community* 11: 86-109. ISSN: 1832-6919.

Gudeman, S. 2001. *The Anthropology of Economy: Community Market and Culture.* Oxford: Blackwell Publishers. ISBN-13: 978-0631225676.

Gudeman, S. 2016. *Anthropology and Economy.* Cambridge: Cambridge University Press. doi.org/10.1017/CBO9781316442739

Hicks, D. 2007. "Community and nation-state in East Timor." *Anthropology Today* 23 (1): 13-16. doi.org/10.1111/j.1467-8322.2007.00484.x

Hicks, D. 2012. "Compatibility, resilience and adaptation: The barlaque of Timor-Leste." *Local-Global: Identity, Security, Community* 11: 124-137. ISSN: 1832-6919

Lameiras-Campagnolo, M. O. 1975. "L'habitation des Fatuluku de Lórehe (Timor Portugais)." PhD diss., Université René Descartes, Sorbonne, Paris.

Loch, A. 2009. "Nation Building at the Village Level: First the House, then the Church and Finally a Modern State." In *East Timor: How to Build a New Nation in Southeast Asia in the 21st Century?*, edited by C. Cabasset and F. Durand, 95-104. Bangkok: Research Institute German Contemporary Southeast Asia (IRASEC & CASE). ISBN: 9786119028203

Meitzner Yoder, L. S. 2005. "Custom, codification, collaboration: integrating the legacies of land and forest authorities in Oecusse enclave, East Timor." PhD diss., Yale University, New Haven.

McWilliam, A. 2005. "Houses of resistance in East Timor: Structuring sociality in the new nation." *Anthropological Forum* 15 (1): 27-44. Doi.org/10.1080/0066467042000336698

McWilliam, A. 2007. "Harbouring traditions in East Timor: Marginality in a lowland entrepôt." *Modern Asian Studies* 41 (6): 1-31. doi:10.1017/S0026749X07002843.

McWilliam, A. 2008. "Fataluku healing and cultural resilience in East Timor." *Ethnos* 73 (2): 217-240. doi.org/10.1080/00141840802180371

McWilliam, A. 2011. "Exchange and resilience in Timor-Leste." *Journal of the Royal Anthropological Institute* 17 (4): 745-763. doi.org/10.1111/j.1467-9655.2011.01717x

McWilliam, A. 2012. "New Fataluku diasporas and landscapes of remittance and return." Special Issue, Nation-Formation, Identity and Change in Timor-Leste, *Local-Global: Identity, Security, Community* 11: 72-85. ISSN: 1832-6919

McWilliam, A. 2013. "Cultural heritage and its performative modalities: Imagining the Nino Konis Santana National Park in East Timor", In *Transcending the Culture-Nature Divide in Cultural Heritage: Views from the Asia-Pacific Region (Terra Australis 36)*", edited by S. Brockwell, S. O'Connor, and D. Byrne, 191-202. 1st ed. Canberra: ANU ePress.

McWilliam, A. 2020. *Post-Conflict Social and Economic Recovery in Timor-Leste: Redemptive Legacies*, London, New York: Routledge Press. ISBN: 9780367366681

McWilliam, A. 2022a. "Making money, missing home: Reflections on Timorese informal labour migration to Britain". *The Asia Pacific Journal of Anthropology* 23 (3): 266-285.

McWilliam, A. 2022b "Distilling Livelihoods in Timor-Leste: Fataluku Ecologies of Practice". *Human Ecology* 50: 605–615. https://doi.org/10.1007/s10745-022-00328-2y

McWilliam, A., and C. d S. Monteiro. 2019. "On Brexit Worries: Migration and Remittance Landscapes in Timor-Leste." In *The Routledge Handbook of Contemporary Timor-Leste*, edited by A. R. McWilliam and M. Leach, 136-146. London: Routledge. doi.org/10.4324/9781315623177

McWilliam, A., and M. Leach. 2019. *The Routledge Handbook of Contemporary Timor-Leste.* Abingdon: Routledge.

Niner, S. 2012. "Barlake: an exploration of marriage and issues of women's status in Timor-Leste." *Local Global, Identity, Security, Community* 11: 138-155. ISSN: 1832-6919.

Palmer, L. 2015. *Water Politics and Spiritual Ecology: Custom, Environmental Governance and Development.* London: Routledge. Doi 10.4324/9781315883250

Pannell, S. 1997. "From the poetics of place to the politics of space: Redefining cultural landscapes on Damar, Maluku Tengah." In *The Poetic Power of Place: Comparative Perspectives on Austronesian Ideas of Locality*, edited by J. J. Fox, 163-173. Canberra: Department of Anthropology, Comparative Austronesian Project, Research School of Pacific and Asian Studies, The Australian National University. ISBN 1 920942 86 6 (online)

Roll, K. 2018. "Reconsidering integration: Veterans benefits as state-building." In *The Promise of Prosperity: Visions of the Future in Timor-Leste*, edited by J. Bovensiepen, 139-156. Canberra: ANU Press. doi.org/10.22459/PP.2018

Rosa, F. D. 2019. "Catholic luliks or Timorese relics? Missionary anthropology, destruction and self-destruction (C.A. 1910-74)." In *Crossing Histories and Ethnographies: Following Colonial Historicities in Timor-Leste*, edited by R. Roque and E.G. Traube, 155-176. New York/Oxford: Berghahn Books. ISBN-13: 978-1789202717

Silva, K. 2018. "Marriage prestations, gift making, and identity in urban East Timor." *Oceania* 88 (1): 127-147. doi.org/10.1002/ocea.5185

Traube, E. G. 1986. *Cosmology and Social Life: Ritual Exchange among the Mambai of East Timor.* Chicago: University of Chicago Press. ISBN-13: 978-0226811499

Viegas, S. M., and R. G. Feijó. 2017. *Transformations in Independent Timor-Leste: Dynamics of Social and Cultural Cohabitations.* London/New York: Routledge. ISBN: 9781138691438.

Viegas, S. M., and R.G. Feijó. 2019. "Funerary Posts and Christian Crosses: Fataluku Cohabitations with Catholic Missionaries after World War." In *Crossing Histories and Ethnographies: Following Colonial Historicities in Timor-Leste*, edited by R. Roque and E.G. Traube, 177-202. Oxford/New York: Berghahn Books. ISBN-13: 978-1789202717

Wallis, J. 2015. "Assessing the Implementation and Impact of Timor-Leste's Cash Payment Schemes." In *A New Era? Timor-Leste after the UN,* edited by S. Ingram, L. Kent and A. McWilliam, 235-249. Canberra: ANU Press. doi.org/10.22459/NE.09.2015

CHAPTER 14

The *frente ekonomika* (economic front): Timorese perspectives on seasonal work in Australia

Michael Rose

Abstract

This paper looks at how, in Timor-Leste, the ways in which people perceive and experience the Australian Seasonal Worker Program (SWP) are contingent on a range of distinctly Timorese perspectives on life, labour and identity. Those working abroad give meaning to their hard work in Australia by framing it as part of a continuing national struggle for economic justice. Despite this, the widespread perception that patronage and family networks remain instrumental in deciding who gets access to lucrative positions in Australia remains a source of frustration for many. While the policy aims of the SWP are clear enough, in seeking to realise them there is a case for more closely engaging with the subjective experiences of those within it.

Keywords: Timor-Leste; Australia; agriculture; migration

Remittance sending from Timor-Leste–new forms of an old struggle

In their introduction to this volume, Palmer, Silver and Cunha characterise the breadth of scholarship it gathers as united by a concern with 'unmasking community economies'. In a sense the inclusion of a chapter such as mine might seem somewhat counterintuitive. Not only is my work focused primarily on perspectives of people who have made the decision to absent themselves (geographically at least) from their birth communities, but who have done so specially to undertake alienated wage labour in an unapologetically neoliberal Australian agricultural sector. My fellow contributors have, by contrast, largely focused on modes of thought, economic activity and social organisation that can be closely linked to a geographical place. Chapters 1 (Sousa), 2 (Hicks), and 3 (Grainger) interrogate the spatiality of colonial markets and housing developments. Chapters 4 (Barnes), 5 (Fidalgo-Castro and Alonso-Población), 6 (Trindade and Oliveira), 7 (Nogueira da Silva), and 8 (Cunha and Bessa) look at issues related to ritual, authority, exchange, food and (above all) land. Chapters 9 (Crespi), 10 (Palmer and Jackson), and 11

(Barreto Soares) step back from this focus on ritual and agrarian life to focus on an altogether distinct vision of Timor-Leste, one defined by forms of capital investment and engineering, that while decidedly not of the *knua* (village) are most certainly contingent on the physical reality of the *rai* (land).

To a certain extent the final three chapters that focus on labour migration, of which mine is one, are distinct, but perhaps not as much as they might seem to be at first. Although not completely unconcerned with the reality of the Timorese house, whether that be as a literal abode (see Chapter 12, this volume) or as a ritual centre through which (and where) alliances and exchange can be mediated (see Chapter 13, this volume), my colleagues and I all seek to uncover and describe the ways in which Timorese workers, even when literally immersed in neoliberal wage labour, continue to participate in the community economies that typically continue to provide a framework for living in their home communities.

In writing on this, McWilliam, Wigglesworth and Boavida dos Santos and myself come to similar conclusions—Timorese ritual economies that revolve around geographically rooted elements, such as sacred houses (*Uma Lulik*) and holy land (*rai lulik*), remain surprisingly robust in the face of globalised wage labour. In this chapter I draw on research undertaken among young people who have returned to Timor from work in Australia under its Seasonal Worker Program to show how, for most of this cohort, leaving their homeland to work was not so much an opportunity to escape social and ritual duties to which their families hold them accountable as to acquire the wealth to service them better. Paradoxically, the increased participation of Timorese workers in work ordered by neoliberalism abroad may feed into the continued (and even expanded) importance of alternatives to neoliberalism in Timor itself.

Viewed from afar, the reasons why young Timorese might go abroad to work are not hard to see. Timor-Leste's young population is growing fast, its two-speed economy is dominated by resource extraction, and although there is plenty of work to do looking after its large families and small farms, the paying jobs school leavers dream of are vanishingly rare. The clique of leaders that led its famous 1975-99 independence struggle have maintained control ever since and mostly squandered their chance to invest the windfall from nearly depleted petroleum fields on laying the foundation for a diversified economy. With current reserves almost exhausted, the fund being depleted at an unsustainable rate (World Bank 2020), Timor-Leste is a nearly classic example of the paradox that Auty (1995) and Ross (1999) have famously described as the 'resource curse'. A nation that people both refer to as the beloved land (*rai doben*) and try to leave as they see no future there.

Fieldwork for this paper took place in the latter half of 2019 as part of my work as a research fellow at the Australian National University and involved around two months of regular, face-to-face interaction with overlapping, extended networks of people associated with the SWP. In the end I spoke to thirty-three workers, and several times as many who aspired to be part of the program, had family participating, or just had strong opinions about the whole issue and wanted to talk about it. These networks were centred in Dili, and mostly consisted of people who had worked together abroad or studied together in Timor, but included people living as far afield as Oecussi, Same, and Aileu.

While finding people who had returned from Australia took some doing, I was overwhelmed by people who desperately wanted me to help them get there. Some had gone through the application process but never been called for an interview. Others said they would like to apply but either didn't know how or thought there was no use without a personal 'in'. Although constantly telling them otherwise, all of them believed I could make a difference.

Two elements of their experiences are of particular interest. The first is the tendency people have to envisage the SWP as part of a national struggle for development and dignity, contiguous with that carried out by the preceding generation who used their exile to fight for independence. The second is the continuing perception that, in spite of official protestations to the contrary, personal networks within Timor rather than formal, 'merit' based processes are what really matter in gaining access to overseas work in Australia.

In prefacing a discussion of these themes, a broader discussion of the current situation regarding employment in Timor-Leste is in order.

Over the next five years, the ability of Timor-Leste's politicians and policy makers to find jobs for its young may well determine its future as a sovereign state. At present, around 30,000 Timorese reach working age each year (RDTL 2017). Officially youth unemployment is only around 12% (Belun 2018), but for the majority who scrape by in precarious agriculture or commerce (sometimes clinically referred to by outsiders as 'self-employment') the line is blurry. Many of those who identify as jobless actually spend their days working hard on the family farm or at various forms of small scale commerce.

Historically, the most common aspiration for young Timorese graduates has been to find a post with the government. In past times this was not unrealistic, however in an age of mass education there are simply not enough places for everyone. The State of Timor-Leste only employs around 35,000 people (RDTL 2017). This is ominous for two reasons. Firstly, the inefficient and bloated public sector remains Timor-Leste's only major source of salaried work. Secondly, the producing oil reserves that pay for virtually all of it are almost gone and (despite official optimism) the development of new ones is not a sure thing (Cardoso 2019).

For more than a decade now foreign investment envisaged to follow 'front loading' on various infrastructure projects has been touted as a panacea for resource dependency, but little has come of it. Coffee and tourism have both, thus far, failed to thrive, and there is reason to be sceptical of Mr Gusmão's (2017) confident assertion that "Timor-Leste offers a predictable and secure environment for investment and business."

No less an authority than the World Bank (2020) places Timor-Leste at 181 out of 190 on the ease of doing business index and the cost of a ticket from Dili to Darwin can compare to one from Australia to Europe. Although the nation's aging political leaders rarely miss an opportunity to make emotive declarations about the continuing struggle, sometimes dressing in camouflage fatigues while doing it (Leach 2015), the less glamorous question of how the nation's young are going to live has yet to be confronted.

The 2011-2030 'strategic development plan' held superficial promise in this regard but given its lack of costings and/or other details Dalton's (2014, 211) description of it as "a utopian wish list of how life will be in Timor-Leste by 2030" seems justified. Likewise, the previous government's pronouncement that it would create 300,000 new jobs by 2023 (for a population of 1.3 million) had its heart in the right place, but very little connection to reality (Gusmão 2019). Unless they manage to get some sort of job with the state, there are few opportunities for the young in Timor-Leste to find regular, paid work.

Given this situation, the tendency of young Timorese to seek their fortune overseas is not surprising. The numbers, though not precise, are striking. Wigglesworth and Boxer (2017) estimated there could be as many as 19,000 Timorese in the UK, a figure that may well have ticked over to 20,000 in the years since. Brexit will slow the growth of its community but will more likely result in its gradual shift to the Republic of Ireland or elsewhere in the EU than its destruction. Taking a cue from this demonstrated appetite for work abroad, Timor-Leste's government made it their policy to seek inclusion in various guest and seasonal worker schemes. According to official sources, in mid-2018 around 2300 of its citizens were serving as guest workers in Korea, mostly on three-year contracts in fisheries, retail or manufacturing. At around the same time around 1000 were working in Australia, mostly in six-month stints harvesting fruit and vegetables as part of its seasonal worker program (SEFOPE 2018). Thus, as of two years ago we come to a minimum figure of Timorese working abroad that is approaching 24,000. Soon there will be more Timorese making their living from the diaspora than from the state. In 2018, according to the Observatory for Economic Complexity, Timor-Leste earned a total of $67.3 million from exports, mostly of fossil fuels. In the same year, according to the World Bank data that takes into account only formal money transfers, Timor-Leste earned over $96 million from remittances.

Local and global in international work

Globally, Timor-Leste's story of limited prospects at home driving people to seek their fortune abroad is not a new one. At least since the Industrial Revolution the flight of impoverished and disenfranchised folk from hard up or overcrowded rural areas in search of a brighter future has shaped the urban landscapes and cultures we take for granted today.

Because labour migration is such a universal phenomenon and managed/monitored by governments and with an appetite for quantitative data, there remains a danger of neglecting the diversity of ways in which it is experienced, especially by the workers it impacts most directly. "Discussions on globalisation, to borrow the words of Gustavo Lins Riberio (2009) can "tend to focus on processes commanded by powerful agents" (2009). Inspired by the case for using ethnographic methods to address this issue set out in the co-authored 2012 volume, *Globalisation from Below* (Mathews, Ribeiro, and Vega 2012), this research proceeds from the premise that the perspective of Timorese workers within the SWP are not only distinct from those normative to policy makers in Canberra, but sometimes expressed through words, narratives and somatic dispositions that may be incomprehensible to them. While approaches to understanding the SWP that gloss over this diversity in favour of research filtered through metrics and assumptions about life familiar to Australian policy makers are understandable, they are also intellectually disingenuous—and indeed risk complicity in the erasure of subaltern perspectives that can characterise globalisation at its worst. This article seeks to throw into relief how and why, although Timorese perspectives on international work may not be readily comprehensible to outside 'experts', they should not be dismissed.

The ways in which people in Timor-Leste perceive international work are shaped by their position betwixt Southeast Asia and the Pacific and their dramatic recent history of governance by and struggling against Indonesia. Those old enough to participate in the SWP were raised with tales of Timorese abroad advocating for independence prior to 1999 as part of the *frente diplomatika* (diplomatic front). The highly visible presence of the United Nations and various iNGOs since 1999 has also strengthened the perceived value of money from abroad promoting development at home. For Timorese of an earlier generation, studying in Indonesia could be a way of accruing the intellectual resources to continue their fight for a homeland. In a similar way, for the current generation, work abroad that feeds back into household and village economies can be 'reconfigured' (Leach 2018, 294) as contiguous with the heroic efforts of the recent past. Certainly, while commentators who identify the growth of Timor-Leste's diaspora as being driven by the fizzling of its domestic economy have a valid point, from within, the discourse is less negative. "*Luta nafatin*!" My informants would regularly tell each other when facing challenges at home or abroad—'continue the struggle'. As I seek to show further on, through envisaging their lives as part of this historical arc, members of Timor's diaspora can find purpose and optimism even in the face of hopeless odds.

The governance of labour sending in Timor-Leste, in particular the popular and rapidly growing option of going to Australia for seasonal work, is also distinct and worthy of attention. Unlike migration to the UK which is a largely private matter (although, as McWilliam [2020, 106] has shown it is still usually dependent on being able to secure sponsorship to attain a passport from the Government of Portugal), people who go to work in Australia, South Korea, Japan or Canada do so as part of government programs that are, in theory, open to anyone who meets the basic qualifications. In the Australian case, which is my focus, applicants submit their documents to the local SEFOPE office and then undergo a language and physical test before being accepted into a 'work ready pool' from which they can be selected for an interview with a foreign employer, usually in Dili.

In reality, despite support from the Australian government, in Timor the recruitment process is widely perceived to be anything but clear, and whilst on the island I regularly had people sidle up to me and ask how it *really* worked, and if I could put in a good word for them. It is widely believed that personal connections play a role in who is called for an interview, and recurring rumours of bribery are not implausible. This is to say that, although selection to the SWP is officially a merit-based system, in reality access to lucrative international work is believed to be, like access to other forms of work with the government, contingent on local networks of power, patronage and reciprocity. While this perception is generally invisible to outside actors, for Timorese it is taken-for-granted, and in line with their experiences of accessing government services more broadly— an amalgam of norms that draws on both the steep hierarchies of the island's indigenous polities and the socially contingent models of governance prevailing in Indonesia (Peake et al. 2014). The result seems to be that while outsiders usually see the SWP as flattening Timor-Leste's prevailing hierarchies (including those related to social-rank, education and gender) in-so-far as access to this work appears to sometimes leverage patronage networks, at times it may well also perpetuate them instead.

Labour as national struggle

One truly odd but telling feature of my conversations with these frustrated young people in Dili was the regularity with which, in seeking to explain their educational background, they would ask me if I had heard of the Westphalian System. This slightly obscure term refers to the modern system of nation-states and its beginnings in a treaty signed in the German city of Westphalia in 1648—interesting but not a major concern for young folk in Dili in 2020, one would think. In the end I spoke to some 33 returned workers, as well as many more people from their families or communities. While there were exceptions, they were almost all of a certain type—educated and intellectually curious youth who had been among the first in their family to finish school and had then travelled to Dili in search of work, education, diversion, love or some combination of all four. Although they had studied various things, a course in international relations was the most popular choice. A history of the nation-state, including the Peace of Westphalia, seems to have been covered early on, and although their understanding of global affairs was usually cloudy, they were enthused by all things international, something that often went along with a passion for studying English. These energetic *joven* (youth) had been raised on stories about the role of how the *frente diplomatika* which (along with the *frente armada* and the urban pro-independence underground known as the *frente klandistina*) had defied both the Indonesian neighbours and a sceptical world to win their nation's independence. A slogan used by former President and current Prime Minister Taur Matan Ruak captures the zeitgeist well: "in the past we shed our blood for independence, now we must sweat and work hard for a better life" (T: *uluk ho imi fakar ran ba ukun rasik aan, fila fali ho imi, hisik kosar ba moris diak*). Hard work in peacetime, Ruak says, is not just virtuous in itself but also a way of continuing the struggle and sacrifice of those who fought in the war (Anibal 2016).

Speaking to returned or aspiring seasonal workers, I found they were typically sanguine about the extent to which their formal qualifications were not in demand by employers in Timor-Leste, or anywhere else. They expressed little or no sense that menial work in Australia was 'beneath' them. Almost without exception they were either happy they had been selected to pick fruit, or disappointed that in spite of their English language skills and demonstrated determination, they had been unable to find a place in the program. Some of the reasons why my interlocutors wanted this work so badly are common to labour migrants the world over— most notably a need to support themselves and their family. Some younger interlocutors also spoke of a desire to see a land beyond Timor and learn about a way of life other than their own. Yet the degree to which they mostly placed their individual experience within a larger national struggle is distinctive and significant. Almost everyone who had been to Australia agreed that work there was hard, sometimes very hard—entailing long hours, exposure to heat and cold, absence from family or loved ones and sometimes onerous discipline. It was the sense that they endured all this in the service of something bigger that made it bearable. One interlocutor set this out for me directly. "Our fathers were part of the *frente armada*" he explained, "we are of the *frente ekonomika* (economic front)". For the educated young, most of whom had dreams of a life that went far beyond picking fruit, this collective narrative was a way of coming to terms with the menial nature of their work and the shortfall between it and their hopes of becoming an *ema boot* (important person) with an office job. Whatever hardships they had to endure, it was for the greater good. There was a sense that no matter how difficult things were, through their own willingness to work hard in an unfamiliar foreign land the struggle for national development would also be successful.

This tendency of young Timorese workers to position their diasporic labour within a broader narrative of national struggle, has striking parallels with the spirit that pervades life at the Timor-Leste's premier language training centre Science of Life (SOLS) 24/7.[1] There students are explicitly inculcated in the idea that training will not only improve their own prospects but make them better able to contribute to the development of their country. As a regular visitor to their four various residential training centres in Oecussi District over the years, I watched the live-in students begin and end their days raising the flag and reciting the national anthem. They would practice their English by chanting slogans like "I love East Timor very much!" Once they asked me to give a motivational speech on how I thought they could make Timor-Leste an "advanced country like Australia". Although English is taught in Timorese secondary schools, in Timor SOLS has developed a reputation as a cheap and affordable place to acquire this prestigious skill. Most young Timorese who speak English, seasonal workers included, have lived at one of their centres or benefitted from their courses.

For anyone who has spent time in Timor-Leste recently, it would be difficult not to be aware of SOLS, and indeed in collecting data for this paper it was a key research site.[2] It arrived in 2005, and although its size has fluctuated, current members say it has around 30 residential centres and sub-centres throughout the country. Its mission, genuinely non-profit, is to provide people with the chance to improve their lives through education. This consists largely of English lessons, although other subjects including IT and money management are also offered, as well as its eponymous Science of Life System™—a set of golden rules urging diligence, discipline, compassion and positive thinking.

Although it was founded in Cambodia, SOLS in Timor-Leste is strikingly local. Centres consist of thatched huts or reclaimed Indonesian-era ruins with exceptionally simple classrooms (open-air), dormitories (sleeping mats) and kitchens (serving boiled cassava leaf and rice) that run on a minimal budget. Good students eventually become teachers. Fees compare favourably with what it would cost students to live at home.

When asked what brought them to SOLS, students invariably answered, with heart-breaking earnestness, that they hoped English would increase their chances of finding a job. When I started visiting them in 2011, this response was typically more an aspiration than anything else—a plumb NGO position was unlikely to appear, and while migrating to the UK was an option for some it came with daunting social and financial costs. Now most of them do have a plan—to register to pick fruit in Australia. It is noteworthy that, although it is a non-government organisation, life at SOLS is overtly nationalistic. As mentioned above, each day begins and ends with a raising or a lowering of the national flag and the singing of the national anthem. Students pledge that they will strive to become 'leaders with character' in order to 'develop Timor-Leste'. Also interesting is the way in which, alongside language training, SOLS teaches its students other skills specifically (most notably basic accounting and money management) intended to help them get by as respectable wage earners in a market economy—something that is particularly significant given that many of its students are drawn from communities in which subsistence agriculture and ritualised exchange have historically been more important than the cash economy. In this sense, SOLS is arguably engaged not in ideologically neutral instruction in numeracy and language skills, but a form of what Silva (2017) describes as 'economic pedagogy'—'a project intended to 'monopolise the sources of government, prestige and social reproduction via the state, its institutions and projects.' Analysing government sponsored *tara bandu* (ritual prohibition) ceremonies carried out around Ermera in 2012 with the intention of encouraging people to dedicate less of their wealth to ritual exchange, Silva describes how the state was able to effectively appropriate customary authority in order to promote ways of understanding and use wealth that would ultimately undermine its influence. In the case of SOLS we see a comparable situation—an NGO that has successfully mobilised the nationalist, spiritually minded, do-it-yourself ethos of Timorese collectivism in order to promote the idea that individual wage earning is a better way to live.

For all its similarities with its Pacific neighbours, SOLS in Timor-Leste highlights that working abroad is embedded in a distinct context—specifically a tradition of self-organised, nationalist youth. Organisations such as this have had a long history in both fascist Portugal and the Indonesian Orde Baru (Bexley and Tchailoro 2014; Kuin 1993). Archival footage from the early 1970s shows children being drilled by the short lived FRETILIN government (TV New Zealand 1975). Almost fifty years later one of these kids, now my landlord in a coastal village in Oecussi and about 60 years old, delighted in entertaining his own children with a half-remembered Portuguese marching song about how the youth should give everything for their country.

The Indonesian concept of organised nationalist youth has had an even longer lasting impact. The concept of *pemuda* has been central to Indonesian nationalism since its inception, and the generation of Timorese students that absorbed this narrative as part of their education in the 1980s and 1990s were, ironically, able to make it the basis for their own nationalism. Although the armed resistance was never completely wiped out, as the 1990s wore on it was the *frente klandistina*, a mostly urban movement of nationalist youth who became the driving force behind it. One of the most significant components of this was an organisation known as RENETIL (a Portuguese acronym for The National Resistance of Timorese Students) whose main purpose was to organise nationalist activities among Timorese students in Indonesia. Veterans of the movement describe how, although they hoped that studying abroad would give them an edge in the job-market, their activities there were orientated not towards personal gain but collective struggle (Silva 2013).

To an outside observer the future of young Timorese workers abroad, including Australia, is challenging to say the least. The work they do is precarious, the experience of being away from home is often disorientating, the wages they send back tend to get quickly eaten up servicing the needs of those who stay behind, and no matter how well they look after their own families their country's economic future is highly uncertain. And yet, in spite of all this, Timorese workers in Australia persist at their difficult jobs, and thousands wait enthusiastically (if not impatiently) to join them. While this is partially explicable in terms of people simply trying to meet their own needs, the Timorese national story of struggle against all odds (including, notably, pronouncements by outside observers that their cause was hopeless, see Braithwaite, Charlesworth, and Soares 2012, 61-78) clearly plays a part in bolstering their resilience. Regardless of how things might appear to researchers who are unfamiliar with their home context, Timorese can draw on this heritage to envisage their work abroad not primarily as alienated labour within a grossly unequal global system but also as a way of contributing a meaningful part to a national struggle they have been inculcated into since childhood. A struggle which they will eventually win.

The fog of peace: accessing international work through local networks

Just as Timorese seasonal workers in Australia can draw upon their national story in giving meaning to their work abroad, so too are the processes through which they seek to attain such work contingent on local modes of governance. These ways and means of acting are generally not visible to those without a detailed knowledge of the Timorese context.

In theory, the SWP is managed jointly between Australia and Timor-Leste. While recruitment is the preserve of SEFOPE, Australia seeks to support these workers through its Pacific Labour Facility (PLF), currently operated by a contractor, Palladium. Although this work is complex, a significant part of its focus is seeking to ensure that clear information about the Program is publicly available and to put in place measures, "to ensure recruitment processes are fair, transparent and equitable" (DFAT 2019, 12).

Although the good-will of all parties in this can be taken for granted, it is acknowledged that Timor-Leste may lack the 'capacity' to achieve this goal without assistance, and there are a range of materials designed for distribution through social media that aim to answer questions relating to the SWP, including the steps one needs to take to sign up to the program. Identified in neat stages, these steps begin with an initial visit to the SEFOPE office for an interview with an Australian employer. Reading these materials, one could be mistaken for believing that winning a coveted place working in Australia was a straight-forward seven step process and that clarification is just an email away (SEFOPE 2019).

In reality, from talking to returned workers (or, even more often, frustrated prospective workers) it was apparent that this was not how they saw the situation. Whatever the truth about what is happening, there is a widespread sense of confusion about how someone might go about being selected, and a sense of desperation among potential applicants who are convinced that the system is rigged in favour of those with connections.

The nature of this discord quickly became apparent as soon as I arrived in Timor and began seeking out people who could help me better understand this topic. When I put the word out that I was interested in speaking to people who had returned from Australia, my Facebook and WhatsApp messages quickly started piling up.

Despite being clear that I was not a government representative and had no power over who was selected to the SWP, I quickly found that many didn't seem to believe me:

> "Maun (older brother), would very much like to work in Australia. Can you help me?"
> "Maun, I am very sad because I am unemployed. I speak good English. Do you know how I can work in Australia?"
> "Maun, I applied to work in Australia, but I was not called for an interview."

While I eventually also managed to speak with individuals who had come back from Australia and their families, the overwhelming majority of the messages I received were from people who wanted to go to Australia and hoped that I could somehow assist them in doing so. Confronted with this I would attempt to clarify the situation, sometimes by directing would-be applicants to the official material that had been produced by SEFOPE. More than anything else these efforts tended to elicit disappointment. Most gave up quietly, but there were a couple of individuals who didn't get (or ignored) the hint, and continued to badger me, repeatedly asking to meet up with me and insinuating that I was willing to help other people and not them. My protestation that there was already an established process for applying for the seasonal worker program ('just check the website') and that they needed to talk to SEFOPE was clearly not credible to them. Later I asked a number of informants I had known for years why this might be the case. They confirmed what I had already suspected, that people who were behaving in this way felt I had unfairly brushed them off, and that if I really wanted to help them I could.

"Everyone knows that SEFOPE just send their families", I was told by one unhappy young man as he sat miserably in his front yard, 'there's no point in even applying'. Whether this was accurate was impossible to say. Certainly, I met people who did seem to have succeeded in joining the SWP without personal connections. Nonetheless, the idea the process was rigged was widespread—repeated to me by most of the aspiring young workers I spoke to.

The view, normative in Timor-Leste, that regardless of what might be stated officially, access to seasonal work was mediated by personal connections, stands in stark contrast with the perspectives of Australian actors within the program. For them such behaviour is viewed as corrupt and totally unacceptable. Australian actors within the SWP evince an understandably inflexible commitment to the idea that the program sits within a publicly acknowledged and agreed upon set of rules and regulations. Indeed, a major part of the Australian aid effort to Timor-Leste and other countries in the region is its Governance for Development (GfD) program which describes itself as aiming to effect 'poverty reduction in Timor-Leste through economic development and improvement in the delivery of government services' (Cardno 2019). While GfD is separate from the PLF, both reflect Australia's commitment to helping Timorese institutions embody professional, transparent, and apolitical forms of governance.

For Timorese actors involved in the governance of the SWP there are many reasons to be receptive to this well intended agenda. However, although the Timor-Australia relationship tends to be construed as a partnership, in both the specific case of the SWP, and in its dealings with international patrons more generally, there is an unspoken asymmetry of power. Timor-Leste is only one of many countries that sends workers to Australia, and there is an overwhelming number of people waiting to go. This is a relationship in which Australia is in the position of strength and, by extension, the socially contingent Timorese ways of getting things are in a distinctly subaltern position.

It is not the purpose of this article to cast judgment on this situation. Rather my point is that that governance in Timor-Leste reflects what Brown (2014) describes as an "ecology of relations" that can be "described neither by liberal nor customary frameworks" and in which patronage relationships deeply matter. This situation also appears to be reflected in the way people think about the SWP. To put it another way, in the case of the SWP, as with most other Timorese government processes, the formal mechanism is at best a framework, and at least just an acceptable public face for a more complex, culturally contingent reality (Aspinall et al. 2018; Cummins 2015). What foreigners may see as corruption or incompetence is, in some cases, simply the manifestation of a way of getting things done which values relationships over bureaucratic process.

The procedure by which people apply for a place in SWP is worth describing further.

Until last year, people who wanted to join the seasonal worker program had to travel to Dili and submit their documents (*fó dokumentus*) at the central SEFOPE office there. This is a highly stylised process adapted directly from that prevailing in Indonesia whereby applicants muster copies of their identity card, school leaving certificates and a CV written according to a uniform format (all of which takes considerable doing in itself) along with an application form and submit them all in a manila folder. Informants told me that it is very important that these folders are blue. The background of the passport photo that comes along with it has to be a certain type of red. One striking aspect of this is that the applications cannot be in any way personalised, in fact if anything the process is seen as being more about showcasing the ability of applicants to conform with the rules and display deference to authority rather than demonstrating any special aptitude for the job in question. For any sort of government job, but especially for the SWP, the number of applicants is generally overwhelming. Although these numbers are far from official, SEFOPE staff told me they thought that even before the 2018-2019 recruitment almost 9000 new applicants submitted their documents, and there were already 10,000 waiting to go.

What happens after documents are submitted is less clear. Candidates who fit the basic age and health criteria are, in theory, invited back for a physical test intended to ensure that they have the minimum strength and agility to do the work at hand, although the way in which this was carried out seemed inconsistent. Some returned workers chuckled as they described how at their physical test, they had been asked to lift up a box and put it on the table. Others recalled having been put through large sports day style events in which hundreds of candidates were doing push ups and endurance runs—a routine rumoured to have been adapted from that used by the army to select recruits. One returned worker admitted that she had not done the physical test at all but was somehow still selected. There is also supposed to be a written exam intended to ensure that prospective workers have a basic knowledge of English, although once again the degree to which this was effectively applied is questionable. Many workers reported working with people who knew no English at all. Others who were near fluent were rejected. Finally, some, though not all, of the returned workers reported being asked for a short interview (perceived by some as a test of their ability to speak English) in which they were asked about their motivations for working in Australia, although again, what role this played in who got selected was completely opaque.

In theory, workers who passed all these stages were then placed into a 'work ready pool'. from which people would be called upon for interviews with foreign employers. Contact from SEFOPE, if it was to occur, was by telephone, something which caused anxiety in itself. Timor-Leste's mobile network, though extensive, is unreliable, and those who lose their phone or their number cannot always afford to immediately replace it. Many of the people I spoke to lived in terror of missing the call, which could change their life.

The sum result of all of this among prospective seasonal workers was confusion, and a widespread conviction that the unwieldly official path was at best unlikely to provide results and at worst not really intended to. There was widespread puzzlement as to why one person was selected for an interview and not another, and indeed even from an outsider's point of view there was no good explanation for this. When I asked SEFOPE and other figures with an inside knowledge of how government worked in Timor-Leste they would typically chuckle and say something like 'this is not Australia, Mike'. As mentioned above the applications were not personalised, and for each opportunity that comes up there are hundreds of equally qualified candidates to choose from. While there have been widely publicised examples of public servants involved in labour sending being moved for allegedly favouring friends and relatives in the selection process, the degree to which this was politically motivated is hard to say. Actual or aspiring seasonal workers were also a fraught source of information about this. Those who had been waiting for a call back from SEFOPE for years tended to be embittered, often pointing to people they perceived as less qualified (that is to say with less ability to speak English than themselves) but better connected who had been called for an interview. Returned workers, on the other hand, would sometimes concede that getting an interview for a position could be a matter of knowing the right person, although not in their case, or that of anyone they directly knew.

Given the reality that selection to the SWP in Timor occurs within a setting where it is widely accepted that access to jobs or other state resources is contingent on political and social affiliation, it is probably disingenuous to believe it is fully merit based. For outsiders, in particular those working in the policy space, this presents both a challenge and an opportunity. The challenge lies in accepting, non-judgementally, the reality that in Timor-Leste the norms surrounding public governance are different from those prevailing in Australia. The opportunity is that once having recognised this gap exists, work can begin on building a realistic understanding of how recruitment processes in Timor-Leste work. Such an understanding might, eventually, inform a solution to this specific issue that is satisfactory to everyone. While it is all very well for policy to be informed by principle, pre-existing practice must also be considered if it is to be effective.

Conclusion

Labour mobility is a global phenomenon lived through local frameworks. While the movement of labour can be approached through the prism of economic data and high-level policy, the experiences of labourers cannot—a reality that is too often overlooked or glossed over. Top down research approaches to understanding the SWP and similar programs are necessary and no doubt well-intended, but such research needs to also find ways of engaging with the stories of those who do the work, in all their cultural and linguistic distinctiveness.

While the focus of this research has been on the specific case of Timor-Leste, in considering the SWP more broadly the enormous variety of places from which workers come poses a serious challenge. Although all ten participating countries might fairly be placed within Austronesia, from Papua New Guinea to Fiji, they vary greatly in terms of their languages, religion and economic activity. By sketching how the experiences of Timorese SWP workers in Australia are embedded in distinctly Timorese frameworks for being in the world that may not be readily apparent or comprehensible to foreign observers, this paper seeks to gesture to the importance of recognising and engaging with this diversity in thinking about how the SWP works and its impact on sending countries.

Although from an outsider's point of view Timorese participation in the SWP might seem to be primarily about the accumulation of wealth or personal experience, closer engagement shows it is also inspired by a spirit of collective sacrifice and struggle abroad that has roots going back at least forty-five years, arguably longer. In so far as this narrative is important to how workers meet the challenges of toiling in an unfamiliar environment, its existence is of significance to anyone interested in understanding the Program's impact on Timorese individuals and communities. Likewise, whilst an outside observer would likely see recruitment to the SWP as a flawed, though merit-based process, the reality, only perceptible through observation from the inside, is that in Timor there is a widespread belief that it is often contingent upon personal connections and patronage relationships. While the degree to which this is in fact the case is difficult to say, the reality that it is widely believed has a tangible influence on how people think about the SWP and is thus significant regardless.

The idea that policy relating to labour migration should be attentive to the perspectives of those who participate in it, or aspire to, is not a novel one, or at least should not be. While the SWP, and similar programs, can operate without such an awareness (and indeed, to a certain extent, are currently doing so), without it they will struggle to fully appreciate the needs of the workers within it. Expanding the role of ethnographic methods in understanding their experiences would be a great first step towards changing this.

Acknowledgement

This research was undertaken with support from the Australian Government's Pacific Research Program.

Notes

1 In 2019, SOLS 24/7 in Timor rebranded as AHHA Education.

2 My material on SOLS 24/7 became a blog on the subject for the Development Policy Centre (Rose 2019).

References

Anibal, J. 2016. "Povu Viqueque Husu PR Taur Kontinua Kandidata Aan Ba 2017." *Timor Agora*, 19 September. Accessed at https://timor107.rssing.com/browser.php?indx=32109086&item=5493 on 3rd of May 2020 on 3 May 2020.

Aspinall, E., A. Hicken, J. Scambary, and M. Weiss. 2018, "Timor-Leste votes: Parties and patronage." *Journal of Democracy* 29 (1): 153-167.

Auty, R. M. 1995. "Economic Development and the Resource Curse Thesis." In *Economic and Political Reform in Developing Countries*, edited by O. Morrissey, F. Stewart, 55-80. London: Palgrave Macmillan.

Belun. 2018. "Leaving No Youth Behind in Timor-Leste." Accessed at https://timor-leste.unfpa.org/sites/default/files/pub-pdf/03_NEET_ENG_PRINT%20%281%29.pdf on 28 April 2020.

Bexley, A. 2009, "Youth at the crossroads: the politics of identity and belonging in Timor-Leste." PhD thesis, The Australian National University.

Bexley, A and N. Rodrigues Tchailoro. 2013, "Consuming youth: Timorese in the resistance Against Indonesian occupation." *The Asia Pacific Journal of Anthropology* 14 (5): 405-422.

Bovensiepen, J. and F. D. Rosa. 2016, "Transformations of the sacred in East Timor." *Comparative Studies in Society and History* 58: 664-693.

Braithwaite, J., H. Charlesworth and A. Soares. 2012. *Networked Governance of Freedom and Tyranny: Peace in Timor-Leste.* Canberra: ANU E-Press. http://doi.org/10.22459/NGFT.03.2012.

Brown, M. A. 2014. "Formação do Estado e da comunidade política em Timor-Leste – A centralidade do local." *Revista Crítica de Ciências Sociais* 104: 101-122

Cardno. 2019. "Governance for Development." Accessed at https://www.cardno.com/projects/governance-for-development-gfd/ on 4 May 2020.

Cardoso, J. da C. 2019. "Can Timor-Leste Move Away from an Oil Based Economy?" *The Diplomat*, March 06. Accessed at https://thediplomat.com/2019/03/can-timor-leste-move-away-from-an-oil-based-economy/ on 28 April 2020.

Cummins, D. 2015. *Local Governance in Timor-Leste: Lessons in Postcolonial State-building*. London: Routledge.

Dalton, H. 2014. "Still struggling: Market-based approaches to poverty alleviation in rural Timor-Leste." PhD diss., Deakin University.

DFAT (Department of Foreign Affairs and Trade). 2018. *Timor-Leste Workforce Development and Strategic Review.* Canberra: DFAT. Accessed at https://www.dfat.gov.au/sites/default/files/timor-leste-workforce-development-strategic-review.pdf, on 28 April 2020.

DFAT (Department of Foreign Affairs and Trade). 2019. *PLS Policy Handbook.* Canberra: DFAT. accessed at https://www.dfat.gov.au/sites/default/files/pacific-labour-scheme-policy-handbook.pdf on 4 of March 2020

Fox, J. J. 1989. "Category and complement: binary ideologies and the organization of dualism in Eastern Indonesia." In *The Attraction of Opposites: Thought and Society in the Dualistic Mode,* edited by D. Maybury-Lewis and U. Almagor, 33-56. Ann Arbor, MI: University of Michigan Press.

Gusmão, A. 2019. "300,000 New Jobs by 2023', *Tatoli*, October 25. Accessed at http://www.tatoli.tl/en/2019/10/25/300000-new-jobs-by-2023-upma/ on 29 April 2020

Gusmão, X. 2017. "Invest in Timor-Leste." Accessed at https://www.xananagusmao.org/invest on 29 May 2020.

Kuin, S. 1993. "A Mocidade Portuguesa nos anos 30: Anteprojectos e instauração de uma organização paramilitar da juventude." *Análise Social* 28 (122): 555-588

Leach, M. 2015. "The politics of history in Timor-Leste." In *A New Era? Timor-Leste after the UN*, edited by S. Ingram, C. Kent and A. McWilliam, 41-58. Canberra: ANU E-Press.

Leach, M. 2019. "The distinctive character of East Timorese nationalism." *Bulletin of the National Museum of Ethnology* 43 (3): 283-300.

Mathews, G., G. Ribeiro, and C. A. Vega. 2012. *Globalization from Below: The World's Other Economy.* London: Routledge.

McWilliam, A. 2020. *Post-Conflict Social and Economic Recovery in Timor-Leste.* London: Routledge.

Observatory for Economic Complexity. 2018. "Timor-Leste". Accessed at https://oec.world/en/profile/country/tls/ on the 14July 2020.

Peake, G., L. Kent, A. Damaledo, and P. M. Thu. 2014. "Influences and Echoes of Indonesia in Timor-Leste." Discussion Paper presented SSGM 2014/8, Australian National University, Canberra.

RDTL (República Democrática de Timor-Leste). 2011. *Timor-Leste Strategic Development Plan 2011-2030.* Dili: RDTL. Accessed at www.timor-leste.gov.tl/wpcontent/uploads/2011/07/Timor-Leste-StrategicPlan-2011-20301.pd on the 14 July 2020.

RDTL (República Democrática de Timor-Leste). 2015. "Population and Housing Census." Accessed at http://www.statistics.gov.tl/2015-timor-leste-population-and-housing-census-data-sheet/ on the 4 May 2020

RDTL (República Democrática de Timor-Leste). 2017. *Orçamento Geral Do Estado*, Accessed at https://www.mof.gov.tl/category/documents-and-forms/budget-documents/?lang=en on 4 May 2020.

Ribeiro, G. L. 2009. "Non-hegemonic globalizations: Alter-native transnational processes and agents." *Anthropological Theory* 9 (3): 297-329.

Ross, M. 1999. "The political economy of the resource curse." *World Politics* 51 (2): 297-322.

Rose, M. 2019. "Science of Life Systems: learning English and looking outward in Timor-Leste." *Development Policy Blog*, December 9. Accessed at https://devpolicy.org/science-of-life-systems-learning-english-and-looking-outward-in-timor-leste-20191209/ on 3 March 2020.

Rose, M. 2020. *Indigenous Spirits and Global Aspirations in a Southeast Asian Borderland.* Amsterdam: Amsterdam University Press.

Rose, M. forthcoming. "Timorese in the SWP: global labour, local frameworks." *Asia and the Pacific Policy Studies.*

SEFOPE (Sekretaria Estadu Formasaun Profesional no Empregu). 2018. "Labour Market Outlook Timor-Leste." Dili: SEFOPE. Accessed at http://www.laohamutuk.org/DVD/2018/LMONov2018en.pdf on 31 July 2020.

SEFOPE (Sekretaria Estadu Formasaun Profesional no Empregu). 2019. "Factsheet 2 -Prosesu Selesaun Kona-ba Programa Traballador Sazonal." Accessed at http://dnee.sefope.gov.tl/public/images/pdf-1585054258-sefope-factsheet-2--seasonal-worker-program-selection-process--tetun.pdf on 31July 2020.

Silva, C. da. 2013. *RENETIL iha luta libertasaun Timor-Lorosa'e: antes sem título, do que sem pátria! / Carlos da Silva L.F.R Saky*. Dili, Timor-Leste: RENETIL.

Silva, K. 2017. "Managing Resources, Persons and Rituals: Economic Pedagogy as Government Tactics." In *Transformations in Independent Timor-Leste: Dynamics of Social and Cultural Cohabitations*, edited by S. M. Viegas and R. G. Feijó, 193-209. New York: Routledge. doi.org/10.4324/9781315535012-11.

Traube, E. G. 1986. *Cosmology and Social Life among the Mambai.* Illinois: University of Chicago.

TV New Zealand. 1975. "East Timor, 1975. Tony Smith TVNZ" Accessed at https://www.youtube.com/watch?v=pMVGqi1aBjo on 4 May 2020.

Wigglesworth, A., and L. Boxer. 2017. "Transitional Livelihoods: Timorese Migrant Workers in the UK." Discussion paper for the Development Policy Centre. Accessed at https://devpolicy.org/2017-Australasian-Aid-Conference/Papers/Wigglesworth-Boxer_Transitional-livelihoods-Timorese-migrant-workers-UK.pdf on 29 April 2020.

World Bank Group. 2018. "Timor-Leste, Country Data." Accessed at https://data.worldbank.org/country/timor-leste on 18 February 2020.

World Bank Group. 2020a. "Economy Profile Timor-Leste, Doing Business 2020." Accessed at https://www.doingbusiness.org/content/dam/doingBusiness/country/t/timor-leste/TMP.pdf, on 28 April 2020.

World Bank Group. 2020b. *Timor-Leste Economic Report April 2020. A Nation Under Pressure.* Dili: World Bank Group. openknowledge.worldbank.org/bitstream/handle/10986/33749/Timor-Leste-Economic-Report-A-Nation-Under-Pressure.pdf?sequence=1&isAllowed=y. Accessed 10 December 2020.

About the Authors

Enrique Alonso-Población holds a PhD in Social and Cultural Anthropology from the Universidad da Coruña (Spain). He has held senior advisory and managerial positions at several international organisations such as the U.N.'s Food and Aquaculture Organization (FAO) and INGOs, such as the Sustainable Fisheries Partnership.

Susanna Barnes is an assistant professor at the University of Saskatchewan. Her research focuses on customary forms of land tenure and natural resource management as well as customary approaches to health and well-being. She is co-author of an inter-disciplinary study of property relations and social resilience in Timor-Leste (2016, Routledge), and co-director of a visual methods collaboration *Holding Tightly: Custom and Healing in Timor-Leste.*

Laurentina 'Mica' Barreto Soares teaches international relations at the Department of International Relations of the National University of Timor-Leste (UNTL). Mica completed her PhD at the Swinburne University of Technology, Australia in 2021. Her thesis focused on China-Timor-Leste relations. She earned her masters' degrees in Peace Studies from Notre Dame University in the USA in 2003 and International Development Studies from Ohio University in the USA in 2011.

Mina Bessa was born in Eluli in colonial times. She studied in Maubara. After 1975, Mina became an activist within the Timorese diaspora against the invasion and for the independence of her country. Just after the Referendum in 1999 she returned to Timor-Leste and started to recover and rebuild her family land and community.

Abel Boavida dos Santos has been a lecturer at the Faculty of Social Sciences, UNTL, since 2002 and completed his PhD at the Universidade do Porto, Portugal, in 2022. He has been involved in civil society organisations working on various community development and empowerment programs since 2000. From 2000-2006, he worked at the "Sa'he Institute for Liberation" (SIL) in Timor-Leste, an NGO founded by young activists involved in the struggle for independence in Timor-Leste. His area of specialisation is rural community development and peasant social movements. He has consulted on various research projects with international and national researchers including the Labour Mobility Assistance Program, Oxfam, Paz y Desarrollo and The Asia Foundation.

Brunna Crespi is an Anthropologist and Ethnogeographer. She is a Postdoctoral Fellow at Musée du Quai Branly – Jacques Chirac and a Research Associate at UMR 208 Paloc (IRD/MNHN). She has worked with Amazon rainforest local communities and her current research focuses on ASEI communities. She is interested in development-related conflicts, cultural resilience, identity in pluricultural areas, and territorial representations.

Alberto Fidalgo Castro is Assistant Professor in Social Anthropology at the Universidad Complutense de Madrid (Spain) and postdoctoral visiting fellow at the Programa de Pós-Graduação em Antropologia Social at the Universidade de Brasília (Brazil). He holds a PhD in Social and Cultural Anthropology from the Universidade da Coruña (Spain).

Teresa Cunha holds a PhD in Sociology from the University of Coimbra. She is an associate professor at the College of Education and a senior researcher at the Center for Social Studies at the University of Coimbra where she lectures on several PhD Courses and co-coordinates the Gender Workshop Series and the Research Program 'Epistemologies of the South'. In 2017, she received the honorable Order of Timor-Leste.

Alex Grainger is a researcher and interdisciplinary social scientist whose research focusses on land in rural and urban settings and the extractive industries, particularly their influences and impacts on livelihoods, labour and local and regional environments. He is based in the UK.

David Hicks is Professor of Anthropology at Stony Brook University. His six books on Timor-Leste are *Tetum Ghosts and Kin* (1976, 2004); *Structural Analysis in Anthropology* (1978); *A Maternal Religion* (1984); *Kinship and Religion in Eastern Indonesia; Rhetoric and the Decolonization and Recolonization of East Timor* (2015); *Oral Literature, Gender, and Precedence in East Timor: Metaphysics in Narrative* (2021).

Sue Jackson is a professor and cultural geographer based at the Australian Rivers Institute at Griffith University. She has research interests in the social and cultural values associated with water, water governance, customary Indigenous resource rights, and capacity building in environmental management and planning.

Andrew McWilliam is Professor of Anthropology in the School of Social Science at Western Sydney University. He is a specialist in the anthropology of Insular Southeast Asia with ethnographic interests in eastern Indonesia and Timor-Leste as well as Northern Australia. Recent publications include, *Post-Conflict Social and Economic Recovery in Timor-Leste: Redemptive Legacies* (Routledge 2020) and a co-edited volume, *The Routledge Handbook of Contemporary Timor-Leste* (2019). He is current editor of *The Australian Journal of Anthropology* (TAJA).

Renata Nogueira da Silva is a teacher at the Sub Secretariat of Continuing Education for professionals in the Federal District (EAPE-DF), and hold a PhD in Social Anthropology from Universidade de Brasília (UnB). She has been part of the Economy and Globalization Studies Laboratory (LEEG) at the same university. She has been working in the area of cultural heritage, ethno-racial relations, and education.

Ivete de Fatima Sarmento de Oliveira is currently working as Adviser for First Lady Office of Timor-Leste. She has a Master degree in social anthropology and development studies, SOAS, London University, UK. She is the founder of several women's organisations in Timor-Leste including Timor-Leste National Women's Network (Rede Feto) and FOKUPERS. She served as President of the National Women's Network 2009-2015 and worked as an adviser to the Government of Timor-Leste.

Lisa Palmer is professor and human geographer at the University of Melbourne who teaches and researches on human-environment relations and indigenous approaches to environmental and social governance. Her research takes a critical ecological approach and is focused on Timor-Leste and Indigenous Australia.

Michael Rose is a research associate at the University of Adelaide.

Kelly Silva is an associate professor at the University of Brasilia (UnB) and a CNPq (Conselho Nacional de Desenvolvimento Científico e Tecnológico, in Portuguese) research fellow. Since 2000, she has researched processes of invention, transposition and subversion of modernity in Timor-Leste, covering issues such as development praxis, political disputes and economic change.

Lucio Sousa is Assistant Professor in the Department of Social and Management Sciences at Universidade Aberta, and researcher at the Institute for the Study of Literature and Tradition (IELT-FCSH-NOVA). He has a Ph.D. in Social Anthropology with a thesis about ritual practice and social organisation in a Bunak community in Timor-Leste.

Jose "Josh" Trindade is currently working as Socio-Cultural Adviser at the Presidency of the Council of Ministers, Government of Timor-Leste. He has been an active advocate of addressing fundamental issues relating to culture, beliefs and traditional systems, and their relationship to nationalism, social solidarity and rule of law. He has written and published several anthropological papers on Timor-Leste.

Ann Wigglesworth has 30 years of experience in international development, working in Asia, the Pacific, Africa and Latin America, including seven years in Mozambique. She became involved in Timor-Leste in 1997 as Program Manager for Caritas Australia in Timor-Leste. She was awarded a doctorate in 2010 with a thesis focussing on the early years of Timor-Leste's independence through the perspectives of the younger generation. She has published articles on Timorese civil society, gender and labour migration. Her first book 'Activism and Aid: Young citizens' experiences of development and democracy in Timor-Leste' was published in 2016. She is a consultant, researcher, sessional lecturer and an Honorary Fellow at Victoria University, Melbourne.

Index

A

Aboriginal Housing: 93, 94.

ABRI (Armed Forces of the Republic of Indonesia): 77, 78.

Aca: 282.

Acakaka i irinu: 283.

Acakaka nana kafu: 283.

Acakaka: 278, 282, 283, 284, 288, 290, 291.

Ade (Vemasse): 108.

Agency: 21, 22, 107, 108, 116, 118, 162, 166, 172, 187, 270, 289.

Agriculture: 11, 12, 14, 25, 27, 28, 29, 37, 51, 90, 196, 197, 207, 208, 209, 241, 242, 255, 257, 263, 265, 270, 286, 295, 297, 303.

Aha Bu'u House: 113, 114

Aileu: 297.

Ai-bubur: 222.

Ai-kakeu: 222.

Ai-kameli: 222.

Ai-mahoni: 222.

Ai-naa: 222.

Ai-nitas: 222.

Akanu: 119, 279, 291.

Allas: 49.

Aldeamentos: 24.

Aldeia: 112, 125, 132, 143, 163.

Alfase: 67.

Alliance: 24, 119, 120, 123, 124, 135, 144, 149, 164, 165, 198, 200, 275, 289, 296.

Anana: 67.

Ancestors: 18, 21, 23, 33, 75, 112, 113, 117, 118, 120, 131, 135, 137, 144, 161, 162, 163, 164, 168, 170, 171, 172, 173, 178, 197, 201, 210, 275, 276, 282, 283, 287, 288, 289, 290.

Ar Foer: 222, 230.

Arenga Pinnata: 114.

Arenga saccharifera: 279.

Assimilated Timorese: 97, 98.

Asuliar: 112, 119.

Asumanu *Suku*: 126, 127.

Asuwa'in: 69.

Atan: 20, 32, 107, 108, 109, 110, 111, 112, 113, 114, 115, 116, 118, 119, 120.

Atsabe: 62, 70.

Australia: 28, 35, 85, 92, 93, 94, 195, 217, 218, 221, 236, 240, 241, 245, 251, 255, 257, 258, 259, 260, 261, 262, 263, 264, 265, 266, 267, 268, 269, 270, 271, 273, 295, 296.

Austronesia: 109, 276, 309.

Auxiliar: 111, 112, 119.

B

Babulo: 112, 113, 114, 115, 116, 117, 118, 119, 120.

Baçar: 51.

Bagi: 62, 135, 144.

Bagot: 94.

Baguia: 34, 219, 220, 221, 222, 223, 224, 225, 226, 228, 229, 230, 231.

Bailoron: 135.

Balarauain: 75, 80.

Bandos: 51.

Banin: 144.

Barlake: 14, 57, 58, 62, 124, 125, 131, 137, 139, 142, 285.

Barter: 13, 14, 47, 49, 54, 71, 82, 207.

Basar Maubisse: 46.

Basar Turiscain: 46.

Basar: 45, 46, 65.

Batar-da'an: 156

Batar-isin: 144.

Batar: 71.

Baucau: 53, 57, 62, 67, 70, 80, 174, 215, 219, 276.

Bazaar: 24, 31, 45, 46, 47, 49, 50, 51, 52, 53, 54, 55, 56, 57, 58, 59, 60, 61, 62, 185, 187, 188.

Be-Asu: 70.

Beaço: 196.

Beaco: 240.

Becora: 95.

Bee-manas ai-tukan: 138, 140.
Been: 14.
Bei'ala: 33, 161, 162, 171.
Belak: 131, 132, 134, 136.
Belum: 124.
Betano: 169, 174, 196.
Bibi: 73, 137.
Bibiçuçu: 47.
Bibiçiusso: 49.
Bibileu: 75, 80.
Bidau: 95.
Biti:144.
Biti Ho Mama: 131, 137.
Bobonaro: 53, 56, 61, 70, 97, 115, 127.
Boletim do Comércio, Agricultura e Fomento: 52, 53, 54, 62.
Bondage: 32, 108, 110, 112.
Bornal: 140.
Bosok: 161, 167, 169.
BOT (*Boletim Oficial de Timor*): 45, 51, 52, 54, 56, 62, 61,
Bridewealth: 131, 133, 137, 138, 141, 142, 144, 285, 292.
Bua-malus: 126, 131, 167, 174.
Bunaq: 195, 196, 197.

C
Calu ho papu: 287, 289.
Calu: 286, 287, 289.
Câmara Municipal de Díli: 95, 96.
Cambodia: 302.
Cana brava: 97.
Canberra: 299.
Cantinas: 69, 74, 77.
CAPES: 36.
Capitalism: 11, 12, 14, 15, 23, 25, 30, 31, 36, 179, 180, 182, 186, 189.
Caraubalo: 65, 66, 67, 68, 73, 74, 75, 77, 80, 82.
Carbon Credits: 216, 217, 221, 222, 230, 231.
Carbon Offset: 215, 216, 217, 218, 219, 220, 222, 231.
Carbon Trading: 34, 216.
Catholic: 69, 79, 125, 126, 131, 137, 143, 151, 174, 260, 263, 273, 289, 291.
Catholicism: 283, 289, 290.
Ceremonies: 19, 123, 124, 125, 131, 149, 151, 163, 164, 167, 170, 172, 190, 201, 203, 205, 210, 266, 270, 272, 303.
Change: 19, 20, 34, 35, 37, 51, 53, 61, 65, 66, 72, 77, 78, 79, 85, 88, 89, 96, 143, 164, 195, 196, 204, 205, 206, 207, 208, 210, 216, 229, 236, 261, 263, 264, 266, 268, 269, 270, 271, 272, 273, 275, 278, 287, 288, 308.
China: 34, 52, 55, 58, 235, 236, 237, 238, 239, 240, 241, 242, 243, 244, 245, 247, 249, 250, 251.
Chinese Communities: 35, 93, 235, 250.
Chinese: 24, 25, 34, 35, 45, 46, 50, 51, 52, 54, 56, 57, 59, 62, 66, 69, 72, 74, 77, 78, 80, 81, 82, 89, 93, 95, 99, 108, 109, 117, 156, 235, 236, 237, 238, 240, 241, 243, 244, 245, 246, 247, 248, 249, 250, 251, 254, 286.
Christianity: 24, 87.
Cipaios: 55, 60.
CIRC (Center for International Conflict Resolution): 124.
Climate Change: 208, 215, 217.
CNI22 (Chinese Nuclear Industry 22nd): 245.
CNPq (*Conselho Nacional de Desenvolvimento Científico e Tecnológico*): 36.
Co-dependency: 21, 31, 37.
Cockfight: 31, 46, 56, 57, 58, 60, 65, 69, 70, 77, 79, 207.
Colonial Authorities: 24, 31, 45, 46, 47, 50, 59, 66, 87, 88, 90, 95.
Colonial Order: 24, 31, 45, 46, 55.
Colonial Power: 45, 47, 54, 55, 88.
Colonisation: 79, 151, 152, 199.
Comandos: 47, 49, 51, 53, 57, 59, 61.
Combatentes: 283.
Comissão Municipal: 71.
Commensality: 129, 161, 165, 166, 171, 172, 282, 289.
Commodity: 17, 18, 24, 37, 47, 68, 72, 108, 164, 216, 218, 276.
Commons: 21, 30, 198, 205, 210, 229, 289.
Community Forestry: 215, 221.
Community-based System: 20.
Community-based: 13, 14, 15, 16, 17, 22, 23, 29, 30, 37, 119, 120, 220, 249.
Community: 14, 17, 18, 19, 21, 22, 23, 34, 58, 60, 78, 83, 115, 117, 119, 147, 148, 157, 177, 178, 179, 183, 187, 188, 190, 196, 197, 201, 203, 204, 205, 206, 207, 208, 209, 210, 218, 225, 226, 227, 230, 246, 247, 250, 262, 263, 271, 275, 283, 284, 287, 295, 296, 298.

Compensation: 34, 196, 198, 201, 202, 203, 204, 207, 209, 287.
Conflict: 15, 49, 85, 88, 123, 124, 153, 154, 155, 157, 187, 195, 197, 198, 200, 201, 202, 204, 206, 209, 210, 219, 225, 226, 247, 256, 257.
Conservation: 215, 218, 223.
Corypha utan: 203.
CPLP (Community of Portuguese-speaking Countries): 238.
Credit: 12, 25, 81, 123, 137, 141, 143.
Customary Environmental Governance: 216, 224.
Customary Obligations: 265, 266, 270, 285.
Customary Practice: 210, 224, 225, 226, 275, 284, 285, 289.
Customary: 17, 18, 20, 21, 35, 81, 115, 119, 149, 158, 159, 178, 179, 190, 196, 197, 198, 199, 201, 202, 203, 206, 210, 215, 219, 222, 224, 225, 226, 227, 229, 230, 231, 266, 269, 272, 275, 277, 278, 279, 284, 285, 286, 287, 288, 290, 303, 306.

D
Dapkur Lulik: 167.
Darulete *Suku*: 130.
Darwin: 92, 93, 94, 195, 298.
Dato: 67, 68, 69, 78.
Debt: 17, 19, 33, 36, 108, 112, 115, 161, 162, 163, 164, 165, 166, 172, 173.
Decolonisation: 98.
Dependence: 17, 26, 89, 98, 107, 166, 195, 196, 207.
Derok: 67.
Development: 11, 12, 15, 23, 25, 26, 36, 51, 53, 56, 57, 60, 66, 87, 88, 90, 91, 92, 124, 141, 147, 159, 164, 187, 189, 195, 205, 206, 225, 231, 236, 238, 239, 240, 244, 245, 246, 247, 250, 256, 264, 272, 295, 297, 298, 299, 302, 306.
DFAT (Department of Foreign Affairs and Trade): 259, 260, 272.
Dili: 12, 28, 47, 54, 56, 60, 61, 62, 67, 80, 82, 85, 86, 95, 96, 98, 111, 118, 119, 127, 149, 158, 168, 187, 237, 238, 239, 240, 245, 246, 248, 249, 251, 256, 257, 258, 260, 265, 266, 267, 268, 270, 272, 287, 297, 298, 300, 301, 307,
Diversity: 11, 18, 20, 30, 34, 108, 109, 180, 182, 183, 208, 219, 223, 227, 228, 230, 249, 276, 299, 309.
Domestic work: 13, 15.
Dosi: 127.

E
Ecofeminist: 33, 179, 187.
Ecology: 182, 183, 189, 306.
Economic changes: 34, 196, 207, 315.
Economic Development: 124, 164, 206, 236, 238, 244, 246, 247, 306.
Economic Ecologies: 11, 13, 17, 20, 29, 30, 31, 32, 34, 278.
Economic Growth: 12, 26, 85.
Economic Institutions: 14, 15, 20, 23, 29.
Economic Market: 15.
Economic Pedagogy: 303.
Economic Relations: 13, 17, 18, 19, 21, 22, 29, 34, 164, 183, 188, 237, 238, 247, 275.
Economic Sphere: 22, 23, 54.
Economic Transformation: 34, 35, 193.
Economic Value: 37, 66, 147, 148, 153, 158, 197, 229.
Economics: 12, 16, 56, 65, 66, 142, 248.
Economy of Desire: 34, 179, 187, 189.
Economy: 11, 12, 13, 14, 15, 16, 17, 18, 19, 20, 21, 22, 23, 24, 25, 26, 28, 29, 30, 32, 33, 34, 35, 36, 46, 47, 49, 54, 56, 65, 71, 74, 88, 93, 119, 120, 143, 159, 165, 182, 196, 236, 237, 238, 239, 244, 247, 248, 249, 250, 255, 257, 267, 275, 296, 299, 303.
Eluli: 177, 178, 179, 180, 183, 184, 185, 186, 187, 188, 189, 190.
Ema Boot: 302.
Ema Cina: 69, 71.
Ema Dili: 119.
Ema Fehan: 67.
Ema Foho: 67, 119.
Ema Malai: 66, 67, 69, 71, 78.
Ema Mutin: 69.
Ema Reino: 68, 78.
Ema Timur: 67, 72, 74, 77, 78.
Ema: 80, 81, 107, 109, 111, 112, 114, 120.
Epistemologies of the South: 177, 179, 180, 181, 182, 184, 189.
Ermera: 37, 53, 133, 138, 174, 303.
Escudos: 71, 72, 93, 97.
Ete materia: 281.
Ethnicity: 31, 46, 65, 66, 70, 71, 77, 78, 79.
Ethno-linguistic groups: 45, 49, 96, 98, 147, 149, 159, 196, 197, 290.
Etu Sedok: 156.

Exchange: 11, 13, 14, 15, 16, 17, 18, 20, 21, 22, 24, 29, 30, 31, 33, 34, 47, 49, 51, 54, 56, 58, 59, 60, 67, 71, 82, 108, 111, 114, 115, 119, 120, 123, 129, 130, 133, 137, 139, 140, 142, 152, 158, 164, 167, 172, 173, 200, 201, 207, 208, 216, 227, 228, 230, 231, 238, 266, 272, 275, 276, 281, 284, 285, 287, 289, 291, 292, 295, 296, 303.
Expropriation: 15, 197.

F
Faan: 202.
Falintil (Forças Armadas de Libertação Nacional de Timor-Leste): 291, 283.
Fad luli: 291.
Fané: 282, 287.
FAP-DF (Fundação de Apoio à Pesquisa do Distrito Federal): 36.
Fara: 281.
Fataluku: 17, 28, 35, 140, 265, 275, 277, 278, 279, 281, 282, 283, 284, 285, 286, 287, 288, 289, 290, 291.
Fatin Lulik: 168.
Fatu: 285.
Fatuk Lulik: 168.
Faulara: 32, 123, 124, 125, 126, 127, 130, 140.
Fehan: 67, 68, 71, 72, 73, 74, 75, 78, 80, 81, 82.
Feira: 51.
Feminist: 177, 179, 180, 181, 182, 184, 185, 186, 187, 189, 190.
Ferik: 139.
Fertility-giver: 21, 115, 123, 124, 126, 130, 131, 133, 135, 136, 137, 138, 139, 140, 141, 142, 143, 144.
Fertility-taker: 21, 115, 123, 124, 126, 129, 130, 131, 132, 133, 135, 136, 137, 138, 139, 140, 141, 142, 144.
Fetosan: 158.
Fia lafai ukani: 279.
Fia le: 278, 279, 281, 284, 291.
Fiji: 272, 309.
Finta: 71.
Flores: 109.
Fó dokumentus: 307.
Fó han: 165.
Foho: 67, 68, 71, 72, 74, 75, 78, 81, 82, 135.
Fomento: 57.
Fordism: 25, 32, 85, 86, 87.
Frente Armada: 301.
Frente Diplomatika: 299, 301.
Frente Ekonomika: 28, 35, 295, 301.
Frente klandistina: 301, 303.
Fretilin (Frente Revolucionária de Timor-Leste Independente): 113.
Fuik: 199.
Funerals: 163, 270, 287, 289.
Fussu nin: 170.
Futu Manu: 207.

G
Gender: 31, 46, 58, 65, 66, 69, 72, 75, 77, 78, 79, 147, 148, 150, 157, 159, 185, 190, 260, 261, 262, 268, 271, 278, 300.
GfD (Governance for Development): 306.
Gift: 17, 18, 110, 111, 115, 120, 123, 131, 132, 162, 163, 164, 165, 166, 170.
Gift exchange: 17, 33, 120, 142.
Governance: 14, 18, 23, 24, 25, 29, 119, 132, 179, 215, 219, 230, 299, 300, 304, 306, 308.
Governance Practices: 15.
GPS (Global Position System): 222, 230.
GUC (*Gabinete de Urbanização Colonial*): 95.
GUU (*Gabinete de Urbanização de Ultramar*): 95.

H
Hadak Leten: 156.
Halerik: 140.
Halibur maun-alin: 125, 128, 129, 141.
Halo Urat: 131.
Hamanas Kafé: 133, 136, 137, 141.
Hamulak: 167.
Hamutu Moris Hamutu Mate: 18, 19, 20.
Hamutuk: 19.
Hanek: 72.
Hasé Matebian: 131, 137.
Hatuquessi *Suku*: 126.
Heteropatriarchy: 180, 182.
Hiit umane: 140.
Ho Musan Ida: 221, 231.
Hola bensa: 131, 137.
HolaRua *Suku:* 163, 174.
Household: 12, 13, 14, 15, 22, 23, 30, 32, 33, 49, 71, 74, 115, 116, 118, 123, 125, 126, 127, 129, 130, 132, 133, 135, 141, 142, 143, 147, 148, 149, 150, 151, 153, 155, 156, 157, 158, 159, 168, 208, 209, 221, 222, 228, 242, 255, 256, 263, 265, 266, 268, 269, 275, 276, 277, 278, 279, 281, 282, 283, 287, 288, 289, 299.

Household decision-making: 33, 147, 148, 153, 155, 159.
Houses: 22, 26, 33, 111, 112, 113, 114, 115, 116, 117, 118, 126, 135, 137, 142, 163, 164, 165, 167, 168, 169, 171, 178, 185, 201, 276, 277, 278, 279, 281, 282, 283, 285, 286, 287, 288, 289, 290, 291, 292.
Huaqiao Group: 235.
Huaren Group: 235.

I
I Huma'ara: 289.
Ibun ho nanal: 139.
IMF (International Monetary Fund): 16, 26.
Imposto Domiciliário: 71.
Impostos de Capitação: 24, 71.
Indigenous Housing: 85, 87, 88, 93, 96.
Indonesia: 37, 77, 91, 109, 116, 117, 124, 187, 195, 206, 219, 236, 240, 241, 245, 246, 286, 299, 300.
Indonesian invasion: 25, 126.
Indonesian occupation: 60, 78, 81, 107, 116, 124, 140, 178, 203, 207, 227, 275, 276, 278.
Indonesian state: 25, 26.
Industrial Revolution: 299.
Inequality: 32, 119, 184, 186, 261.
Ingondoeiro: 55.
Interdependence: 18, 19, 24.
Investment: 11, 25, 26, 28, 88, 92, 94, 120, 130, 201, 237, 238, 240, 244, 267, 289, 297, 298.
Ipilu tei: 282.
Isin: 139, 144.
Isin ho Been: 139.
Ita Nia Rai: 202.

J
Jakarta: 91, 92, 93, 94.
Japanese occupation: 90, 95, 251.
Java: 108.
JKP (*Jajasan Kas Pembangunan*): 92.
José Celestino da Silva: 49.
José Ramos-Horta: 239, 251, 271, 273.

K
Kaben: 131.
Kafana: 129.
Kahlin: 94.
Kakaluk: 198.
Kalen: 277, 285.
Kamanasa Kingdom: 34, 195, 196, 197, 198, 199, 201, 202.
Kampung Baru: 117.
Kankun Malai: 67.
Karau: 137.
Kebayoran Baru: 91, 92.
Keramik: 277.
Kilat no Musan: 108, 113.
Kinship Relations: 21, 116, 120.
Kinship: 21, 22, 26, 32, 33, 107, 108, 115, 116, 123, 125, 142, 143, 178.
Kioks: 77, 78, 169.
Kios: 77, 78, 82.
Knua: 296.
Kokoreli: 223, 231.
Kolen: 132.
Kontas: 223, 227.
Korea: 28, 255, 256, 257, 258, 264, 265, 269, 270, 298.
Kota: 68, 80.
Kristu Rei: 289.
Kultura: 167.
Kumpul: 129.
Kupang: 108.

L
La'o Hamutuk: 201, 203, 209, 245.
La'o Mane-foun: 133.
Labarik: 131.
Labis Laran: 164.
Labour Mobility: 255, 256, 309.
Lafuru tei: 278, 282, 283, 285, 287, 290.
Lafuru: 282.
Lakluta: 149.
Lalu cu: 277, 290.
Larantuka: 108.
Lauhata: 127.
Lautém: 53, 257, 265, 276, 277, 278, 283, 284, 285, 287, 288, 291.
Le amarua: 278, 280.
Le ia valu: 277, 278, 279, 282, 283, 288, 291.
Le lohai: 279.
Le o'o utu-natana: 282.
Le pitine: 277.
Le tein: 283, 288, 290.
Le tein(u): 283.
Le varaca: 277.

Leadership: 66, 117, 152.
Lehe: 223.
Leotelá *Suku:* 126.
Lere Dalan: 133, 136, 137, 138, 141, 142.
Leu Loporu: 281, 291.
Leura tei: 282.
Lia mate no lia moris: 156, 158,
Lia-na'in: 130, 131, 132, 133, 135, 136, 137, 139, 140.
Lifau: 108.
Liliru: 281.
Liquiçá: 32, 119, 123, 126, 127, 143.
Lisan: 179, 190, 206.
Lisuk: 127.
Liurai rai nain: 114, 117.
Liurai-feto: 178, 179, 184, 187, 190.
Liurai: 60, 67, 68, 69, 74, 78, 81, 97, 107, 109, 110, 111, 112, 113, 114, 115, 117, 119, 199, 211.
Livro de Aldeia: 125, 143.
LMAP (Labour Mobility Assistance Program): 257, 259, 260, 262, 264, 271.
Local economy: 11, 13, 14, 16, 32, 34, 59, 221, 222, 229, 247, 248, 250, 271, 286.
Local market: 31, 61, 169, 208, 248.
Lolon: 72.
Lonia: 282.
Lorehe Village: 278.
Loron matebian: 143.
Lospalos: 169, 266, 284, 286, 287.
Luhu: 167.
Lulik: 18, 136, 144, 162, 170, 291.
Lusotropicalism: 25, 32, 56, 85, 86, 87, 88, 96, 99.
Lutu-hun: 110, 111.

M

Ma'arau: 279.
Macau: 108, 239, 246, 249.
Makassae: 67, 80, 113, 147, 149, 223.
Malais: 49.
Malaya: 88.
Malus: 71, 174.
Manan: 140.
Manatuto: 46, 108, 112.
Mane-foun: 123, 124, 133, 135, 136, 138, 139, 140.
Manu-ain: 133, 135.
Manufahi: 33, 52, 53, 161, 162.
Market Economy: 11, 12, 13, 14, 23, 24, 28, 29, 31, 34, 35, 37, 124, 140, 141, 142, 246, 275, 287, 303.
Market Operation: 23.
Market Opportunities: 28.
Market Society: 12, 17, 25, 26, 28, 37.
Market space: 70.
Market Transactions: 32, 82, 124.
Market-based: 13, 17, 18, 34, 215, 216, 218, 229.
Market-driven Economy: 13, 15, 30.
Market-driven Institutions: 11, 13, 23.
Market-driven: 11, 13, 229.
Market: 12, 13, 15, 16, 17, 23, 24, 25, 26, 28, 31, 32, 34, 45, 46, 48, 49, 50, 51, 53, 54, 55, 56, 60, 61, 62, 65, 66, 67, 68, 69, 70, 71, 72, 73, 74, 75, 76, 77, 79, 80, 81, 140, 164, 197, 203, 215, 216, 230, 241, 247, 267, 276, 286, 289.
Maromak oan: 152.
Maromak: 33, 161, 162, 163, 170, 170, 171, 172, 173.
Marriage Exchanges: 14, 31, 115, 124, 158, 292.
Marriage-based Exchange: 20.
Mass Production: 85, 86, 87, 92.
MAT (*Missão Antropológica de Timor*): 96.
Matabixu: 136.
Matadalan ba Rai NGO: 248.
Matak Malirin: 21.
Matak: 130.
Matebian Mountain: 34, 215.
Matebian: 170, 171.
Matrilocality: 142.
Maubara: 177, 183, 184, 185, 187, 190.
Maun-alin: 133.
MCP (Malayan Communist Party): 90.
MCP (Malayan Communist Party): 90.
Mercado: 45, 46, 57, 62.
Migration: 35, 99, 119, 237, 244, 255, 256, 257, 258, 272, 300.
Minangkabau House: 92.
Ministério do Ultramar: 85.
Miscegenation: 87.
Missa Agradesimentu: 290.
Modernization: 206, 207.
Modo: 169.
Monetary Exchange: 129, 207.
Money: 15, 16, 23, 24, 28, 29, 32, 33, 35, 51, 54, 56, 71, 93, 117, 124, 127, 129, 130, 132, 135, 148, 156, 158, 159, 169, 202, 203, 206, 207, 208, 209, 210, 221, 228, 249, 262, 263, 265, 266, 267, 268, 270, 271, 272.
Moradias Econômicas: 95.

Moradores: 52, 55, 95.
More-than-human care: 21.
More-than-human economy: 21, 32, 33.
More-than-human: 20, 21, 30, 31, 173.
Morteen: 140.
MSR (Maritime Silk Road): 238, 239.
Mua Ocawa Ratu: 279.
Mutuality: 17, 20, 23, 26, 28, 30, 35, 36, 275, 276, 287, 289.
Mu'u-fuka totole: 282.

N
Nahe-biti: 143.
Natar: 147, 148, 157.
Nation-building: 28, 32, 66, 79.
Nation-state: 13, 15, 79, 284, 300, 301.
National Economy: 13, 14, 16, 23, 29, 79, 256.
Native Market: 47.
Naueti: 67, 81, 113, 147, 149.
Neoliberal Economy: 18, 119.
Neoliberal: 12, 26, 34, 119, 179, 215, 216, 219, 225, 295, 296.
Neoliberalism: 296.
New Singapore: 206.
NGO: 78, 124, 201, 203, 209, 216, 218, 221, 223, 231, 245, 248, 299, 302, 303.
Non-humans: 33, 161, 162, 163, 190, 197, 199.
Non-market: 31, 182, 215.
Nona System: 57, 58.
Nossa Senora: 289.
Northern Ireland: 257, 258, 262, 263, 272.
Northern Territory: 93, 251.

O
Oan Hakiak: 115.
OBOR (One Belt One Road): 238, 239.
Observatory for Economic Complexity: 298.
Occupation: 25, 31, 45, 49, 59, 69, 211, 235, 247.
Oecussi: 52, 97, 236, 240, 297, 302, 303.
Ordenança: 112.
Ornassa: 112.
Osan Funan: 130.
Ossu sub-district: 66, 67, 69, 70, 73, 74, 149, 157.
Offering: 14, 131, 135, 136, 137, 138, 139, 140, 162, 163, 164, 166, 167, 168, 170, 171, 173, 183, 265, 281, 282, 288.
Obligations: 20, 21, 22, 28, 142, 185, 266, 278, 282, 287, 290.

P
Palappa: 97.
Palu: 283.
PAP (People's Action Party): 88, 90.
Papua New Guinea: 272, 309.
Pataka: 131.
Patriarchal: 151, 184, 186, 188.
Patrilocal: 22, 178, 188.
Pecuário: 68.
Pemuda: 303.
PES (Payment for Ecosystem Services): 217.
PKI (*Partai Komunis Indonesia*): 91.
PLF (Pacific Labour Facility): 304.
Pokala: 285, 291.
Portugal: 24, 58, 187, 240, 241, 245, 303.
Portuguese Administration: 25, 70, 85, 246, 249.
Portuguese Authority: 47, 49, 54, 58, 59, 88.
Portuguese Colonialism: 47,
Portuguese Colonisation: 152, 199.
Portuguese Timor: 24, 25, 32, 45, 47, 57, 61, 85, 98, 111.
Post-colonial: 68, 79, 86, 87, 91, 98, 168, 174, 184, 190.
Post-conflict: 26, 27, 34, 140, 195, 226, 229, 276, 288.
Post-Independence: 17, 18, 34, 35, 124, 230, 235, 246, 275, 277.
Posto Sede: 66, 81.
Posto: 55, 56, 114.
Povo: 107, 114.
Povoações: 66.
Prenda: 130.
Property: 19, 20, 32, 34, 37, 95, 108, 110, 127, 142, 198, 201, 202, 204, 205, 208, 216, 219, 223, 224, 226, 228, 229, 230, 231, 246, 248, 249.
Public Housing: 85, 86, 87, 88, 89, 90, 91, 92, 94, 98.

R
Racism: 25, 32.
RAEOA (Special Administrative Region of Oecussi): 26,
Rai Doben: 296.
Rai Lulik: 296.
Rai Nain: 198, 199, 200, 211.
Rai teen: 199.
Rai: 190, 198, 210, 211, 296.
Ratu: 279, 282, 283, 285, 291.

Reciprocity: 19, 20, 21, 36, 108, 109, 110, 130, 188, 217, 275, 300.
REDD+ (Reduced Emissions Through Avoided Deforestation and Forest Degradation): 218.
Redistribution: 18, 32, 123, 124, 132, 140 141, 142, 143.
Regime of Accumulation: 85, 87, 91.
Regime of Exchange: 24, 33, 142.
Regime of Private Property: 229.
Regime: 13, 11, 18, 24, 31, 78, 99, 119, 123, 124, 140, 141, 143, 164, 202, 203, 205, 226, 246, 279, 283.
Regulamento do Trabalho dos Indígenas: 24.
Regulamento do Trabalho Indígena na Colônia de Timor: 24.
Rei: 110.
Reinos: 111.
Remittances: 35, 36, 248, 249, 255, 256, 258, 262, 265, 266, 267, 270, 272, 295, 298.
Repollu: 67.
Reproduction: 13, 14, 22, 28, 30, 37, 86, 162, 163, 164, 165, 166, 168, 277.
Republic of Ireland: 298.
Resilience: 14, 28, 34, 185, 210, 275, 304.
Resources: 14, 15, 21, 22, 23, 24, 28, 31, 33, 34, 35, 114, 117, 118, 119, 123, 124, 126, 141, 142, 148, 153, 154, 155, 156, 157, 159, 179, 182, 197, 198, 199, 200, 205, 206, 207, 215, 218, 219, 221, 222, 224, 225, 226, 229, 256, 267, 272, 275, 276, 277, 279, 284, 285, 286, 289, 290, 296, 297, 299, 308.
Rights-in-person: 109, 110.
Ritual Exchange: 33, 123, 124, 126, 140, 141, 142, 143, 144, 303.
Ritual Obligations: 141, 143.
Ritual Practices: 12, 33, 124, 143, 164, 206, 287.
Ritual: 13, 14, 21, 22, 28, 32, 33, 57, 75, 79, 111, 113, 115, 117, 118, 123, 124, 125, 128, 129, 130, 131, 133, 137, 138, 140, 141, 142, 143, 149, 150, 151, 152, 156, 158, 159, 162, 163, 165, 167, 168, 172, 178, 179, 202, 203, 205, 210, 224, 225, 226, 230, 231, 276, 277, 278, 279, 281, 282, 283, 284, 285, 286, 287, 288, 289, 295, 296, 303.
Roma Hamlet: 113, 114, 117.

S

Sabraca-lotuk: 67.
Sabraca: 67.
Sacred Food: 161, 167.
Sacred House: 33, 36, 120, 147, 161, 162, 163, 164, 165, 167, 168, 170, 171, 172, 173, 183, 275, 283, 289, 291.
Saka: 282.
Sala fuka: 285.
Same: 33, 52, 60, 161, 162, 163, 168, 169, 297.
São Tomé e Príncipe: 94.
Sapaio: 68, 74.
Sau-batar: 143.
Seasonal Works: 35, 255, 257, 259, 260, 295, 296, 298, 300, 301, 302, 304, 305, 306, 307, 308.
SEFOPE (Secretariat of State for Vocational Training and Employment Policy): 257, 3000, 304, 305, 306, 307, 308.
Segunda linha: 69.
Sei-mecen le: 279.
Serimónia: 129, 143.
SERVE (Timor-Leste's Service for Business Registration): 245, 254.
Sharing: 112, 152, 164, 167, 190, 206, 228, 262, 270.
Singapore: 87, 88, 89, 90, 91, 92, 93, 206, 236, 246.
SIT (Singapore Improvement Trust): 89, 93, 97, 99.
Slave: 20, 32, 54, 68, 107, 108, 109, 110, 111, 112, 114, 115, 116, 117, 118, 120, 279.
Slavery: 32, 107, 108, 109, 110, 111, 112, 115, 116, 118, 119, 120.
Social Reproduction: 16, 19, 22, 86, 94, 142, 162, 303.
Social Stratification: 119.
SOLS (Science of Life): 302, 303, 310.
South Korea Temporary Workers Program: 257.
South Korea: 241, 245, 255, 257, 258, 260, 271, 300.
Squatters: 90, 99.
State-building: 15, 16, 23, 24, 26.
Suai Supply Base Project: 34, 195, 196, 201, 202, 205, 206.
Suai-Covalima: 196.
Suai: 70, 97, 195, 196, 198, 245.
Subsistence Economy: 35, 272.
Suku: 60, 61, 65, 66, 67, 68, 71, 73, 74, 75, 77, 79, 80, 82, 112, 113, 126, 127, 130, 133, 147, 149, 163, 199, 211.
Swietenia macrophylla: 222.
SWP (Australian Seasonal Worker Program): 255, 256, 257, 258, 259, 260, 262, 263, 264, 265, 266, 267, 268, 269, 270, 271, 272, 273, 295, 297, 299, 300, 304, 305, 306, 307, 308, 309.

T

Tabako: 71.
Tais: 47, 48, 69, 131, 137, 140.
Taiwan: 241, 249.
Tali Metan: 114.
Tara Bandu: 14, 206, 224, 225, 226, 230, 303.
Tara Horok: 226.
Taru: 279, 291.
Tasak: 130.
Tasi Mane Project: 195, 196, 197, 205, 208, 209, 210, 211, 236, 245.
Tasmania: 261.
Taur Matan Ruak: 301.
Territory: 24, 25, 31, 45, 47, 49, 50, 54, 56, 59, 93, 98, 109, 178, 180, 195, 196, 198, 199, 200, 201, 204, 206, 246.
Tetum Terik: 18, 147, 149, 202.
Tetum: 18, 32, 45, 62, 67, 80, 96, 109, 110, 120, 144, 147, 149, 170, 174, 190, 195, 196, 197, 221, 224, 226, 250, 269, 276, 283, 292.
Tetun Terik: 67.
Tim Alfa: 277.
Timor Gap: 195, 196, 198, 201, 202 203, 204, 207, 208, 210, 211, 240.
Timorese-Chinese: 35, 236, 237, 241, 246, 247, 248, 250, 251.
To'os: 147, 148, 157.
Tokodede: 129, 144, 177.
Topasses: 108.
Tourism: 208, 220, 238, 260, 277, 297.
Trade: 24, 25, 29, 34, 37, 47, 48, 49, 50, 51, 52, 59, 60, 61, 62, 69, 70, 71, 73, 74, 77, 80, 81, 86, 108, 109, 196, 207, 208, 216, 222, 236, 237, 237, 238, 240, 241, 242, 243, 262, 286.
Tradition: 20, 35, 36, 51, 60, 89, 96, 97, 98, 112, 140, 143, 170, 188, 195, 204, 205, 206, 266, 277, 278, 284, 285, 287, 290.
Transformation: 13, 14, 77, 164, 166, 168, 171, 173, 180, 196, 208.
Transmigration: 25, 60, 126, 197.
Tropical Architecture: 32, 86, 87, 98, 99.
Tua Hakarak: 282.
Tua Mo: 290.
Tua: 135, 136, 144,
Tuaca: 54.
Tuak: 131.
Tuku Odamatan: 131.
Tutu kaka: 281, 282.
Tutu: 285.

U

Uato Carabou: 66, 74.
Uato-Lari Leten: 114.
Uato-Lari: 66, 67, 74, 81, 82, 112, 117.
Uatolari: 149, 157.
UK (United Kingdom): 28, 255, 256, 257, 258, 260, 262, 265, 268, 269, 270, 272, 298, 300, 302, 287.
Ular: 199.
Ulsuku: 131.
Ulun-houris: 110.
Uma Kik: 73, 80, 82,
Uma Lisan: 23, 97, 130, 149, 150,
Uma Lulik: 33, 112, 123, 126, 290, 149, 150, 151, 183, 184, 185, 275, 276, 277, 278, 283, 287, 290, 291, 296.
Uma Malae: 170.
Uma Yanamli: 170.
Umane: 130, 135, 136, 138, 139, 140, 158.
Umane/mane-foun relation: 123, 124.
UN (United Nations): 78, 79, 92, 207, 237, 249, 299.
United Nations World Food Program: 208.
Unu: 114.
Urban Planning: 25, 32, 85, 86, 87, 88, 94, 95, 96, 98.
Urbanisation: 28, 86, 94, 95, 99.
USAID: 78.
Utu-Natana: 282.

V

Valahana: 285.
Vata ira: 282.
Vata'asa le: 279.
Venilale: 67, 70, 74, 81, 82.
Victoria: 261, 273.
Violência doméstica: 269.
Viqueque: 31, 33, 61, 62, 65, 66, 67, 68, 69, 70, 71, 73, 74, 75, 77, 78, 79, 80, 81, 82, 97, 108, 110, 111, 147, 149, 150, 155, 157, 159, 240, 245.

W

Wai hula: 282.
Walin: 115.
Warung: 77, 78, 82.
Wealth in Knowledge: 21, 31.
Wealth in People: 22, 31, 32.
WithOneSeed Program: 215, 219, 221, 222, 223, 224, 225, 228, 229, 230, 231.
World Bank: 16, 26, 78, 79, 245, 298.
WWII (World War II): 25, 32, 54, 251.

X

Xefe de aldeia: 132.
Xefes de Suku: 67, 79, 114, 117.
Xefe suku: 113.

Z

ZEEMS-TL (Special Zone of Social Market Economy of Timor-Leste): 26.

FSC
www.fsc.org
MIX
Papier | Fördert
gute Waldnutzung
FSC® C083411

Kolibri 360 GmbH
Ferdinand-Jühlke-Straße 7
99095 Erfurt, Deutschland
produktsicherheit@kolibri360.de